Jesus Son of Mary in the Qur'ān and According to the Teachings of Ibn 'Arabī

Jesus Son of Mary in the Qur'ān and According to the Teachings of Ibn 'Arabī

By
Maurice Gloton

Translated by
Edin Q. Lohja

Title of the original:
Jésus le Fils de Marie dans le Qur'ân et selon l'enseignement d'Ibn 'Arabî,
Beirut: Albouraq, 2006. ISBN 2-84161-275-9

FONS VITAE

First published in 2016 by
Fons Vitae
49 Mockingbird Valley Drive
Louisville, KY 40207
http://www.fonsvitae.com
Email: fonsvitaeky@aol.com

Library of Congress Control Number: 2015960376

ISBN 978-1887752-817

Printed in Canada

The most profound gratitude goes to Jane Casewit, without whose editing, proofreading, and tireless service this important volume would not have come to be. Great appreciation is extended to Sarah Swetzkoff for her careful editing.

Contents

Introduction

A comprehensive study of Jesus and Mary according to the Islamic revelation and the teachings of Ibn 'Arabī must situate the holy pair in a context particular to the last Divine descent. The study must not separate them from the descent (of the message of Islam), or from the final Prophet, Muḥammad, upon whom God sent down the revelation.

Therefore, the "Christic" perspective of Islam is intimately related to the original, holistic, and recurring figure of Muḥammad. He is the seal of legislating prophecy sent by God as the bearer of Islam, a form of the universal Divine Law.

The present study will take into account all of these considerations. We are thus required to contemplate the significance of the Qur'ānic revelation as the last cyclic and universal manifestation of the Divine Word. This Divine Revelation contains numerous themes on eschatology, ethics, legal and ritual prescriptions, and so on. It concisely presents knowledge concerning the previous revelations, which are validated by the authentic, essential, and current values that they contain, and otherwise invalidated or abrogated. Considering the diverse and ever-changing dispositions which humans carry within themselves, they must serve God by heeding that knowledge which He provides in the Qur'ān—His word descended upon the Prophet—and eventually in other inspired Books, according to new cyclical conditions within which humanity evolves. The study must also show the reality of Muḥammad, the Messenger, Prophet and servant of God, seal of the prophets, who synthesizes all other prophetic typologies until the Day of Resurrection.

As the final Revelation, Islam teaches us that the Qur'ān considers as God-willed revelation all the Divine descents which have taken place during various phases of the human cycles, with all the prophetic types they brought to the fore. Divine revelation is permanent but manifests itself in varying forms appropriate to place and time.

Muslim commentators on the Qur'ān, including certain great masters of Muslim spirituality such as Ibn 'Arabī, emphasized these aspects of Islam and developed them in accordance with the Qur'ān and the traditions of the Prophet. Their scholarship draws from the multiple interpretations allowed by the fundamental Texts according to literal and symbolic modes of expression. The final section of this book cites extracts from two of the main works of Ibn 'Arabī that illustrate the themes of our study. These themes have been nourished and inspired by his writing, as well as by that of certain great Qur'ānic commentators who also wrote on the present subject dedicated to the anointed one, Jesus, Son of Mary.

These preliminary remarks render null the claim that Islam is a Christian heresy, as some have asserted more or less explicitly since the origin of Islam over fourteen centuries ago. Misunderstandings are common even in our own day, despite the fact that an increasing number of non-Muslims possess sufficient understanding to facilitate constructive dialogue and exchange. It is hoped that a broad and profound rapprochement between increasingly qualified persons will be established at all levels: metaphysical, theological, ethical, scientific, and sociological, provided that we recognize the authentic and permanent values of the Revelation promulgated in different forms by the messengers and the prophets that God has sent for mankind's salvation.

The Prophet of Islam received the Revelation in diverse forms that he and certain members of his faithful Companions described. When Revelation would descend upon him, no acquired and specialized knowledge could compete with, reduce, or change the Divine word which manifested itself in him. Muḥammad was perfectly *ummī*, unlettered, of virgin and diaphanous substance, in a state akin to the one in which his mother brought him into this world, as related in an authentic prophetic tradition. The Divine Word passed into him and through him like limpid water, and remains unaltered and unalterable. The exceptional and diverse knowledge that he could have acquired through personal experience never interfered with the Divine descent. When the revelation intervened on him in a moment of perfect plenitude and concentration, it was a total Divine presence that filled him completely. For example, his knowledge of Christianity through representatives of the Church never altered the Divine words he received, and they never substituted the latter whenever Jesus, Mary, and a particular

Christianity are mentioned by God in the sacred scripture of Islam.

The Qur'ānic text presents the previous Revelations transmitted by their respective prophets in the form of essential recapitulations. The text is not encumbered with their exhaustive contents and chronology, for this is neither the vocation nor the purpose of the Qur'ān. What God says in the Qur'ān about Jesus and Mary must be necessary and sufficient to enable spiritual individuals at the interior of Islam to meditate on both figures without neglecting or ignoring anything from the Muḥammadan reality and the contents of the universal Message that he transmitted.

We can therefore anticipate the value of such studies for the West, which largely belongs to the Christian tradition. From this perspective, Islam, or more precisely the Qur'ān, provides knowledge on earlier revelations in keeping with their fundamental values. It suggests to the Muslims, and more broadly to the members of other authentic Traditions, the essential and sufficient themes for the development of all spiritual life. This scriptural perspective justifies that the bearers of a sacred scripture preceding Islam must take into account the last and necessary cyclical position of Islam, willed providentially by God, as well as its presence in the world.

From this perspective arises a second implication. The knowledge presented by the Qur'ānic revelation regarding the prophets before the advent of historical Islam is necessarily true and sufficient because it was revealed by God. Although discrepancies appear, for example, between the Christian and Islamic formulations, one must always bear in mind that the Islamic revelation cannot but be the expression of Truth, even if an identical or similar fact generates additional enunciations according to the perspective of other Revelations: this occurrence is enriching, not conflicting. If different points of view persist, they must, if possible, be examined and resolved as facts that God Himself has put forward and postulated. Such an attitude will only be achieved through perfect trust in the revealed text, which is indisputable and true in itself and in its multiple implications. Profound meditation, a certain intuition, and total sincerity of the spiritual person will help him or her to understand the inexhaustible, and often difficult to decipher, contents of the scripture under study.

This attitude requires that one never lose sight of the fact that each Divine revelation is fundamentally complete in itself and hence sufficient for the communities which it was called to govern. According to this principle, none of the revelations must be denigrated; Divine Revelations are necessarily perfect because God originates them for the salvation of their adherents. Representatives of a certain Revelation can always try to show its "superiority", but ultimately God's multiple formulations of truth will only point to the difficulty of this approach which requires much competence in numerous disciplines. The increasingly significant intermingling of cultures and religions characterizes the present condition of humanity. Thus there is great interest in trying to understand the revealed Truth of the other without seeking to denigrate, diminish, or distort it, while at the same time preserving a perfect intellectual conviction, exemplary moral integrity and commitment to one's own adopted path. Effective rapprochement, at once spiritual, theological, ethical and sociological, between representatives of various religions is not possible except under the aforementioned conditions, by the grace of God.

Finally, we must not lose sight of a final point. In the Revelation to the Prophet, the language used by God is clear Arabic, which therefore acquires a sacred value. The translation of the sacred Text requires great care, profound respect and propriety regarding the Truth, as well as a total sincerity. The translation must reproduce the polyvalent, literal, and symbolic meanings of the Original by considering the fundamental semantics of sacred Arabic and its original philology as a providential means of expressing the Qur'ānic Revelation. According to this perspective, an original study becomes established as a method of interpretation, without necessarily having to conform itself to existing translations and commentaries, and without falling into the numerous traps associated with a reproduction of the sacred Text translated according to inherited conventions. This study will address the Scripture in keeping with the perspective that it is completely original and authentic, that it does not imitate previous Revelations, and that it must be understood in and of itself and located in the context of this Revelation—not in those which representatives of other confessions sometimes promote as preeminent. Hence, the translator and presenter must be a faithful interpreter who effaces himself before the word of God in order to produce a more recognizable, true and transparent result. For these various reasons, the translations of certain Qur'ānic terms proposed in this work may differ from common translations. Our approach toward the subject is based on the technique used by the majority of Muslim scholars to learn from the polysemic value of the Qur'ānic roots. The origin of these roots resonates in their etymology but the roots have also been continually developed to accommodate new accepted meanings; although they effectively carry this host of meanings, not all have been clearly identified. This Qur'ānic language comprises a sacred dimension and enables multiple interpretations of the Divine Word that have yet to be established.

***

At the beginning of Christianity, the Christic, Marian, and Trinitarian perspective posed valid and delicate questions to the Church fathers, and until today it continues to raise numerous issues. The dogmas pertaining to the two Natures of Christ, the three Persons of the Trinity, and "the Mother of God" (*theotokos*) have been elaborated upon by the Church throughout the centuries, even in recent times, and very often involving confusion, discord, and bloody repressions. The first great Councils, such as those of Nicea, Ephesus, and Chalcedon, which established the most seminal positions concerning the Trinity, Christ, and Mary, were far from attaining the unanimous support of both the Eastern and the Western Churches. The monophysite crisis, which spanned many centuries, was not complete at the time of the first important conquests of nascent Islam, and the latter certainly facilitated the mass conversion of Christian communities in Syria, Mesopotamia, Arabia, Egypt, North Africa and even Spain.

Christianity, whose first representatives were Semites, prospered to a greater degree in geographical and cultural zones wherein the Greek and Latin pantheons had triumphed. During the first centuries of the Christian era, the Greek and Latin theologians and fathers elaborated a theological *summa* by using philosophical and philological methods particular to Greek culture and its logic.

On the contrary, the Christians of Semitic origin were fundamentally less apt and hence less inclined to receive this mode of expression. The controversies concerning the Trinity and the "two natures" affected them less and their monophysism enabled them to accept with ease Islam's simpler formulation of monotheism.

These Christological, Trinitarian, and Marian controversies are reflected in the Qur'ānic text which warns against categorical, excessive, and fixed doctrinal positions. Although the two Natures of Christ are suggested by several passages of the Qur'ān, and although it contains the injunction to not say "Three" about God, and despite the fact that the Divine Reality at the level of Unity (*tawḥīd*) can be envisaged under essentially different "aspects," the difficulty does not become less real. The Qur'ānic text takes account of it in a subtle way that is subject to numerous interpretations, especially if the Qur'ānic context is envisaged with multiple facets. The same problems that caused dogmatic conflicts within the Church can be equally treated through the verses that address these difficulties, as we shall see many times in this study. However, the overwhelming majority of Muslims consider the Divine word of the Qur'ān to be infallible, paramount, indubitable, and indisputable, and therefore we will never question it in this study. We will accept it completely without any preliminary.

From early on and until the present day, the Muslim jurist-theologians and commentators had to familiarize themselves with the particulars of the Christian tradition in a detailed manner. Nevertheless, the Qur'ānic verses regarding certain aspects of the reality of Jesus have been interpreted in divergent and sometimes contradictory manners in accordance with the respective schools. Our approach to the themes of the study has been formulated in accordance with the interpretations of the great commentators of the sacred text and according to the teaching of Ibn 'Arabī as specified early in this introduction.

On the other hand, and this is crucial, the Islamic doctrines of the Divine Unity, and of the legislating and universal Mission of the Prophet Muḥammad, allow us to refrain from occupying ourselves exclusively with the privileged and exceptional case of the Anointed One, Jesus, Son of Mary. Unlike Christianity, Islam retains all the virtue of being an original, integral, and autonomous Divine descent, a synthesis of previous revelations. Among other subjects, it mentions certain elements of the previous Revelations, as seen through the prism of Islam, to inspire motivation and meditation.

The second part of our study will attempt to elucidate these delicate points with the help of the body of Qur'ānic verses, in accordance with the verse order retained by the version of the Caliph 'Uthmān, which present Jesus, Mary, and Christianity according to the vision of Islam.

We solicit the Grace of God to lead this delicate and long-postponed work to successful completion. The subject now seems to have become particularly useful and necessary, in light of the more open positions recently expressed by the Church and certain Muslim initiatives. We wish to facilitate the proliferation of bilateral contacts and dialogues with the aim of engendering a deeper understanding of certain crucial facts that is both reciprocal and continually striving for perfection.

Chapter I

Universality of Islam

According to the Qur'ān, the Sunna, and the authoritative knowledge of the Muslim tradition, Islam is the last Revelation or Divine descent (*tanzīl*) and its Messenger, Muḥammad, is the Seal of the prophets: *Muḥammad is not the father of any man among you, but he is the messenger of Allah and the Seal of the Prophets; and Allah is ever Aware of all things* (Qur'ān, 33:40). Thus the last Revelation seals and recapitulates the previous Revelations and addresses itself to the whole of humanity on the authority of this verse: *We sent thee* (addressing first of all the Prophet Muḥammad) *not save as Mercy for all creatures* (Qur'ān, 21:107).

According to Anas b. Malik, the Prophet said: "The two legislating and prophetic missions have reached their term, and there is neither a Messenger nor a Prophet after me . . .." (Tirmidhī). From the revealed text, we quote the following verse which confirms the universal vocation of Islam to pervade contemporary humanity: *Say: O mankind! Lo! I am the Messenger of Allah to you all—[the messenger of] Him unto Whom belongeth the Sovereignty of the heavens and the earth. There is no god save Him: He that giveth life and He that giveth death. So believe in Allah and His messenger, the primordial* (or unlettered) *Prophet, who believeth in Allah and in His Words, and follow him that haply ye may be led aright* (Qur'ān, 7:158). *He it is Who hath sent His messenger with the guidance and the Religion of Truth, that He may cause it to prevail over all religion. And Allah sufficeth as a Witness* (Qur'ān, 48:28). *He it is Who hath sent His messenger with the guidance and the Religion of Truth, that He may cause it to prevail over all religion, however much the associators may be averse* (Qur'ān, 9:33).

Therefore, in the entire cycle of the ceaselessly renewed Divine Revelation Islam is the final Tradition expressing both the universal and primordial character of this Revelation. The message of

Islam was initially addressed to humankind by the Prophet Adam and was renewed during each important phase of the historical human cycle by an uninterrupted series of prophets and messengers of God.

Abu Hurayra reports to have heard the Prophet say: "I was kindled from the best of all the generations of the sons of Adam since their Creation, until I appeared in the generation which is mine" (Bukhārī).

As we shall demonstrate through Qur'ānic verses, in this continued sequence of prophets and messengers, Abraham plays a fundamental role in the economy of the cycle.

To this essential notion of Islam's universal character is added that of the axial or permanent Religion (*dīn qiyam*), the immutable or perennial Tradition (*dīn qayyim*), and of the primordial Nature or differentiation (*fiṭra*). These Qur'ānic expressions possess direct, mutually dependent relationships. They cannot be dissociated from the notion of the essential and permanent service because they concern an attitude of worship which every human being must uphold before their Lord and Creator, *for thy Lord hath decreed, that ye worship none save Him* (Qur'ān, 17:23).

The following verse constitutes the most significant mention of the principal elements of this primordial and universal aspect of Islam:

Set thy face (*wajh*) *to the pure, upright Religion* (*dīn*) *as a theotrope*[1] (*ḥanīf*) *in view of the original form* (*fiṭra*) *according to which Allah created* (or *differentiated*) (*faṭara*) *human beings. There is no altering of Allah's creation* (*khalq*). *That is the immutable religion, but most men know not [how to discern]* (Qur'ān, 30:30). In this verse, the two terms which we have translated as "conforming," or differentiated, and "the original form" both issue from the same root, *f-ṭ-r*, meaning to split, to set about, cut in two, differentiate, conform, have breakfast, or do something first. It therefore refers to a primordial and essential differentiation that exists, *in divinis* with all its potentialities and predispositions, even before it emerges from the universal manifestation. The Divine Name *al-Fāṭir* refers to He who actu-

1. The neologism "theotrope," a translation of the word *ḥanīf*, comes from two Greek roots: *theo*, God, and *trepein*, to turn; that is, one who turns spontaneously to God. (author's note)

The term *ḥanīf* refers to those who practiced original, primordial monotheism in the pre-Islamic Arabian milieu. (editor's note)

alizes the virtualities of each entity by generating their passage from potential to act.

In Arabic, the term *islam* comes from a root meaning to be safe and protected, to be intact, or wholesome. The fourth derived verbal form, foundation of the verbal noun *islam*, means: to preserve intact, to give entirely, to submit, to safeguard oneself or to surrender. In religious terminology, Islam is the active and conscious Submission to God and to His normative Will (*irāda*) which prescribes a certain revealed Law in relation to the cyclical conditions of human evolution.

Other verses illustrate this notion of spontaneous orthodoxy or *theotropism* and the innate (*ḥanīf*) wisdom, aligning with the integral submission to the Divine will which characterizes the prophets Abraham and Muḥammad in the Qur'ān. They safeguard as well as define Islam in accordance with this term's etymology.

> *Say: Lo! As for me, my Lord hath guided me unto a straight path, a permanent religion (dīn qiyam), the rule of wisdom (milla) of Abraham, the upright, who was not of the associators (mushrikīn)* (Qur'ān, 6:161).

> *Abraham was not a Jew, nor yet a Christian; but he was a theotrope (ḥanīf) surrendered [to Allah], and he was not of the associators* (Qur'ān, 3:67).

> *As for me, I have set my face as a theotrope towards Him who separated (fāṭir) the heavens and the earth, and I am not among the associators* (Qur'ān, 6:79).

> *Who is better in religion than he who surrendereth (aslama) his face (wajh) to Allah while doing good, and conforms to the rule of wisdom (milla) of Abraham, the upright? Allah chose Abraham as intimate friend (khalīl)* (Qur'ān, 4:125).

> *Lo! religion with Allah* [is] *the Surrender [to His Will and Guidance]* (Qur'ān, 3:19).

> *Seek they other than the religion due to Allah (dīn Allāh), when unto Him submitteth (aslama) whosoever is in the heavens and the earth, willingly or unwillingly, and unto Him they will be returned* (Qur'ān, 3:83)?

> *Say: We have faith in Allah and that which is revealed unto us and that which was revealed unto Abraham and Ishmael and Isaac and Jacob and the tribes, and that which was vouchsafed unto Moses and Jesus and the*

> *prophets from their Lord. We make no distinction between any of them, and unto Him we have surrendered (muslimūn)* (Qur'ān, 3:84).
>
> *And whoso seeketh as religion other than the Surrender it will not be accepted from him, and he will be a loser in the Hereafter* (Qur'ān, 3:85).
>
> *O ye who have faith! Bow down and prostrate yourselves, and worship your Lord, and do good, that haply ye may prosper.*
>
> *And strive for Allah with the endeavour which is His right. He hath chosen you and hath not laid upon you in religion any hardship; the tradition (milla) of your father Abraham [is yours]. He hath named you muslims of old time and in this (Scripture), that the messenger may be a witness against you, and that ye may be witnesses against mankind. So establish prayer (ṣalāt), pay the poor-due (zakāt), and hold fast to Allah. He is your Protecting friend, a blessed Patron, and a blessed Helper* (Qur'ān, 22:77-78)!

Emanating from these verses are numerous teachings concerning the universality of Islam and the word "Islam" which is primordially and semantically the submission or the act of surrendering oneself, safeguarding, and abandoning oneself to God without reservation.

Before we develop the theme of submission and tackle the question of the axial religion, the original nature or form, and natural orthodoxy or theotropism, which as we saw earlier are Qur'ānic expressions, let us examine more deeply the religion of Allah which—according to the verse 3:19 quoted above—is Islam understood in its most universal sense.

The term *dīn*, translated here as religion, has multiple translations in French: tradition, cult, religion, etc.

In the Arabic lexicon, this noun means: remuneration, loan, borrowing, obedience, accounting, judgment, habitual state, submission, surrender.

The ternary root of this noun, *d-y-n*, further connotes: becoming a debtor, acquiring debt, loaning and borrowing, obliging, subjugating, remunerating, being loyal, and judging.

It follows from these numerous, but closely related meanings, that *dīn* is the remuneration that God grants to His servants for their comportment towards Him and His creatures. *Dīn* is also the debt of existence that the servants who submit willingly or unwillingly owe to God, a debt which they must return to Him. According to the latter connotation, *dīn* is a loan from God to His creatures. Therefore they must return to Him as a trusted deposit (*amānah*) that they have preserved intact through their recognition of Him. For ultimately nothing truly and definitively belongs to the servants, who remain completely indebted to their Lord. As subjects of God, they owe Him everything: existence, goods, virtues, and faculties. In reality nothing belongs to them insofar as God is the Real Being (*wujūd haqqī*). He has said: *Allah is the rich, and ye are the poor* (Qur'ān, 47:38).

Dīn therefore implies the recognition by the creatures of their Existentiator who gives them existence on a provisional basis. They must respond to this gift of existence and justify their use of it. Such is veritable worship or servitude (*'ibāda*). The profound meaning of this term therefore implies a preliminary recognition and an acceptance.

The previously quoted verse—*the religion* (*dīn*) *with Allah* (*is*) *Islam*—is, grammatically speaking, a nominal phrase wherein the subject *dīn* necessarily encompasses its absolute attribute ISLAM which is less extensive than its subject. That is why the *dīn* is ISLAM or submission; however, in this double relationship of both linguistic and religious character, Islam is one of the elements of religion.

According to an authentic *ḥadīth*, the veritable and complete religion rendered by Allah includes Islam, or submission; faith (*īmān*), or certainty in or through Allah, according to the etymology of the root *'-m-n*; and perfection of comportment (*iḥsān*).

The Religion in its three principal aspects therefore appears as the act of one's will and intelligence translated into the external and internal behavior of the sincerely worshipping being, dedicated to his or her only Lord.

In summary, Islam thus understood is essentially an attitude of safeguarding, or submission to, the Divine will which concerns all beings without exception and especially human beings, for they were created to submit themselves, willingly or unwillingly, to the creating Divine will and to the infinite All-Possibility (*mashī'a*).

However, all beings are inexorably surrendered to the effectuating Divine will (*mashī'a*) insofar as they are created in the original design of God. Once they are projected into universal existence, they become free to conform to the existentiating Divine Order (*'amr*) or to turn away from the Divine Will (*irāda*). Conformity to the Will imposes certain obligations which produce in the human being an attitude consistent with the original human state.

The Islam revealed to the Prophet Muḥammad states that human beings are originally in God, they issue from God, are willed by God, and that they are ultimately reintegrated unto Him: *Verily we are for Allah, and unto Him are we returning* (Qur'ān, 2:156). They were primordially issued from Divine Unicity (*waḥdāniyya*) and they are the object of Divine Mercy or the Divine universal love, therefore they all preserve a more or less living reminiscence of their origin in God.

This indelible mark of the Divine Unity and Compassion exists in everyone, but it is more or less altered and diminished in the world of multiplicity by a number of distractions and catalysts. These many veils cloud the wholesome consciousness of God that we once possessed. Mankind also needs the reminder provided by God's Mercy. This will be the function of the messengers and the prophets of God who will awaken in humans His permanent and total remembrance, and who will encourage them and invite them to submit themselves consciously and willingly to His Will (*irāda*). In this respect, all revealed religions have no other goal, even though the consequences of God, their holy Legislator, vary by virtue of the various traits taken on by His universal Manifestation.

The term *Islām* then takes another meaning, one that specifies and distinguishes the first notion that we are going to examine. To this universal and permanent Islam, completely aligned with the original divine intention of producing the created beings, there will correspond, in this human cycle, a revealed Islam that will cause creatures to cease forgetting their divine origin. They will worship the One God and Creator, and recognize their Lord and Master in order to serve Him in sincere and exclusive worship, completely abandoning themselves to Him.

The fact that the last Revelation was delegated to the whole of humanity through the term ISLAM brings into focus the importance of submission to the Divine will for a human being.

It is in fact through an act of disobedience (cf. Qur'ān, 20:21)—the tasting of the tree of differentiation (*shajara*)—that Adam was cast out of the paradisiacal Garden (*janna*). Thus the historical and cosmic fall into multiplicity, implying universal Manifestation (all of creation), took place. Adam's fall led inexorably to the fall of his offspring according to verse 2:36: *But Satan caused them both to deflect therefrom [the paradisiacal Garden] and to get out from the state in which they were; and We said: "Fall down (plural, not dual), some of you foes unto the other! There shall be for you on earth a habitation and provision for a time."* The following passage is very explicit in this regard: *And verily We made a covenant of old with Adam, but he forgot, and We found no constancy in him. And when We said unto the angels: "Fall prostrate before Adam," they fell prostrate [all] save Iblīs; he refused. Therefore we said: "O Adam! This is an enemy unto thee and unto thy wife, so let him not drive you both out of the Garden so that thou come to toil. It is [vouchsafed] unto thee that thou hungerest not therein nor art naked, and that thou thirstest not therein nor art exposed to the sun's heat." But the devil whispered to him, saying: "O Adam! Shall I show thee the tree of perpetuity and kingdom that wasteth not away?" Then they twain ate thereof, so that their shame became apparent unto them, and they began to hide by heaping on themselves some of the leaves of the Garden. And Adam disobeyed his Lord, so he went astray. Then his Lord chose him, and relented toward him, and guided him. He said: "Go down hence, both of you, some of you (plural, not dual) foes unto others. But when there come unto you from Me a guidance, then whoso followeth My guidance, he will not go astray nor come to grief. But he who turneth away from remembrance of Me, his will be a narrow life, and I shall bring him blind to the assembly on the Day of Resurrection"* (Qur'ān, 20:115-124).

This revealed Islam, new in its expression but not in its Truth, concerns the present human cycle. It is witnessed by those who adhere to it through affinity. The Islam that interests us more, particularly in this work which is primarily dedicated to the Anointed One, Jesus, Son of Mary, will naturally be that which was revealed to the last Prophet, Muḥammad. This Islam has kept the same appellation that God gave to the religion Abraham rendered to Him, as He has said in one of the previously quoted verses, the revealed Islam which expresses this submission in a language eminently and providentially convenient to the conditions of present humanity.

That is why the first condition of entering or adhering to the revealed Islam is to testify to or recognize the Divine Unity and the sacred Mission of the Messenger of Allah, sent as a mercy for all creatures, according to the Qur'ānic verse 21:107. This testimony is thus formulated: *I bear witness that there is no god but God, and I bear witness that Muḥammad is the Messenger of God* (*Ashhadu an lā ilāha illā 'Llāh, wa ashhadu anna Muḥammadan Rasūlu 'Llāh*). This is why the first of the five pillars of Islam consists of this two-part profession of faith.

In Chapter III, we will demonstrate the significance attached to the two terms *ilāh* and Allāh in this testimony, and we will draw certain conclusions regarding the reality of Jesus under different aspects as it is expressed in the Qur'ānic text.

It is also in the form of testimony that the offspring of Adam recognized the veracity of God's Lordship when all his descendants were in the reins of this first Prophet before the terrestrial advent. Allah mentions it in the Qur'ān: *And (remember) when thy Lord brought forth from the Children of Adam, from their reins, their seed, and made them testify of themselves, (saying): "Am I not your Lord?" They said: "Yea, verily. We testify." Lest ye should say at the Day of Resurrection: "Lo! of this we were unaware"* (Qur'ān, 7:172).

In this primordial condition, every human being as a conscious servant had to testify to the essential Reality of his Lord and his own distinct, God-given original nature or form (*fiṭra*). This principal recognition constitutes the axial and permanent Religion (*dīn qiyām*), through which he made his rule of wisdom (*milla*) following the example of the Patriarch Abraham, whom he must take as a prophet in addition to the Prophet Muḥammad, as related in the following two verses: *Verily in the Messenger of Allah ye have an excellent pattern for him who looketh unto Allah and the Last Day, and remembereth Allah much* (Qur'ān, 33:21); *There is a goodly pattern for you in Abraham and those with him . . .* (Qur'ān, 60:4). It is owing to this degree of excellence that one is veritably, spontaneously, and adequately theotropic (*ḥanīf*), fully conscious of this lordly Reality which is originally and ultimately his. For the servant who submits himself most perfectly to the Will of his Master and Lord finds himself in this metacosmic instant adorned with all His Attributes. All of the inward and outward comportments then become the fulfilled expression of this divine will, which is realized by him in perfect consciousness.

Chapter II

The Two-Part Profession of Islamic Faith, or the *Shahāda*

The first pillar of Islam and the first article of Islamic faith both concern the affirmation of Divine Unity, but they are envisaged in different modalities. In fact, the first pillar of Islam specifies that one testify to this Unity, whereas the first article of faith engages the believer only with God—to trust in Him, to have faith in Him. Moreover, this first foundation of Islam comes with a two-part profession of faith: not only in the existence of the Divine Unity, as we shall see, but also in the mission of Muḥammad, the Messenger of God. According to a certified *ḥadīth*, the first part of the profession declares faith in Divine Unity, the first pillar of Islam. The doctrine of Divine Unity simply postulates that there is only one god or *ilāh*, and that is Allah. The Revelation and the Sunna, or Prophetic Tradition, explain the Reality of this One God, as expressed by God Himself and affirmed in the *shahāda*.

The domain governed by these two principal themes, as well as that which pertains to the mission of the Messenger of Allah, are so vast that we shall only tackle certain essential elements of this double testimony of Islamic faith. May God assist us in this fundamental but difficult question of presentation, for the Reality of God as well as that of His Prophet do not lend themselves to definition. We shall also tackle this two-part profession of faith uniquely with respect to the two fundamental sources of authority, the Qur'ān and the Sunna.

We can already offer a first observation: the two notions of Islam (submission to the Divine will) and of Faith (assent, adherence, conviction) seem distinct, even though they cannot be dissociated from each other, and even though one necessarily implies the other.

According to certain *ḥadīth*, Islam is defined by the following five pillars: the two-part testimony to Divine Unity and the mission of the Messenger of God (*shahāda*), the prescribed prayer or action of unifying grace (*ṣalāt*), the purifying tithe (*zakāt*), fasting during the month of Ramadan (*ṣiyām*), and pilgrimage (*hajj*). Therefore Islam comprises an outward practice of rites which may or may not imply sincerity and adherence, since we cannot exclude the possibility of hypocrisy. The realization of true faith demands the adherence of one's intelligence and a great conviction attached to the essential truths expounded upon in the Revelation. The prophetic tradition specifies that one must have faith in God the One, in His Angels, in His revealed Scriptures, in His Messengers, and in the measuring out of both good and evil. The following verse highlights this distinction: *The Bedouins say: We have faith. Say [unto them, O Muḥammad]: Faith ye have not, but rather say "We submit," for the faith hath not yet entered into your hearts . . .* (Qur'ān, 49:14).

The subject of concern is not the existing difference between Submission (*Islām*) and Faith (*īmān*). Ghazālī has masterfully expounded upon that in the first volume of his great *summa* "The Revival of Religious Sciences," or *Iḥyā' 'ulūm al-dīn*.

Let us quickly identify some facts on this subject. These two ways of speaking about God are clearly related to the distinction that one can make, in a general manner, between active submission to the Divine will and certitude engendered by faith in God. Submission to the Divine will implies the servant's total confidence in God and His creation, whereas Faith calls for an innate disposition to understand the revealed truths and adhere to them with all one's being. Islam appeals above all to the will and to the love of the believer, and to his or her faith inscribed on the innermost self. It urges his intelligence and behavior toward knowledge. It is impossible for a servant who is conscious of his faith and love of God to dissociate them from the will and intelligence that mobilize him to act justly on account of the ultimate goal. If the human being carries faith within himself, and has a sound mind and normal constitution, he cannot act without bringing into play the motive which incites him to do something or abstain from it, and without having some knowledge of the goal which that particular act suggests. These two attitudes form the basis of human activity and proceed from a single approach, for ultimately, those who have faith are determined to achieve a goal they have cause to pursue. The attraction of the ultimate goal is the love and knowledge of the worshipping servant for his Lord and Master who is his Origin and End. In fact, according to the divine word: *Say, [O Muḥammad, to mankind]: If ye love Allah, follow me; Allah will love you and forgive you your sins. Allah is Forgiving, Merciful* (Qur'ān, 3:31).

***

Revelation contains the formula of Divine Unity in thirty-six variations. Let us consider a few examples:

And your God is One, not deity but He, the All-merciful (Qur'ān, 2:163). *Allah! There is no deity save Him, the Alive, the Eternal* (Qur'ān, 2:255). *Allah [Himself] is Witness that there is no god save Him. And the angels and the men of learning . . .* (Qur'ān, 3:17). *He sendeth down the angels with the Spirit of His command unto whom He will of His bondmen, [saying]: Warn mankind that there is no deity (ilāh) save Me, so keep your duty unto Me* (Qur'ān, 16:2). *He [Jonas] cried out in the darkness, saying: There is no god save Thee. Be Thou Glorified! Lo! I have been a wrong-doer* (Qur'ān, 21:87). *So know that there is no god save God* (Qur'ān, 47:19).

The prophetic traditions report the following words: "Whoever dies conscious that there is no god but God enters Paradise." The Prophet told Mu'ādh ibn Jabal: "O Mu'ādh, there is no servant who bears witness that there is no god but God and that Muḥammad is the Messenger of God without God preserving him from the Fire." "The most excellent word uttered by myself and the preceding prophets is *lā ilāha illā 'Llāh wahdahu lā sharīk la* (there is no god but God, who is One, without any partner)." The Prophet said to Abū Hurayra: "Whomever you see bearing witness that there is no god but God with sincerity of heart, give them the tidings of Paradise."

These few verses and *ḥadīth* allow for a first remark. God bears witness, as do the Angels and those who know that there is no deity save God. On the other hand, those who bear witness know Him about whom they testify, *So know that there is no god save God*, and the Prophet has also said: "He who dies being conscious that there is no god but God enters the Garden."

What is, then, this testimony that God makes concerning Himself and the faithful offer to Him in turn?

Let us refer to the Arabic language to better understand the meaning we must ascribe to this testimony. The verb "to testify," or *shahīda*, also means, both in common speech and in the revealed language of the Qur'ān, to be present for something, to bear witness about something, or to attest.

Testimony is therefore an act of presence, and thus an act of immediate knowledge or a clear realization. Furthermore, from a linguistic perspective, testimony is always information given with full cognizance by one who is present. From the dual character of this definition—the acts of both presence and information—it follows that when one bears witness to His Unity, God is present and conscious of the Knowledge which He maintains in respect to His own unique and singular Reality. Allah therefore can witness Himself only through Himself, as He is alone and without associate according to a Qur'ānic as well as prophetic formula. However, He can bear witness to Himself. The Angels and those possessing knowledge, who, according to the verse we quoted earlier, also bear witness to the Divine Unity, are conscious of this Unity through an act of presence. A being only testifies in full sincerity to that which it recognizes, and never to that which is absent to its consciousness or nonexistent.

Thus another question arises: What is the nature of this testimony performed by a human being and concerning the subject of Divine Unity about which he has some knowledge?

This testimony is possible only because the servant has known this truth since eternity when he attested to his Lord through Adam. When present before his Lord, he recognized Him. Has God not said in that eternal instant: *And [remember] when thy Lord brought forth from the Children of Adam, from their loins, their seed, and made them testify concerning themselves, [saying]: "Am I not your Lord?" They said: "Yea, verily. We testify"* (Qur'ān, 7:172).

This knowledge that human beings had about their Lord from eternity, even before they were manifested on earth, can never be sincerely and intimately negated. In one's innermost self, there remains the indelible mark of God's Unity and Being. Consequently it is a question of a truth engraved forever upon man's intimate being, constituting the very principle of his permanent reality in God. The same *shahāda* could therefore be translated and interpreted: It is present in my consciousness and I recognize that there is no god present and worthy of being worshiped but God.

The fall of Adam and of his spouse, their exit from the paradisiacal Garden, and the fall of their progeny, who they brought with them forever, increasingly diminished this realization of divine Unity. In the previous chapter, we recalled one of the Qur'ānic episodes referring to the fall of Adam.

It is here that the second *shahāda* becomes relevant, as it concerns the sacred and divine Mission of the Envoy mentioned in the first Pillar of Islam: "I bear witness that Muḥammad is the Messenger of God." This can also be translated as: It is thoroughly present in my consciousness and I recognize that Muḥammad is the Messenger of God.

Without the providential intervention of the Prophet Muḥammad—God's Blessing and Peace be upon him—who was sent by God out of pure clemency and mercy, and therefore love, the descendants of Adam could not recognize fully—in all aspects of their being—the truth of the first shahāda: *No god but God*. In fact, this universal truth, forever inculcated in the being, is actualized through the Revelation transmitted by the Prophet and the conformity of the faithful to the perfection of his nature. Muḥammad is the light shining in the heart of the creature who was enveloped by darkness following the fall to earthly manifestation: *O Prophet! Lo! We have sent thee as a witness and a bringer of good tidings and a warner. And as a summoner unto Allah by His permission, and as a lamp that giveth light* (Qur'ān, 33:45-46).

That is why the faithful servant who submits himself to God's Law must attest and verify in himself, as an evident truth, the divine mission of the Messenger of God. And that is also why the Prophet, before being charged with this mission, was invested with all the divine qualities needed to fulfill it. God says of Muḥammad in His Holy Book: *Verily, you are of a tremendous nature* (Qur'ān, 68:4). Hence, one can better understand that without the intervention and the intercession of the Prophet, the son of Adam has but little chance to fully recognize, in the manner which saves him from the consequences of the fall into manifestation, the Unity and the universal Existence of God which are the essence and the raison d'être of all manifested beings. The emulation of the impeccable and perfect Prophet, adored with all the characteristics of God, has no other goal but to enable the servant to recognize in himself this fundamental truth, and in turn to remain faithful to the primordial Pact which he made with his Lord for ever. God says: *Verily in the Messenger of Allah ye have an excellent pattern for him who looketh unto Allah and the Last Day, and remembereth Allah much* (Qur'ān, 33:21). Speaking of himself, the Prophet also informs us that he constitutes a model for all of mankind: "I have been given the all-comprehensive words." Without the Prophet and total love for him, one cannot become fully present before God and recognize Him as the Lord, as one's Lord. Through the love that God brings to us with His mercy, God says: *Say, (O Muḥammad, to mankind): If ye love Allah, follow me; Allah will love you and forgive you your sins. Allah is Forgiving, Merciful. Say: Obey Allah and the messenger. But if they turn away, lo! Allah loveth not the disbelievers* (Qur'ān, 3:31-32).

One of the consequences of our obligatory love toward the prophet who was sent out of the pure mercy of love for all the worlds, according to the Qur'ānic verse, is that this love for the Messenger of God becomes necessary for the worshipper. It is necessary to his irresistible attraction towards his Creator who is his Origin and End. The love for the Prophet awakens the love that God placed in the human being for eternity when He created him out of pure love. And this love for the Prophet will ultimately be none other than the love that the worshipper carries to his Lord. The more he loves the Prophet and the more he loves his Lord, the more attracted he will be to God. The following verse illustrates this vital point and gives total authority to this argument: *Yet of mankind are some who take unto themselves rivals to Allah, loving them with a love like [that which is the due] of Allah [only]—those who believe are stauncher in their love for Allah . . .* (Qur'ān, 2:165). *O ye who believe! Choose not your fathers nor your brethren for friends if they take pleasure in disbelief rather than faith. Whoso of you taketh them for friends, such are wrong-doers. Say: If your fathers, and your sons, and your brethren, and your wives, and your tribe, and the wealth ye have acquired, and merchandise for which ye fear that there will no sale, and dwellings ye desire are dearer to you than Allah and His messenger and striving in His way: then wait till Allah bringeth His command to pass. Allah guideth not wrongdoing folk* (Qur'ān, 9:23-24). It is through the emulation of the Prophet that the worshipper intensifies his love for him to the point of loving the Prophet more than his own soul. This is because the Prophet represents, in a certain way, the Master, the Lord, whom he must not only serve but also love and recognize to the extent of his innate, individual capability.

It is therefore evident that the instruments of grace that God gave to each member of the community of Muḥammad were instituted through him. They were defined in the Revelation and in the Prophetic Sunna, and they were promulgated out of pure mercy so that human beings may get progressively closer to God. The realization thus obtained through sincere and complete adherence to the double *shahāda* would be developed through the religious practices that God reveals to that end. Their meanings stem from the truth contained in this double testimony.

Thus understood, the two-part testimony of Divine Unity and the Mission of Muḥammad concerns *iman* just as much as *islam*, meaning deliberate submission is as important as the Faith which engenders beneficial acts. According to a *ḥadīth*, "whoever says *Lā ilāha illā 'Llāh, Muḥammad Rasūl Allāh* protects his life and his goods." He who recognizes the truth of this testimony saves his own soul, and he who realizes the perfection of these two outward and inward attitudes embellishes the testimony and accomplishes the completion of submission and of faith. This perfection of *islām* and *īmān* is called *iḥsān*, meaning embellishment or excellence. According to a famous *ḥadīth*, it is ". . . that thou shouldst worship God as if thou sawest Him; for if thou seest Him not, yet He seeth thee." The servant who realizes this state achieves certitude which, according to another *ḥadīth*, is the entirety of faith.

The servant who testifies that Muḥammad is the Messenger of God does not say that he is the Chosen One or the Prophet, although he is nonetheless. It is as Messenger of God that one attests to Muḥammad in this witnessing of faith. The person who has faith therefore must recognize the revealed message not only as divine revelation, but also in the totality of its contents including all the aspects comprised by this message.

The two-part *shahāda* recapitulates all the fundamental facts of the Islamic Revelation. It contains all the doctrinal elements on God and His Being, His manifestation, and the raison d'être of the creation. It enables us to understand how the sincere servants achieve sanctity or nearness to God by conforming to the Muḥammadan reality.

To conclude this brief account, we will say that the consequence of this two-part testimony, articulated by the servant with an increasingly perfect consciousness, will be the recognition of the Reality of God and of His universal Presence in His Creation. Who, then, is conscious of this Presence if not God Himself, the Witness of all beings? We cannot but recognize Him as the unique Witness of all, simultaneously present within us, for we are the receptacles of His Presence. Contemplation or *mushāhada*—a word coming from the same root as *shahāda*—directed towards God as Lord and towards God who is present in His creation, is an immediate realization of the being which ascertains or attests to the Presence of the witness who observes him. It is also the realization of everything, without causing God to cease being transcendent with respect to His Creation, and without Him losing His incommensurability with this creation which would be instantly annihilated if He did not vivify it with His permanent Presence. Without exception, all beings contemplate God as Witness, but with varied realizations, depending on their degree of purification obtained through the means of grace embodied by the religious obligations. God has said: *What thing is of most weight in testimony? Say: Allah is Witness between me and you. And this Qur'ān hath been inspired in me, that I may warn therewith you and whomsoever it may reach. Do ye in sooth bear witness that there are gods beside Allah? Say: I bear no such witness. Say: He is only One Allah. Lo! I am innocent of that which ye associate [with Him]* (Qur'ān, 6:19).

In the following two chapters, we will expound upon the contents of these two sacred professions. It is God who expresses the Truth and guides the Way (cf. Qur'ān, 33:4).

Chapter III

On the Formula of Divine Unity
"No Deity but God"
Lā ilāha illā 'llāh

There is an important difference between the following two sacred formulae:

i) "I testify that there is no deity but God," or *Ashhadu an lā ilāha illā 'Llāh.*
ii) "No deity but God," or *Lā ilāha illā 'Llāh* does not include any oath and by this very fact does not necessarily engage the person, as one can very well say *no deity but God* without acknowledging the role of personal faith in this truth. Testifying to the Divine Unity engages the person to recognize the latter and to feel directly and necessarily concerned with it. By not including this oath of faith, the formula *Lā ilāha illā 'Llāh* is simply an expression negating every deity beside God. We are going to expound on some of the doctrinal aspects this implies and, in order to do that, we will proceed with an analysis of its constituent elements.

The revealed word *Lā ilāha illā 'Llāh* presents four elements. The first two express an absolute negation *Lā ilāha*, "no deity," and the last two a categorical affirmation, *illā 'Llāh*, "but God," or "except God." Moreover, the two nouns translated as god are different in Arabic: *ilāh* and *Allāh*. We will explain the difference between these two nouns in order to reach some doctrinal conclusions of great importance. Beginning with these remarks, we will see what comportment the servant of God adopts in order to recognize in himself the truth implied by this Islamic formulation of the Divine Unity.

The grammarians specify that the negation *lā* is absolute and it means *no*. According to the grammarians, the particle *illā*—composed of *il*, if, and *lā*, not—which can be translated as "if not," always takes the meaning of *other than, except*. The formula of Divine Unity can therefore be translated as: *no deity but God*. An even more accurate translation would perhaps be, *no deity if not God*. The same grammarians bring to light the fact that the particle of exception *illā*, "if not, except," which comes after the absolute negation *lā*, or "none," does not necessarily imply an affirmation. That is why the sacred formula *lā ilāha illā 'Llāh* can also be rendered: *If there is a god, it is God*. This is the same rule of Arabic grammar that allows us to correctly interpret the following prophetic *ḥadīth*: *Lā ṣalāta illā bi tahūr*, or "no prayer without purification." This last formula does not necessarily mean that there is no prayer, but that if the latter exists then it must be preceded by the purifying ablution. Similarly, the sacred formula in question does not necessarily affirm the existence of God; it indicates that, if there is a god, it is God.

The last conclusion does not suggest that this formula affirms the Existence of God for it does not contain an expressed or implied verb. It merely postulates His Unity. Furthermore, the pronunciation, articulated either outwardly or inwardly, must awaken in the faithful the consciousness of his origin in God, Creator of everything to Whom all things are attached. The more the servant recites this formula the more he will recognize that there is none other than God in the principle of his own being, or in the permanent reality of his essence in God. This act of faith corresponds to his knowledge of the revealed Qur'ānic statements on God.

This analysis of the two terms *ilāh* and *Allāh* leads us to consider their semantic meanings. In French, *ilāh* and *Allāh* are generally rendered both as "god," or "divinity."

What is, then, the difference in meaning between the two terms, seeing as God Himself distinguishes them in His revealed Scripture?

Grammarians and theologians have their differences on the question of the name *Allāh*. Is it a proper noun which does not derive from anything, or is it a name derived from a determined reality?

Those who state that the name *Allāh* does not stem from any derivation, and that it therefore has no etymology, advance the following arguments concerning the Qur'ānic verse: *Knowest thou a homonym for it?* (Qur'ān, 19:65). Knowest thou one that is named

Allah along with Him? Knowest thou anyone who wouldst have the right to the perfection of the Names and the Attributes which only *Allāh* can claim? Who can sincerely claim to be truly qualified by them? Is there a name which encompasses more universal realities than this incomparable name? Does it derive from the name of a creature, when it is known that nothing is like unto Him? In reality, this name *Allāh*, through which everything subsists, alludes to the Divine Essence. Therefore, from this perspective, it is a proper name that designates a reality without stemming from that which it names. Being Itself indefinable, it gives everything its definition.

While the name *Allāh* is considered to pertain to the absolute, transcendent, unconditioned Divine Essence, it can never be appropriated to mankind because this name does not derive from anything and therefore does not share a common value/framework/category/classification with the names of determined and qualified beings. The name *Allāh* also does not admit any relation in its absoluteness. In this respect, the name *Allāh* is identical to the named, the name thus being considered as the very reality of the named, which is Allāh *qua* absolute, unconditional Reality.

However, certain legal experts assert that an etymological derivation is possible. In this case they envisage the different meanings taken by the root of the name *Allāh*, which is *A-L-H* or *W-L-H*. The second root means to worship as one god, to be overwhelmed by love, to be dismayed, to have nostalgia and to be sad, to be high and shiny, to be veiled, or to be permanent.

All of these meanings are interesting for two main reasons:

—Firstly, they all encourage the soul to orient itself more perfectly towards God.

—Secondly, the person who invokes God through this sacred name *Allāh* must do so with the appropriate attitude consisting of veneration, humility, nostalgia, and love towards tradition. This name is pronounced with an emphasis. It should not be said *Allāh* but rather *Allōh*, the *ā* becoming almost an *ō*. This outward and/or inward pronunciation or articulation must provoke the irresistible call of all the energies of the person towards Allāh through the nostalgia that the worshiping servant retains from his origin in Him. He keeps present in his consciousness that Allāh constitutes all reality and the only reality.

However, these apparently contradictory points of view concerning the derivation or non-derivation of the Name *Allāh* are not incompatible. While the Name *Allāh* suggests the Divine Essence which transcends all created reality, it also means that Allāh is present in His Work, in the universal Manifestation, and that it can awaken the consciousness that Allāh is the permanent and only Truth worthy of worship in the servant. Yet, since human beings can recognize this true Reality in themselves, they experience an irresistible love attracting them towards Allāh, which is subtlety present in all things while remaining transcendent and immutable in Its essential solitude.

By virtue of this verse of the Qur'ān, *Thy Lord hath decreed, that ye serve none save Him* (Qur'ān, 17:23), all beings cannot but submit themselves to Allāh, their Lord; they are all attracted willingly or unwillingly, consciously or not, towards Him. The infidel or the non-believer, whether he misdirects his faith or stifles it [*kāfir* being etymologically he who stifles (faith) or the farmer who stifles grain], will identify himself illusively—never veritably and essentially—with the countless and particular idols or gods who will be for him as many foci of attraction. Such an attitude is called associating (*shirk*) false and vain gods with God—gods who seem to rival Him. The servant who is faithful to his principal origin will never cease orienting himself, with exclusive dedication, towards his Principle and Master, under the double influence of the divine knowledge and love that transform and sanctify him. The meanings contained in the possible derivations of the Name *Allāh* imply all these qualities on the part of the worshipper. The *Name* Allāh is thus a remembrance (*dhikr*) of the Divine Presence and of the Love of God for His creatures. It is also their remembrance of their origin in Him.

Having recognized the various possible meanings of the Name *Allāh*, let us strive to identify the existing differences between the two nouns *ilāh* and *Allāh*.

When the Name *Allāh* is taken as a proper noun, it does not derive from anything. It is, as we shall illustrate, the perfect symbol of the ultimate Reality of all the things with which it can never be compared.

But when this same Name *Allāh* is considered a derived noun, we discover that one of its potential etymologies according to the grammarians and theologians is *a-l-h*, source of the term *ilāh*. This root *a-l-h.* means to adore, to be in amazement, to remain in awe out of the respect, fear or love inspired by someone, to take refuge with someone, or to be protected.

The theologians claim that this *ilāh* as a determined reality other than God, even if invested with divine power, must be methodically and existentially excluded from consciousness. This *ilāh* is then, according to this point of view, felt and recognized as a reality distinct from God. It is also recognized as illusory, a reality which may well be a particular created being like all the creatures, from the most important to the most insignificant. From this determined, autonomous, and limited quality, *ilāh* takes on a quasi negative character of meaning beside, above or instead of Allāh, for if there is an *ilāh*, it can only be Allāh. That is why, ultimately, the true worshipper, the person who directs his faith properly, does not consider anything in the Creation of God as a god or an autonomous and exclusive *ilāh.* For the true worshipper, this *ilāh*, linked as it is to Allāh, is none other than Him. The human being becomes aware of this through regular spiritual and methodical work, every day and each instant acknowledging intimately that this *ilāh* is the servant himself with respect to God, whom he serves and upholds as the object of his worship.

In the clear formula of all testimony, *lā ilāha illā 'Llāh, No deity but Allāh*, the deity or *ilāh*[a] that is completely negated is the deity which implies all beings, in a general manner, since this negation has an absolute character, as we noted earlier. In certain Qur'ānic formulations, this *ilāh* concerns more particularly each one of us. Thus, in Surah Tāhā God says: *This is your [worshiped] god* (*ilāhukum*) *and the god of Moses, but he hath forgotten* (Qur'ān, 20:88). Here, the word *[worshiped] god* is of course *ilāh*, and God says again: *Lo! thy [worshiped] God is surely One* (Qur'ān, 37:4). *And He it is Who in the heaven is [worshiped] God* (*ilāh*)*, and in the earth [worshiped] God* (Qur'ān, 43:84). Elsewhere in the Qur'ānic text it is said: *He is Allāh in the heavens and on the earth* (Qur'ān, 6:3). In the last verse, the term used is *Allāh* and not *ilāh*, because Allāh, in His unconditioned and undetermined Reality is subtly present in what He has created and He necessarily encompasses the *ilāh* of all possible beings.

From these few considerations of the term *ilāh* we can extract three possible interpretations, each of which takes into account a different point of view.

1) Firstly, when *ilāh* is taken and worshiped as an autonomous,

independent, delimited and ephemeral reality, it then constitutes the object of idolatrous worship. In Islam, such worship is considered to neglect attachment to God. It is called association, or *shirk*, the only sin that cannot be forgiven or erased. God says thereof: *If there were therein gods beside Allah, then verily both (the heavens and the earth) had been disordered. Glorified be Allah, the Lord of the Throne, from all that they ascribe [unto Him]. He will not be questioned as to that which He doeth, but they will be questioned. Or have they chosen other gods beside Him? Say: Bring your proof. This is the Reminder of those with me and those before me, but most of them know not the Truth and so they are averse. And We sent no messenger before thee but We inspired him: There is no god save Me, so serve Me* (Qur'ān, 21:22-25). *Hast thou seen him who maketh his desire his god, and Allah sendeth him astray purposely* (Qur'ān, 45:23).

2) Secondly, one may consider the term *ilāh* to represent *Allāh* in His divine function. Allāh reveals this "aspect" of Himself in the following verses: *Allah hath not chosen any son, nor is there any god along with Him; else would each god have assuredly championed that which he created, and some of them would assuredly have overcome others. Glorified be Allah above all that they allege* (Qur'ān, 23:91). Allāh Himself specifies that there is no *ilāh* but God Himself, Alone, Unique, One and without anyone sharing in His Existence: *Is there a god with Allah? Exalted be Allah above what they associate [with Him]*, (Qur'ān, 27:63), and, *And cry not unto any other god along with Allah. There is no deity* (ilāh) *save Him* (Qur'ān, 28:88).

3) Finally, one may envisage the term ilāh as representing the manifestation of a divine function (*tajallī*): *Has Allah not said: And He it is Who in the heaven is God (ilāh), and in the earth God (ilāh). He is the All-Wise, the All-Knower* (Qur'ān, 43:84). It is this same God, in His active capacity, to whom beings submit willingly or unwillingly, and to whom they are faithful. Thus it is Him that they recognize as their God, after having driven from their souls all the gods claiming autonomy, and after the divine Grace has taken hold of them to the point that they contemplate none but the Existence and the presence of God in His Theophany. It is in this contemplation (*mushāhada*) that pure, saintly, and guided servants were able to say: "I have not seen

anything without seeing Allāh before that thing," as Abū Bakr, the first successor of the Prophet, said. "I have not seen anything without seeing Allāh after that thing," said 'Umar, the second Caliph. "I have not seen anything without seeing Allāh with it," said 'Uthmān, the third Caliph.

Each of these three points of view draws a unique commentary:

—According to the first meaning of the word *ilāh*, the believer strives best to remove everything that is other-than-Allāh. He achieves this through a methodical war, called the Great Holy War (*jihād akbar*), against his soul that incites to evil. His struggle culminates in the recognition of God, who is present in him, as his God and Lord. He detaches himself from all individual and fragmentary realization, and qualifies himself with the character traits of God, to use the words of a famous tradition.

—In the second approach to the noun *ilāh*, the same believer worships God in God, because his god is none other than God who is one and without associate. He recognizes in God his God and Lord, and also his Origin.

—The third facet of the noun *ilāh* is spoken by the person sanctified by the Sanctity of Allāh when he or she testifies in all consciousness and certitude that *there is no deity (ilāh) but Allāh*, and that the divine Manifestation is but the external representation of the possibilities implied in His infinite and eternal Knowledge. For . . . *is there a god with Allāh* (cf. Qur'ān, 27:60-64) and beside Him? For this person, God is present in His Work without however ceasing to transcend what He is created of, and without being affected by it. According to the prophetic *ḥadīth*, "Allah was and there was nothing with Him." In His Sacred Book, Allah says: *He is with you wheresoever ye may be* (Qur'ān, 57:4). He also says, *whithersoever ye turn, there is Allah's Countenance* (Qur'ān, 2:115). These persons, who have a constant awareness of God, in themselves and in His Creation, know veritably that their God is One God, since they know with a particular certainty that God is the unique Real Being and that they are the receptacles of the possibilities which include His Existence, which no longer is modified by them, just like the ocean waves produced by the breath of the Spirit do not really affect the ocean in its unity.

In addition, the formula of Divine Unity *Lā ilāha illā 'Llāh* covers and uncovers all the essential doctrinal aspects of God and His universal Existence, and the "impermanence" of the world which does not cease evolving and renewing at each breath of the All-Radiating with Love (*raḥmān*). *Lā ilāha illā 'Llāh* reveals the immutable Knowledge of God as well as the means to reach His knowledge.

The faithful and sincere servant who has witnessed Divine Unity, and who therefore keeps this knowledge of God present in himself continuously, deepens this knowledge thereafter. This is why he will not cease repeating this divine formula spontaneously, thus aligning himself with the truth it expresses, and identifying himself, in a certain manner, with the Reality it postulates. For, according to the Qur'ānic Revelation, *There is no deity* (*ilāh*) *save Him. Everything perishes save His Face* (Qur'ān, 28:88). Certain commentators consider this Face to be that of Allah but also that of the person in his permanent divine Reality.

That is why this sacred formula is the most perfect expression of Divine Unity and of the essential and permanent Reality of the person. In order to recognize that it is precisely so, the worshiping servant who submits himself faithfully will repeat it tirelessly in order to remain integrated with the Truth which he contemplates and witnesses (*shāhid*) in all the constituent elements of his integral being which is vivified and sanctified by it.

In the course of this book we shall see that the Qur'ān situates Jesus in relation to the noun *ilāh*. The preceding analysis of *ilāh* and *Allāh* already suggests what can be variously considered the reality of the Anointed One, Jesus Son of Mary, in the Qur'ānic Revelation.

Chapter IV

On the Formula
Muḥammad is the Messenger of God
Muḥammad Rasūl Allāh

We have commented on the formula of Divine Unity, No god but God (*lā ilāha illā Allāh*), in its simple form, not as part of the testimony. We will now present some characteristics of the second formula of Islamic faith, *Muḥammad rasūl Allāh*, likewise considering it aside from its relationships with the testimony of faith. We will proceed to the analysis of each of its three constituent terms in order to clarify their principal meanings, as well as those meanings resulting from the joining of three sacred words in a single phrase. However, we cannot aspire to exhaust the countless meanings of such a revealed formula.

Certain authors interpret the name *Muḥammad* to mean glorified, praised. The root Ḥ-M-D, from which the name Muḥammad derives, clearly means to praise, to thank, to celebrate the perfections of something or someone. *Muḥammad* is the passive participle of the second derived verbal form, which means: to produce praise, to make praiseworthy. The name *Muḥammad* therefore means: he who has been made praiseworthy or he in whom praise is produced. Moreover, in Arabic, the form corresponding to the name Muḥammad qualifies nouns of place and time. Grammarians call these nouns "names of vase" or "of countenance." The derived name *Muḥammad*, which is at once a passive participle and a noun of time and of place, then takes on the meaning: he who is the place—or support—in whom praise is manifested during a given time or cycle. This interpretation is interesting, as we shall see later, for it enables us to give to the function of the divine Envoy a universal meaning which is perfectly and providentially fulfilled by the Prophet of Islam, as well as by all the prophets and persons—each in the magnitude which God has determined for them—who are nothing but the bound receptacles of the universal Praise of God. From this perspective, the name Muḥammad is linked with praise (*al-ḥamd*) and to the Divine Name *al-Ḥamīd*, constructed in the *fa'īl* scheme with the double, passive and active meaning concerning the transitive verbs. *Al-Ḥamīd* means 'the All-Praised All-Praiser.' The name *Muḥammad* can thus have the meanings of a proper noun which applies only to a being, and those of a name which is derived from the root 'to praise.'

The name *Muḥammad* therefore concerns first and foremost the Prophet in his reality. This reality is distinguished from that of other creatures because in this respect he constitutes a unique reality envisaged in the mode of praise. *Muḥammad* is therefore a privileged being who receives the universal Praise of God; the latter concerns him particularly. To paraphrase a Qur'ānic verse, Muḥammad, viewed as Envoy—or Messenger—out of his Lord's pure Mercy of love for the beings of the universe, must fully realize the divine Praise in order for it to be spread to all the members of humankind and the Muslim Community through his providential intermediary until the Day of Resurrection.

There is more! A third doctrinally important meaning follows inexorably. *Muḥammad*, in whom a permanence of the praise of God is produced, for always and forever, is none other than the actual Existence or Being of God encompassing the whole of His Praises or Beautiful Names (*el-asmā' al-ḥusnā'*) which He manifests in order to make known, through love, all the possibilities or predispositions implied by His infinite Foreknowledge.

To better understand and delve deeper into the meanings of the name Muḥammad, let us try to define, to the greatest extent possible, praise in general and divine Praise in particular.

Let us first consider some examples in the revealed Book, the Qur'ān. Allāh says: *Praise belongs to Allāh, the Lord of all beings* (Qur'ān, 1:2). *The seven heavens and the earth and all that is therein celebrate His Glory, and there is not a thing but glorifies (God) by His (or its) praises; but ye understand not their glorifying. Lo! He is ever Forbearing, Forgiving* (Qur'ān, 17:44). *And whosoever giveth thanks, he giveth thanks for his soul. And whosoever refuseth—Lo! Allah is Absolute, Owner of Praise* (Qur'ān, 31:12).

Praise can therefore be defined: the expression, proclamation or celebration of the perfection of a thing. Allāh proclaims His infinite Perfections implied in His limitless Knowledge. The creatures are nothing but the expression of the divine All-Possibility. Every manifested being cannot but celebrate the divine Glory through His own Praise. The creatures of God express Praise, for they represent as many perfections as He manifests. It is for this reason that each being is seen as a set of divine praises, or a set of divine perfections which make explicit or manifest "aspects" of God (*ilāh*). This praise reveals the Treasure buried in the profound and unfathomable mystery of His Knowledge.

Such an interpretation of the universal divine praise enables the verse quoted above to accommodate a double meaning. Allāh clarifies: *there is not a thing but glorifies God] by its praise* (Qur'ān, 17:44). The commentators of the Qur'ān who specialize in syntax note that the pronoun "its" in the expression "its praise" concerns Allāh or the praise of Allāh, but also applies to the creature. This is because the grammatical analysis of this pronoun refers to the nearest name, which in this verse is the masculine word "thing," whereas the name *Allāh* is not mentioned explicitly. This verse therefore accommodates two principal meanings which ultimately merge: either the "things" proclaim divine Praise, or things are nothing other than the proper Praise or the proper infinite Perfections of God. Each thing expresses the divine Possibilities and, by this very fact, the praises made by the "things" are nothing but the things themselves envisaged according to the perfections they express. They are the locus or the receptacle of divine Praise and each of them expresses an aspect thereof. This is why, with respect to praise, each thing is *Muḥammad* interpreted as the one in whom the divine Perfections or Possibilities are revealed in the cosmic and historical cycle where he evolves.

Therefore Muḥammad was and is the worthiest being to receive the Divine Attributes. Let us recall that it was his grandfather 'Abd al-Muttalib who, under inspiration from 'Amīna, the mother of the Prophet, named him with this name which was rarely if ever used before. He was the first servant able to receive and realize in the fullest manner all the perfect Divine words contained in the Revelation. Whereas his name *Muḥammad* implies this truth in and of itself, a famous *ḥadīth* further confirms it. The Prophet said of himself: "I have been given the all-comprehensive words." It is possible that the Muslims who bear the name Muḥammad, or who call their sons by this name, feel more or less consciously that the name Muḥammad *does* contain all-embracing words. The Tradition recommends that Muslims name their children Muḥammad.

The Prophet, the most excellent being and the most capable of receiving praise, and the most appropriate and active receptacle in whom the perfections are manifested permanently, had to serve as a role model to his Community. In expressing his own human possibilities, he also had to encompass all the human possibilities of his Community, so that he might serve them as a living law and role-model and thus enable them to realize with full consciousness the divine Praise which was manifested in the Community through him. This name Muḥammad, therefore is destined to be the best and most satisfactory among those who describe him. For this very reason, he is mentioned by that name in the two-part Islamic profession of faith, even though the Tradition recognizes him by other names as well.

The virtue of his name Muḥammad is also closely linked to that of his name ʿAbd Allāh, or the Worshipper, Servant of God. Because of the infinite perfections that God has placed in him, he is truly and totally the servant-worshipper of his Lord. In order for him to manifest the Divine perfections, he had to be completely receptive to Divine favour: he had to be like a polished mirror, bare and unadorned by images, so that he might integrally reflect the set of Divine Names without altering their actualization.

The name and the character of Muḥammad thus defined enables us to better understand the second element of the phrase *Muḥammad Rasūl Allāh*, *rasūl* meaning messenger.

The root of the word *rasūl* has multiple meanings. That which particularly interests us is the meaning of envoy or messenger. The other connotations of the root *r-s-l* are: to have a soft, gracious, and balanced pace like that of a camel; to have abundant milk from a large flock; or to have long, flowing hair. The *rasūl* is therefore first of all the messenger, the envoy, the one sent with a mission. He is entrusted with a mission or a purpose, but his mission includes an unwavering consistency in bringing about abundance and well-being. He disperses difficulties or oppositions. Muḥammad, the Messenger, is therefore a privileged being who is realized through God Himself. God sends him to reinstill consciousness in human beings, in the entirety of their constitution made in the image of God, so that they realize that they come from Him and that they must return unto Him according to the status which He has determined for them.

When the two nouns *Muḥammad* and *Rasūl* are thus interpreted, the formula *Muḥammad Rasūl Allāh* expands to the following: He who is the fullest receptacle of the divine perfections is the Messenger whom God sends by instilling in him a permanent mission of grace and prosperity.

This sacred statement thus concerns every being, but it applies first and foremost to the Prophet. It reveals his exceptional and incomparable quality which rendered him capable of receiving and transmitting the Divine Message. The latter consists of the divine Perfections expressed and communicated through the Prophet Muḥammad. Allāh is the God who praises and is praised by Muḥammad. Yet Allāh can only be praised and give praise through that which was sent with Muḥammad: the universal Message which he brings from the Lord of all beings of the universe. The Muḥammadan function of the divine envoy then must be to serve as an intermediary and sacred vicegerent between God and the creatures so that they regain consciousness that they do aught but chant the very Praise of God and that they express His All-Possibility. Glorifying God by His own praise allows created beings to fulfil the divine plan. Allāh again announces this truth in another formulation, saying: *We sent thee not save as Mercy for all creatures* (Qur'ān, 21:107). This verse refers primarily to the Prophet and his universal Mission, but it also concerns all the beings that are created to spread the Mercy of God which *encompasses all things*, to quote the Qur'ānic expression. In the verse 21:107, Allāh does not reveal this truth by bringing into action, through the use of the pronoun *We*, the set of Beautiful Names and the Divine Functions, for that would require the combination of all the Divine Names in order for the Prophet Muḥammad to be imbued—and by extension we too—with all the qualities which distinguished him as the envoy encapsulating the Virtues and the Words of Allāh.

The possessor of faith who has submitted to the law of Islam will repeat the formula *Muḥammad Rasūl Allāh* by making present in his consciousness that it is true and that it addresses him. This permanent testimony of the Reality of the Prophet and his own reality forged in the unity of his Lord will become more and more real, sincere and efficacious. The increasingly perfect emulation of the Prophet Muḥammad will make the man of faith conform to the most perfect reality of the envoy, and he will ultimately identify with the Prophet depending on the God-granted potential which he unknowingly carries within himself from eternity. Through the universal Law revealed to Muḥammad the possessor of faith will ultimately come to understand intimately that he is the locus where the Divine Perfections are manifested. He will then know in an increasingly evident and immediate way that in the universal Existence of God there is but One Praised-Praiser, Allāh. All created beings are inexhaustible receptacles of His perfect Names who, whether willingly or unwillingly, glorify Him with infinitely varied forms of praises.

Understood in this manner, the sacred formula thus enables us to accept that each prophet is also Muḥammad through one of the latter's attributes. His attributes imply, according to his all-inclusive and universal reality, the reality of each prophetic type. The Message which he transmits from God represents the synthesis of all other revelations. According to this perspective, Muḥammad, the seal of the Prophets, preeminently encompasses the prophetic virtue of the other divine envoys.

Allāh reveals that *there is no deity but Allāh* and that *Muḥammad is His Messenger*. He also bears witness to the Unity of His being and of His universal existence. In this way, all beings are like perfect forms which express Him. One of the most adequate symbols alluding to this truth is that of the ocean and the waves produced by the Breath of the Spirit. The water of the sea is one, the Muḥammadan spirit is also one, but it communicates to this homogenous Water an infinity of qualities. Each wave produced by the Breath of the Spirit is one of the praises which would have not existed if the Spirit did not spread the divine possibilities.

The teachings contained in the two-part profession of Islamic Faith are inexhaustible. We have only considered a few fundamental aspects. These brief glimpses will suffice to show how much the truth implied in the two-part *Shahāda* concerns us all. They enable us to better understand why the person who repeats it as often as possible, sincerely, in all purity, and with the required faith, has no other reward but the paradisiacal abode by his Lord, as a *ḥadīth* states.

This universal and all-embracing quality which *Muḥammad, the Messenger of Allāh*, possesses is of importance to all of us and is expressed in certain significant verses which will serve as a conclusion:

> *And how would ye deny Faith, when it is ye unto whom Allah's Signs are recited, and His messenger is in your midst* (or *in you, fī-kum*)? *He who holdeth fast to Allah, he indeed is guided unto a right path* (Qur'ān, 3:101).

> *And know that the messenger of Allah is among you* (or *in you, fī-kum*). *If he were to obey you in many a matter, ye would surely be in difficulty; but Allah hath endeared the faith to you and hath beautified it in your hearts, and hath made disbelief and lewdness and rebellion hateful unto you. Such are they who are the rightly guided* (Qur'ān, 49:7).

> *But Allah would not chastise them while thou wast with them, nor will He punish them while they seek forgiveness* (Qur'ān, 8:33).

Chapter V

The Prayer on the Prophet
Al-Ṣalāt 'Alā-n-Nabī

The preceding chapter, dedicated to the formula *Muḥammad Rasūl Allāh*, enabled us to glimpse a fundamental aspect of the reality of the Prophet of Islam, through certain characteristics of the Arabic language of the revelation and the Qur'ānic verses. The present chapter will demonstrate another facet of the Prophet Muḥammad in relation to what is usually translated as "the prayer on the Prophet." We are going to tackle this theme by once again turning to Arabic semantics and certain verses dealing with this subject.

The ternary verb root of the noun *ṣalāt* is *s-l-w*. This root has the following principal meanings: to hit on the back, to finish second in a horse race, to perform an action of grace which unites or brings one closer, to make a bond of grace, or to pray. Considering the various coherent meanings, he who makes the "prayer" or action of grace, the *musallī*, is always second in relation to the one who is taken for a target and the one which we try to overtake in this competition. On the other hand, the root *s-l-w* is outwardly related through form and meaning to the root *w-s-l* which includes the same radicals presented in a different order. This root means: to achieve, to unite, to join, or to bind.

This theme is present in certain verses which will enable us to better understand the action of grace that links and/or unites. The scheme following the provided translation shows the mode of action of this *ṣalāt*.

> *And of the desert-dwellers are those who believe in Allah and the Last Day, and take that which they expend as means of bringing them near to Allah (qurubāt) and [obtaining] the uniting graces of the Messenger (ṣalawāt al-Rasūl). Lo! verily it is a means of nearness (qurba) for them. Allah will bring them into His mercy. Lo!*

> *Allah is Oft-forgiving, Merciful* (Qur'ān, 9:99).
>
> *Of their goods, take alms, wherewith thou mayst purify them and mayst make them grow, and effectuate the link of grace on them (ṣalla 'alay-him). Lo! thy link of grace (ṣalāt-ka) is a haven of peace for them (sakan^{un} la-hum). Allah is Hearer, Knower* (Qur'ān, 9:103).
>
> *Who say, when a misfortune striketh them: 'Verily we are for Allah, and unto Him are we returning.' Such are they on whom are unifying graces from their Lord (ṣalawāt min Rabbi-him), and mercy. Such are the rightly guided* (Qur'ān, 2:156-157).
>
> *Say: Lo! my action of unifying grace (ṣalātī) and my sacrifice and my living and my dying are for Allah, Lord of the Worlds* (Qur'ān, 6:162).
>
> *Hast thou not seen that all [who are] in the heavens and the earth, and the birds in their flight celebrate the Glory of Allah? Each of them has known His act of unifying grace, and the proclamation of His Glory; and Allah is Aware of what they do* (Qur'ān, 24:41).
>
> *He it is Who operates the link of grace upon you (yuṣallī 'alaykum), as well as His angels, that He may bring you forth from darkness unto Light; and He is ever Merciful to those who have faith* (Qur'ān, 33:43).
>
> *Lo! Allah and His angels effectuate the link of grace on the Prophet (yuṣallī 'alā al-nabī). O ye who have faith! Operate the link of grace on him and submit yourselves entirely* (Qur'ān, 33:56).

Ṣalāt's mode of action according to the verses above is shown on the facing page.

The verses quoted above are directed towards various 'addressees' on whom or for whom this *ṣalāt* takes place. Let us examine each of these verses in order to show the different actors concerned with this *ṣalāt* as well as the elements which comprise these Qur'ānic references.

The "key" verse is 33:56, in which Allāh and His angelic functions make the *ṣalāt*:

> —on the Prophet Muḥammad who is then directly endowed with its virtues;
>
> —on the Muslims who have faith according to Islam and who receive the divine order to make the *ṣalāt* on him.

Verse 9:103 orders the Prophet to bestow the link of grace upon

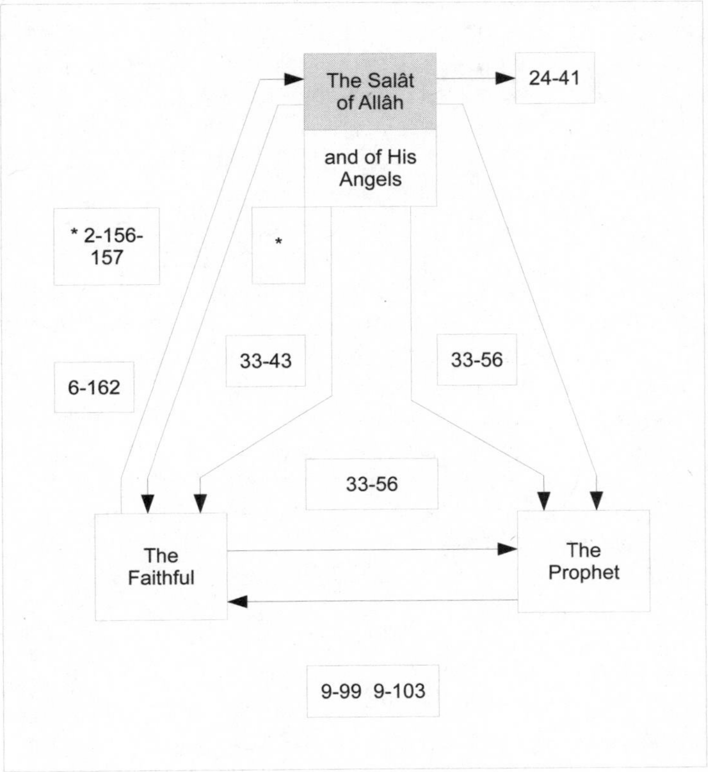

them, for his *ṣalāt* is permanent peace for them (*sakan la-hum*).

On the other hand, verse 33:43 specifies that Allah and His angels make the *ṣalāt* on the believers, but unlike verse 33:56 which does not restrict prayers concerning the Prophet, this verse affirms that through *ṣalāt* the Believers will be *brought forth from darkness into light*. This is a sign of Allah's mercy or radiating love for them. Indeed, in the same chapter, the Prophet is addressed in the following manner: *O Prophet! Lo! We have sent thee as a witness and a bearer of good tidings and a warner. And as a summoner unto Allah by His permission, and as a torch that brings light* (Qur'ān, 33:45-46). He is a torch that brings the Divine light and therefore has no need to pass from darkness into light.

In these verses, it is Allah and His Angels who make the *ṣalāt* on the Prophet and the believers, and the Prophet also makes the *ṣalāt* on the Believers, as well as the Believers on the Prophet. But the reverse is never mentioned in the revealed text, for neither the Prophet nor the believers make *ṣalāt* on Allah and His angels. On the contrary, in verse 6:152, Allah uses the expression *My ṣalāt* to address each and every Creation and He tells those beings that their *ṣalāt*, their commitment, their life, and their death are for Allah (*lil-Lāh*), the Lord of all the worlds. The *ṣalāt* of Allah and of the angels is carried out on the creatures, and the *ṣalāt* of the creatures takes place for Allah. It is addressed to Him, for they receive the divine and angelic *ṣalāt* which occurs upon them, and they cannot but intend it for Him and return it to Him, as the two-part exegesis of verse 24:41 confirms above. We have translated the verse by identifying the third-person singular pronoun *hu* (he or him) as pertaining to Allah: *Each of them has known His act of unifying grace, and the proclamation of His Glory* . . .. According to this translation the pronoun "His" therefore corresponds to Allah, implying that the *Ṣalāt* and the *tasbīḥ* pertain to Him. However, this verse element can be interpreted differently if the two expressions *his ṣalāt and his tasbīḥ* each concern the term, for grammar dictates that the nearest word determines the subject of the pronoun under discussion. We wish to remark that the Arabic pronoun accords with the possessor just as in English. Of the terms making up this verse, we will retain only *ṣalāt*, which is the object of this chapter. In this second interpretation, the term *ṣalāt* leads to envisaging all beings, or each of them—a notion implied by the Arabic term *kull*—as having their own manner of ascending the celestial hierarchy and ultimately reaching God: *The Exalter of Ranks, the Lord of the Throne. He causeth the Spirit of His command upon whom He will of His slaves, that He may warn of the Day of Meeting, the day when they come forth [as they are], nothing of them being hidden from Allah. Whose is the Sovereignty this day? It is Allah's, the One, the Almighty* (Qur'ān, 40:15-16). *Allah will exalt to high ranks those who believe among you, and those who have been granted knowledge* . . . (Qur'ān, 58:11).

Verse 6:162 is preceded and followed by other verses showing the value of *ṣalāt* and the degrees of proximity to God that it enables: *Whoso bringeth a good deed will receive tenfold the like thereof, while whoso bringeth an ill-deed will be awarded but the like thereof; and they will not be wronged. Say: Lo! As for me, my Lord hath guided me unto a straight path according to a right religion: the tradition of Abraham, theotrope, who was not among the associators. Say: Lo! my worship and my sacrifice and my living and my dying [are] for Allah, Lord of the Worlds. He hath no partner. This am I commanded, and I am first of those who surrender [unto Him]. Say: Shall I seek another than Allah for Lord, when He is Lord of all things? Each soul earneth only on its own account, nor doth any laden bear another's load. Then unto your Lord is your return and He will tell you that wherein ye differed. He it is Who hath placed you as viceroys of the earth and hath exalted some of you in rank above others, that He may try you by that which He hath given you. Lo! Thy Lord is swift in prosecution, and Lo! He verily is Forgiving, Merciful* (Qur'ān, 6:160-165)

The *ṣalāt*, as a means of divine grace which allows the believer to reach the greatest proximity to God, takes on diverse forms. The Prophet Muḥammad described *ṣalāt*: "*Ṣalāt* is the Ascension (*mi'rāj*) of the believer." The Revelation alludes to the Prophet's Ascension, describing his distance from the Lord as: *two bow lengths or even nearer, and He revealed unto His slave that which He revealed* (Qur'ān, 53:9-10).

This *ṣalāt* may take many forms: (i) ritual in the five daily prayers; (ii) performed in dedication to the Prophet; or (iii) in the innate form of that which is obligatory for all beings. In every form it is an intimate dialogue between the servant and his Lord. The *ṣalāt* is also a divine and human act in a sacred place, during which the Divine Plan is distilled and developed by those who maintain the required ritual orientation during the act of prayer. The human being is the vicegerent (*khalīfa*) of God who has been entrusted with the Safe-keeping (*amāna*) of all other creation (Qur'ān, 33:72). He who "prays" in this way turns towards the spiritual Center of Islam—Mecca—and develops in three dimensions according to the various positions of the body he observes in his ritual prayer. In the vertical position (*qiyām*), which represents the immutability of God and His attribute of Absolute Independence (*qayyūm*), he is like the universal pole corresponding to the celestial hierarchy and spiritual elevation. In the position of bowing, he develops into the boundless immensity of the possibilities contained in each of the hierarchical worlds. In prostration, he effaces himself in the divine proximity. Finally, in the sitting position he bears witness, through God, of this proximity that affects the whole of his being. The hands which collect and orient the spiritual energies and the presence of God with full consciousness are the primary catalyst for the penetration of this presence into the whole physical, psychic, and spiritual being. Thus, when the worshipper raises his hands (*yad, yadayn*, also meaning oriented active force) at the moment of sacralising himself for the rite of prayer by pronouncing *Allāhu Akbar* (Allah is infinitely great), he must have an intense awareness of carrying out a divine process that will make him a receptacle for divine descent. He may fold his hands on his chest, thus channeling the divine energies to the centre of his whole being, or he may loosen his hands to let the energies descend to the deepest foundations of his being. During this action of unifying and transforming grace, he advances into three worlds: the physical, the psychic, and the spiritual. When the unifying prayer is performed with intuitive awareness of these different meanings, it affects the whole being, leading to a state of permanent grace thus described by God: *Those who remain constant at their unifying prayer, and in whose wealth [is] a right acknowledged* (Qur'ān, 70:23-24).

The action of unifying grace as such belongs to God but its accomplishment is the making of the believer who is merely the place where the "praying" act of God appears. This place is called *musallā*, the locus upon which this divine act of unifying grace is carried out, and where beings stand in prayer. This prayer, including as it does movements, words, and specific and unalterable gestures, remains what it is for God first and foremost before being canonical: a pure action of unifying Grace that He performs on His creatures who are its supports. The descent of the "operating" and transforming grace will vary according to the divinely predetermined receptacles.

There exists another type of action of unifying grace mentioned in two verses which we quoted earlier: the act of grace and the benediction which God, His Angels and the believers perform on the Prophet. In this last type, as we have pointed out in the previous chapter, the name *Muḥammad* is a passive participle of the second derived form, which also applies to names of place and time. *Muḥammad* qua derived noun thus means: "he who is the support upon whom the praise or the proclamation of the divine perfections and qualities is manifested during a given cycle." This semantic interpretation is particular to the revealed and sacred Arabic, and provides us with another means of understanding the universal function of the divine Messenger and his aptitude to receive divine praises, from the beginning of the human cycle up to its end. It also helps us grasp why the prophet who carried the name *Muḥammad* was "before Adam was between water and clay" in the words of an authentic tradition. This name *Muḥammad* concerns essentially the Prophet of historical Islam and universal Islam in its particular reality. But when this name is envisaged as a derived noun that can be applied to anyone, it specifically concerns each being who is gifted with a set of divine attributes in which he participates more or less consciously. When God, His Angels, and the believers "pray" on the Prophet Muḥammad, it is also in view of his total and synthetic perfection which includes that of all humans, a perfection in which they cannot but participate and develop in themselves by performing the act of unifying grace on him. For the Qur'ān says, *And know that the messenger of Allah is in you* (fī-kum). *If he were to obey you in many a matter, ye would surely be in difficulty; but Allah hath endeared the faith to you and hath beautified it in your hearts, and hath made disbelief and lewdness and rebellion hateful unto you. Such are they who are the rightly guided* (Qur'ān, 49:7). When human beings who have faith make the *ṣalāt on Muḥammad*, the act realizes certain possibilities particular to the Prophet who can thus hope to be granted the *Praiseworthy Station* mentioned by God in this verse: *It may be that thy Lord will raise thee to a Praiseworthy Station* (*maqām maḥmūd*) (Qur'ān, 17:79).

There are numerous prophetic traditions showing the distinguished value of this *ṣalāt* which the Believers perform upon the Prophet. We will quote a few of them here: "Whoever performs the *ṣalāt* upon me once, Allah performs the *ṣalāt* upon him ten times." "I met the Archangel Gabriel who told me: 'I announce this glad tiding to thee: Allah has said, I transmit my salutations of peace to whoever expresses his salutations of peace to thee, and I perform the *ṣalāt* upon whoever performs the *ṣalāt* on thee.'" "On the Day of Resurrection, my intercession (*shafā'atī*) will reach whoever has performed the *ṣalāt* upon me ten times in the morning and ten times in the evening. Whoever performs the *ṣalāt* upon me, Allah purifies his heart from hypocrisy just like water purifies the cloth." "When you hear the muezzin calling to prayer, repeat what he says and perform the *ṣalāt* upon me. For whoever performs the *ṣalāt* upon me, Allah performs the *ṣalāt* ten times upon him. Then ask for me to be granted the station of mediation (*ṣallū liya al-wasīla*) for it is a position (*manzila*) in the Garden which is only granted to one of the servants of Allah, and I hope to be that one. Intercession (*shafā'a*) will be given to whoever asks the degree of mediation (*wasīla*) for me." The term *wasīla* is not an easy one to translate. The *Lisān al-'arab* dictionary defines it under the root *w-s-l*: "It is to reach a position (*manzila*) beside the king, it is a degree (*daraja*) and nearness (*qurba*). So and so seeks access (*wassala*) to Allah while working to get near to Him." *Wasīla* means to have credit and influence, gathering around someone, the means of reaching him through the best way of reaching affinity.

The *Ṣalāt 'alā al-nabī* is the means of approach and access to God through the intermediary of the Seal of the Prophets, Muḥammad, synthesis of all prophetic typologies. This is why, in the tradition of Islam, it is he who God, the Angels and the Believers all address, even if the latter must take recourse to additional prophetic types in order to seek the granting of their requests. But Allah knows best!

Chapter VI

General Themes Concerning Jesus, Mary, and the Christians in the Qur'ān and Prophetic Tradition According to the Surahs in Which They Appear

In this chapter, we will present the principal themes dealing with Jesus ('Īsā), Mary (Maryam), Zachary, Yaḥyā' (John the Baptist), and the Christians (al-naṣārā) by discussing the different Qur'ānic sequences in which they appear, ordered chronologically whenever possible, or otherwise ordered thematically. This method strives to respect the Qur'ānic context wherein chapters and verses are presented in a manner that situates their characteristic events. Most of the verses may be analyzed according to where in the Qur'ān Allah mentions them, but other verses which are often apparently unrelated and which carry essential teachings must be commented upon independently. Generally speaking, the Qur'ānic style is rather concise and numerous verses contain different themes. We will notice this trait repeatedly in examining our current topic concerning the "Christic" perspective of the Qur'ān. In the following lengthy chapter, we will summarize a translation of all the verses under discussion opposite their Arabic text. We will then comment upon them in the usual order of their classification according to the method generally used by the Qur'ānic commentators.

A. The family and the progeny of 'Imrān down to Jesus

1. Who constitutes the family of Jesus through his mother?
2. His election
   —among all beings of the World

3. The announcement made to Zachary
   —his request to have a progeny (3:38, 3:40)
   —annunciation of Yaḥyā's birth by the Angels (3:39)
   —his request for a sign (3:41)
4. The prophet John the Baptist (Yaḥyā'): see above and 3:39, 6:85, 19:7, 19:12.
5. Invocation of pregnant Anne (Hanna), mother of Maryam (3:35)

B. Maryam—Mary

1. Birth of Mary
   —her mother Anne (Hanna) delivers her (3:36)
   —her mother names her Maryam (3:36, the meaning of this name)
   —her mother asks that she be protected from Satan (3:36)
2. Her childhood
   —her perfect belief (3:37)
   —her guardianship under Zachary (3:37, 3:44)
   —her divine sustenance (3:37)
   —her seclusion from her people (19:17)
3. The Annunciation
   —as tidings of things unseen (3:44)
   —an envoy of the Spirit of God in the likeness of a perfect form (19:17)
   —her request to seek refuge in God (19:18)
   —Annunciation of the Anoint, Jesus, Son of Mary by the angels (3:45)
   —Mary never touched by a man (3:47, 19:20)
   —tidings of the gift of a pure son (19:19)
4. The conception
   —the Word (from God) unto Mary (4:171)
   —by the Spirit (19:17, 19:21, 21:19, 66:12)
   —God and His Spirit (*rūḥ*): See the verses on the Spirit. Who is the Father of Jesus? (66:12)
   —The Divine Order or Command (*'amr*) (19:21)
   —The virginal conception (21:91, 66:12)
5. Her pregnancy and the birth of Jesus
   —her seclusion with Jesus (19:22)
   —the signs of parturition (19:23)
   —her remarks (19:23)
6. Miracles accompanying the birth of Jesus

—he speaks to his Mother (19:24)
—he speaks in the cradle (19:29)

7. Reactions of the people around her
—her own people (19:27)
—the title of sister of Aaron they give to Mary (19:28), a link of spiritual lineage, not parentage.
8. Her election, her privileges, and her qualifications
—immaculate, transparent or diaphanous (3:42)
—chosen above other women (3:42)
—her reverence (3:43, 66:12)
—her truthfulness (5:75)
—the favours of God bestowed upon her (5:110)
—screened by protection (19:17)
—not driven by desire (19:20)
—sister of Aaron (19:28)
—a sign for all the beings of the Universe (21:91)
—forever virgin (21:91, 66:12)
—testifies to the truth of the Words of her Lord (66:12)
—perfect servant (3:35, 19:21)

C. Jesus and Mary

1. Genealogy of Jesus according to the Qur'ān
2. The names of Jesus
—Jesus—'Īsā (6:85, 42:13, 43:63)
—The Anointed One or the Messiah—*al-Masīh* (9:30)
—The Anointed One or the Messiah, Jesus Son of Mary—*al-Masīh 'Īsā ibn Maryama* (3:45, 4:171)
—The Anointed One or the Messiah, Son of Mary—*al-Masīh ibn Maryama* (5:17, 5:72, 5:75, 9:31)
—Son of Mary—*Ibn Maryama* (23:50, 43:57)
—Jesus Son of Mary—*'Īsā ibn Maryama* (5:78; 5:110, 112, 114, 116; 19:34; 33:7; 57:27; 61:6, 14)
—Mary is the one who bore him (*wālidatī*) (19:32)
—Do not hold up me and my mother as deities alongside Allah (5:116)
—the Anointed One, Son of Mary; and his mother *al-Masīh ibn Maryama wa Ummu-hu*: 5:17
—Son of Mary; and his mother—*Ibn Maryama wa Ummu-hu* (23:50)
3. The exceptional birth of Jesus

4. The childhood of Jesus
5. Their common qualities
   —they used to eat food (5:75)
   —they constituted a single Sign (23:50)
   —their elevation (23:50)
   —by the Spirit: the Divine Name *Raḥmān* whose root is divided into *Rūḥ* and *Mā.*

D. Jesus

1. His nature and his attributes
   —his existence from the *Kun* (exist! be!) (3:47)
   —his original similarity or semblance (*mathāl*) to Adam (3:59)
   —the Word of God (*kalimat Allāh*) (4:171)
   —Spirit from God (*Rūḥ min-Hu*) (4:171)
   —strengthened by His Breath, the Holy Spirit (2:87, 5:110) cf. the Gospel of John XX, 22
   —Statement of the Truth (*qawl al-Ḥaqq*) (19:34)
   —Servant of God (*'Abd Allāh*) (4:172, 19:30, 43:59)
   —Prophet (*nabiyy*) (19:30)
   —gifted with clear proofs (2:87, 2:253, 5:110, 43:63)
   —Knowledge of the scripture (Torah and Gospel) (3:48, 5:110)
   —confirms the Torah (that which was not updated/renewed by him and his followers) (3:50, 5:46, 61:6)
   —brings glad tidings of a Messenger whose name is *Aḥmad* (61:6)
   —Muḥammad is the Paraclete: see the Gospel of John XIV, XV, XVI, 1st epistle of John
   —Messenger (*rasūl*) (2:87, 4:171, 5:75)
   —Messenger unto the Children of Israel (3:49)
   —received Scripture (19:30)
   —received the Gospel (57:27)
   —received Wisdom (*ḥikma*) (3:48, 55, 59; 5:47, 48, 110; 43:63)
   —illustrious (3:45)
   —of those brought near (3:45)
   —of the righteous (3:46)
   —receiver of blessings (19:31)
   —detached from those who disbelieve—purification (3:55)

—Sign of God (3:49, 19:21, 21:91, 23:50)
—Witness on the Day of Resurrection (4:159)
—Soul (*nafs*) of God and of Jesus (5:116)
—Mercy from God (19:21)
—offers the *ṣalāt* and the *zakāt* (19:31)
—dutiful to his mother (19:32)
—not arrogant or unblessed (19:32)
—Salām (peace) upon him . . . (19:33)
—a model (43:57, 59)
—example for the Children of Israel (43:59)
—gifted with favours (43:59)
—a sign (for the coming) of the Hour (43:61)

2. His miracles
—raising the dead and healing (3:49, 5:110)
—speaks in the cradle (3:46, 5:110, 19:30)

3. His Message, the Gospel and/or the Gospels
—Comprehensive/universal descent of the Gospel (3:3)
—Abraham and the Gospel (3:65)
—Guidance (3:3)
—placing those who follow him above those who disbelieve until the Day of Resurrection (3:55)
—The Gospel is guidance and light (4:46)
—the name *Muḥammad* mentioned in the Gospel (7:157)
—Gospel received by Jesus (47:27)
—parables (48:29)

4. His disciples
—His Helpers (*ansār*) (3:52, 61:14)
—the *Ḥawāriyyūn*—who are they? (3:52, 5:111, 112, 61:14)
—Muslimūn (3:52, 5:111)
—witnesses (3:53, 5:111)
—their conformity to Jesus (3:53)

5. The Eucharist and the Table-Spread (*Mā'ida*)
—the disciples' question to Jesus about the descent of a table (5:112)
—Jesus invokes his Lord (5:114)
—this Table is frequent reiteration and feast (*'īd*) (5:114)
—a promise to the truthful (5:119)—the meaning of the term *nafs*.

6. His "Completeness"
—his faithful fulfilling of the Promise (3:55)

7. Crucifixion and his death? His rising from the dead
    —Was he crucified or not, and by whom? (4:157)
    —Who was crucified then?—the formula *Shubbiha la-hum* (4:157)
    —His being risen up unto God (3:55, 4:158)
8. His relationship with the end of time and the coming of the Hour (43:61)
9. His logias according to the Qur'ān, the Sunna, and Traditions
10. His non-superiority with respect to other Messengers and/or Prophets
11. Difference between the names *Allāh* and *Ilāh*
    —*Ilāh*: deity which reveals itself—used for God and for creatures (3:2, 62)
    —one God who reveals Himself (4:171, 5:73, 9:31)
    —commentary on the Surah 112 of the Qur'ān
12. Difference between the noun *ibn* and *walad* (2:87)
13. Faith in Jesus
    —who are the People of the Scripture? (2:105, 3:64)
    —the People or Possessors of the Scripture (4:159)
    —his possible "destruction," as well as that of his mother and everyone on earth (5:17)
14. Followers in the footsteps of the Prophets
    —in the capacity of truthful confirmers (5:46)

E. Christianity and the Christians before the Islamic Revelation

1. Christianity and Christians
    —formula of equivalence in the two Revelations: worship of One God (*Ilāh*) without any partner or equivalent—rejection of any form of idolatry (3:64)
    —they claim they are sons of God and His loved ones (5:18)
    —the nearest (in affection) to the (Muslim) Believers are the Christians . . . (5:82)
    —those who uphold the Anointed One, Son of Mary as a lord beside God (9:31)
2. Qur'ānic term for denoting the Christians
    —*Nasārā* (2:62, 111, 120, 135, 140; 5:14, 18, 51, 69, 82; 9:30; 22:17)
3. Trinity, ternary, triad, three, dyad
    —say not "Three" (4:171)

—Allah is not the third of the three (5:73)
—Jesus and his mother as two gods? (5:116)

4. God: genesis, generation and filiation
   —the existentiating *Kun* (19:34)
   —Allah has no child (*walad*) (4:171, 19:34)
   —their claim that the Messiah is the Son (*ibn*) of Allah, and its consequences (9:30, 32)
5. Monastic life and priesthood
   —the priests and their behavior (5:82)
   —the monks and their behavior (5:82)
   —monasticism (57:27)
6. The state of Christianity and the Christian birth at the time of the rise of Islam (3:67)
7. Abraham neither Jew nor Christian (3:67)
8. Confusion of those who differ concerning Jesus
   —their knowledge (4:157)
   —their conviction or their conjectures (4:157)
9. The People of the Gospel
   —must stand out in wisdom or else they shall be transgressors (5:47)
   —among them there are people who are moderate (5:66)
   —Aḥmad and the Paraclete (61:6 and John XIV, XV, and XVI, and the 1st epistle of John)

F. Jesus and the Children of Israel; Jews and men

1. The Banū Isrā'īl
   —who are they (3:49)
   —their disbelief or their obscuring (of faith) (3:52)
   —cursed for their disbelief, by the tongue of David and of Jesus, Son of Mary (5:78)
   —God's wrath and chastisement of them for their behavior (5:80)
   —God restrained them from Jesus (5:110)
   —they considered the miracles as magic (due to the double nature of Jesus) (5:110)
   —calumny of Jews towards Mary (4:156)
2. The Jews
   —they say they are children of God and His loved ones (5:18)
   —they are the most vehement in enmity to those who have faith (5:82)

—their claim: 'Uzayr is the Son of Allah (9:30, 9:32)
—'Uzayr and the implied consequences (4:157, 158)

3. The men
   —The reaction of Jesus before the expression *Take me and my mother for two gods* (5:116)
   —Depreciation of the worship due to God (5:116)
   —polytheistic worshiping (43:58)

G. The People of the Scripture

1. Those who obscure the faith (*kāfirīn*)
   —they say that God is the Messiah, Son of Mary (5:17)
   —they do not love the sending down of the good (2:105)
   —they obscure the Signs of God (3:70)
   —they remain aloof from the faith until the coming of the Evidence (98:1)
2. Those who have faith and guard themselves
   —they have the Garden (of bliss) (5:65, 9:111)
   —it is best for them (3:110)
   —their humility (3:199)
3. Respecting the Scripture
   —in order to conform to the divine order (5:68)
   —their alteration of Scriptures (3:78)
4. Their attitude towards religion (*Dīn*)
   —there must be no extreme attitudes in the expression of the Truth
   —attitudes not to be emulated (5:77)
5. Their legal status with respect to Islam
   —indebted to the Religion of Truth (9:29)
   —indebted for the tribute (*jizya*) (9:29)
6. Some wish to see the Faithful turn into disbelievers (2:109, 3:69)
7. Approach for a profession of common faith (3:64)
8. Their dispute about Abraham (3:65)
9. Some people conceal the truth (3:71)
10. Their declarations (3:72)
11. Orthodox community (3:113)
12. The coming of the Messenger with proofs after an interval (5:11)
13. Their blaming of the Believers (5:59)
14. Transformation into monkeys, swine, and idol-worshippers (5:60)
15. Modalities of controversy with them (29:46)

H. The Disbelievers or those who obscure Faith Regarding God

—He is the Anointed One, Son of Mary (5:7, 72)
—He is the third of the Three (5:73)

I. The relations of the Prophet Muḥammad with the Christian world

1. The Prophet before the Qur'ānic revelation
2. His family ties
3. His occupation as caravan tender, the Meccan period.
4. His relationship with the Christians of Najrān
   —mutual imprecation (3:61)
   —real expiatory formula (*qaṣaṣ al-Ḥaqq*) (3:62)
5. Immigration of the first Muslims to Abyssinia—Surah 19 (Maryam)

Chapter VII

Commentary by Surah

Surah 2

Qur'ān, 2:62. *Lo! Those who believe [in that which is revealed unto the Prophet], and those who are Jews, and Christians, and Sabaeans—whoever believeth in Allah and the Last Day and doeth right—surely their reward is with their Lord, and neither fear shall come upon them nor shall they grieve.*

إِنَّ الَّذِينَ آمَنُوا وَالَّذِينَ هَادُوا وَالنَّصَارَىٰ وَالصَّابِئِينَ مَنْ آمَنَ بِاللَّهِ وَالْيَوْمِ الْآخِرِ وَعَمِلَ صَالِحًا فَلَهُمْ أَجْرُهُمْ عِنْدَ رَبِّهِمْ وَلَا خَوْفٌ عَلَيْهِمْ وَلَا هُمْ يَحْزَنُونَ

In the presumed order of revelation, the second chapter was the eighty-seventh to be revealed, and the above verse is the first to mention the Nazarenes (translated here as Christians). It is inserted into a sequence of verses whose themes are apparently independent from its content. On the contrary, verse 69 of Surah 5, which is number 112 in the presumed order of the revelation, uses terms identical to the verse cited above. Surah 5 ends in a sequence of several verses (65-69) dealing with related themes, which we will comment upon later.

Certain commentators, following Ibn 'Abbās, a companion of the Prophet, have considered this verse to be abrogated by verse 85 of chapter 3, which was the eighty-ninth to have been revealed; that is, after verse 2:62 above, but before verse 5:69. For this chronological reason, it could not have been abrogated by verse 3:85, which says: *And whoso desires as religion other than the Surrender (al-islām) it will not be accepted from him, and he will be among the losers in the Hereafter.*

On the other hand, as we have already shown in the chapter dedicated to the universality of Islam, the term Islam accommodates several interpretations. Universal Islam concerns all forms of revelation, in contrast to historical Islam, while each has to provide every truly spiritual person access to this trans-historical Islam which is ultimately beyond all forms taken by Revelation throughout history. As the final revelation, Islam then synthesizes the diverse forms of previous revelations; such should therefore be the outcome of each revelation and each of their members. The ultimate goal towards which each person adhering to a particular form of revelation strives is situated beyond the latter and thereby surpasses it. Verse 2:135 refers to this finality: *And they say: Be Jews or Christians, then ye will be rightly guided. Say: Nay, but [follow] the religion of Abraham, the theotrope who was not of the associators.* This notion of "theotropism" will be commented upon within the same verse. The central aspect of the primordial Tradition which transcends all revealed forms without abolishing them, the concept of theotropism finds expression in these two additional verses: *Abraham was not a Jew, nor yet a Christian; but he was a theotrope who had surrendered (muslim), and he was not of the associators. Lo! those of mankind who are closest to Abraham are those who followed him, and this Prophet and those who have faith; and Allah is the Protecting Guardian of the believers* (Qur'ān, 3:67-68). These verses place emphasis on notions of theotropism, the undifferentiated universal orientation, and the exclusive and primordial worship such as that performed by Abraham beyond the Jewish and Christian forms issuing forth from him like two branches of the same trunk. Islam as the last revelation synthesizes the different forms that the perennial Revelation acquired during the course of the history of humankind. The Qur'ānic text expresses in a concise manner all kinds of divine precepts and universal wisdoms whose enunciations are concentrated in the Divine Names. The Names are necessary for God's presence in His work to accord with the most differentiated and often antinomian aspects. For this reason, in the historical cycle inaugurated by Islam, the most dissimilar human attitudes are mentioned so that the believer who adheres to them may put them to good use.

There exist several interpretations of verse 2:62 in accordance with possible divisions of these sequences and according to the meaning that has been given to the expression *those who have faith*. Generally, the verses comprising this formula concern all those who have adhered to divine revelations throughout history, in one form or another, and who have realized the ultimate goal that those revelations offer: the return to Allah beyond all conditioning. When they become depositaries of this faith, they may be called People of the Book (*ahl al-kitāb*). This expression, considered alongside the etymological meanings of its two compositional terms, can also be applied to human beings who adhere to the last form of the universal Revelation, Islam.

The rest of this verse specifies that the undifferentiated believers (*mu'minūn*), the Jews, the Christians, and the Sabaeans, must all put their faith in Allah and in the Last Day, and they must behave with integrity to receive their reward with Him with no fear or affliction. The universal value of this Qur'ānic declaration is remarkable.

The following verses, which we will quote later in this work, refer implicitly to this universality of faith over the course of different revelations from Adam to Muḥammad: *If only the People of the Scripture (ahl al-kitāb) would have faith and ward off [evil], surely We should remit their negative dispositions from them and surely We should bring them into Gardens of Delight. If they had observed the Torah and the Gospel and that which was revealed unto them from their Lord*[1] *they would surely have been nourished from above them and from beneath their feet. Among them there are people who are moderate (min-hum ummat*^{un} *muqtaṣidat*^{un}*)*,[2] *but many of them are of evil conduct. O Messenger! Make known that which hath been revealed unto thee from thy Lord, for if thou do it not, thou wilt not have conveyed His message. Allah will make thee immune against mankind. Lo! Allah guideth not the disbelieving folk. Say O People of the Scripture! Ye have naught [of guidance] till ye observe the Torah and the Gospel and that which was revealed unto you from your Lord. That which is revealed unto thee [Muḥammad] from thy Lord is certain to increase the contumacy and disbelief of many of them.*

1. Including the Qur'ān and other revealed Scriptures, according to some commentators such as Qurṭubī.

2. Those who are found among the People of the Book are considered by these same Muslim commentators of the Qur'ān as being those who have faith, the Believers (*mu'minūn*) in a general sense before Islam, including also the Muslims (cf. the commentary of Qurṭubī).

But grieve not for the disbelieving folk (Qur'ān, 5:65-68).

Although the expression *ahl al-kitāb* refers to human beings possessing a scriptural tradition before the close of the Qur'ānic revelation, it would be later considered by certain commentators to also apply to those who have adhered or adhere to Islam, the last Divine descent.

Another term concerning those who have faith is a vocative expression occurring 90 times in the Qur'ān: *O you who have faith* (*yā' ayyuhā al-ladhīna āmanū*, literally *O you who have believed*). Those referred to are the believers who adhere to Islam, the last revelation, although sometimes this expression is used in contexts concerning persons who follow other revelations as well.

The Qur'ānic occurrences of four religious categories. The verses in gray cells of the first column concern the verses wherein only one religious category is mentioned					
Verses	Surahs	Naṣārā	Alladhīna Hādū	Hūd	Yahūd
2:62	Medinite 87th	1	1		
2:111	Medinite 87th	2		1	
2:113	Medinite 87th	3&4			1&2
2:120	Medinite 87th	5			3
2:135	Medinite 87th	6		2	
2:140	Medinite 87th	7		3	
3:67	Medinite 89th	8			4
4:46	Medinite 92nd		2		
4:160	Medinite 92nd		3		
5:14	Medinite 112th	9			
5:18	Medinite 112th	10			5
5:41	Medinite 112th		4		
5:44	Medinite 112th		5		
5:51	Medinite 112th	11			6
5:64	Medinite 112th				7
5:69	Medinite 112th	12	6		

5:82	Medinite 112th	13			8
6:146	Meccan 55th		7		
9:30	Medinite 113th	14			9
16:118	Meccan 70th		8		
22:17	Medinite 103rd	15	9		
62:6	Medinite 110th		10		

A. The Arabic term *naṣārā*, which occurs fifteen times in the Qur'ānic text, is a plural applying only to Christians, depending on the contexts in which it occurs. This will be easily recognizable each time we come across the term in the quoted verses. *Naṣārā* has a direct etymological relationship with the ternary root *n-ṣ-r* meaning to help, assist, rescue, support, or to be a helper of. In verses 3:52 and 61:14, 'Īsā (Jesus) is assisted by his disciples; the term used for them is *anṣār*, a plural which is derived from the same root *n-ṣ-r*.

The Disciples of Christ were originally called "Christians" around the year 44 in Antioch, about a dozen years after the rising of Jesus.

B. The expression *alladhīna Hādū*: *those who follow Judaism,* occurs ten times in the Qur'ān and includes the verb *Hāda*, from the ternary root *h-w-d* which means to repent.

C. The name *hūd*, from the same root *h-w-d*, occurs thrice in the Qur'ān and is always used in the direct case (*hūd*[an]), meaning 'the Jews.'

D. Another term, *yahūd*, which occurs nine times, comes both from the root *y-h-d* and *h-w-d* mentioned above, and also serves to qualify the Jews. This denomination was introduced during the period 940-586 B.C. to describe the citizens of Judas' kingdom starting from the prophet-king David (cf. Old Testament in II Kings XVI, 6). The term is still in use. It followed the ancient term Hebrew, from the Hebraic root *'a-b-r*, meaning "those from beyond" similar to the meaning of the Arabic root which connotes: to go beyond, to traverse, to cross, consider, interpret, translate, explain, shed tears. *Yahūd* was also used to refer to Semitic tribes of the Middle East who were attached to Seth through the intermediary of Eber, who corresponds to the Haribu/Apiru of the Egyptian and Mesopotamian texts. These tribes migrated from Ur, in Chaldea, all the way to the Aramean country and mixed with the people of Canaan.

The Qur'ān includes the additional term *Banū Isrā'īl*, or Children of Israel. The expression occurs 41 times and we shall comment upon it when discussing verse 3:49.

The Sabaeans would have descended from a Semitic tribe originally from Babylonia before the advent of Islam. They still have representatives in today's Iraq. The root *s-b-'*, the origin of this name, means to progress, to change religion, to rise (as in a star).

> Qur'ān, 2:87. *And verily We gave unto Moses the Scripture and We caused a train of messengers to follow after him, and We gave unto Jesus, son of Mary, clear proofs (or distinctions), and We supported him with the Holy spirit. Is it ever so, that, when there cometh unto you a messenger [from Allah] with that which ye yourselves desire not, ye grow arrogant, and some ye disbelieve and some ye slay?*

وَلَقَدْ آتَيْنَا مُوسَى الْكِتَابَ وَقَفَّيْنَا مِنْ بَعْدِهِ بِالرُّسُلِ ۖ وَآتَيْنَا عِيسَى ابْنَ مَرْيَمَ الْبَيِّنَاتِ وَأَيَّدْنَاهُ بِرُوحِ الْقُدُسِ ۗ أَفَكُلَّمَا جَاءَكُمْ رَسُولٌ بِمَا لَا تَهْوَىٰ أَنْفُسُكُمُ اسْتَكْبَرْتُمْ فَفَرِيقًا كَذَّبْتُمْ وَفَرِيقًا تَقْتُلُونَ

Let us note beforehand the multiplicity of forms addressed in this relatively short verse.

1. Moses, Messenger and Prophet: his revealed Law and the Messengers who followed him

This refers first of all to Moses who received the Scripture, and to the Messengers who followed his Law but who received sacred Scriptures themselves. It may concern David with the Psalms and Solomon with the Books of Wisdom. In Islam, the *Rasūl*, or the Messenger, is the man who is perfectly realized in Allah and who is sent by Him, from Him, with a revealed Law, to a more or less important community that is most often called upon to expand. The Messenger or the Envoy is also a prophet (*nabī'*), but a prophet does not necessarily bring a Law from Allah and is therefore not called a Messenger in most cases. The *nabiyy*, from the root n.b.' or *n-b-y* of this noun, is a man of God who brings news of a high order.

We have already dealt with the function of the *rasūl* in the chapter dedicated to the study of the formula *Muḥammad Rasūl Allāh.*

2. The Scripture or *kitāb*

The term *kitāb*, translated here as Scripture, comes from the ternary root *k-t-b*. It is a noun of action, namely the act of writing, as well as a simple noun referring to the writing that constitutes is the final or progressive result of this act. This root implies the following meanings: to write, to designate, to tie and tighten the orifice with a string, to cork, to sew, and to stitch. It also may refer to a texture, a structure, etc. The *kitāb* can therefore be interpreted as being a set of organized and effective signs, all parts of which are held together to make a coherent whole, a well-structured tissue in its diverse constituent elements. This term's references to the root are not detached from a cosmic symbolism of the warp and the weft, to the texture of other Traditions. Moses received from his Lord the Tablets of the Law according to the verse 145 of Chapter 7: *And We wrote (katabnā) for him, upon the Tablets (alwāḥ), an exhortation and clear explanation of all things, then [bade Moses]: 'Hold it fast; and command thy people [saying]: Take the better [course made clear] therein. I shall show thee the abode of evil-livers.'* In this verse, God addresses Moses in the vocative, as if he remained ever-present in the economy of the human cycle.

3. 'Īsā ibn Maryam or Jesus, the son of Mary

In the Qur'ānic text, we find the following names concerning Jesus and Mary:

A. For 'Īsā

a. 'Īsā is used nine times alone and/or named in a list of prophets in the following verses: 2:136; 3:52, 55, 59, 84; 4:163; 6:85; 42:13; 43:63.

b. al-Masīh, "the Anointed One," or "the Messiah," Christ, occurs twice in the Qur'ān, 4:172 and 5:72.

c. al-Masīh, Ibn Allāh, "the Anointed One, son of Allah," occurs only once, in 9:30.

d. al-Masīh, 'Īsā ibn Maryam, "the Anointed One, Jesus, Son of Mary," occurs three times in the Qur'ān, in 3:45, 4:157, and 4:171.

e. al-Masīh ibn Maryam, "the Anointed One, Son of Mary," occurs five times in verses 5:17 (twice), 5:72, 5:75, and 9:31.

f. al-Masīh ibn Maryam wa Umma-hu, "the Anointed One, Son of Mary, and his Mother," occurs once in verse 5:17.

g. Ibn Maryam, "Son of Mary," is used once in the Qur'ān, verse 43:57.

h. Ibn Maryam wa Umma-hu, "Son of Mary, and his Mother," occurs once in verse 23:50.

i. 'Īsā ibn Maryam, "Jesus, Son of Mary," occurs thirteen times between six different chapters of the Qur'ān; 2:87, 253; 5:46, 78, 110, 112, 114, 116; 19:34; 33:7; 57:27; 61:6, 14.

B. For Mary

a. Maryam: This name is used eleven times in the Qur'ānic verses 3:36, 37, 42, 43, 44, 45; 4:156, 171; 19:16, 27; and 66:12.

b. in diverse compositions: See the names concerning 'Īsā above.

c. Wālida: Meaning "mother, engenderer, one who generates." This form is a present, participle or active substantive from the root *w-l-d*: to engender, to procreate, to mother.

d. Umm: Meaning "mother, she who presents, or brings forth, she who produces, who 'intends.'"

C. Meanings of these diverse names

a. al-Masīh: According to Muslim philologists, this term might originate from one of the following two roots: *m-s-h* or *s-y-h*. It occurs eleven times in the Medinite chapters.

The first root, *m-s-h*, means: to anoint, to rub, to coat, to wipe, or to remove something with the hand. In this form *masīh* is an adjective-name, constructed upon the *fa'īl* scheme, which also includes both an active and a passive meaning. The Anointed One is therefore he who receives the unction and whom Allah fashions with His two hands by imbuing him entirely with Himself. He is the Anointed One but also he who gives or transmits the received divine unction. In the tradition of Israel, this meant unction with oil whose meaning included a consecration to God for the service of people. This notion extends thereby to the unction in the Holy Spirit or the Breath of God, and it becomes the sign of the coming of the Anointed One whom Israel awaited. In the Old Testament, the name of Masīh is given to King Cyrus, who ruled Persia from 558-528 B.C. and who liberated the Jews from their captivity in Babylonia. Many of the liberated then returned to Jerusalem, in Judea. *Thus saith IHVH* (*Yahweh*) *to his anointed one* (*mashīh*, in Hebrew), *to Cyrus, whose right hand I have holden, to subdue nations before him . . .* (Isaiah, 45:1).

The second root, *s-y-h*, means principally: to cast on the

ground, to pour, to spread, to travel, or to cover a distance. *Masīh* is then constructed upon the rarely used scheme *maf'īl* to derive the meaning: one who is constantly moving and changing place.

The more common translations of this name come from Arabic (*masīh*) in accordance with a common Semitic stock, from Latin (the Anointed One), and from Greek (Christ).

The Qur'ānic title Masīh is given to 'Īsā throughout all the stages of his life, and even before his birth, as in verse 3:45: *Behold, the angels said: O Mary! Lo! Allah giveth thee glad tidings of a word from Him, whose name is al-Masīh, 'Īsā ibn Maryam, illustrious in the world and the Hereafter, and one of those brought near.* This verse implies that the person of Christ was included from the beginning in the Divine design in accordance with a unique and privileged function.

b. 'Īsā: In Arabic, there is no clear origin for this proper name. It is composed of the following letters: *'ayn, yā', sīn, wāw.* Some believe it has Hebrew or Aramaic origin in the word *Yèsū'* or *Yèshū'* which is composed of the consonants *yā', sīn* or *shīn*, and *'ayn* arranged in a quasi-inverse order compared to the Arabic name. After the exile of the Jews to Babylonia, this name was interpreted as "Yahweh saves." One comes across anagrams in both languages, for example *ma'a* in Arabic and *'āmma* in Hebrew, each meaning *with.* This inversion of the letters in the name 'Īsā can be interpreted as the respective predominance of the human or divine aspect of Christ in the two revelations, Islamic and Christian.

From another perspective, the Qur'ānic revelation, while presenting certain prophetic figures such as Abraham, Moses, and Jesus, brings in new elements characterizing these prophets with respect to both Testaments. For example, the Qur'ān does not mention all the events listed in the Bible that involve these three prophets. Rather, it mentions other events which are not found in the Bible. Qur'ān is characterized by concise edifying accounts, most often without an historical will on the part of the Divine Author. In the sacred texts quoted above, there is no intention to create a biography of great characters whose existence cannot be verified according to the criteria of the modern science of history; these texts therefore engage with the question of "mythical figures."

c. Son (ibn): In commentaries and translations, a distinction between the two terms *ibn* and *walad* is rarely made.

The root *b-n-y* from which the word *ibn* is derived means: to build, to construct, to prop up, to structure. From this semantic perspective, the term *ibn* is the being which receives its economy and constitution from its two parents (*abwānī* or *wālidānī*), and is therefore formed by those two words. *Ibn* is composed of the same root as *ab*, father, to which the final *n* (*nūn*) is added. This term corresponds to the feminine *bint* (daughter) and its common plural *banūn*. In Sufism, the following adage is often mentioned: "The son is where the secret of father is manifested." In the Qur'ān the term always conveys a positive connotation.

The root *w-l-d*, from which the collective name *walad* derives, means: to engender, to mother, to procreate, or to bring to the world. *Walad* concerns all mothered beings, be they male or female. In the Qur'ānic text, it often has very negative connotations, in contrast to the term *ibn*.

In the case of 'Īsā, his origin through his mother, the perfect woman, is identified and undisputable. The Angel (Gabriel) who manifests in her presence breathes the Spirit into her, as described by the verses 19:17-21 quoted in the commentary below. 'Īsā is therefore the perfect being in his simple humanity, issued from a perfect mother and a perfectly harmonious angel (cf. 19:17). We shall later return to this question in much more detail.

d. Maryam: This name was often given among the Hebrews. Was not the sister of Moses called Maryam? This proper noun, which certain commentators maintain originates in Hebrew or Aramaic, was arabicized by the Qur'ānic revelation. In Hebrew it means "she who worships, she who is devout and pious, she who has vowed her life to God."

The proper noun *Maryam* accommodates two Arabic etymologies. It relates to both the root *r-w-m*: to desire ardently, and the root *r-y-m*: to incline, to have a penchant for something or someone. The term *raym* derives from this second root and refers to surplus or remainder. The first *m* (*mīm*) of the name *Maryam* renders it a noun of place: she who carries an immense inspiration, she who contains in herself love that proliferates in overabundance. Moreover, the two *m*'s of her name, the initial and the final, each holding a numerical value of 40, imply a perfect receptivity that she possessed right from the time of her birth. This receptivity continued through the annunciation of the birth of Jesus and the time of her acceptance of her ultimate function: that of unceasingly giving birth in faith to a multitude of persons who thereby constitute an aspect of her descent through Jesus, her son. We shall have the occasion to return to this subject later in the commentaries on certain verses.

D. The evident proofs or clear distinctions (*al-bayyināt*)

This feminine term is the plural of *bayyina* deriving from the root *b-y-n*: to be separated, to be evident, and to be eloquent. This root includes the double meaning of separation and union. It generated the preposition *bayna* which means 'between,' fulfilling the function of an isthmus that simultaneously unites and separates two distinct realities. This meaning applies to subtle intermediary realities that participate in the formless spiritual world and the domain of the forms. Allah uses the plural form in the conjugated verb *We have given* to communicate that He confers the *Bayyināt* to 'Īsā ibn Maryam through His Beautiful Names. It is not a question of a simple plural of politeness or majesty, but of a veritable investiture given to Jesus, the Son of Mary through the totality of Divine Names.

E. We have helped him through the Spirit of Sanctity

The term *qudus* which we have translated as "sanctity" is considered by numerous Muslim commentators of the Qur'ān as a Divine Name in the same capacity as *Quddūs*. *Quddūs* means All-Holy and derives from the same ternary root *q-d-s*: to be pure, spotless, unmixed, immaculate, and holy.

The Arabic noun *rūḥ*, meaning spirit, wind, air, or from Semitic stock, is related through its root *r-w-ḥ* to the dual qualities of the evening air which is refreshing in temperature and soothing in fragrance. The *rūḥ* is the spiritual breath that transmits life: the spiritual principle of life and the divine Spirit. The following verse is the most representative, allowing us to interpret this rich word of diverse implications as being the Reality at the Divine level: *They are asking thee concerning the Spirit. Say: The Spirit is by command of my Lord, and of knowledge ye have been vouchsafed but little* (Qur'ān, 17:85). A similar presentation of these three names, namely, those of the Divine Command or Order, the Spirit, and God, is found under different terms in verses 16:1-2, 40:15, and 42:52 which accommodate this interpretation: *[Inevitable] cometh [to pass] the Command of Allah: seek ye not then to hasten it: Glory to Him, and far is He above all that they associate [with Him]! He sendeth down the angels through the Spirit from His command unto whom He will of His bondmen, [saying]: Warn mankind that there is no deity save Me, so keep your duty unto Me* (Qur'ān, 16:1-2). *The Exalter of Ranks, the Lord of the Throne. He causeth the Spirit of His command upon whom He will of His slaves, that He may warn of the Day of Meeting* (Qur'ān, 40:15). *And thus have We inspired in thee [Muḥammad] a Spirit of Our command* (Qur'ān, 42:52). Let us note that in these three verses we find three expressions for qualifying God: *Rabb* (Lord), Allah (Name of the Divine Essence and Its universal function), and We (applying to the totality of Divine Names which cooperate so that the Divine Order or Command may transmit the Spirit to the Prophet Muḥammad, as illustrated in the last verse). We will have the occasion to readdress the Function of the Spirit and the Divine Command more profoundly in the commentary on verse 4:171. In this verse the Order or the Command is closely related to the exceptional case of the Anointed One, Jesus Son of Mary, through the Word (*kalīma*).

The expression *Rūḥ al-Qudūs*, or "the Spirit of Sanctity," occurs four times in the Qur'ān. It is applied to Jesus, Son of Mary in 2:87, 2:253, and 5:110, and once in verse 16:102 to those who have faith: *Say: The Spirit of Sanctity hath delivered it (the Qur'ān) from thy Lord in Truth, that it may confirm those who have faith, and as guidance and good tidings for those who have surrendered* (Qur'ān, 16:102).

In these verses, we note that the Spirit proceeds both directly from Allah as in 16:102, and from the Divine Command, which is comparable to the Divine Word, as in verses 17:85, 16:1-2, 40:15, and 42:15.

Thus understood, *Rūḥ al-Qudūs* also applies to both the Holy Spirit of Allah and to the manifestations of this Spirit, in all the possible worlds, in formal or non-formal roles which are appropriate to the circumstances determining its modes of apparition and action. Can it be deduced that the non-human function that marks the origin of the engendering of Jesus has a direct relationship with the apparition of the Angel to Mary in perfect human (*bashar*) form (cf. 19:17)?

F. Concerned individuals' reaction to the messengers

The end of this verse addresses individuals concerned with the divine Messenger, which is transmitted in various forms depending on the human beings concerned. Hesitating to accept or refuse a new form of Revelation is a fairly common attitude, and the

Qur'ānic text revisits this theme repeatedly. This is the reason why the prescriptions imposed by God, be they new or old, outward or inward, are often accepted collectively or individually with many a reservation and reticence.

> Qur'ān, 2:105. *Neither those who disbelieve among the people of the Scripture nor the associators love that there should be sent down unto you any good thing from your Lord. But Allah chooseth for His radiating Love whom He will, and Allah is of Infinite Bounty.*

مَا يَوَدُّ الَّذِينَ كَفَرُوا مِنْ أَهْلِ الْكِتَابِ وَلَا الْمُشْرِكِينَ أَنْ يُنَزَّلَ عَلَيْكُمْ مِنْ خَيْرٍ مِنْ رَبِّكُمْ ۗ وَاللَّهُ يَخْتَصُّ بِرَحْمَتِهِ مَنْ يَشَاءُ ۚ وَاللَّهُ ذُو الْفَضْلِ الْعَظِيمِ

The expression "people of the Scripture" was discussed in connection with verse 2:62, and further illustrated by verses 5:65-68. The later verses confirm that the expression is addressed to the communities who have received, through the mediation of Messengers, scriptures from God transmitted orally and/or in writing. In other words, the notion of *kitāb* (Scripture) is not necessarily confined to a book, a scroll, a writing, or a collection but rather characterized by divine formulations containing an appropriate teaching. It is also to be noted that this term *kitāb* is not mentioned in the Qur'ānic text for the prophets and messengers before Abraham who did not have writing (*khatt*) at their disposal or who did not need a scripture to transmit the divine notifications. The Qur'ān does not give any information on this subject.

Difference between *kufr* and *shirk*

The word *kufr*, according to the etymology *k-f-r*, connotes the following physical meanings: to cover, conceal, bury, make disappear, to hide, to inter, and to sink. Its corresponding figurative notions include forgetting, rejecting, being ungrateful, renouncing, refusing, disbelieving, and depreciating. The *kāfir*, a term deriving from the active participle, rejects or buries faith either completely or partially. He is a disbeliever but not necessarily a polytheist or idolater. *Kufr* is most often juxtaposed with faith (*īmān*), a term which implies confidence, security, and adherence to the givens of Revelation.

Shirk comes from the root *sh-r-k* meaning: to be associated with, to co-partake, to share, to have a part, to have broken belts or to have laces loose. In religious vocabulary a *mushrik* is he who associates others unto Allah; it is the idolater whose faith in distinct gods could be either more or less complete. This notion is the opposite of the unity of faith in one God, and it leads to the diffusion of the world of multiplicity.

These two notions are therefore both condemned in the Qur'ān in different respects leading to distinct sanctions relevant to this life and the next.

Qur'ān, 2:109. *Many of the people of the Scripture long to make you disbelievers after your belief, through envy on their own account, after the truth hath become manifest unto them. Forgive and be indulgent [toward them] until Allah give command. Lo! Allah is Able to do all things.*

وَدَّ كَثِيرٌ مِنْ أَهْلِ الْكِتَابِ لَوْ يَرُدُّونَكُمْ مِنْ بَعْدِ إِيمَانِكُمْ كُفَّارًا حَسَدًا مِنْ عِنْدِ أَنْفُسِهِمْ مِنْ بَعْدِ مَا تَبَيَّنَ لَهُمُ الْحَقُّ ۖ فَاعْفُوا وَاصْفَحُوا حَتَّىٰ يَأْتِيَ اللَّهُ بِأَمْرِهِ ۗ إِنَّ اللَّهَ عَلَىٰ كُلِّ شَيْءٍ قَدِيرٌ

Qur'ān, 2:110. *Establish the action of unifying grace [prayer], and pay the poor-due; and whatever of good ye send before for your souls, ye will find it with Allah. Lo! Allah is Seer of what ye do.*

وَأَقِيمُوا الصَّلَاةَ وَآتُوا الزَّكَاةَ ۚ وَمَا تُقَدِّمُوا لِأَنْفُسِكُمْ مِنْ خَيْرٍ تَجِدُوهُ عِنْدَ اللَّهِ ۗ إِنَّ اللَّهَ بِمَا تَعْمَلُونَ بَصِيرٌ

Qur'ān, 2:111. *And they say: None entereth the Garden unless he be a Jew or a Christian. These are their own desires. Say: Bring your proof if ye are truthful.*

وَقَالُوا لَنْ يَدْخُلَ الْجَنَّةَ إِلَّا مَنْ كَانَ هُودًا أَوْ نَصَارَىٰ ۗ تِلْكَ أَمَانِيُّهُمْ ۗ قُلْ هَاتُوا بُرْهَانَكُمْ إِنْ كُنْتُمْ صَادِقِينَ

Qur'ān, 2:112. *Nay, but whosoever surrendereth his face to Allah while doing good, his reward is with his Lord; and neither fear shall come upon them nor shall they grieve.*

بَلَىٰ مَنْ أَسْلَمَ وَجْهَهُ لِلَّهِ وَهُوَ مُحْسِنٌ فَلَهُ أَجْرُهُ عِنْدَ رَبِّهِ وَلَا
خَوْفٌ عَلَيْهِمْ وَلَا هُمْ يَحْزَنُونَ

Qur'ān, 2:113. *And the Jews say: "The Christians follow nothing [true]"; and the Christians say: "The Jews follow nothing [true]." Yet both are readers of the Scripture. Even thus speak those who know not. Allah will judge between them on the Day of Resurrection concerning that wherein they differ.*

وَقَالَتِ الْيَهُودُ لَيْسَتِ النَّصَارَىٰ عَلَىٰ شَيْءٍ وَقَالَتِ النَّصَارَىٰ لَيْسَتِ
الْيَهُودُ عَلَىٰ شَيْءٍ وَهُمْ يَتْلُونَ الْكِتَابَ ۗ كَذَٰلِكَ قَالَ الَّذِينَ لَا يَعْلَمُونَ
مِثْلَ قَوْلِهِمْ ۚ فَاللَّهُ يَحْكُمُ بَيْنَهُمْ يَوْمَ الْقِيَامَةِ فِيمَا كَانُوا فِيهِ يَخْتَلِفُونَ

Verse 2:112 of this sequence again illustrates Islamic universalism, as we previously emphasized in the commentary on verse 2:62. Authentic, universalist Islam recognizes all the divine descents that intervened in different historical phases of humanity. The "face" in this verse effectively symbolizes the essential aspect of the person who maintains a certain affinity with the Divine Face which is subtly present in the whole of creation: *Unto Allah belong the East and the West, and whithersoever ye turn, there is Allah's Face. Lo! Allah is All-Embracing, All-Knowing* (Qur'ān, 2:115).

To this essential orientation or worship represented by the face, Allah enjoins perfect behavior of the same type as that He describes in verse 2:62. This well-founded universalism holds the potential to end religious dissensions through the dialogue referred to in the following verses: *Call unto the way of thy Lord with wisdom and fair exhortation, and reason with them in the better way. Lo! thy Lord is Best Aware of him who strayeth from His way, and He is Best Aware of those who go aright* (Qur'ān, 16:125). *And argue not with the People of the Scripture unless it be in [a way] that is better, save with such of them as do wrong; and say: We believe in that which hath been revealed unto us and revealed unto you; our Allah and your Allah is One, and unto*

Him we surrender (Qur'ān, 29:46).

Allah makes this necessary recommendation toward this good end: *Repel evil with that which is best . . .* (Qur'ān, 23:96).

He who adheres to the universal and historical Islam as we mentioned in the verse 2:62 commentary does not or should not enter into these polemics. For this reason, Allah has established authentic Islam with the following verse: *Thus We have appointed you a middle community (ummat^an wasat^an), that ye may be witnesses over mankind, and that the messenger may be a witness over yourselves . . .* (Qur'ān, 2:143).

Qur'ān, 2:116. *And they say: Allah hath taken unto Himself an offspring. Be He glorified! Nay, but whatsoever is in the heavens and the earth is His. All are subservient unto Him.*

وَقَالُوا اتَّخَذَ اللَّهُ وَلَدًا ۗ سُبْحَانَهُ ۖ بَل لَّهُ مَا فِي السَّمَاوَاتِ وَالْأَرْضِ ۖ كُلٌّ لَّهُ قَانِتُونَ

In our commentary on verse 2:87 we noted the semantic and qualitative difference between the two terms *walad* (child), and *ibn* (son). In this verse and others (3:47, 4:171, 6:101, 10:68, 18:4, 19:35, 88, 91, 92, 21:26, 23:91; 25:2; 43:81) that reflect this distinction, *walad* is used in the sense of a physical progeny, issued from a father and a mother in a process incompatible with the level of the Divine and Unity. The root *'-kh-dh*, meaning to take or to seize, is given here in its eighth verbal form. It is often explained by the Arabic commentators with the verb *tabannā*, or to adopt. The verb *ittakhadha* may also be translated: to choose, to take for oneself, and to attribute to oneself.

Those referred to as the speakers are not necessarily the Christians and the Jews, but anyone who does not know or who cannot discern, and they are mentioned together in verse 2:113.

In Chapter 112, entitled the Absolute Purity (*al-Ikhlāṣ*), Allah has said: *Say, He, Allah [is] One, Allah, the Impenetrable universal Support. He begetteth not, nor is begotten, and none is like Him.* This Divine statement refutes all notions of plurality applied to Allah and affirms Allah's transcendence as One, infinite, eternal Divine Essence, and as a subtle and unadorned immanent Presence that supports His entire creation; an Essence without which the worlds and all that they contain would either rest unmanifested or be reabsorbed in Her.

> Qur'ān, 2:119. *Lo! We have sent thee with the Truth, a bringer of glad tidings and a warner. And thou wilt not be asked about the companions of Hellfire.*

إِنَّا أَرْسَلْنَاكَ بِالْحَقِّ بَشِيرًا وَنَذِيرًا ۖ وَلَا تُسْأَلُ عَنْ أَصْحَابِ الْجَحِيمِ

> Qur'ān, 2:120. *And the Jews will not be pleased with thee, nor will the Christians, till thou follow their creed (milla). Say: Lo! the guidance of Allah is Guidance. And if thou shouldst follow their desires after the knowledge which hath come unto thee, then wouldst thou have from Allah no protecting guardian nor helper.*

وَلَنْ تَرْضَىٰ عَنْكَ الْيَهُودُ وَلَا النَّصَارَىٰ حَتَّىٰ تَتَّبِعَ مِلَّتَهُمْ ۗ قُلْ إِنَّ هُدَى اللَّهِ هُوَ الْهُدَىٰ ۗ وَلَئِنِ اتَّبَعْتَ أَهْوَاءَهُمْ بَعْدَ الَّذِي جَاءَكَ مِنَ الْعِلْمِ ۙ مَا لَكَ مِنَ اللَّهِ مِنْ وَلِيٍّ وَلَا نَصِيرٍ

The first verse essentially concerns the Prophet and Messenger Muḥammad. The Messenger is he who brings a new Law from Allah. In enabling the divine Descent, which is also his own, he is a Prophet for he is entrusted with proclaiming the tidings he brings from Allah and conveying the Message. That is why each messenger is a prophet whereas a prophet is not necessarily a messenger; in most cases the former will confirm the contents of Revelation already received by a divine messenger. For example, most of the Prophets of Israel have authenticated the inexhaustible contents of the Mosaic Law. This function of prophet messenger does not make the person invested with it responsible for the individuals he must warn. Each human being manages their own case as they understand it, depending on the possibilities they carry within themselves from eternity.

The Qur'ān mentions certain facts about the Laws that descended before the apostolate of the seal of the prophets, Muḥammad. It also expounds upon other facts not contained in previous revelations. It sums up the essence of the previously received Messages, while introducing new elements in such a manner that the prophetic typologies do not necessarily correspond in every way to those contained in Scriptures originating prior to historical Islam. The famous historical or mythical accounts, whether in the sacred books or profane literature, are related to isolated and representative select elements only to convey a lesson.

> Qur'ān, 2:135. *And they have said: 'Be Jews or Christians, then ye will be rightly guided.' Say: 'Nay, but [we follow] the religion (milla) of Abraham, the theotrope, and he was not of the associators.'*

وَقَالُوا كُونُوا هُودًا أَوْ نَصَارَىٰ تَهْتَدُوا ۗ قُلْ بَلْ مِلَّةَ إِبْرَاهِيمَ
حَنِيفًا ۖ وَمَا كَانَ مِنَ الْمُشْرِكِينَ

The expression "they have said" refers to the Jews and the Christians whose first religion (*milla*) refers to the prophet Abraham. The Islamic revelation considers Abraham as possessing of an original, primordial disposition or orientation towards Allah that does not differ from that attributed to Judaism and to Christianity.

The term *theotrope* is a neologism corresponding to the word *ḥanīf*; it comes from Greek and it means "he who turns to Allah at every instant and in all circumstances." The first meaning of the root *ḥ-n-f*, source of the adjective-noun *ḥanīf*, is "to turn to, incline to, or lean towards." We have modelled this word on the term heliotrope, or "sunflower," whose meaning is "to turn towards the sun by a natural attraction." In the Qur'ānic text, this term occurs ten times in the singular and twice in the plural (*ḥunafā*). It is used primarily in reference to Abraham and those following him, for the Prophet Muḥammad, and also for those who turn only to Allah. In the following section we discuss this term in verses 3:67 and 98:5, which are related to verse 2:62 (see commentary above).

> Qur'ān, 2:136. *Say: We have faith in Allah and that which is revealed unto us and that which was revealed unto Abraham, and Ishmael, and Isaac, and Jacob, and the [twelve] tribes, and that which Moses and Jesus received, and that which the prophets received from their Lord. We make no distinction between any of them, and unto Him we have surrendered.*

قُولُوا آمَنَّا بِاللَّهِ وَمَا أُنْزِلَ إِلَيْنَا وَمَا أُنْزِلَ إِلَىٰ إِبْرَاهِيمَ وَإِسْمَاعِيلَ
وَإِسْحَاقَ وَيَعْقُوبَ وَالْأَسْبَاطِ وَمَا أُوتِيَ مُوسَىٰ وَعِيسَىٰ وَمَا أُوتِيَ
النَّبِيُّونَ مِنْ رَبِّهِمْ لَا نُفَرِّقُ بَيْنَ أَحَدٍ مِنْهُمْ وَنَحْنُ لَهُ مُسْلِمُونَ

The end of this verse accommodates two different translations which reinforce each other's meaning: the man of faith cannot recognize the intrinsic reality of each prophet insofar as he has not received the privilege of prophethood. He is therefore not in a position to make such distinctions between the different prophets, and to exclude some while privileging others. Here we encounter yet again the universalism enunciated in numerous passages of the Qur'ān. This comportment promises an immense spiritual benefit for the man of faith provided that he adheres to the Divine Will with profound conviction and complete submission. He must also adhere to the authentic contents of the Messages sent down during the different phases of humankind—as the essential contents of these messages are mentioned ceaselessly in the sacred text of Islam. For the man of faith, these actions constitute his participation in the universal Message conveyed by the last of the messengers and the prophets, Muḥammad; a Message which takes into account the previous revelations which the Prophet includes in the whole comprehensive extent of his being and his function until the Day of Resurrection.

The imperative *say* concerns the Jews and the Christians who had previously been asked to remain faithful to that which was revealed—without specifying the contents of this Divine descent—to Abraham, Ishmael, Isaac, and the [twelve] Tribes (*asbāṭ*). They were also asked to adhere to the Divine Messages conveyed by Moses and Jesus. The phrase *and that which the prophets received* refers to all who might be considered prophets, regardless of whether they are mentioned in the Qur'ān. Verse 7:160 concerns the twelve tribes of the times of Moses, with several centuries separating them from Jacob and his twelve sons mentioned in Chapter 12, Yūsuf (Joseph): *We divided them into twelve tribes; and We inspired Moses, when his people asked him for water, saying: Smite with thy staff the rock! And there gushed forth therefrom twelve springs . . .* Verse 4:163, quoted earlier, first mentions the Prophet Muḥammad. It then situates Jesus in a line of prophets, and it also mentions the twelve tribes. However, it is not the verb "send down," conjugated in its passive form (*unzala*), but the verb "inspire" in the past tense of the active form (*awhaynā*) which is used in the last verse. In this conjugated form the verb comes from the root *w-h-y*, meaning: to inspire, to suggest, to breathe, or to insufflate. In the Qur'ān, this verb is conjugated 72 times in the fourth form, and is used four times as a verbal noun not only to qualify the divine action which inspires the prophets but also others, such as the mother of Moses (20:38 and 28:7), the bees, etc. It is therefore an interiorisation or an actualization of a reality which one possesses and which Allah uncovers. This is contrary to the term "send down" (*anzala*) which does not necessarily imply the realization of the truth of His manifestation's contents as well as the prescriptions and rulings of all orders concerning human beings. It also does not always render in a satisfactory manner the Qur'ānic modalities of the Divine descent, or the Divine act of sending down (*tanzīl*), as pertaining to the realization of the Qur'ānic message or of a divine message addressed to some persons in the particular modalities concerning them. However, the term "revelation" often proves to be useful considering the meaning it conveys in most of the translations of both sacred and profane Arabic literature.

> Qur'ān, 2:137. *If they believe in the like of that which ye believe, then are they rightly guided. But if they turn away, then are they in schism, and Allah will suffice thee [for defence] against them. He is the Hearer, the Knower.*

فَإِنْ آمَنُوا بِمِثْلِ مَا آمَنْتُمْ بِهِ فَقَدِ اهْتَدَوْا ۖ وَإِنْ تَوَلَّوْا فَإِنَّمَا
هُمْ فِي شِقَاقٍ ۖ فَسَيَكْفِيكَهُمُ اللَّهُ ۚ وَهُوَ السَّمِيعُ الْعَلِيمُ

Although this *like* is not specified explicitly, one may infer from the already quoted verse 2:62 that the members of the communities mentioned therein must have faith in Allah and in the Last Day, and perform righteous works, these three inward and outward attitudes being fundamental and universal for every authentic believer. In verse 2:112, Allah also specifies that a believer must guard his face solely for Him. The term "like," which we have used as translation of the term *mithl*, indicates but one general adherence to faith and to an original orientation to the One God corresponding to potentially varied forms of worship.

Qur'ān, 2:138. (according to the) *dye from Allah, and who is better than Allah at dyeing. We are His servants.*

صِبْغَةَ اللَّهِ وَمَنْ أَحْسَنُ مِنَ اللَّهِ صِبْغَةً وَنَحْنُ لَهُ عَابِدُونَ

The active noun *ṣibgha*, translated as "dyeing," comes from the root *s-b-gh*, which occurs four times in the Qur'ān. This root means to dye (a fabric), to stain, to color, to dip into dye, to plunge (for example the hand into the water), to moisten, to be inflated, to immerse, to soak, or to dye. Generally it connotes any modification of the color or an attribute of a thing by introducing another thing. More precisely, the dye allows the tissue to reflect the color that we see for it absorbs all the other colors. For the majority of Muslim commentators this term serves to designate Christian baptism, the word baptism deriving from the Greek word for "to dye." The Arabic-speaking Christians use the term *ta'mīd*. In verse 23:20, the word *ṣibgh* refers to a condiment for the seasoning of cooked dishes: *. . . and a tree that springeth forth from Mount Sinai that groweth oil* (*duhn*) *and condiment* (*ṣibgh*) *for the eaters*. Moreover, the term *ṣibgha* at the beginning of verse 2:136 appears in the direct case and may, according to the majority of commentators, specify how each person receives faith. For each individual carries faith according to his or her eternal predispositions that are contained in the Knowledge of God and actualized by virtue of their tendencies. A number of interpretations have been applied to the term *ṣibgha* such as religion (*dīn*), primordial nature (*fiṭra*), or active submission (*islām*).

The term *ṣibgha* has often been considered a metaphor; however, where does the literal meaning end and the metaphorical or figurative sense begin? Word roots in ancient Semitic languages and particularly in Qur'ānic Arabic usually have a primary, material meaning before serving as the basis for symbolic interpretation. This prevents one from envisaging meaning in an exclusively figurative sense and instead obliges a hierarchy of non-arbitrary meanings and analogical, or better, anagogical correspondences, in different orders of reality understood through the universal Divine order. Moreover, the Qur'ānic revelation has permitted the extension of the abstract and its corresponding notions to a large quantity of concrete connotations embraced by that root.

For example, the root *k-f-r* generates the word *kāfir* which designates in a religious context: the disbeliever, the infidel, and the ungrateful. However, its etymology reveals that its original meaning was "to bury," such as when the cultivator sows grain to grow crops. Verse 57:20 contains a good example of the primary semantic meaning of *k-f-r*; in this verse, the word *kuffar*, one of the plural forms of *kāfir*, clearly translates as "cultivator." The noun *kāfir* may therefore be rendered "dissimulator," or he who hides his faith, so as to preserve the first etymological meaning while simultaneously allowing other semantic interpretations that refer to this primary connotation in levels of meaning permitted by language and analogical truths. This important knowledge will be applied to our commentary on terms like *kalima* (word), *rūḥ* (spirit), breath (*nafs*), soul, and animated entity.

We are His servants: or rather one might say "worshippers" (*'ābidūn*), a term composed of an active participle that is used as a noun. This term connotes the perfectly realized servant, as in the case of Jesus who is called *'abd Allāh*, or servant of God, in verse 19:30. The worshipper is the being who, in realizing the perfect servitude or the condition of the servant, actualizes total submission to the Lord. None of his individual attitudes presents an obstacle to his reception of the qualities of the Lord (*Rabb*). He becomes and remains, with full consciousness, the locus where the Divine Names act continually without limitation. For these reasons and others, those who are realized in God, such as the prophets and especially the Prophet of Islam, Muḥammad (see for example verse 72:19), are perfect servants of a lordly nature. We cannot but worship Him, as in the following verses: *Thy Lord hath decreed, that ye worship none save Him . . .* (17:23); *I have not created the jinn and humankind except that they might worship Me* (51:56) or *that they might know Me* according to a predominant interpretation. Furthermore, the two terms *Rabb* and *'abd* are always in correlation, for the Lord cannot exist without a servant, and the servant cannot exist without a lord. In this work, we have often translated the word *Rabb* as "Lord." The root of this noun, *r-b-b*, connotes the ideas of mastery, education, and teaching, and may also be elevated to the potential meanings: to have control over something or someone, to exercise authority, to gather, to unite, to be chief or master.

Qur'ān, 2:139. *Say: Dispute ye with us concerning Allah when He [is] our Lord and your Lord? Ours are our works and yours your works. We are dedicated to Him sincerely.*

قُلْ أَتُحَاجُّونَنَا فِي اللَّهِ وَهُوَ رَبُّنَا وَرَبُّكُمْ وَلَنَا أَعْمَالُنَا وَلَكُمْ أَعْمَالُكُمْ وَنَحْنُ لَهُ مُخْلِصُونَ

Allah is the Lord of lords who embraces all beings, each of whom is the servant of his Lord according to his particular circumstances, as we noted earlier. In addition to the notion of universalism contained in this verse and others, we also find therein the diversity of attitudes and orientations of the servants depending on their Divine predispositions. For the unity of God does not challenge the multiplicity of convictions and attitudes; Allah is at the origin and finality of the most diverse vocations. It might even be stated that the Universality of God prefers to manifest itself as multiple aspects in each one of us.

Qur'ān, 2:140. *Or say ye that Abraham, and Ishmael, and Isaac, and Jacob, and the (twelve) Tribes were Jews or Christians? Say: Do ye know best, or doth Allah? And who is more unjust than he who hideth a testimony which he hath received from Allah? Allah is not unaware of what ye do.*

أَمْ تَقُولُونَ إِنَّ إِبْرَاهِيمَ وَإِسْمَاعِيلَ وَإِسْحَاقَ وَيَعْقُوبَ وَالْأَسْبَاطَ كَانُوا هُودًا أَوْ نَصَارَىٰ ۗ قُلْ أَأَنْتُمْ أَعْلَمُ أَمِ اللَّهُ ۗ وَمَنْ أَظْلَمُ مِمَّنْ كَتَمَ شَهَادَةً عِنْدَهُ مِنَ اللَّهِ ۗ وَمَا اللَّهُ بِغَافِلٍ عَمَّا تَعْمَلُونَ

The testimony in question here is often interpreted as being the *ḥanifiyya* or "theotropism" characterizing the Patriarchs named in this verse, while the Jews and Christians are not referred to as *ḥunafā* in the Qur'ān. It may also relate to the universal orientations of the believers implied in verses 2:62, 2:112, and 2:137.

Qur'ān, 2:141. *Those are a people who have passed away; theirs is that which they earned and yours that which ye earn. And ye will not be asked of what they used to do.*

تِلْكَ أُمَّةٌ قَدْ خَلَتْ ۖ لَهَا مَا كَسَبَتْ وَلَكُم مَّا كَسَبْتُمْ ۖ وَلَا تُسْأَلُونَ عَمَّا كَانُوا يَعْمَلُونَ

Some considerations linked to the notion of "community"

This community is represented by the prophets and patriarchs Abraham, Ishmael, Isaac, Jacob, and the twelve tribes whose chiefs were Jacob's twelve sons. The story of Joseph (Yūsuf), one of Jacob's sons, is related in the twelfth chapter and that chapter bears his name. After those mentioned above came the great prophetic figure Moses, whose father-in-law Shu'ayb, named Jethro in the Old Testament, is considered a prophet in Islam.

The root of the term which we have translated as community is *'a-m-m*, meaning to be ahead, to take or be taken in front, to head towards, to have an intent, or to be a mother. From this root derives the substantive *'umm*, meaning source, origin, principle, prototype, or mother, as well as the term *'umma*, meaning community or people. According to the derivative semantic and doctrinal perspective, the mother is evidently not considered virgin and immaculate, but rather as producing, giving birth to a more or less limited number of beings or to an unlimited number if one considers the divine Prototype. The feminine, maternal Principle is envisaged as productive when it is impregnated by the masculine Principle and produces a common product. This fruit of their union is the child or the engendered being (*walad*).

Thus the Mother of the Scripture (*Umm al-Kitāb*, cf. Qur'ān, 3:7), "impregnated" by the Divine Principle, symbolizes the latter in its productive, "feminine" or "maternal" aspect which contains all possible Scriptures. Within this notion, revelation may distinguish one or several particular Scriptures, just like a mother of several children might also be accurately called the mother of one of them.

From the hidden Scripture (*kitāb maknūn*, cf. Qur'ān, 56:78) or the original Text emerge the Scriptures sent to the member of the Community (*'umma*) by God as sustenance for meditation and invocation. In the context of Qur'ānic Arabic, the term *'umma* may then be interpreted as meaning the productive source of human beings who are sacralised or "sacralisable" by the Muḥammadan Revelation.

The Prophet Muḥammad himself is called *'ummī*, a term which is usually translated imprecisely as unlettered or illiterate. According to the etymology of the form *naba'a*, the Prophet (*nabī'*) is the human being chosen by Allah. He proclaims exalting tidings, as he has been sent by Allah with a sacred Scripture and therefore acts as the productive source of a Community sacralised by the divine Revelation. In the following two Qur'ānic passages Allah calls him by this epithet *'ummī*:

> *. . . He (Allah) said: I smite with My punishment whom I will, and My mercy embraceth all things, therefore I shall ordain it for those who ward off [evil] and pay the poor-due, and those who believe Our Signs; Those who follow the messenger, the community-generating (or unlettered) Prophet, whom they find described in the Torah and the Gospel [which are] with them. He enjoins on them that which is right and forbid them that which is wrong. He makes lawful for them all good things and prohibits for them only the foul; and he relieves them of their burden and the fetters that they used to wear. Then those who believe in him, and honour him, and help him, and follow the light which is sent down with him: they are the successful. Say [O Muḥammad]: O mankind! Lo! I am the Messenger of Allah to you all—Him unto Whom belongeth the Sovereignty of the heavens and the earth. There is no deity (ilāh) save Him. He quickeneth and He giveth death. So believe in Allah and His messenger, the community-generating (or unlettered) Prophet, who believeth in Allah and in His Words, and follow him that haply ye may be led aright* (Qur'ān, 7:156-158).

The Prophet is described as 'unlettered' or 'illiterate.' He receives the Revelation in a condition of perfect availability and receptivity, without the capability to alter the divine Message through individual human intervention. The Prophet himself gave a definition of what he understood by the term *'ummī*: "Verily, we are an illiterate community (*'innā 'ummat^{an} 'ummiyyat^{an}*), we neither write nor count." Commenting upon this prophetic tradition related by Ibn 'Umar, al-Zajjāj explains that the name *'ummī* describes the person who has retained the same disposition as that he had when his mother brought him into this world; that is, he knew neither how to read nor how to write, and had not yet received the imprint of any human knowledge.[3]

It is the Prophet Muḥammad who conveys the Book—the

3. See Ibn Manẓūr, *Lisān al-'arab*, root 'a-m-m.

Text or Scripture—by Divine inspiration (*waḥy*), after receiving it from the Archangel Gabriel. Gabriel possesses its spiritual paternity, whereas Muḥammad possesses its hallowed maternity. It is this celestial Scripture that the Angel of Revelation, Gabriel, ordered him to recite. If the Prophet had not recited this Scripture beginning from that timeless moment, if he had not formalized it and rendered it sensible, then it would have remained dead or purely virtual. Its Message would have remained unknown to the Community that he was destined to lead by representing all of its members and knowing every individual from the first to the last, according to his words. The Angel did not tell him "Read!" but rather "Recite!" (*iqra'*), for recitation generally implies a "re-citation" or re-actualization of previous knowledge. This re-actualization appeals to the active and selective memory and to the clear and distinct consciousness of this previous knowledge. This is why the Angel did not tell him to read, for reading implies drawing knowledge from an established collection, marked by letters, reserved for those who know how to write and read. The Prophet is a being realized in God, by God, but he did not know of the Scripture or the act of faith (*īmān*), according to what God Himself says in the Qur'ān: *And thus have We inspired in thee a Spirit of Our Command. Thou knewest not what the Scripture was* (*mā al-kitāb*, the Quidity of the Book) *nor the act of faith* (*al-īmān*). *But We have made it a light whereby We guide whom We will of Our bondmen. And lo! thou verily dost guide unto a right path, the path of God, unto Whom belongeth whatsoever is in the heavens and whatsoever is in the earth. Do not all things reach God at last?* (Qur'ān, 42:52-53).

Moreover, Allah specifies regarding the Prophet of Islam: *Thus We have sent down unto thee the Scripture. Those unto whom We gave the Scripture aforetime have faith in it; and of these [who have not received the Scripture] there are some who have faith in it. And none deny Our signs save the disbelievers. And thou (O Muḥammad) wast not a reader of any scripture before it, nor didst thou write it with thy right hand, for then might those have doubted, who follow falsehood* (Qur'ān, 29:47-48).

In these verses God specifies that before the Divine descent, Muḥammad discerned neither the Quidity of the Scripture in one form or another, nor that of faith, given his virgin nature and his state of comprehensive consciousness. Because he was a prophet before the manifestation of humankind, and even before Adam, according to a famous ḥadīth, he possessed the supreme Realization without having to categorize knowledge. He did not need to situate things in a relational manner, nor did he need to align his faith with a particular revealed Scripture. For these reasons, he replied to the Angel of Revelation, Gabriel (Jibrīl)—who ordered him twice to recite—that he did not know how. The Angel grasped Muḥammad and engraved upon his virginal and pure soul the subtle sacred Word which the Prophet then articulated. He was completely available and receptive by nature, and the celestial Recitation left an indelible impression upon his whole being. On the Night of Power (*laylat al-qadr*), the Prophet received in its entirety this primordial Recitation which God communicated to him anew. It came to him through the Mediation of the Archangel of Revelation, in a fragmentary manner according to the providentially arranged circumstances of the progressive Descent of His Word. *Lo! We revealed it in the Night of Power* (Qur'ān, 97:1); *A revelation from the Beneficent, the Merciful, a Scripture whereof the verses are expounded, a Recitation in Arabic for people who have knowledge* (Qur'ān, 41:2-3). These are the words he recited to his Companions. The faithful impression they left permitted the Companions not to read the sacred text, but rather to recite it and to ritually convey it to others chiefly through oral transmission.

Qur'ān, 2:253. *Of those messengers, some of whom We have caused to surpass others, and of whom there are some unto whom Allah spake, while some of them He exalted in degree; and We gave Jesus, son of Mary, clear proofs and We supported him with the Spirit of Sanctity. And if Allah had so willed it, those who followed after them would not have fought one with another after the clear proofs had come unto them. But they differed, some of them believing, and some disbelieving. And if Allah had so willed it, they would not have fought one with another; but Allah doeth what He will.*

تِلْكَ الرُّسُلُ فَضَّلْنَا بَعْضَهُمْ عَلَىٰ بَعْضٍ ۘ مِنْهُمْ مَنْ كَلَّمَ اللَّهُ ۖ
وَرَفَعَ بَعْضَهُمْ دَرَجَاتٍ ۚ وَآتَيْنَا عِيسَى ابْنَ مَرْيَمَ الْبَيِّنَاتِ وَأَيَّدْنَاهُ
بِرُوحِ الْقُدُسِ ۗ وَلَوْ شَاءَ اللَّهُ مَا اقْتَتَلَ الَّذِينَ مِنْ بَعْدِهِمْ مِنْ
بَعْدِ مَا جَاءَتْهُمُ الْبَيِّنَاتُ وَلَٰكِنِ اخْتَلَفُوا فَمِنْهُمْ مَنْ آمَنَ وَمِنْهُمْ
مَنْ كَفَرَ ۚ وَلَوْ شَاءَ اللَّهُ مَا اقْتَتَلُوا وَلَٰكِنَّ اللَّهَ يَفْعَلُ مَا يُرِيدُ

In the commentary on verse 2:87, we references the part of this verse which is related to ʿĪsā ibn Maryam.

The beginning of this verse refers to the preceding verse and concerns first of all the Prophet Muḥammad: *These are the portents of Allah unto which We recite with truth, and lo! thou art one of the messengers* (Qur'ān, 2:252).

As an illustration to the contents of this verse, let us quote two examples: *And messengers We have mentioned unto thee before and messengers We have not mentioned unto thee; and Allah spoke directly unto Moses* (Qur'ān, 4:164). *And make mention in the Scripture of Idrīs. Lo! he was a truthful one, [and] a prophet. And We raised him to a lofty station* (Qur'ān, 19:56-57).

The last part of verse 2:253 could be translated as: . . . *Some of them kept the faith, and others concealed it.*

Two Divine wills?

Two verbs are used at the end of the verse: the verb *shā'a* from the root *sh-y-*ʿ, meaning to will something in a universal and comprehensive manner, and the verb *yurīd*, from the root *r-w-d*, meaning to will something by selecting and distinguishing its characteristics in existence. From these two distinct notions emanate two aspects of the Divine Will. The first root gives the word *shay'*, or the thing willed, the act of the will: the primordial act of the unconditioned and undifferentiated Divine Will (*mashī'a*), and the metaphysical locus of all possible things, meaning all the permanent realities in God.

The "thing" (*shay*) thus understood according to its semantic and metaphysical meaning is "anterior" to the Divine function (*ulūhiyya*) which includes in its Principle the Divine Names and Attributes. *Mashī'a*, a non-Qur'ānic term, is a name of action which shows itself as a name of place. It comes from the same root as *shay'* and it refers to the unconditioned Divine Will, therefore it is envisaged as a metaphysical Locus where the essential "things" remain immutable. From this perspective, *Mashī'a* is not a divine attribute because it stands beyond the Divine Being or the Divine Function.

Tradition distinguishes another quality attributed to the Divine Will called *Irāda*. This term comes from the second root in question, and means to come and go with a precise motivation. It is one of the seven attributes of the Divine Function (*ulūhiyya*) together with life, knowledge, power, speech, seeing, and hearing. This Will (*irāda*) gives a distinct and normative intention to the first Will, *Mashī'a*. In unison with the Knowledge, Power, and Divine Act, the former actualizes the things contained in God from eternity through the existentiating Order. According to this interpretation, these things (*ashyā'*) cannot but manifest, in cosmic degrees, their essential predispositions established in the Divine Presence.

Two fundamental notions correspond to these two "aspects" that the Divine Will manifests: *Qaḍā'*, or the Divine decree which concerns *Mashī'a*, and *Qadar*, or the measuring out which implies the progressive actualization of the immutable entities or the permanent realities present in God. The following two verses illustrate the distinctions that characterize these two aspects of the Divine Will: *Had Allah intended ('arāda) to choose a son, He could have chosen what He would of that which He hath created. Be He Glorified! He is Allah, the One, the Ever-Subduer* (Qur'ān, 39:4). *Whoso desireth (yurīdu) the ephemeral, We hasten for him therein what We will (nashā'u) for whom We please. And afterward We have appointed for him hell; he will endure the heat thereof, condemned, rejected* (Qur'ān, 17:18).

Surah 3

Qur'ān, 3:1-2. *Alif Lām Mīm. No deity save Him, the Living, the Immutable.*

الم اللَّهُ لَا إِلَٰهَ إِلَّا هُوَ الْحَيُّ الْقَيُّومُ

Qur'ān, 3:3. *He hath sent down unto thee the Scripture with truth, confirming that which was before it, even as He revealed the Torah and the Gospel*

نَزَّلَ عَلَيْكَ الْكِتَابَ بِالْحَقِّ مُصَدِّقًا لِمَا بَيْنَ يَدَيْهِ وَأَنْزَلَ
التَّوْرَاةَ وَالْإِنْجِيلَ

Qur'ān, 3:4. *Aforetime, as guidance to mankind; and hath sent down the Criterion (furqān). Lo! those who disbelieve the Signs of Allah, theirs will be a heavy doom. Allah is Mighty, Able to Requite.*

مِنْ قَبْلُ هُدًى لِلنَّاسِ وَأَنْزَلَ الْفُرْقَانَ ۗ إِنَّ الَّذِينَ كَفَرُوا
بِآيَاتِ اللَّهِ لَهُمْ عَذَابٌ شَدِيدٌ ۗ وَاللَّهُ عَزِيزٌ ذُو انْتِقَامٍ

The testimony of Divine Unity in verse 3:2 was afforded extensive commentary in the previous chapter that we dedicated to the study of this sacred formula which occurs thirty-six times in the Qur'ānic text and takes various forms.

Verse three concerns the Prophet Muḥammad in particular, but also refers to the Believers who actualize the divine Word in themselves through ritual recitation and mediation on its teachings. This Word is the Scripture in the universality of its reality and its truth. It was received by the Prophet and it contains the essence of the Messages that God has conveyed to different divine messengers. The Scripture only contains that which remains actual in the cadre of universal Islam, the last revelation in the human cycle which synthesizes the other forms of divine descent. The Qur'ān confirms the previous revelations, as described by many verses (2:101; 3:39, 50, 81; 4:47; 5:46, 48; 6:92; 35:31, 46:12, 30; 61:6), such as *Say: Whoever is an enemy to Gabriel—or he it is who hath brought down this (Scripture) to thy heart by Allah's leave, confirming that which was before it, and a guidance and glad tidings to believers* (Qur'ān, 2:97).

Furqān and Qur'ān

The criterion in question here is evoked by the term *furqān*, whose verbal root *f-q-r* means: to split, separate, divide in two, to distinguish, to expound clearly, and to decree. The noun *furqān* is constructed according to the scheme *Fu'LāN* which indicates intensive value. *Furqān* therefore implies the following meanings: total discernment, complete distinction, decisive separation, peremptory criterion, and argument. It is related to the revealed Scripture in its distinct and intelligible qualities as well as in the inexhaustible meanings it contains. It differs from the term *qur'ān* which is constructed on the same paradigm *Fu'LāN* and whose verbal root *q-r-'a* encompasses the following meanings: to recite, to read before someone, to transmit, to learn, to gather the scattered parts and to reunite them. The Qur'ān is primordially the recitation or re-citation of this same Scripture and it contains the notion of reunion, synthesis, gathering, collecting, and immediate apprehension. Contrary to the current and most generally accepted opinion, the

Qur'ān is not just "the Writing" or "the Book;" it undergoes continuous primordial actualization in the prototype of the Scripture (*umm al-kitāb*) and in the ritual utterance of the Divine word by the Believers. The Qur'ān is therefore not the materialized or bound (*muṣḥaf*) book as is usually implied.

We will comment on the term Gospel (*Injīl*) in our discussion of verse 3:48.

> Qur'ān, 3:33. *Lo! Allah chose* (or elected = *iṣṭafā'*) *Adam and Noah and the Family of Abraham and the Family of 'Imrān above [other] creatures.*

> إِنَّ اللَّهَ اصْطَفَىٰ آدَمَ وَنُوحًا وَآلَ إِبْرَاهِيمَ وَآلَ عِمْرَانَ عَلَى الْعَالَمِينَ

> Qur'ān, 3:34. *Descendants one of another. Allah is the All-Hearer, All-Knower.*

> ذُرِّيَّةً بَعْضُهَا مِنْ بَعْضٍ وَاللَّهُ سَمِيعٌ عَلِيمٌ

The verb *iṣṭafā'* is conjugated in the eighth verbal form of the root *ṣ-f-w* which means: to be pure, limpid, clear, and immaculate, decant and neat; to skim the cream off something, or to take the best part. In the eighth form, *ṣ-f-w* acquires the following meanings: to select, choose, prefer, elect, skim the cream off, and to become clear. In other verses, God chooses or elects other beings, prophets or messengers: *He (Allah) said: O Moses! I have preferred thee above (other) men by My messages and by My speaking [unto thee]. So hold that which I have given thee, and be among the thankful* (Qur'ān, 7:144). *Allah chooseth from the angels messengers, and (also) from mankind. Lo! Allah is Hearing, Seeing* (Qur'ān, 22:75). *And make mention of Our bondmen, Abraham, Isaac and Jacob, men of power and vision. Lo! We purified them with a pure thought, remembrance of the [final] Abode—Lo! in Our sight they are verily of the elect, the excellent* (Qur'ān, 38:46-47).

The Family of 'Imrān

Who, then, is the family of 'Imrān, mentioned in this verse without further details? One may infer from the two verses 3:35 and 66:12

that ‘Imrān was the father of Mary. Knowledge of the descendants of Abraham according to the Old Testament allows one to suppose that ‘Imrān here is linked to the offspring of Abraham through Isaac, one of his sons, and through Jacob, son of Isaac, then through Levi the third son of Jacob, and through Lea and Qehat, the first of four sons of Levi. ‘Imrān is therefore identified in the Old Testament with the name of *Amran*, father of Aaron, Moses, and Miryam, from the tribe of Levi. Following this Biblical lineage, the family of ‘Imrān started with Abraham and ended with Aaron and Moses, passing through Isaac, Jacob, Levi, Qehat, and Amran. Only Abraham, Isaac, Jacob, Moses and Aaron are mentioned in the Qur’ān.

Synopsis of the genealogies of Jesus and John the Baptist according to Islam

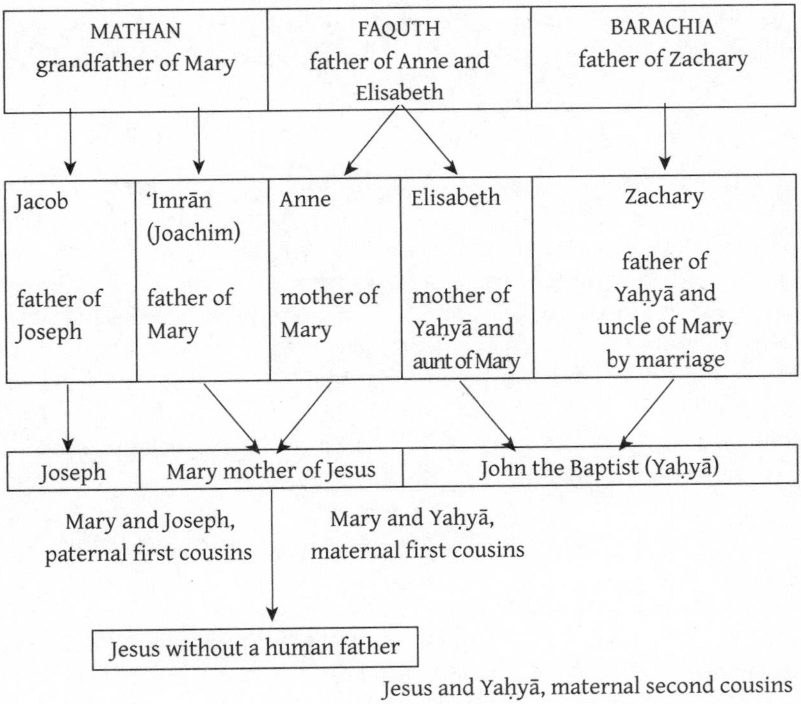

Levi was one of the twelve sons of Jacob and he is included in the Qur’ānic denomination of *asbāṭ*, referring to the twelve Tribes of Israel or their twelve eponymous chiefs. This denomination of

asbāṭ is found five times in the sacred book, in verses 2:136, 2:140, 3:84, 4:163, and 7:160.

The first four verses situate the *asbāṭ* or eponymous chiefs in a fixed lineage starting from Abraham and passing through Isaac and Jacob. This lineage justifies the mentioning of the following verse (3:35). 'Imrān, or Amran according to the New Testament, could also be an eponymous ancestor from whom a continuous lineage descends, transmitting the quasi prophetic virtue without interruption from one generation to the another down to the 'Imrān mentioned in the following verse. This appellation of 'Imrān would conceal a divine secret which makes the father of the perfect woman Maryam a spiritual "entity" transmitted in a subtle and providential manner. This entity would form the integral being of Mary and *ipso facto* that of Jesus. Jesus was engendered by the Spirit of Sanctity who presented himself in the perfect form of the Archangel of the universal Revelation, assimilated into Gabriel by Tradition.

The Family of Jesus Son of Mary

The Qur'ānic text furnishes us with limited commentary on the family of Jesus, Son of Mary. Mary (Maryam), the only woman whose name appears in the Qur'ān, is a daughter of 'Imrān—corresponding to Joachim of the Christian tradition—and is mentioned by name in verse 35 of Surah 3. In contrast, the name of his wife Anne (Hanna), who in the same verse invokes her Lord asking him to consecrate the fruit of her womb, does not appear anywhere in the Qur'ān. We know it is Anne speaking because of the exegetical traditions. Zachary, considered a prophet in Islam, is mentioned in several verses to which we shall have the occasion to return later. He takes Mary into custody in the absence of her father Joachim; she would never have the opportunity to know him, for he died before her birth.

In order to find the links of parenthood between Mary and Zachary, one must refer to certain Islamic traditions which are in agreement with the Christian narrative. According to the commentary of al-Ṭabarī, 'Imrān b. Mathan, or Joachim, is a descendant of Solomon and David. The father of Anne, mother of Maryam, was Fakudh b. Katil. Zachary, or Zachariah, son of Barachiah, father at seventy of John the Baptist (Yaḥyā) in the Qur'ān, is the maternal uncle of Maryam and her first tutor after Joachim's death. Elisabeth (Ishā'), wife of Zachary and mother of John the Baptist (Yaḥyā) is the maternal aunt of Maryam. Joseph the Carpenter (Yūsuf al-Najjār), who is not mentioned in the Qur'ān, is the nephew of Zachary. In his advanced age, he becomes the tutor of Maryam through the delegation of Zachary. Anne, the mother of Maryam, entrusted her to the Levis, a family from among the progeny of Aaron and the custodians of the Temple of Jerusalem.

The table below summarizes these various familial links. It shows that Mary and John the Baptist were first cousins through the two sisters Anne and Elisabeth, and that Jesus was second cousin to John the Baptist.

The Arabic and Qur'ānic name of 'Imrān, as we shall see in the commentary, corresponds to Joachim, father of Mary. Its etymological meaning is "he who is very prosperous." This is a very close intensive form of dual, which may suggest that prosperity extends to this world and the next. The name Anna, Hanna in Arabic, means: "she who sighs with compassion, whose heart is tender and merciful." The root of this beautiful name principally evokes the meaning "making a sound like the relaxed bow." The divine and merciful love of Hanna had to be so strong as to overflow from her and fill others. We can already see that God prepared Mary, through the divine predisposition of her parents, to be the receptacle of the divine Word which would later manifest in and through Jesus. Moreover, Tradition relates that Hanna was barren and sad in her old age before Mary's birth. We are confronted again with the miraculous intervention of God, a phenomena which affected Sara, Rebecca, and other outstanding women of the Old Testament who were considered barren, and which suggests an exceptional destiny reserved for Mary.

Qur'ān, 3:35. *[Remember] when the wife of 'Imrān said: My Lord! I have vowed unto Thee that which is in my womb as a consecrated [offering]. Accept it from me. Lo! Thou, only Thou, art the Hearer, the Knower!*

إِذْ قَالَتِ امْرَأَتُ عِمْرَانَ رَبِّ إِنِّي نَذَرْتُ لَكَ مَا فِي بَطْنِي
مُحَرَّرًا فَتَقَبَّلْ مِنِّي ۖ إِنَّكَ أَنتَ السَّمِيعُ الْعَلِيمُ

The invocation that Mary's mother Hanna addresses to her Lord, *I have vowed unto Thee that which* (*mā*) *is in my womb as a consecrated [offering]*, includes the neutral relative pronoun *mā*. Because of its fundamental non-determination, this pronoun does not exclude any potential connotations, masculine as well as feminine. The pronoun would be actualized in the form of a female being, Mary, who is a perfect receptacle of Divine grace and who would later form or give birth to the Perfect, the Realized, Jesus—Peace be upon him. The express demand of 'Imrān's wife ends with the mentioning of two Divine Names which are used in the absolute sense with the universal article *al*, implying complete adherence of faith and her perfect submission to the Divine Hearing in accordance with the Knowledge that Allah possesses from pre-eternity. From this very pithy and concise verse one may deduce that God responded favorably to the intense desire of Hanna to have descendants, and that He received and accepted the vow of this aged and barren woman.

> Qur'ān, 3:36 *And when she was delivered she said: My Lord! Lo! I am delivered of a female—Allah knew best of what she was delivered—the male is not as the female; and lo! I have named her Maryam, and lo! I crave Thy protection for her and for her offspring from Satan the outcast.*

فَلَمَّا وَضَعَتْهَا قَالَتْ رَبِّ إِنِّي وَضَعْتُهَا أُنثَىٰ وَاللَّهُ أَعْلَمُ بِمَا
وَضَعَتْ وَلَيْسَ الذَّكَرُ كَالْأُنثَىٰ ۖ وَإِنِّي سَمَّيْتُهَا مَرْيَمَ وَإِنِّي
أُعِيذُهَا بِكَ وَذُرِّيَّتَهَا مِنَ الشَّيْطَانِ الرَّجِيمِ

The Qur'ānic context seems to imply that perhaps Hanna expected to have a boy. Her miraculous conception, taking place in an advanced age, did not permit her to hope for another child who could have been male and, according to the Hebrew tradition, destined to serve in the Temple, whereas daughters could not fulfil this function. In this lineage chosen by God, it was Mary who would be the mother a son, Jesus.

It is remarkable that it was Mary's mother who gave her this name and not her father, as is the custom in the Mosaic tradition. As we noted earlier, Mary's exceptional paternal and eponymous line had to play a completely providential role in her already miraculous birth due to her mother's advanced age. She was born into a family whose ancestry was made pure and preserved. Moreover, she remained exempt from the "touch" of Satan (Ar. Shayṭān, whose etymological meaning is malicious, revolted, and distant) on every new-born. An authentic narration from the Prophet states that, "every new-born son of Adam is touched by Satan, except for the son of Mary and his mother; at this touch, the child cries its first cry."

Who is this progeny of Mary that her mother Hanna asks to also be protected from Shayṭān? It is firstly and essentially Jesus, her son, who was himself born miraculously without a father. It also concerns those who are mentioned in verse 4:159, *There is not one of the People of the Scripture but will believe in him (Jesus) before his death, and on the Day of Resurrection he will be a witness against them.* Verse 43:57, which will be commented upon later, specifies that Jesus is quoted as a model (*mathal*[an]): *And when the son of Mary is quoted as a model, behold! the folk [around Prophet Muḥammad] raise a clamor in ridicule . . ..*

According to tradition, Mary very soon became an orphan and was taken into custody by her maternal uncle Zachary, who is considered a prophet in Islam and whose only son Yaḥyā (John the Baptist) is the maternal cousin of Mary. The prophet Yaḥyā, whose name in Arabic means "he lives, or shall live," would also come into this world miraculously, his father being of old age and his mother barren.

Let us note in passing that this family of close kinship was destined to an exceptionally providential life bestowed upon them by intercessions of Divine grace; they would initiate a new traditional era in the human cycle. According to verse 43:61, Jesus is a Sign of the Hour. According to certain traditions, he will have this role at the end of times as well, when he will reappear on the occasion of his second coming. He will kill the Antichrist and re-establish peace on earth for a short time.

> Qur'ān, 3:37 *And her Lord accepted her with perfect acceptance and vouchsafed to her a goodly growth; and made Zachariah her guardian. Whenever Zachariah went into the sanctuary where she was, he found that she had food. He said: O Mary! Whence cometh unto thee this? She answered: It is from Allah. Allah giveth without stint to whom He will.*

فَتَقَبَّلَهَا رَبُّهَا بِقَبُولٍ حَسَنٍ وَأَنْبَتَهَا نَبَاتًا حَسَنًا وَكَفَّلَهَا زَكَرِيَّا ۖ كُلَّمَا
دَخَلَ عَلَيْهَا زَكَرِيَّا الْمِحْرَابَ وَجَدَ عِنْدَهَا رِزْقًا ۖ قَالَ يَا مَرْيَمُ أَنَّىٰ لَكِ
هَٰذَا ۖ قَالَتْ هُوَ مِنْ عِنْدِ اللَّهِ ۖ إِنَّ اللَّهَ يَرْزُقُ مَنْ يَشَاءُ بِغَيْرِ حِسَابٍ

Let us note that Zachary (or Zachariah), who is considered as Mary's maternal uncle by marriage, bears a name whose etymology—both in Hebrew and Arabic—comes from the root *z-k-r* or *z-ch-r*. This root evokes memory and reminiscence, but also an aspect of virility, of impregnation. In Arabic, the root *dh-k-r*, which is very close to *z-ch-r* in its phonetics, principally means: (i) to strike with the male organ, to sharpen, render masculine, give birth to males; (ii) to remember, mention, recall, memorize, invoke. The corresponding substantives are therefore: (i) male organ, sharp edge, force, robustness, male palm-tree; (ii) *dhikr*, or remembrance, recollection, evocation, invocation, recital, re-naming, praise, reading of the Qur'ān, etcetera. *Dhikr* stands out from the list as the Divine word which carries the seeds contained in the Divine consciousness. Thus it possesses an eminently impregnating virtue, whether articulated by God Himself in His Revelation or formulated by a human being. It is one of the divine characteristics, an attribute related to God's Being. It expresses the original qualities of the active Principle which penetrates universal manifestation, or the matrix of the forms of the world, by ordaining this matrix through the action of the seeds of wisdom and of love. In its operative "virtue," *dhikr* is a sharp and illuminating fine point that penetrates into the darkness of human constitution as yet not harmonized and vivifies it with its motherly seed.

In the commentary on verse 2:138, we pointed out that Lord (*Rabb*) and servant (*'abd*) cannot but exist in correlation, the Lord always being envisaged in terms of adjoining or attachment and correlation. If one disappeared, the other would do too. In the Qur'ān, the name "Lord" is never found with the universal article *al* (the); its forms indicate absolute value through always being adjoined, for example: Lord of the heavens and the earth (*rabb al-ṣamawāt wa al-arḍ*), your Lord (*rabbu-kum*), etcetera. Such examples confirming this correlation are very numerous.

Mary, a perfect servant, is invested in all her being with the character traits of her Lord and she realizes all their modes. She is therefore the perfect but active receptacle of Divine presence, totally willing and predisposed to receive the Word of God (*kalimatu-Hu*). As a consequence of this reception of that which comes from God, the being of Mary in all her constitution is harmoniously designed to receive, fully consciously, the Spirit of Sanctity who transmits the Divine Word (*kalima*) to her. Verse 4:171 illustrates this particularly important mystery in the complex set of divine and human relationships which concern Mary, Jesus, the Spirit of Sanctity or Divine Spirit, and the Word of God.

As a child, Mary is taken under guardianship by the prophet Zachariah who is also her maternal uncle by marriage, as we pointed out earlier. The exceptional guardianship of Mary was assigned to Zachariah because she was entrusted to him by God Himself. For Zachariah, the guardianship is like a test that God imposes upon him because of the question he posed to her. As a prophet, he must have understood that Mary was sustained by God directly, but perhaps he wanted to know from Mary herself how she understood her own situation! Yet again, God shows us the quasi-prophetic virtue of Mary who, through her integral receptivity and the very essence of her being, is the one who inspires prophethood. She is the prototypal figure *par excellence*. Through her universal presence, she serves to support the prophetic mission.

The *Miḥrāb*

The word *miḥrāb*, translated here as "sanctuary," is a noun of place deriving from the root *h-r-b*, meaning: to lay bare, sharpen (also for cutting), or to be in conflict. The *miḥrāb* is the place of bareness, wherein conflicting or complementary tendencies are presented or absorbed. It may refer to a sanctuary reserved for spiritual retreat, the designated place where the divine Mystery is realized in the temple of perfect man in integral inner silence and with the concentration of all energies and the unification of all tendencies. Certain commentators have imagined this *miḥrāb* as the Saint of saints situated in the temple of Jerusalem and constructed by the prophet Solomon. We find this term applied to David in yet another occasion in verses 38:21-23, *And hath the story of the litigants come unto thee? How they climbed the wall into the sanctuary; How they burst in upon David, and he was afraid of them. They said: Be not afraid! [We are] two litigants, one of whom hath wronged the other, therefore judge aright between us; be not unjust; and show us the fair way.*

Lo! this my brother hath ninety and nine ewes while I had one ewe; and he said: Entrust it to me, and he conquered me in speech. In this verse, the *miḥrāb* in question cannot be assimilated to the Saint of saints because the Temple had not yet been constructed at the time of David. He had already designed its construction and his son Solomon would accomplish it later. This term *miḥrāb* conceals numerous secrets related to the exceptional choosing of the prophets in question. Together they play a role in the fundamental economy of the cycle of revelation. One always admires the richness of meanings in the concise Qur'ānic text: the formulations and the scenes follow each other rigorously, and one is also amazed at the extent of providentially arranged events which tally from a group of verses to another.

It is interesting to note the symbolism of the numbers 99 and 1, mentioned in this verse. One may relate them to the prophetic narration indicating that God has 99 Names (100 minus 1), and whoever memorizes them enters the Garden (*janna*), number one designating Divine Unity and the mysterious Supreme Name.

Qur'ān, 3:38. *There Zachariah prayed unto his Lord and said: My Lord! Bestow upon me of Thy bounty goodly offspring. Lo! Thou art the Hearer of Prayer.*

هُنَالِكَ دَعَا زَكَرِيَّا رَبَّهُۥ قَالَ رَبِّ هَبْ لِي مِنْ لَدُنْكَ ذُرِّيَّةً طَيِّبَةً إِنَّكَ سَمِيعُ الدُّعَاءِ

It is in the mystery and intimacy of this sanctuary that, according to tradition, Zachariah, an old man with no offspring and a barren wife, would pray to his Lord with all his being to bestow upon him a goodly offspring. Here too Mary plays a fundamental role, as she stays in the same sanctuary of Divine mystery, in the intimacy of her innermost secret centre. With such an arrangement of circumstances, could Zachariah's prayer not be granted?

Qur'ān, 3:39. *And the angels called to him as he stood praying in the sanctuary: Allah giveth thee glad tidings of [a son whose name is] Yaḥyā (i.e. John the Baptist, who cometh) to confirm a word from Allah, lordly, chaste, a prophet, of the righteous.*

فَنَادَتْهُ الْمَلَائِكَةُ وَهُوَ قَائِمٌ يُصَلِّي فِي الْمِحْرَابِ أَنَّ اللَّهَ يُبَشِّرُكَ بِيَحْيَىٰ مُصَدِّقًا بِكَلِمَةٍ مِنَ اللَّهِ وَسَيِّدًا وَحَصُورًا وَنَبِيًّا مِنَ الصَّالِحِينَ

Qur'ān, 3:40. *He said: My Lord! How shall I have a son when age hath overtaken me already and my wife is barren? [The angel] answered: So [it will be]. Allah doeth what He will.*

قَالَ رَبِّ أَنَّىٰ يَكُونُ لِي غُلَامٌ وَقَدْ بَلَغَنِيَ الْكِبَرُ وَامْرَأَتِي عَاقِرٌ قَالَ كَذَٰلِكَ اللَّهُ يَفْعَلُ مَا يَشَاءُ

In the chapter dedicated to the *ṣalāt* on the Prophet (*al-ṣalāt al-nabī*), we have mentioned the etymology of the term *ṣalāt* which is usually translated as "prayer" but which we have rendered as "effecting the link of grace" due to the meaning of the root *ṣ-l-w*. Zachariah, a prophet, is in a relationship of grace with Allah while the Angels communicate to him glad tidings of the coming of a son named Yaḥyā ("he lives," or "he will live"). It is at the Site of the Divine Mystery, where Mary also resides, that he is announced to have a descendant despite his wife's infertility and his advanced age. Moreover, the Angels inform him of the birth of a son who, according to the Qur'ān, will be a prophet confirming the coming of Jesus, the Word of God, just as God announces it to the People of the Scripture (*ahl al-kitāb*) in verse 4:171, . . . *The Messiah, Jesus son of Mary, was only a messenger of Allah, and His word which He conveyed unto Mary, and a spirit from Him*. We shall offer further commentary later.

The expression which we have rendered as *confirmer of a Word* (*muṣaddiq^an bi-kalimat*) might be translated in another way because of the preposition *bi*, an article which marks contiguity, proximity, and, by extension, instrumental action. For this reason, the Qur'ānic expression *muṣaddiq^an bi* can be translated "confirmer through (or thanks to)" or also, in this Qur'ānic context, "*regarding a Word from Allah,*" or "*confirming by virtue of a Word from Allah.*" According to this last translation, one might suppose that being a perfect person the prophet Yaḥyā confirms the coming of Christ. This is consistent with what is known from the New Testament in which John the Baptist announces and prepares the coming of his cousin, the Anoint. Yaḥyā will be a liege (*sayyid*) invested with prophethood, chaste, and without physical offspring, for he is said to have been celibate. He shall be among the Righteous (*ṣaliḥīn*), meaning faultless, virtuous, and perfectly constituted, according to the root of the plural active participle *ṣ-l-ḥ*. Once again we note the excellence and the divine favour bestowed upon this chosen prophetic family.

The information that Zachariah received is not directly and initially given by God Himself, but rather by the Angels. Surprised by this announcement, Zachariah addresses God directly to inform Him of his amazement and perhaps his doubt. God tells him that it will be so, with or without his immediate willingness. In the following verse (3:41) he asks God to grant him a "Sign."

> Qur'ān, 3:41. *He said: My Lord! Appoint a Sign for me. [The angel] said: The Sign unto thee [shall be] that thou shalt not speak unto mankind three days except by signals. Remember thy Lord much, and praise [Him] in the early hours of night and morning.*

قَالَ رَبِّ اجْعَل لِّي آيَةً قَالَ آيَتُكَ أَلَّا تُكَلِّمَ النَّاسَ ثَلَاثَةَ
أَيَّامٍ إِلَّا رَمْزًا وَاذْكُر رَّبَّكَ كَثِيرًا وَسَبِّحْ بِالْعَشِيِّ وَالْإِبْكَارِ

Why does his Lord impose upon him three days of silence? Certain commentators consider it a sanction provoked by Zachariah's doubt, perhaps referring to the Gospel of Luke (Luke I, 20). One might also suggest that it was an extension corresponding to the three worlds—the physical, the psychological, and the spiritual—so that all the actors of this miraculous event, linked to one another through family bonds of both blood and spirit, might reach full acceptance. Furthermore, the two Arabic expressions used here—*la tukallima*, literally *thou shalt not speak*, and *ramz*, meaning discrete eye signals, hand or head gestures, or symbolic allusions—imply a question of a language based on allusion (*ishāra*), a specific language which suggests more to those who are present than audibly articulated words. The mysteries stemming from this miraculous situation must only be communicable through this symbolic manner of expression willed by God Himself. The invocation or remembrance (*dhikr*) of his Lord, commanded of Zachariah by God in the early hours of night and morning, stems from an intimate and inward call without any outward articulation of sounds. The "Sign" in question indicates that God is always Present in the Qur'ānic text; His Epiphany comes through everything that He manifests in all possible realms and His revealed Word in one form or another. However, one must note that verse 19:10 mentions three *nights* of silence imposed upon Zachariah, not three days. Must one understand that the day includes the night or that the night includes the day?

> Qur'ān, 3:42. *And when the angels said: O Mary! Lo! Allah hath chosen thee and made thee entirely pure, and hath preferred thee above the women of the universe.*

وَإِذْ قَالَتِ الْمَلَائِكَةُ يَا مَرْيَمُ إِنَّ اللَّهَ اصْطَفَاكِ وَطَهَّرَكِ
وَاصْطَفَاكِ عَلَىٰ نِسَاءِ الْعَالَمِينَ

The episode concerning Mary, which starts at verse 3:35 and is interrupted in verses 3:38-41, continues here in a long passage.

Let us note the repetition of the verb "choose" applied to Mary in this verse. In the first sequence, Mary is chosen in a non-relational manner through her unique quality as a person, whereas in the other passage, she is chosen as superior in relation to all possible women.

The Arabic term *'alamīn*, translated here as "universe," is a regular plural that is generally applied to living beings gifted with knowledge, i.e. both jinn and human beings. It comes from the root *'a-l-m*, meaning "to be a sign of, mark, distinguish through a mark, discern, establish a link between different signs, to know, to distinguish things from each other." The Arabic term *'ilm*, found numerous times in the Qur'ān and applied to Jesus in certain verses, comes from the same root and is often translated as "knowledge." According to its etymology, when applied to God this noun connotes the infinity of permanent realities present in Him. When it concerns the human being, it represents the elements he discerns in the universal creation and binds together by his intellect (*'aql*) in order to constitute a coherent ensemble called "knowledge, science." Thus interpreted, the knowledge that human beings acquire or possess is knowledge of God's Order and Wisdom in different realms.

The general teaching concerning Mary consists of considering her free from all impurity, and in particular free from sin in all its forms, for she is a veritable servant of her Lord without any limitation. Thus, the expression "entirely pure" must be understood in an integral sense. Certain commentators suggest that she was even exempted from menstrual periods and the pains of childbirth!

Muslim commentators point out that the plural *malā'ika*, or "angels," is used for a singular subject, namely the Angel of the Revelation, Gabriel. This term can also be translated as "the choir of the angels," as occasionally mentioned in the religious literature.

Qur'ān, 3:43. *O Mary! Be obedient to thy Lord, prostrate thyself and bow with those who bow [in worship].*

يَا مَرْيَمُ اقْنُتِي لِرَبِّكِ وَاسْجُدِي وَارْكَعِي مَعَ الرَّاكِعِينَ

Mary is a perfect woman according to both the references of the Qur'ānic text, as previously noted, and a Prophetic tradition. The Prophet Muḥammad names Mary as one of the perfect women, alongside Āsiya, the Pharaoh's wife from the time of Moses; Khadīja, the Prophet's first wife; and Fāṭima, his daughter who was married to the Prophet's cousin and the fourth Caliph 'Alī ibn Abī Ṭālib. She is bound with the prescriptions of Mosaic Law. God recommends three fundamental attitudes.

The first, which is purely inward, consists of mustering all her energies and faculties, all of her being for her Lord, so that nothing distracts her from the essential worship which she owes Him as a completely submitted creature. This reverence encompasses all aspects of her immaculate being. It renders her entirely receptive to the Presence of her Lord within her and within creation, but it also renders her eminently active.

The Prophet of Islam, despite his essential and existential perfection, is nevertheless obligated to adhere to the prescriptions of the Law. His Lord conveyed to him this Law for himself and his community, and he has been charged with it until the Day of Resurrection, as we have already shown.

The second is the prostration, implying a complete re-absorption of the whole being through the folding of the body.

The third attitude is the bowing down which could mean

expansion through the hierarchy of cosmic degrees, as certain mystics have pointed out.

These two postures represent universal worshipping gestures and must not be interpreted, as certain commentators mistakenly do, as being calculated according to certain postures of Muslim ritual and canonical prayer. We shall have the occasion to return to this subject in the commentary on verse 19:31. Muslim commentators have noted that prostration (*sujūd*) is mentioned before the bowing down (*rukū'*), these two postures of the ritual prayer occurring in the reverse order. One may understand that in order to reach the position of prostration, one must pass uninterruptedly and obligatorily through the position of bowing down.

Qur'ān, 3:44. *This is of the announcements of things unseen. We reveal it unto thee. Thou wast not present with them when they threw their pens [to know] which of them should be the guardian of Mary, nor wast thou present with them when they contended [thereupon].*

ذَٰلِكَ مِنْ أَنۢبَآءِ ٱلْغَيْبِ نُوحِيهِ إِلَيْكَ ۚ وَمَا كُنتَ لَدَيْهِمْ إِذْ
يُلْقُونَ أَقْلَٰمَهُمْ أَيُّهُمْ يَكْفُلُ مَرْيَمَ وَمَا كُنتَ لَدَيْهِمْ إِذْ يَخْتَصِمُونَ

From verse 3:33 onwards, we notice that the Divine mystery affects this Family that has been privileged by God's favour, causing it to providentially play a role in the economy of the Divine plan which would be at the origin of a new expression of the Revelation. This verse is primarily addressed to the Prophet of Islam, but also concerns every true believer. By direct inspiration, the verse is informed of the components of this Mystery that concern him due to his universal and all-comprehensive reality.

Tradition teaches that Zachariah, assisted by God, was chosen after this throwing of the pens to be the guardian of Mary. She was a child that had been orphaned very early in her life. The guardianship of Mary by competent persons in this exceptional context clearly constituted an issue of considerable importance. We may also deduce the quality of those who participated in this mysterious scene. Mary's unique case must have attracted the attention of all those wanted to have the distinguished privilege of taking care of her.

The style used by the Divine Author in this verse also bears witness to both the Mystery surrounding this Family and the providential mission Mary was charged with and which she would fulfil.

Qur'ān, 3:45. *[And remember] when the angels said: O Mary! Lo! Allah giveth thee glad tidings of a word from him, whose name is the Anoint, Jesus, son of Mary, illustrious in the world and the Hereafter, and one of those brought near [unto Allah].*

إِذْ قَالَتِ الْمَلَائِكَةُ يَا مَرْيَمُ إِنَّ اللَّهَ يُبَشِّرُكِ بِكَلِمَةٍ مِنْهُ اسْمُهُ الْمَسِيحُ
عِيسَى ابْنُ مَرْيَمَ وَجِيهًا فِي الدُّنْيَا وَالْآخِرَةِ وَمِنَ الْمُقَرَّبِينَ

The Anointed One, Jesus, son of Mary, Word of Allah

In Arabic, the word *kalima*, or "word," to which we shall return on several instances in the commentary on verse 4:171, is in the undetermined singular feminine form. This term can be interpreted as in the previously mentioned verse 3:39, or alternatively in the following manner:

The expression that we have translated as *whose name* should be rendered as "the name of him." This word is in the masculine form and therefore cannot but relate to Allah, the only masculine name in this part of the verse.

What should one understand by "him"? 1) Is it the name of Allah, as we just said, or 2) the personalized name of the word which is then the complete name of Jesus?

1) In Arabic grammar, the pronoun *Hu* (in reference to *ismu-Hu*, His Name), must normally be of the same gender as the name to which it is related, in this case 'Allah' which is masculine. Therefore the complete name of Jesus, *the Anoint, Jesus, son of Mary*, would be one of God's Names.

2) Otherwise, it is possible that the noun 'word,' feminine in Arabic, represents the personification of Jesus and therefore requires a masculine accord: *ismu-hu*. This type of meaning occasionally occurs in the Qur'ān as well as in classical poetry. In the latter exegetical commentaries, *ismu-hu* is interpreted as being the name of this word, that is, *the Anointed One, Jesus, son of Mary*.

In another case, it is difficult put forth a definite opinion regarding choice of interpretation in the Qur'ānic context. One might also assert that the two interpretations both turn out to be possible owing to the mysteriously complex case of the person of the Anointed One, Jesus, son of Mary.

In the commentary on verse 2:87, we have already analyzed the meaning of each word included in the complete name of Jesus in the Qur'ān.

The adjective noun in the adverbial case *wajīh*[an], which we have translated as "illustrious," comes from the root *w-j-h:* to touch on the face, to surpass in rank, dignity, and consideration, to enjoy respect, to turn, to orientate oneself, to head towards. Due to the *fa'īl* scheme on which this word is constructed, it acquires both an active and a passive meaning. It can therefore be translated according to the following lexicon: having a well-constituted face, eminent, illustrious, esteemed, notable, distinguished, honoured, noble, chief, and principal.

The Anointed One, Jesus, Son of Mary, brought near unto God

The Anoint, Jesus, Son of Mary is among those brought near (*muqarrabūn*). But what must one understand from this term? It comes from the verbal root *q-r-b* which means: to walk during the night until dawn, to travel during the night, to find oneself in front of somebody, to approach, to be near, to be imminent, to be close, to be intimate with, to be pleased, to put the sword in the sheath (which fits it perfectly). In the passive participle of the second verbal form it acquires the meaning: to draw close those which constitute objects of offerings, intimate ones, honoured ones, or esteemed ones. Let us quote the set of verses in order to better grasp the meaning of this expression: *And the Foremost! The Foremost? Those are the ones brought near* (*muqarrabūn*)*—in the Gardens of Bliss* (Qur'ān, 56:10-12). In this context and in verse 4:172 mentioned later, the *muqarrabūn* are the Intimate ones, who enjoy the greatest nearness and intimacy with Allah. Such are the Messengers and the Prophets, of whom Jesus is one. However, all human beings are ultimately destined to return to God through the spiritual realization in the Path that Allah has traced out and which is different for each of them. Therefore we all benefit from this intimacy, such as mentioned by the verse . . . *Verily we are for Allah, and unto Him are we returning* (Qur'ān, 2:156). The mystics will evoke the Gardens (or Paradises) of the Essence or of the primordial Source (*jannāt al-'ayn*), the ultimate unsurpassable degree.

The Announcement made to Mary by the Angels

According to the Arab lexicographers, the word angel—sing. *malak*, pl. *malā'ika*—can come from two verbal roots: (i) *m-l-k*, meaning to contain, hold, possess, detain, use, control, keep in possession, exercise authority, dominate, govern—marry a woman, or knead. A *malak* is therefore a spiritual being gifted with power, authority, control, handling; (ii) *l-'a-k*: to send with a mission, the prefix *ma* in *malā'ika* indicating nouns of instruments and functions in grammar. According to this second etymology, the angel is a spiritual entity sent with a mission or exercising a certain regular or random function. The exegetes of the Qur'ān state that each angel represents a kind unto itself. For this reason, the plural used here or in other verses seems to concern both many kinds of angels and a collective function.

The announcement of the coming of the Anoint, Jesus, Son of Mary, which the Angels make to Mary, resembles that which we find in verse 19:17 et passim where the Spirit assumes for Mary, who is surprised by this unusual visit, the form of a being looking like a perfectly made human being, assimilated into Gabriel, the Angel of Revelation by Tradition. Let us point out that this assimilation of the Spirit, which integrates a human form into the Angel Gabriel, does not necessitate the use of plural as in verse 3:45 and 3:42 where the announcement made to Mary takes place through the angels.

In this verse, however, the angels in question do not take the human form and Mary is neither on guard nor fearful, the announcement having to be made here in the imaginary or purely spiritual world. We can therefore note the different modalities that this announcement takes on and the characteristic and multiple phases implied. This non-incarnate and purely spiritual angelic intervention prefigures that to be taken on formally and humanly, by the Spirit assimilated into the Angel Gabriel, whose form will be decisive in the coming of the Anointed One. Let us point out that therefore, in this Surah, the passages concerning the annunciation made to Mary carry moments and modalities which are not the same as in Surah nineteen, even though they include an identical ending. This ending is the incorporation of the Anoint into this world, through his mother Mary. There he would grow until, according to verse 4:158, God would raise him to heaven to await his second coming near the end of times.

> Qur'ān, 3:46. *He will speak unto mankind in his cradle and in his manhood, and he is of the righteous.*

وَيُكَلِّمُ النَّاسَ فِي الْمَهْدِ وَكَهْلًا وَمِنَ الصَّالِحِينَ

The Anointed One, Son of Mary, is the Word of Allah and Spirit from Him, according to verse 4:171. He spoke from his birth, as in verses 19:24 and 19:30-33. At the time of his effective coming into existence, he utilized a perfectly articulate language like a human being with a completely developed phonetic apparatus. The phrase "he is of the righteous" goes to show that he is perfect in his integral constitution, the "Righteous" being considered in mysticism as persons who are intimately present in God. The root of this word, *ṣ-l-ḥ*, implies the following meanings: to be integrated, without defects, in a good state, or virtuous, as we noted in the commentary on verse 3:39.

> Qur'ān, 3:47. *She said: My Lord! How can I have a child when no being [made] of flesh* (bashar) *hath touched me? He said: So [it is for you]. Allah createth what He will. When He decreeth a thing, He but saith unto it: Be! and it is.*

قَالَتْ رَبِّ أَنَّىٰ يَكُونُ لِي وَلَدٌ وَلَمْ يَمْسَسْنِي بَشَرٌ قَالَ كَذَٰلِكِ
اللَّهُ يَخْلُقُ مَا يَشَاءُ إِذَا قَضَىٰ أَمْرًا فَإِنَّمَا يَقُولُ لَهُ كُنْ فَيَكُونُ

How should we understand the word *bashar*?

In verse 2:87 we analyzed the term *walad* which applies to both genders and which can be translated as: child, engendered being, and progeny.

The term *bashar*, which we have translated as "being (made) of flesh," comes from the root *b-sh-r* meaning: to take off the skin or tree bark, to peel or grate, to delight someone with news, to cohabit with a spouse, to rejoice at something. A *bashar* is a being of human stature, born from a father and a mother, whose outward appearance expresses his belonging to the human race without being biased towards total spiritual realization. The latter can be attained because of his all encompassing constitution, made in the divine Form, according to verse 95:5, *Surely We created man in the best constitution*, and to the Prophetic tradition, "Allah created man in His form." This definition of *bashar* enables us to understand that the Prophet Muḥammad is a being of human stature conceived by a father and a mother like every human being. He is perfectly human, even though most people see in him only this specific outward quality without perceiving and contemplating his double reality, an outward and inward totality. The following verse, which concerns firstly and essentially the Prophet, emphasizes this perspective: Say (unto them O Muḥammad): *I am only a being of human stature like you. It is inspired in me that your God is One God, therefore take the straight path unto Him and seek forgiveness of Him. And woe unto the associators* (Qur'ān, 41:6). In the Qur'ān, this term *bashar* is never applied to Jesus. The only occasion on which it is mentioned in relation to the genesis of the human nature of Jesus is the appearance, to Mary, of the Spirit of God which temporarily assumes for her a *perfect human likeness* (*bashar sawiyy*, cf. 19:17). In Surah Nineteen, which is entitled "Mary," Allah mentions the exceptional constitution of Jesus who was conceived without a human father. He did not appear according to the habitual engendering of a human being, and for this reason he is not called *bashar sawiyy*. However, one must not deduce that the messenger and prophet Jesus is superior to the messenger and prophet Muḥammad. May God protect us from making distinctions between the prophets; the previously quoted verse 2:286 is very explicit in this regard.

The appellation *bashar* in the Qur'ān

In the Qur'ān, several prophets after Adam are qualified by the term *bashar*. Although Adam is not called a prophet in the Qur'ān, the Tradition recognizes him with this title. Let us quote the verses that refer to the prophets in question with this noun, according to the presumed order of their apparition:

1. For Adam, Qur'ān 15:33 and 38:71, *When thy Lord said unto the angels: Lo! I am about to create a bashar out of mire. And when I have fashioned him and breathed into him of My Spirit, then fall*

down before him prostrate (Qur'ān, 38:71-72).

2. For Noah, Qur'ān, 10:11, 11:27, 14:9, 23:24, 23:33.

3. For Hūd and Thamūd, Qur'ān, 10:11, 14:9.

4. For Ṣāliḥ, Qur'ān, 26:154; 54:24.

5. For Shu'ayb, Qur'ān, 26:186.

6. For Moses and Aaron, Qur'ān, 23:47.

7. For the Prophet Muḥammad, Qur'ān, 17:93-94; 18:110, 21:3, 41:6, 74:25.

8. In its other Qur'ānic occurrences, this term is used in the general sense to refer to a human being, or one who belongs to mankind. Sometimes it acquires a collective meaning and the verb qualifying it takes on the plural (masculine) form: *And of His signs is this: He created you of dust, and behold you human beings, ranging widely* (*bashar tantashirūn*)*!* (Qur'ān, 30:20)

We have translated the expression we find in 19:21 as *So [it will be] for you* (*ka-dhalī kī*). By breaking down each element, we may better approach the meaning of this pithy and nominal (that is, without a verb) phrase. We note that it specifies a characteristic which is addressed only to the Virgin Mary, due to the fact that her constitution is of a unique purity and a total readiness to receive the Spirit carrying the Word (*kalima*) of God. The Arabic demonstrative *dhālika* sometimes declines depending on the persons it designates. This is why we encounter expressions such as *dhālikum*, so it is for you (plural), *dhālikunna*, so it is for them (feminine), and *dhālikī* (not *dhālika*), so it is for you (singular feminine), to designate only Mary in verses 3:47 and 19:21.

Allah creates [or gives the norm (*yakhluqu*) to] everything He desires. When He decides or decrees an order (*amr*) or a willed reality (*shay*) stemming from His Divine Order or Degree, He commands this entity to come into existence. It manifests in the created world the possibilities that God places in them. The Order is first composed and not created in the divine design before being produced in the world to which it is destined. The expression *kun fa-yakun* will be dealt with in more detail in the commentary on verse 3:59. The existentiating *kun* is primordially the unique uncreated Word which produces the manifested beings.

Qur'ān, 3:48. *And He will teach him the Scripture and wisdom, and the Torah and the Gospel*

وَيُعَلِّمُهُ الْكِتَابَ وَالْحِكْمَةَ وَالتَّوْرَاةَ وَالإِنْجِيلَ

A. How should one understand the term "Scripture"?

Allah Himself will teach or teaches to Jesus the Scripture (*kitāb*), but how should one understand "Scripture," a term which we have already encountered and commented upon in a variety of contexts? In relation to the different Qur'ānic occurrences of the term kitāb—which we do not consider to have figurative or metaphoric meanings, but rather polysemic or anagogical ones—we may identify several interpretations.

1) Firstly and primordially, Scripture refers to the *kitāb* found with God in which rests His knowledge of all realities. In it their destiny is included or "written" from pre-eternity. Is this *Kitāb* accessible to human beings? *Allah effaceth what He will, and establisheth [what He will], and with Him is the source of ordinance* (Qur'ān, 13:39). *By the Scripture which maketh plain. Lo! We have made it a Recitation in Arabic that haply ye may understand. And Lo! It is in the Mother of the Book, which We possess, sublime, full of wisdom* (Qur'ān, 43:2-4). Such is the Scripture that Allah teaches to Jesus directly.

2) Secondly it refers to the *kitāb* which Allah sends down or reveals to the Messengers who receive it. This scripture takes shape first by the voice and then by the written word so as to constitute a book, a collection which will enable its material conservation and facilitate the study of its contents. *It is not meet for any human being unto whom Allah had given the Scripture and wisdom and the prophethood that he should afterwards have said unto mankind: Be slaves of me instead of Allah; but [he would say]: Be ye faithful servants of the Lord by virtue of your constant teaching of the Scripture and of your constant study thereof.*

3) Scripture also relates to the *kitāb* in which the outward and inner comportments of human beings are written, and for which they shall be judged in complete equity: *Nay, but the record of the righteous is in 'Illiyīn—And what will make you know what the highest 'Illiyīn is?—[It is] a Register inscribed* (Qur'ān, 83:18-20).

In verse 3:48, it is Allah who communicates the knowledge of the Scripture to Jesus. The word used and conjugated is in the incomplete form, for here it refers to the simple annunciation that Allah makes to Mary about the coming of Jesus which is not yet actualized. However, in verse 5:110 Allah speaks to Jesus, Son of Mary in the first person singular of the same verb "teach," but this time in the complete form, for then Jesus has been engendered: "*. . . and how I taught thee the Scripture and Wisdom and the Torah and the Gospel . . ..*" Not only does Allah teach the Scripture to Jesus but He also gives it to him in this verse that speaks about it, *He spake: Lo! I am the servant of Allah. He hath given me the Scripture and hath appointed me a prophet* (Qur'ān, 19:30). He also gives him the Gospel, which is already a differentiation of this Scripture found in Allah from eternity, as we noted earlier: *We bestowed on him the Gospel wherein is guidance and a light, confirming that which was [revealed] before it in the Torah—a guidance and an admonition . . .* (Qur'ān, 5:46) *. . . We gave him (Jesus) the Gospel . . .* (Qur'ān, 57:27). Here the plural, represented by *We*, concerns Allah and His beautiful Names. The Prophet Muḥammad receives the Scripture and Wisdom (*ḥikma*) as well, according to this phrase of the verse: *. . . Allah sendeth down unto thee the Scripture and wisdom, and teacheth thee that which thou knewest not. The grace of Allah toward thee hath been immense* (Qur'ān, 4:113).

The numerous meanings acquired by the term *kitāb* are due to the supercomposition of meanings and the eminently anagogical linguistic qualities of Arabic or Arabicized words used by Allah in the Qur'ān. In the majority of cases it is not a question of metaphorical or figurative meanings, for metaphor is a figure of style through which a word receives a meaning different from the one attributed to it in common parlance. Quite often the commentator and the translator remain powerless—but can it be otherwise?—in evaluating the polysemic range of the terms that God uses in His Revelation. Therefore they tend to sometimes understand a term in its proper meaning and sometimes in a figurative meaning according to the idea they form about these terms in the Qur'ānic context. We have already spoken about the terms *kalima*, word, and *rūḥ*, spirit. We shall return to the polysemic and anagogical meanings of Qur'ānic words in more detail in the commentary on verse 4:171.

B. How should one understand "Wisdom"?

The term *ḥikma*, translated here as wisdom, comes from the root *ḥ-k-m* which means: to muzzle a horse and put the martingale under its chin in order to tame it and make it go where one wishes, to hold, to contain, and to prevent one from doing something, to arbitrate, to judge, decide, declare, to resolve, administrate, regulate, govern, to give a ruling, to master, to be cautious, to have a sound judgment. From these numerous but related meanings stems the translation of *ḥikma* as "wisdom." This wisdom is the adequate knowledge of things, of the order which presides over their existence and the purpose they have been assigned with. This purpose consists of conferring upon them their existential status according to God's Plan and which must be applied in all fairness. The sage (*ḥakim*) is he who, out of his knowledge of things, assigns them their right place in relation to the others. Wisdom therefore implies a dualistic quality incorporating both science or knowledge and practice or application.

There are numerous verses in which it is God Himself who teaches or grants Scripture and Wisdom and in which the latter are intimately and inseparably associated with each other, such as for Jesus, for certain prophets or messengers, and also for other human beings. In verse 4:113 it is Allah who brings down the Scripture and Wisdom upon the Prophet Muḥammad, and He teaches him what he knew not: *But for the grace of Allah upon thee, and His mercy, a party of them had resolved to mislead thee, but they mislead only themselves and they hurt thee not at all. Allah descendeth unto thee the Scripture and wisdom, and teacheth thee that which thou knewest not. The grace of Allah toward thee hath been infinite.* (4:113) In verse 2:129, Abraham and Ishmael ask God: *Our Lord! And raise up in their midst a messenger from among them who shall recite unto them Thy revelations, and shall instruct them in the Scripture and in Wisdom and shall make them grow. Lo! surely Thou art the Mighty, the Wise.* This wisdom is granted by Allah to whomever He wishes good according to the verse: *He granteth wisdom unto whom He will, and he unto whom wisdom is granted, he truly hath received abundant good. But none remember except men of understanding* (Qur'ān, 2:269)

In other verses, the term "Scripture" is associated with the word "*ḥukm*" from the same root as "*ḥikma*." It may therefore be translated as: authority, judgment, statute, norm, sentence, appropriate application. For example, the following verse in which scripture, appropriate application, and prophethood are mentioned: *It is not [meet] for any mortal unto whom Allah had given the Scripture and Appropriate Application and the prophethood that he should afterwards have said unto mankind: Be slaves of me instead of Allah; but: Be ye faithful servants of the Lord by virtue of your constant teaching of the Scrip-*

ture and of your constant study thereof (Qur'ān, 3:79). According to this perspective, he who recites the Scripture applies it according to the norms of wisdom.

C. How should one understand "Thora"?

Depending on the sacred context, the commentators of the Qur'ān unanimously consider this term to designate the Scripture given to Moses directly by God. This Scripture had first been transmitted orally and it was put to writing a long time after the death of Moses.

D. How should one understand "Gospel"?

The Muslim commentators and the Orientalists have generally considered the Qur'ānic term "Injīl" to be derived from the Latin word "evangelicum" and the Greek "euaggelion." Both terms mean "good news." Their corresponding word in Arabic is *bishāra*, from the Arabic root *b-sh-r*, which conveys the same meaning in Greek, namely "glad tiding." If this is accurate, then this strange term would be considered to belong to the vocabulary that was Arabicized by the Revelation. Certain scholars consider *bishāra* to be derived from the Arabic root *n-j-l* which includes the following meanings: to throw, to launch, to pierce with a javelin, to mistreat someone, to make a gaping wound, to plough the earth, to remove the skin, to highlight, to manifest, and to erase the writing or the traces of something, to extract, to be green, to be covered in green, and to have big eyes. These numerous meanings evoke some of the traits of Jesus. It is from this root that the Arabic lexicographers derive this word that is mentioned in twelve verses (all of which are quoted in this work).

The commentators of the Qur'ān are of the opinion that only the words attributed to Jesus in the gospels constitute the Injīl, properly speaking. These sayings, however, are not those which Jesus pronounced in his mother tongue, Aramaic, or in his cultural tongue, Hebrew, for they no longer exist in the original language are only known through their Greek and Latin translations, as well as additional translations to a number of vernacular languages.

Qur'ān, 3:49. As a Messenger to the Children of Israel: . . . *Lo! I have come unto you with a sign from your Lord. Lo! I fashion for you out of clay the likeness of a bird, and I breathe into it and it is a bird, by Allah's leave. I heal him who was born blind, and the leper, and I raise the dead, by Allah's leave. And I announce unto you what ye eat and what ye store up in your houses. Lo! herein verily is a Sign for you, if ye are to be believers.*

وَرَسُولًا إِلَىٰ بَنِي إِسْرَائِيلَ أَنِّي قَدْ جِئْتُكُمْ بِآيَةٍ مِنْ رَبِّكُمْ ۖ
أَنِّي أَخْلُقُ لَكُمْ مِنَ الطِّينِ كَهَيْئَةِ الطَّيْرِ فَأَنْفُخُ فِيهِ فَيَكُونُ
طَيْرًا بِإِذْنِ اللَّهِ ۖ وَأُبْرِئُ الْأَكْمَهَ وَالْأَبْرَصَ وَأُحْيِي الْمَوْتَىٰ
بِإِذْنِ اللَّهِ ۖ وَأُنَبِّئُكُمْ بِمَا تَأْكُلُونَ وَمَا تَدَّخِرُونَ فِي بُيُوتِكُمْ ۚ إِنَّ
فِي ذَٰلِكَ لَآيَةً لَكُمْ إِنْ كُنْتُمْ مُؤْمِنِينَ

JESUS, MESSENGER OF ALLAH

In commenting on the contents of verse 2:87, we have already brought to light the known difference between *rasūl* (messenger), and *nabiyy* (prophet). The *nabiyy* is charged with proclaiming the tidings that Allah has made known through the sending of a messenger. In Islam, the *Rasūl* is the person who is sent by God, from God, with a Message coming from Him, updated in its form and addressed to a community to which the prophet must announce the content of this Message. The messenger is also a prophet, as is the case with Jesus, who is called a Messenger (*rasūl*) in this verse and Prophet (*nabiyy*) in verse 19:30. As a Messenger-Prophet, the Message that Jesus must transmit is addressed first of all to persons around him as stated in the Qur'ān.

The message that God continuously communicates to human beings has been transmitted to them by other messengers too, for example Moses and the Prophet Muḥammad. It is therefore remarkable that the two juxtaposed qualifiers, *rasūl* and *nabiyy*, concern Moses in verse 19:51, Ishmael in verse 19:54, and the Prophet in verses 7:157 and 7:158: *And make mention in the Scripture of Moses. Lo! he was purified (murlas), and he was a messenger, a prophet* (Qur'ān, 19:51). *And make mention in the Scripture of Ishmael. Lo! he was a keeper of his promise (ṣādiq al-wa'd), and he was a messenger, a prophet* (Qur'ān, 19:54). *Those who follow the messenger, the Prophet of a primordial nature (ummiyy), whom they will find described in the Torah and the Gospel . . .* (Qur'ān, 7:157). In the last verse, the expression "messenger-prophet" represents a general character and a universal meaning due to the universal article *the* (al), whereas in the previous two verses these two qualifications are grammatically undetermined: "a messenger, a prophet."

The Children of Israel

Who are the children of Israel to whom Jesus was originally sent? Does this mean that his intended audience includes, or will include, only the Children of Israel before, during and after the mission of Jesus?

Of the forty-three occurrences of the word Israel in the Qur'ān, forty-one deal with the children of Israel (*banū Isrā'īl*, a notion which implies both sons and daughters) and only two verses mention this noun alone: *These are they unto whom Allah bestowed favour from among the prophets, of the seed of Adam and of those whom We carried [in the ship] with Noah, and of the seed of Abraham and Israel, and from among those whom We guided and chose . . .* (Qur'ān, 19:58). *All food was lawful unto the Children of Israel, save that which Israel forbade himself, before the Torah was revealed . . .* (Qur'ān, 3:93).

In the Old Testament, the Hebrew noun "Israel" means "whom God fights, and proves strong;" it is given to prophet Jacob during his fight with God: *And he said, Thy name shall be called no more Jacob, but Israel (he who fights El): for as a prince hast thou power with God and with men, and hast prevailed.* (Genesis 32:28). *And God (Elohīm) appeared unto Jacob again, when he came out of Padan-Aram, and blessed him. And God said unto him, Thy name [is] Jacob: thy name shall not be called any more Jacob, but Israel shall be thy name: and he called his name Israel* (Genesis 35:9-10). God's revelation for Abraham, blessed by Him, *And he brought him forth abroad, and said, Look now toward heaven, and tell the stars, if thou be able to number them: and he said unto him, So shall thy seed be* (Genesis, 15:5) would be accomplished through the posterity of his two sons: Ishmael, son of Hagar, who was his first born, and Isaac, son of Sara. Ishmael's progeny would beget the Arabs and Islam, and Isaac's progeny would produce the Hebrew Tradition and Christianity. According to this interpretation, one may deduce that the expression "children of Israel" is a general denomination that applies first to the Hebrews then to the Jews, starting from their captivity in Babylonia. It would be applied to Jesus and those who followed him in his lifetime and shortly thereafter.

In Arabic, the proper noun "Israel" can be divided into two words: *Isrā*—from the root *s-r-y*, to travel in the dark, and the root *'-y-l*, referring to God's act of creation.

Other accounts in the Qur'ānic text feature a messenger who is sent to his people as well as to other communities that are foreign to him. Moses in his mission is principally sent to his own people, but also to Pharaoh and to his notables (cf. Qur'ān, 7:103, 10:75, 11:97, 20:24, 20:43, 23:46, 26:11, 28:3, 29:39, 40:24, 43:46, 44:17, 51:38, 73:15). The same is true of Solomon, a prophet-king who followed the Law of Moses along with the people of Bilqis, the Queen of Saba (cf. Qur'ān, 27:22).

The twelve sons of Jacob according to the Old Testament

God's covenant with Abraham and Isaac was renewed with Jacob and his twelve sons. The sons constitute the ancient eponyms of the twelve tribes or clans of Israel (*asbāṭ*), designated five times in the Qur'ān by the term *asbāṭ*, such as in verse 2:140.

According to Genesis 29:32, 30:25, 37:17, 35:22-26, and 46:8-24, the names of these twelve sons were: 1. Sons of Lea = Ruben, Simeon, Levi, Juda, Issachar, and Zabulon; 2. Sons of Rachel = Joseph, and Benjamin; 3. Sons of Bilha, maid of Rachel = Dan and Nephtali; 4. Sons of Zilpa, maid of Lea = Gad and Asher.

Levi's descendants were gradually adopted by the other lines because of their specialization in sacerdotal functions. These sacraments were inaugurated by the prophet Aaron, the first great priest of Israel.

A Sign from your Lord

The sign in question consists of miracles performed by Jesus as the *Word of Allah* whom He *strengthened with His Spirit*. The Spirit gives life, supports it, and restores it during every moment, through the intermediary of forms and beings constantly manifesting it universally and particularly. The story of the golden calf is one example of the invigoration of the forms by the Spirit, performed by certain human beings with the knowledge of its cause. Sāmirī makes a golden calf who has the quality of bellowing like the Bovidae. This episode is related in Surah 20, verses 85-97. The Sāmirī says, *I perceived what they perceive not, so I seized a handful from the footsteps of the messenger* (Gabriel), *and then threw it in. Thus my soul commended to me* (Qur'ān, 20:96). One might also mention other

Qur'ānic episodes in which the Spirit intervenes in one form or another depending on the circumstances.

This same sign is addressed by the Lord to the children of Israel, each one interpreting the content of this Sign according to their point of view and their knowledge of their Lord. Indeed, in the Qur'ān and in the current Arabic language, the word *rabb*, or lord, is related to the term *'abd*, meaning servant, worshipper, or one who expresses the qualities of his Lord and realizes them intimately. However, it happens that one says "the Lord" but only when one envisages that He totalizes symbolically the set of particular lords, otherwise the expression "the Lord" would be used improperly. Thus, one finds the correlation lord/servant a great number of times in the sacred text. For example, when Jesus says: *Lo! Allah is my Lord and your Lord . . .* (Qur'ān, 3:51); *. . . Worship Allah, my Lord and your Lord . . .* (Qur'ān, 5:117), or again *. . . Lord of the heavens and the earth . . .* (13:16). The word "Lord" is rarely used in an undetermined way, and never in an absolute mode: *Shall I seek another than Allah for Lord, when He is Lord of all things?* (Qur'ān, 6:164)

The miracles of Jesus

The miracles or prodigies that Jesus performed are presented in four different forms in this verse and in three forms in verse 5:110 which we shall comment upon later:

1. The creation of the form of the bird is the pure and simple act of Jesus. To this act the invigorating breath of the Spirit is added; Jesus casts the breath on this form and it bestows life to the bird. The act of Jesus is performed by Allah's leave (*bi idhn Allāh*). The term *idhn*, which we have rendered as "leave," comes from the root *'a-dh-n* meaning: to lend an ear to, to listen, to permit, to find out, to know, to approve. When Jesus professes the Word of Allah—because he is *His Word and a Spirit from Him* (cf. Qur'ān, 4:171), Allah hears, and permits or authorizes.

In the oral tradition, the word is creative; it generates the myriad forms of expression. That is why we could have translated the term *idhn* as "listens" and not as "leave." Thus we note a close affinity between the command pronounced by His Word, Jesus—corresponding with the creative or existentiating "Be!" (*kun*)—and Allah's integral and undistorted response.

This Qur'ānic expression concerning the miraculous action of Jesus *bi-idhn Allāh* has often been criticized by representatives of the Christian church who consider that the Anointed One, or as they say, "the Son of God," performed miracles by his own initiative. Yet in the Gospel of John, Jesus says: *Then answered Jesus and said unto them, Verily, verily, I say unto you, The Son can do nothing of himself, but what he seeth the Father do: for what things soever he doeth, these also doeth the Son likewise* (John, 5:19).

2. The healing of those born blind, as well as the leprous, is not said to have been done "according to Allah's permission" in this verse, unlike in verse 5:110. It could therefore be a question of a wonder, the restoration of an order that should be normal in the human constitution, but has been disqualified by an anomaly. Therefore, there is no act of creation as in the first miracle we mentioned.

3. The act of breathing new life constitutes a divine prerogative performed by the Spirit. It is therefore made "with God's permission," as in the first case.

4. The act of predicting what is ingested and what is secretly accumulated in homes comes from a privileged development of human faculties that Jesus must have manifested spontaneously since his miraculous birth by the Spirit of Sanctity. This is not said to take place "thanks to God's leave." However, it presupposes God's agency since the set of these four prodigies constitutes "a single sign" in itself and for those who believe.

In this verse, it is Jesus himself whom God causes to speak in the first person singular. In verse 5:110, it is God Himself who speaks to Jesus. The chronology seems to differ between the two verses. The sequence of verses from 3:45 to 3:49 regards the annunciation of the coming of Christ to Mary by the Angels. Verse 3:49 graduates from this simple annunciation to the words that the adult Jesus pronounces and to certain miraculous acts he performs. The historical aspect is irrelevant to the elements constituting this sequence, for the foremost purpose of the Divine word is to teach and enlighten.

> Qur'ān, 3:50. *And [I come] confirming that which was before me of the Torah, and to make lawful some of that which was forbidden unto you. I come unto you with a sign from your Lord, so keep your duty to Allah and obey me.*

وَمُصَدِّقًا لِمَا بَيْنَ يَدَيَّ مِنَ التَّوْرَاةِ وَلِأُحِلَّ لَكُم بَعْضَ الَّذِي

حُرِّمَ عَلَيْكُمْ وَجِئْتُكُم بِآيَةٍ مِّن رَّبِّكُمْ فَاتَّقُوا اللَّهَ وَأَطِيعُونِ

JESUS CONFIRMS

The expression translated as *confirming that which was before me of the Torah* is literally expressed in the Qur'ānic text as: confirming in favour of that which (is) between my two hands in the Torah. The word *yad* of the expression *yadayya*, or "my two hands," means hand, wing, or front foot. It also means active force, vigor, intensity, influence, or faculty. In current Arabic, the expression *bayna yadayya* means "that which is before me." In Qur'ānic Arabic, the proper meaning of an expression must be prioritized. In this Qur'ānic occurrence in particular, the elements of previous revelations which Jesus must conserve and which enter into his providential "amplitude" are confirmed. Former possibilities that no longer maintain in a new form of revelation are the only components to be erased or abrogated. Our translation takes into account this meaning. The part following this verse confirms this point of view and supports Jesus' annulment of certain prescriptions of the Mosaic law in this new form of revelation. The "sign" accompanying Jesus' arrival will confirm him in his Mission. This "sign" is comprised of different miraculous events, words, teachings, facts, and gestures which will take place during his apostleship.

Coming as it does from the Lord of the persons to whom this "sign" is addressed, it must bring the evidence to them in a realization which is not identical in each person but which is imposed upon each one according to their receptivity.

Qur'ān, 3:51. *Lo! Allah is my Lord and your Lord, so worship Him. That is a straight path.*

إِنَّ اللَّهَ رَبِّي وَرَبُّكُمْ فَاعْبُدُوهُ ۗ هَٰذَا صِرَاطٌ مُّسْتَقِيمٌ

This is "a straight path," or rather "that which demands uprightness," according to the first meaning of the tenth verbal form issuing from the root *q-w-m* which connotes the following meaning: to stand up, to get up, to stand erect, to take a vertical position, to exist, etc. Our translation takes into account the "desirative" meaning of this tenth verbal form which is an inner reflection of the first form:

to seek or demand for oneself what is expressed by the root.

> Qur'ān, 3:52. *But when Jesus perceived their hiding, he cried: Who will be my helpers in [the cause of] Allah? The disciples said: We will be Allah's helpers. We believe in Allah, and bear thou witness that we have surrendered.*

فَلَمَّا أَحَسَّ عِيسَىٰ مِنْهُمُ الْكُفْرَ قَالَ مَنْ أَنْصَارِي إِلَى اللَّهِ ۖ قَالَ
الْحَوَارِيُّونَ نَحْنُ أَنْصَارُ اللَّهِ آمَنَّا بِاللَّهِ وَاشْهَدْ بِأَنَّا مُسْلِمُونَ

The word "*kufr*," which we have translated as "hiding," comes from the root *k-f-r* whose first meaning is to cover, to conceal, to make disappear, to bury (such as the farmer sowing seed), to hide, or to reject. In the current religious interpretation, the root *k-f-r* signifies: to be a disbeliever, infidel, to be ungrateful, to refuse, to depreciate, etc. However, the Revelation bestows Arabic words with explicit or implicit meanings contained in the meaning of their root. In verse 57:20, one of the terms which designates the farmers is "*kuffār*," plural of *kāfir*, a word derived from the same root: *Know that the life of the world is only play, and amusement, and pageantry, and boasting among you, and rivalry in respect of wealth and children; as the likeness of vegetation after rain, whereof the growth is pleasing to the husbandman (kuffār), but afterward it drieth up and thou seest it turning yellow, then it becometh straw. And in the Hereafter there is grievous punishment, and* (also) *forgiveness from Allah and His good pleasure, whereas the life of the world is but matter of illusion.*

Throughout the centuries and in accordance with theological and mystical schools, the reality of Jesus has posed numerous difficulties of interpretation that have generated contrasting commentaries. The term "*kufr*" used by God in this verse can be interpreted in several ways, depending on how one interprets the words "word, spirit, servant of God" with which Allah describes the Anointed one, Jesus son of Mary, in different ways. Certain Sufis, such as Ibn 'Arabī and his followers, have envisaged four principal perspectives on Jesus:

1. As the Word of God who orders and creates, and Spirit coming from Him (cf. Qur'ān, 4:171), the Anointed one comprises an entity issuing from the Divine.

2. As the Angel (Gabriel), bringer of the Divine Word, who intervenes with Mary, through affinity and harmony, in the form of a perfectly constituted human being assuming in a certain manner a nonhuman paternal function, Jesus acquires a perfectly developed spiritual quality and can thereby give life and perform miracles (with God's leave, cf. Qur'ān, 3:49, 5:110, and 19:17). According to tradition, the Angel Gabriel transmits the Revelation by taking diverse forms. For example, once when the Prophet Muḥammad was in retreat in a cave on Mount Ḥirā' near Mecca, the Angel Gabriel manifested to him in a majestic form, his wings spreading from the East to the West. He also manifested himself to the Prophet in the form of Diḥya al-Kalbī, a greatly handsome Arab.

The Qur'ānic name of Gabriel, Jibrīl, is composed of two different elements:

a) the root *j-b-r*, to re-establish an order with constraint, to put back (a broken bone), to force, to restore, to put something back in a good state, or in its initial condition;

b) the term *Īl*, God present in His Work. He brings, by the Order of God, a new form of revelation that is necessarily adapted to the human cyclical conditions which have deteriorated and which must therefore be opposed and remedied.

3. Because his mother Mary is a human being, the Son of Mary acquires a human body and is recognized as a truly perfect man.

4. The most complete position but also the most difficult to discern and to recognize as being reunited in the Anoint, Jesus, Son of Mary is the three orders of reality. These are expressed below without dissociating, rejecting, or hiding any of them.

Jesus perceived or had plenary consciousness of what the people surrounding him imagined about his exceptional case. Those who voluntarily recognized his total reality without having to hide certain aspects thereof helped him in the cause of Allah. It is particularly remarkable that the Qur'ānic word denoting the helpers (*anṣār*) of Jesus comes from the same root as the word *naṣārā*, which denotes the Christians in the Qur'ān.

The Disciples of Jesus

Who were the Disciples of Jesus, and what is meant by their Arabic nomenclature, *ḥawāriyyūn*? This has proven difficult to both translate and interpret. One may suppose that it concerns first the Apostles, and then those who gathered around Jesus in his peregrinations through Galilee. The term *ḥawāriyyūn* appears five times in Qur'ānic passages related to Jesus. In verse 5:111, Allah declares: *And when I inspired (or revealed, awhaytu) the disciples, [saying]: Believe in Me and in My messenger . . ..* It comes from the root *h-w-r* which means: to be astounded, to be disoriented, to have the sclera and the cornea of the eyes very pronounced, and to whiten (clothes); hence the connotation of opposition or contrast. Certain commentators opine that these close companions of Jesus might have been Essenes or persons dressed in white. Due to the strong meaning of this root, we believe that it refers to persons of a very great spiritual status who had recognized the real value of Jesus; their spiritual realization caused them to reach the degree in which the contradictions are integrated and the oppositions are resorbed.

One may also remark that the Disciples' positive attitude towards the personality of Jesus safeguarded them, and this is precisely the meaning of the root *s-l-m*: to remain safe and sound, to safeguard oneself, to preserve intact, to be delivered, to enjoy safety, or to submit. From this root is derived the active participle used to refer to the Disciples: *muslimūn*, or those who safeguard themselves.

Qur'ān, 3:53. *Our Lord! We believe in that which Thou hast revealed and we follow him whom Thou hast sent. Enrol us among those who witness [to the truth].*

رَبَّنَا آمَنَّا بِمَا أَنْزَلْتَ وَاتَّبَعْنَا الرَّسُولَ فَاكْتُبْنَا مَعَ الشَّاهِدِينَ

What does the active participle *shāhidīn*, translated here as *those who witness*, mean? It comes from the root *sh-h-d*: to be present, to assist in, to be a witness, to bear witness, to observe, to attest, to testify, to confirm, to certify, to recognize, to contemplate. The truthful disciples of Jesus are those who have recognized both inwardly and outwardly the different aspects of his person, have strived to emulate him, and have transmitted the Message in their turn.

Qur'ān, 3:54. *And they (the others) schemed, and Allah schemed: and Allah is the best of schemers.*

وَمَكَرُوا وَمَكَرَ اللَّهُ ۖ وَاللَّهُ خَيْرُ الْمَاكِرِينَ

One may also translate the verb "*makara*" as to trick, dissimulate, to dupe, to use stratagems, or to plot. Those who behaved in such a way are perhaps those who either: followed Jesus and had to hide or dissimulate their profound conviction and intuition of the degrees of reality concerning him; or those who doubted the true reality of Jesus. Taking into account the following verse, one may deduce that the terrestrial mission of Jesus concerns his end and that those who did not recognize his value and his function bore a grudge against him.

Qur'ān, 3:55. *(And remember) when Allah said: O Jesus! Lo! I am gathering thee and causing thee to ascend unto Me, and am cleansing thee of those who disbelieve and am setting those who follow thee above those who disbelieve until the Day of Resurrection. Then unto Me ye will return, and I shall judge between you as to that wherein ye used to differ.*

إِذْ قَالَ اللَّهُ يَا عِيسَىٰ إِنِّي مُتَوَفِّيكَ وَرَافِعُكَ إِلَيَّ وَمُطَهِّرُكَ مِنَ الَّذِينَ كَفَرُوا وَجَاعِلُ الَّذِينَ اتَّبَعُوكَ فَوْقَ الَّذِينَ كَفَرُوا إِلَىٰ يَوْمِ الْقِيَامَةِ ۖ ثُمَّ إِلَيَّ مَرْجِعُكُمْ فَأَحْكُمُ بَيْنَكُمْ فِيمَا كُنْتُمْ فِيهِ تَخْتَلِفُونَ

Qur'ān, 3:56. *As for those who hide (or conceal) the faith I shall chastise them with a heavy chastisement in the world and the Hereafter; and they will have no helpers.*

فَأَمَّا الَّذِينَ كَفَرُوا فَأُعَذِّبُهُمْ عَذَابًا شَدِيدًا فِي الدُّنْيَا وَالْآخِرَةِ وَمَا لَهُمْ مِنْ نَاصِرِينَ

Qur'ān, 3:57. *And as for those who believe and do good works, He will pay them their wages in full. Allah loveth not wrong-doers.*

وَأَمَّا الَّذِينَ آمَنُوا وَعَمِلُوا الصَّالِحَاتِ فَيُوَفِّيهِمْ أُجُورَهُمْ ۗ وَاللَّهُ لَا يُحِبُّ الظَّالِمِينَ

Qur'ān, 3:58. *This [which] We recite unto thee is a revelation and a wise reminder.*

ذَٰلِكَ نَتْلُوهُ عَلَيْكَ مِنَ الْآيَاتِ وَالذِّكْرِ الْحَكِيمِ

In verse 3:55, in the expression *innī mutawaffī-ka* which we have rendered as *I am gathering thee*, the word *mutawaffī* is an active participle derived from the fifth verbal form of the root *w-f-y*. This root's first form means: to be faithful (in one's word and engagement), to discharge (one's responsibility and promise), to pay (on the due date), to reimburse, to be sufficient, to complete, to accomplish, to be integrated. In its fifth form it means: to receive something in full, to receive repayment of the entire debt, to discharge on the due date, to complete something on term, to bring to completion, to receive the deceased (God), to die. This root therefore comprises the idea of a completion, conclusion. Certain Muslim commentators and translators render this expression as "I am calling you to Me." One of the derived meanings of this root, "die," is accepted by Arab lexicographers through the association of ideas; one may remark that certain verses contain at the same time this fifth conjugated form of *w-f-y* as well as and the noun *mawt*, or death, from the root *m-w-t*. For example, *Allah receiveth* (*yutawaffā*) *souls at the time of their death* (*mawt* from the root *m-w-t*) . . . (39:42). This seems to prove that here one cannot translate *yatawaffā* as 'dying,' otherwise the translation would read: "Allah makes the souls die at the moment of their death . . .."

One may therefore consider that in this verse Allah is at the point of bringing the terrestrial Mission of Jesus to completion. The subsequent verses specify that God is causing Jesus to ascend unto Him. In this instance nothing specific indicates the significance of the mission's completion or of the gathering thanks to which Allah raises him up. In the absence of a future marker, this active participle can be translated into either present tense or near future: I am going to gather thee. We will have the occasion to return to Jesus' circumstances in commenting upon verse 4:157: Has he been killed or not? Did he die, and how? And what does this rising mean after the completion of his Mission? In verse 3:57, the same root *w-f-y* is conjugated in its second verbal form, thus acquiring the meaning: to pay in full, to complete a duty perfectly, to give in full, or to repay exactly.

Let us note the progression of four elements which constitute the first part of verse 3:55: (i) the completion which concludes an aspect of the terrestrial mission of Jesus until his return "at the end of times;" (ii) his rise to Allah; (iii) as a result of his rising, his purification (*mutahhir*), or his freedom from those who have renounced him; (iv) finally, the destiny of those who follow him until the Day of Resurrection.

In his great commentary *Mafātīḥ al-ghayb*, or "The Keys to the Unseen," Fakhr al-Dīn al-Rāzī indicates that the verb *tawaffā* means to receive something or someone in their totality. He then specifies that Jesus was elevated with his whole being to God: body, soul, and spirit.

Qur'ān, 3:59. *Lo! the likeness of Jesus with Allah is as the likeness of Adam. He created him of dust, then He said unto him: Be! and he is.*

إِنَّ مَثَلَ عِيسَىٰ عِنْدَ اللَّهِ كَمَثَلِ آدَمَ ۖ خَلَقَهُ مِنْ تُرَابٍ ثُمَّ
قَالَ لَهُ كُنْ فَيَكُونُ

This verse has been largely commented upon by both exegetes and Sufis, such as Ibn 'Arabī in his immense work *al-Futūḥāt al-Makkiyya*, "The Meccan Openings." From this work we have translated long extracts concerning Jesus and Mary. Ibn 'Arabī also discusses this verse in his celebrated work *Fuṣūṣ al-Ḥikam*, "The Ringstones of Wisdom," from which we have translated three chapters dealing with Jesus, Zachary, and Yaḥyā. Mary, Adam, and Eve are mentioned as well.

The meaning of the expressions *mathal* and *'inda 'Llāh*

1) The term *mathal*, translated here as "likeness," comes from the root *m-th-l* which means: to resemble, to compare to, to consider as similar, to seem, to constitute an example, and so on. *Mathal* can therefore be translated: similitude, resemblance, symbol, allegory, adage, comparison, parable, proverb, example, and model. Resemblance does not imply identity, whether in the case

of beings or possibilities in the Divine degree, or innumerable beings of all kinds found in the universal Manifestation.

This verse envisages resemblance or similitude to God Himself (*'inda 'Llāh*). At this level, there is not yet a question of creation; Jesus is the Word or Speech of Allah (*kalimat Allāh*, cf. Qur'ān 4:171). Like Adam, he is not yet manifested and in God's presence. In the following part of the verse, only Adam is said to have been created from a fertile fine substance. In Arabic grammar, the personal pronoun is applied to the nearest noun, therefore it concerns Adam who is mentioned after Jesus. Indeed, Jesus is formed (i) through his mother in his perfect corporeal and psychological constitution, (ii) through the angelic Spirit in his spiritual constitution, and (iii) as the Word and Spirit of Allah, for he resides in the Divine Principle. It is as the Word of Allah that he can pronounce the existentiating *kun* through which all realities are exteriorized, whereas Adam, who is made of clay, is nevertheless dependent on the Divine order which all of them manifest. In their original principle, Jesus, like Adam, remains in God from eternity.

2) On the other hand, at a simpler level the resemblance between Jesus and Adam lies in the fact that none of them has a human father. Adam has neither father nor mother; he is fashioned by the *Two hands of Allah: He said: O Iblīs! What hindereth thee from falling prostrate before that which* (*mā*) *I have created with both My hands? Art thou too proud or art thou of the high exalted?* (Qur'ān, 38:75). Jesus is without a human father but he is a perfect man through his mother Mary, herself a perfect woman.

3) The two share more than corporeal morphology; they also resemble each other in their spiritual constitution. Indeed, the divine Spirit was breathed into Adam after the complete formation of his body, whereas the body of Jesus was constituted at the very moment when Gabriel breathed his breath into Mary: *When thy Lord said unto the angels: Lo! I am about to create a mortal* (*bashar*) *out of mire, and when I have fashioned him and breathed into him of My Spirit, then fall down before him prostrate* (Qur'ān, 38:71-72; 15:29). Jesus took shape after this breathing, not before, and then the divine Spirit strengthened him, as we have already pointed out when discussing verse 2:253.

4) The majority of commentators and translators make an ellipsis of the repeated term *mathal*, thus distorting for the most part the profound meaning of this verse. Moreover, none of them interprets the expression *'inda 'Llāh* according to its strong and precise mean-

ing of "with Allāh." Some of these translations read: *For Allah, Jesus is like Adam whom He created from clay . . .. For God, the case of Jesus is just like Adam's whom He created from clay . . .. Jesus, with Allah, is in the image of Adam: He created him from clay . . .. Yes, the case of Jesus is like that of Adam with God: God created him from the earth . . ..* However, the commentators are unanimous in their general opinion that this Qur'ānic text, revealed by God in its literal, grammatical, and syntax expression, contains neither redundancy nor deficiency. It must therefore be evaluated according to all its own terms, even if this approach might lead to an unusual translation that a French scholar would not recommend. In a similar manner, the translation must take into account and respect the formulation of the Arabic text, as it is heavy with meanings intended by God.

Kun fa-yakūn (Be! and it is)

In the Qur'ānic expression "*kun fa-yakūn*," the verb of existence *kāna*, coming from the root *k-w-n*, is conjugated in the imperfective (*yakūn*). We have rendered this verb in the present tense. The Arabist commentators and most of those who translate into French, English, or Spanish consider this imperfective to have the value of a perfective. This expression is then interpreted: Be and it was. There is no temporal "space" in the Divine discourse concerning this episode. As soon as the Divine Order is announced by this Word *kun*, the human being who is not yet invigorated by the Divine spirit comes to existence. Insofar as the Spirit animates his corporeal aspect, only the human being evolves in time and space here below. Along the same line of thought, verses 3:49 and 5:110 express in the imperfective the different phases which constitute the formation and invigoration of the fowl created by Jesus and animated with the Divine leave.

This complete constitution of the Adamic being comprises an analogy with the created bird. Its corporeal form was by Jesus; he invigorated with its spirit thanks to the leave of God by uttering the creating Word *kun*, as we have seen in verse 3:49. Only those who have the divine capacity to produce forms enlivened by the existentiating Word *kun* can do it legitimately with the permission of Allah. The latter reflection enables us to understand why, in Islam, making forms of animate beings which man cannot give life is forbidden and will find its sanction in the afterlife. In the paradisiacal conditions of human life, man will effectively be able to say "become!" to a thing through the breathing of the Spirit, and it will be, as can be seen in a certain prophetic tiding.

Qur'ān, 3:60. *The truth [comes] from thy Lord, so be not of those who waver.*

الْحَقُّ مِنْ رَبِّكَ فَلَا تَكُنْ مِنَ الْمُمْتَرِينَ

The exceptional circumstances concerning Jesus and Adam seem difficult to accept only through the rational faculty; faith must then accept them and make them more easily accessible, without discussion, so that doubt does not settle in the soul. The Lord of every being teaches man these truths in the most intimate depths of his being. The truths are disconcerting to reason but open rich and numerous new perspectives, both doctrinal and intuitive.

Qur'ān, 3:61. *And whoso disputeth with thee concerning him (Jesus), after the knowledge which hath come unto thee, say: Come! We will summon our sons and your sons, and our women and your women, and ourselves and yourselves, then we will pray humbly [to our Lord] and [solemnly] invoke the curse of Allah upon those who lie.*

فَمَنْ حَاجَّكَ فِيهِ مِنْ بَعْدِ مَا جَاءَكَ مِنَ الْعِلْمِ فَقُلْ تَعَالَوْا
نَدْعُ أَبْنَاءَنَا وَأَبْنَاءَكُمْ وَنِسَاءَنَا وَنِسَاءَكُمْ وَأَنْفُسَنَا وَأَنْفُسَكُمْ
ثُمَّ نَبْتَهِلْ فَنَجْعَلْ لَعْنَتَ اللَّهِ عَلَى الْكَاذِبِينَ

In this verse, God essentially addresses the Prophet, although everyone is or should be interested in the complex and exceptional case of Jesus. After Allah reveals information regarding him, the Prophet Muḥammad directly receives from Him knowledge of the true nature of the Anointed One, Jesus Son of Mary.

The imperative *ta'ālaw* comes from the root *'a-l-w*. In its sixth verbal form it means: to be raised, to come forward, to approach, to arrive, to appear bigger or higher, to become larger, and so on. Thus conjugated, this verb has acquired and retained the meaning of "come."

The delegation of the Christians from Najrān to the Prophet

The leading Muslim Qur'ān commentators and many others following in their footsteps explain this verse through the account of its application by the Prophet shortly thereafter: they report that in the year nine of the Hijra (631 A.D.), a very important delegation consisting of some sixty representatives of the Christians of Najrān, including a bishop, came to see the Prophet so that he could inform them about his Mission and the relations he sought to maintain with Christianity and its local branches. Najrān is a region of Arabia located in northern Yemen. Even though we lack absolute historical evidence, certain experts assert that these Christians had a Monophysite orientation that recognized the single divine nature of the Anoint and caused them to reject the terms of the council held in 451 in Chalcedon, a town in Asia Minor. The dogmatic content of this council may be summarized as follows: Christ is a unique person who possesses two natures, one divine and one human, united "without confusion or change, without division or separation," the properties of each of these two natures being preserved and concurring in a single Person or hypostasis. After lively discussions between the representatives of the type of Christianity that was being practiced in the region and the Prophet regarding the reality of Jesus, the Prophet proposed to the bishop—who refused—the divine trial by mutual imprecation (*mubāhala*).[4]

Of this solemn scene, it is reported that the Prophet came before the Christians of the delegations. He held the hand of Ḥasan on one side and Ḥusayn on the other, his two grandsons by 'Alī ibn Abī Ṭālib. His daughter Fāṭima walked behind him, followed by 'Alī. Met with the imposing majesty of these eminent members of the family of the Prophet, the delegation withdrew and refused this trial; as compensation they accepted to pay a tax permitting them to practice their religion and protect their lives and properties.

According to the majority of the Muslim commentators, the plural used for describing the persons mentioned in this verse seeks to address all those who might be concerned with such a situation, even though the essential points of the traditional account we presented only mentions the Prophet, his daughter, his son in law, and his two nephews.

4. This was a mutual "calling down of divine curses." Those who were certain of their knowledge of a particular issue could call down divine punishment upon themselves if they were in error. This would indicate that they were in the right, as they were willing to undergo divine punishment if they were wrong. (Ed. note)

Qur'ān, 3:62. *Lo! This verily is the true narrative. There is no god* (*ilāh*) *save Allah, and lo! Allah, He* (*Huwa*), *[is] verily the Mighty, the Wise.*

إِنَّ هَٰذَا لَهُوَ الْقَصَصُ الْحَقُّ ۚ وَمَا مِنْ إِلَٰهٍ إِلَّا اللَّهُ ۚ وَإِنَّ اللَّهَ لَهُوَ الْعَزِيزُ الْحَكِيمُ

Qur'ān, 3:63. *And if they turn away, then lo! Allah is Aware of the corrupters.*

فَإِنْ تَوَلَّوْا فَإِنَّ اللَّهَ عَلِيمٌ بِالْمُفْسِدِينَ

The formula *there is no god save Allah* (*mā min ilāh*[in] *illā-Llāh*) is another way of expressing the Unity of Allah. This doctrine excludes all polytheism (or association, multiplicity—called *shirk*), hidden or patent, performed latently or openly. However, the end of verse 3:62 brings out the absoluteness of God through the use of the expression *Allah* and *Huwa* (He). *Huwa* is the pronoun of unconditioned Ipseity but also the subtle Presence of Allah mysterious in His universal Work of wisdom. This verse announces both God's transcendence and immanence.

The immediate punishment for associating others with God is disorder on earth. This takes the greatest range of forms, some of which are not easily discernible in institutions and among individuals. *Corruption hath appeared on land and sea because of [the evil] which men's hands have done, that He may make them taste a part of that which they have done, in order that they may return* (Qur'ān, 30:41).

Qur'ān, 3:64. *Say: O ye familiar with the Scripture! Come to an agreement between us and you: that we shall worship none but Allah, and that we shall ascribe no partner unto Him, and that none of us shall take others for lords beside Allah. And if they turn away, then say: Bear witness that we are they who have surrendered [unto Him].*

قُلْ يَا أَهْلَ الْكِتَابِ تَعَالَوْا إِلَىٰ كَلِمَةٍ سَوَاءٍ بَيْنَنَا وَبَيْنَكُمْ أَلَّا نَعْبُدَ إِلَّا اللَّهَ وَلَا نُشْرِكَ بِهِ شَيْئًا وَلَا يَتَّخِذَ بَعْضُنَا بَعْضًا أَرْبَابًا مِنْ دُونِ اللَّهِ ۚ فَإِنْ تَوَلَّوْا فَقُولُوا اشْهَدُوا بِأَنَّا مُسْلِمُونَ

In the commentary on verse 2:62, we have already explained the expression *ahl al-kitāb*, translated as "Those familiar with the Scripture." It is also often translated as "People of the Book." We have mentioned the verses 5:65 to 68 in order to show that "those familiar with the Scripture" were not just the Jews and the Christians, but all those who possessed a sacred, inspired, or revealed scripture. As long as the Koranic revelation was not terminated, the Muslim believers could not be described as possessing the whole of the Scripture. The revelation was completed shortly before the Prophet's passing. After the end of the Revelation, the Muslims could be compared to those who possessed the Scripture and were part of the "people of the Book" on the condition that each of the terms making up this expression be given their lexical meanings.

The root of the word *ahl*, translated here as "those familiar with," means: to get accustomed, to get used to something or someone, to get married. The noun *ahl* means: family, house, the head of the household (man or woman), people, persons, members of a community, and inhabitants from the same place. *Ahlan* is used to salute the visitors. If one takes into account the preceding sequence, the concerned individuals are those who lay claim to a certain form of Christianity. The *equivalent word* or formulation is primordially divine in its inspiration and its meaning insofar as God Himself pronounces it in this verse; it is therefore included in this particular form in the Revelation. It specifies one of the possible meanings contained in the formula of Divine Unity mentioned previously.

We are they who are surrendered, we are *muslimūn*, we are surrendering, we are submitting. This active present participle comes from the root *s-l-m*, to be safe and sound, to be or remain intact, to preserve in good state, to be exempt of, to avoid. In the fourth verbal form used here (*aslama*), it has a factitive meaning: to preserve intact, safe and sound, to surrender, to submit completely, to enjoy security, to profess Islam—to pay in advance, to have someone climb the ladder. It is an active participle and it should not be translated as "submitted." Submission to God is always a renewed act entailing an eminently active attitude. The act is always challenged and capable of greater perfection; the outcome of this comportment as a servant before the Lord implies a provisory and precarious skill that will definitely be positive for the believer in the future.

The following verses, namely 3:65 to 3:73, concern certain inadequate attitudes of those familiar with the Scripture. God warns against such attitudes:

Qur'ān, 3:65. *O ye familiar with the Scripture! Why will ye argue about Abraham, when the Torah and the Gospel were not revealed till after him? Do you not use your intellect then?*

يَا أَهْلَ الْكِتَابِ لِمَ تُحَاجُّونَ فِي إِبْرَاهِيمَ وَمَا أُنْزِلَتِ التَّوْرَاةُ وَالْإِنْجِيلُ إِلَّا مِنْ بَعْدِهِ ۚ أَفَلَا تَعْقِلُونَ

Qur'ān, 3:66. *Lo! ye are those who argue about that whereof ye have some knowledge: Why then argue ye concerning that whereof ye have no knowledge? Allah knoweth. Ye know not.*

هَا أَنْتُمْ هَٰؤُلَاءِ حَاجَجْتُمْ فِيمَا لَكُمْ بِهِ عِلْمٌ فَلِمَ تُحَاجُّونَ فِيمَا لَيْسَ لَكُمْ بِهِ عِلْمٌ ۚ وَاللَّهُ يَعْلَمُ وَأَنْتُمْ لَا تَعْلَمُونَ

Qur'ān, 3:67. *Abraham was not a Jew, nor yet a Christian; but a theotrope who had surrendered, and he was not of the idolaters.*

مَا كَانَ إِبْرَاهِيمُ يَهُودِيًّا وَلَا نَصْرَانِيًّا وَلَٰكِنْ كَانَ حَنِيفًا مُسْلِمًا وَمَا كَانَ مِنَ الْمُشْرِكِينَ

The verb in verse 3:65, translated as "to intellect," comes from the root *'a-q-l* which means: to bind, to attach, to tie, to rein in, to limit, to tighten, to connect ideas to each other, to understand, to discern, or to use one's intelligence. In the Qur'ān, this root is always conjugated. The active noun *'aql*, meaning intelligence, intellect, reason, and the act of linking words to each other, goes back to the vocabulary of *'ilm al-kalām*, philosophy, and science, not from the Qur'ān. The *'aql* is the faculty which enables a human being to make connections between the signs (*'alamāt*) in order to reach knowledge, a science (*'ilm*).

Those described as *familiar with the Scripture* are the Jews and the Christians, even though all the other communities who have received a sacred or revealed scripture are part of the "People of the Book" as well, as explained in the commentary on verses 2:62 and 5:68.

Qur'ān, 3:68. *Lo! those of mankind who have the best claim to Abraham are those who followed him, and this Prophet and those who believe [with him]; and Allah is the Protecting Guardian of the believers.*

إِنَّ أَوْلَى النَّاسِ بِإِبْرَاهِيمَ لَلَّذِينَ اتَّبَعُوهُ وَهَٰذَا النَّبِيُّ وَالَّذِينَ آمَنُوا ۗ وَاللَّهُ وَلِيُّ الْمُؤْمِنِينَ

This Prophet cannot but denote the Prophet Muḥammad. But who are the believers who are closer to Abraham, the "theotrope" constantly oriented towards God? With few details given about them, one may refer to verse 2:62 which mentions those *who have faith. Whoever hath faith in Allah and the Last Day and doeth right* have therefore adhered to the givens of the divine Revelation throughout history. However, certain Muslim commentators are of the opinion that this verse concerns only believers who have adhered or adhere to the last form of revelation, historical Islam.

Qur'ān, 3:69. *A party of those familiar with the Scripture long to make you go astray; and they make none to go astray except themselves, but they perceive not.*

وَدَّت طَّائِفَةٌ مِّنْ أَهْلِ الْكِتَابِ لَوْ يُضِلُّونَكُمْ وَمَا يُضِلُّونَ إِلَّا أَنفُسَهُمْ وَمَا يَشْعُرُونَ

Qur'ān, 3:70. *O ye Familiar with the Scripture! Why disbelieve ye in the revelations of Allah, when ye [yourselves] bear witness [to their truth]?*

يَا أَهْلَ الْكِتَابِ لِمَ تَكْفُرُونَ بِآيَاتِ اللَّهِ وَأَنتُمْ تَشْهَدُونَ

Qur'ān, 3:71. *O ye Familiar with the Scripture! Why confound ye truth with falsehood and knowingly conceal the truth?*

يَا أَهْلَ الْكِتَابِ لِمَ تَلْبِسُونَ الْحَقَّ بِالْبَاطِلِ وَتَكْتُمُونَ الْحَقَّ وَأَنْتُمْ تَعْلَمُونَ

Qur'ān, 3:72. *And a party of those Familiar with the Scripture say: Believe in that which hath been revealed unto those who believe at the opening of the day, and disbelieve at the end thereof, in order that they may return;*

وَقَالَتْ طَائِفَةٌ مِنْ أَهْلِ الْكِتَابِ آمِنُوا بِالَّذِي أُنْزِلَ عَلَى الَّذِينَ آمَنُوا وَجْهَ النَّهَارِ وَاكْفُرُوا آخِرَهُ لَعَلَّهُمْ يَرْجِعُونَ

Qur'ān, 3:73. *And believe not save in one who followeth your religion—Say: Lo! the guidance is Allah's Guidance—that anyone is given the like of that which was given unto you or that they may argue with you in the presence of their Lord. Say: Lo! the bounty is in Allah's hand. He bestoweth it on whom He will. Allah is All-Embracing, All-Knowing.*

وَلَا تُؤْمِنُوا إِلَّا لِمَنْ تَبِعَ دِينَكُمْ قُلْ إِنَّ الْهُدَىٰ هُدَى اللَّهِ أَنْ يُؤْتَىٰ أَحَدٌ مِثْلَ مَا أُوتِيتُمْ أَوْ يُحَاجُّوكُمْ عِنْدَ رَبِّكُمْ ۗ قُلْ إِنَّ الْفَضْلَ بِيَدِ اللَّهِ يُؤْتِيهِ مَنْ يَشَاءُ ۗ وَاللَّهُ وَاسِعٌ عَلِيمٌ

Qur'ān, 3:78. *And lo! there is a party of them who distort the Scripture with their tongues, that ye may think that what they say is from the Scripture, when it is not from the Scripture. And they say: It is from Allah, when it is not from Allah; and they speak a lie concerning Allah knowingly.*

وَإِنَّ مِنْهُمْ لَفَرِيقًا يَلْوُونَ أَلْسِنَتَهُمْ بِالْكِتَابِ لِتَحْسَبُوهُ مِنَ الْكِتَابِ وَمَا هُوَ مِنَ الْكِتَابِ وَيَقُولُونَ هُوَ مِنْ عِنْدِ اللَّهِ وَمَا هُوَ مِنْ عِنْدِ اللَّهِ وَيَقُولُونَ عَلَى اللَّهِ الْكَذِبَ وَهُمْ يَعْلَمُونَ

Qur'ān, 3:79. *It is not [meet] for any human being unto whom Allah had given the Scripture and wisdom and prophethood that he should afterwards have said unto mankind: Be slaves of me instead of Allah;*

but [what he said was]: Be ye faithful servants of the Lord by virtue of your constant teaching of the Scripture and of your constant study thereof.

مَا كَانَ لِبَشَرٍ أَنْ يُؤْتِيَهُ اللَّهُ الْكِتَابَ وَالْحُكْمَ وَالنُّبُوَّةَ ثُمَّ يَقُولَ لِلنَّاسِ كُونُوا عِبَادًا لِي مِنْ دُونِ اللَّهِ وَلَكِنْ كُونُوا رَبَّانِيِّينَ بِمَا كُنْتُمْ تُعَلِّمُونَ الْكِتَابَ وَبِمَا كُنْتُمْ تَدْرُسُونَ

Qur'ān, 3:80. *And he commanded you not that ye should take the angels and the prophets for lords. Would he command you to disbelieve after ye had surrendered?*

وَلَا يَأْمُرَكُمْ أَنْ تَتَّخِذُوا الْمَلَائِكَةَ وَالنَّبِيِّينَ أَرْبَابًا ۗ أَيَأْمُرُكُمْ بِالْكُفْرِ بَعْدَ إِذْ أَنْتُمْ مُسْلِمُونَ

Qur'ān, 3:81. *When Allah made [His] covenant with the prophets, [He said]: Behold that which I have given you of the Scripture and knowledge. And afterward there will come unto you a messenger, confirming that which ye possess. Ye shall believe in him and ye shall help him. He said: Do ye agree, and will ye take up My burden [which I lay upon you] in this [matter]? They answered: We agree. He said: Then bear ye witness. I will be a witness with you.*

وَإِذْ أَخَذَ اللَّهُ مِيثَاقَ النَّبِيِّينَ لَمَا آتَيْتُكُمْ مِنْ كِتَابٍ وَحِكْمَةٍ ثُمَّ جَاءَكُمْ رَسُولٌ مُصَدِّقٌ لِمَا مَعَكُمْ لَتُؤْمِنُنَّ بِهِ وَلَتَنْصُرُنَّهُ ۚ قَالَ أَأَقْرَرْتُمْ وَأَخَذْتُمْ عَلَىٰ ذَٰلِكُمْ إِصْرِي ۖ قَالُوا أَقْرَرْنَا ۚ قَالَ فَاشْهَدُوا وَأَنَا مَعَكُمْ مِنَ الشَّاهِدِينَ

Qur'ān, 3:82. *Then whosoever after this shall turn away: they will be miscreants.*

فَمَنْ تَوَلَّىٰ بَعْدَ ذَٰلِكَ فَأُولَٰئِكَ هُمُ الْفَاسِقُونَ

Qur'ān, 3:83. *Seek they other than the religion of Allah, when unto*

> *Him submitteth whosoever is in the heavens and the earth, willingly or unwillingly, and unto Him they will be returned?*
>
> أَفَغَيْرَ دِينِ اللَّهِ يَبْغُونَ وَلَهُ أَسْلَمَ مَنْ فِي السَّمَاوَاتِ وَالْأَرْضِ طَوْعًا وَكَرْهًا وَإِلَيْهِ يُرْجَعُونَ
>
> Qur'ān, 3:84. *Say: We believe in Allah and that which is revealed unto us and that which was revealed unto Abraham and Ishmael and Isaac and Jacob and the tribes, and that which was vouchsafed unto Moses and Jesus and the prophets from their Lord. We make no distinction between any of them, and unto Him we have surrendered.*
>
> قُلْ آمَنَّا بِاللَّهِ وَمَا أُنْزِلَ عَلَيْنَا وَمَا أُنْزِلَ عَلَىٰ إِبْرَاهِيمَ وَإِسْمَاعِيلَ وَإِسْحَاقَ وَيَعْقُوبَ وَالْأَسْبَاطِ وَمَا أُوتِيَ مُوسَىٰ وَعِيسَىٰ وَالنَّبِيُّونَ مِنْ رَبِّهِمْ لَا نُفَرِّقُ بَيْنَ أَحَدٍ مِنْهُمْ وَنَحْنُ لَهُ مُسْلِمُونَ

Verse 3:84 is similar to verse 2:136 which we have commented upon previously.

> Qur'ān, 3:85. *And whoso seeketh as religion other than the Surrender [to Allah] it will not be accepted from him, and he will be a loser in the Hereafter.*
>
> وَمَنْ يَبْتَغِ غَيْرَ الْإِسْلَامِ دِينًا فَلَنْ يُقْبَلَ مِنْهُ وَهُوَ فِي الْآخِرَةِ مِنَ الْخَاسِرِينَ

The active noun *dīn*, translated here as religion, comes from the verbal root *d-y-n* primarily meaning: to be or to become a debtor, to owe, to borrow, to be indebted, to owe something to someone, to remunerate, to judge someone, to submit, to obey, to subject, etc. Depending on the context, this term can therefore be translated as: the act of owing something, the due religion, payment, remuneration, custom, engagement, tradition, path, religion, judgement, belief, a relationship one person has with another, and obedience. We have commented upon this term as well as the word "islam" in the chapter entitled "Universality of Islam."

Qur'ān, 3:110. *Ye are the best community that hath been raised up for mankind. Ye enjoin right conduct and forbid indecency; and ye believe in Allah. And if those Familiar with the Scripture had believed it had been better for them. Some of them are believers; but most of them are evil-livers.*

كُنْتُمْ خَيْرَ أُمَّةٍ أُخْرِجَتْ لِلنَّاسِ تَأْمُرُونَ بِالْمَعْرُوفِ وَتَنْهَوْنَ
عَنِ الْمُنْكَرِ وَتُؤْمِنُونَ بِاللَّهِ ۗ وَلَوْ آمَنَ أَهْلُ الْكِتَابِ لَكَانَ
خَيْرًا لَهُمْ ۚ مِنْهُمُ الْمُؤْمِنُونَ وَأَكْثَرُهُمُ الْفَاسِقُونَ

This excellence is the one we have already discussed in the commentary on verse 2:62. It concerns the last community embodying the historical Islam. *Thus We have appointed you a middle nation (ummat^{an} wasat^{an}), that ye may be witnesses against mankind, and that the messenger may be a witness against you. And We appointed the qibla which ye formerly observed only that We might know him who followeth the messenger, from him who turneth on his heels. In truth it was a hard [test] save for those whom Allah guided. But it was not Allah's purpose that your faith should be in vain, for Allah is Full of Pity, Merciful toward mankind.* (2:143)

The expression *right conduct* derives from the passive participle *ma'rūf* which is related to the verbal root *'-r-f*: to distinguish something from above, the idea of expanding, or the concept of diffusing (like perfume); to know, to learn, to distinguish, discern, know, and admit. Thence comes the Qur'ānic term *'urf*, meaning that which is known or recognized, an established use, a custom, a tradition, or an elevated place from where one may discern the components. The expression *ma'rūf* therefore potentially concerns all the rights recognized by the revealed law or the firmly established custom for the common good when no civic law exists.

That which we have translated as *indecency* is a passive participle of the fourth verbal form of the root *n-k-r*: to misread, negate, disavow, disapprove, reject, deny, object, condemn, reprove, find reprehensible, or contest. Thus the expression "forbid indecency" is evidently the opposite of what precedes it: *enjoin right conduct*.

Qur'ān, 3:113. *They are not all alike. Of the Familiar with the Scrip-*

ture there is a staunch community who recite the revelations of Allah in the night season, falling prostrate.

لَيْسُوا سَوَاءً ۗ مِنْ أَهْلِ الْكِتَابِ أُمَّةٌ قَائِمَةٌ يَتْلُونَ آيَاتِ اللَّهِ آنَاءَ اللَّيْلِ وَهُمْ يَسْجُدُونَ

Qur'ān, 3:114. *They believe in Allah and the Last Day, and enjoin right conduct and forbid indecency, and vie one with another in good works. These are of the righteous.*

يُؤْمِنُونَ بِاللَّهِ وَالْيَوْمِ الْآخِرِ وَيَأْمُرُونَ بِالْمَعْرُوفِ وَيَنْهَوْنَ عَنِ الْمُنْكَرِ وَيُسَارِعُونَ فِي الْخَيْرَاتِ وَأُولَٰئِكَ مِنَ الصَّالِحِينَ

Qur'ān, 3:115. *And whatever good they do, they will not be denied the meed thereof. Allah is Aware of those who ward off [evil].*

وَمَا يَفْعَلُوا مِنْ خَيْرٍ فَلَنْ يُكْفَرُوهُ ۗ وَاللَّهُ عَلِيمٌ بِالْمُتَّقِينَ

Qur'ān, 3:199. *And lo! of the Familiar with the Scripture there are some who believe in Allah and that which is revealed unto you and that which was revealed unto them, humbling themselves before Allah. They purchase not a trifling gain at the price of the revelations of Allah. Verily their reward is with their Lord. Lo! Allah is swift to take account.*

وَإِنَّ مِنْ أَهْلِ الْكِتَابِ لَمَنْ يُؤْمِنُ بِاللَّهِ وَمَا أُنْزِلَ إِلَيْكُمْ وَمَا أُنْزِلَ إِلَيْهِمْ خَاشِعِينَ لِلَّهِ لَا يَشْتَرُونَ بِآيَاتِ اللَّهِ ثَمَنًا قَلِيلًا ۗ أُولَٰئِكَ لَهُمْ أَجْرُهُمْ عِنْدَ رَبِّهِمْ ۗ إِنَّ اللَّهَ سَرِيعُ الْحِسَابِ

Qur'ān, 3:200. *O ye who believe! Endure, outdo all others in endurance, be ready, and observe your duty to Allah, in order that ye may succeed.*

يَا أَيُّهَا الَّذِينَ آمَنُوا اصْبِرُوا وَصَابِرُوا وَرَابِطُوا وَاتَّقُوا اللَّهَ لَعَلَّكُمْ تُفْلِحُونَ

The teaching contained in these few verses is without any ambiguity; it results primarily from the teachings outlined by Allah in the verses we commented upon previously.

SURAH 4

JESUS AND CRUCIFIXION

Although the following series of verses spanning from 4:153 to 4:159 concerns those Familiar with the Scriptures, the Divine account deals essentially with the Jews. The culminating point occurs in verse 4:157, several aspects of which will be commented upon.

> Qur'ān, 4:153. *The people of the Scripture ask of thee that thou shouldst cause a Scripture to descend upon them from heaven. They asked a greater thing of Moses aforetime, for they said: Show us Allah plainly. The storm of lightning seized them for their wickedness. Then they chose the calf after clear proofs had come unto them. And We forgave them that! And We bestowed on Moses evident authority.*

يَسْأَلُكَ أَهْلُ الْكِتَابِ أَنْ تُنَزِّلَ عَلَيْهِمْ كِتَابًا مِنَ السَّمَاءِ ۚ فَقَدْ سَأَلُوا مُوسَىٰ أَكْبَرَ مِنْ ذَٰلِكَ فَقَالُوا أَرِنَا اللَّهَ جَهْرَةً فَأَخَذَتْهُمُ الصَّاعِقَةُ بِظُلْمِهِمْ ۚ ثُمَّ اتَّخَذُوا الْعِجْلَ مِنْ بَعْدِ مَا جَاءَتْهُمُ الْبَيِّنَاتُ فَعَفَوْنَا عَنْ ذَٰلِكَ ۚ وَآتَيْنَا مُوسَىٰ سُلْطَانًا مُبِينًا

The Jews of Medina asked the Prophet to rise to heaven in a manner visible to all. They also requested that he descend a book in order to confirm that he was truthful; in imitation—so they thought—of Moses, who received from God the two Tablets upon which the essence of the Law was written.

The people of Moses asked him to make them see God manifestly, in an episode mentioned in the Qur'ān, verses 2:55-56—*And when ye said: O Moses! We will not believe in thee till we see Allah plainly; and even while ye gazed the lightning seized you. Then We revived you after your extinction, that ye might give thanks.*

The episode concerning the making of the golden calf, and the worship thereof by the people of Moses while he was contemplating on the mount Horeb and preparing to receive the Tablets of the

Law, is mentioned in verse 2:54: *And when Moses said unto his people: O my people! Ye have wronged yourselves by your choosing of the calf so turn in penitence to your Creator, and kill (the guilty) yourselves. That will be best for you with your Liberator and He will relent toward you. Lo! He is the Relenting, the Merciful.*

> Qur'ān, 4:154. *And We caused the Mount to tower above them at (the taking of) their covenant: and We bade them: Enter the gate, prostrate! and We bode them: Transgress not the Sabbath! and We took from them a firm covenant.*

وَرَفَعْنَا فَوْقَهُمُ الطُّورَ بِمِيثَاقِهِمْ وَقُلْنَا لَهُمُ ادْخُلُوا الْبَابَ سُجَّدًا
وَقُلْنَا لَهُمْ لَا تَعْدُوا فِي السَّبْتِ وَأَخَذْنَا مِنْهُم مِّيثَاقًا غَلِيظًا

> Qur'ān, 4:155. *Then [We cursed them] because of their breaking of their covenant, and their disbelieving in the revelations of Allah, and their slaying of the prophets wrongfully, and their saying: Our hearts are hardened—Nay, but Allah set a seal upon them for their disbelief, so that they believe not save a few.*

فَبِمَا نَقْضِهِم مِّيثَاقَهُمْ وَكُفْرِهِم بِآيَاتِ اللَّهِ وَقَتْلِهِمُ الْأَنبِيَاءَ
بِغَيْرِ حَقٍّ وَقَوْلِهِمْ قُلُوبُنَا غُلْفٌ ۚ بَلْ طَبَعَ اللَّهُ عَلَيْهَا بِكُفْرِهِمْ
فَلَا يُؤْمِنُونَ إِلَّا قَلِيلًا

Muslim commentators remain puzzled as to the meaning that ought to be attributed to the passage about entering the gate. The Old Testament speaks about a boundary which the people of Moses must not transgress, and God asks the Ancients to prostrate from a distance, as only Moses can approach it from near. (cf. Exodus 19:12-13, and 24:1.)

One may identify a symbolic meaning in this expression by considering *gate* to imply the surrounding wall of a cave which was found in the vicinity of the place where Moses received the revelation. It could also refer to the tents' entrance where his accompanying disciples camped in this sacred place. There is every reason to believe that the blessed site wherein Moses encountered his Lord became sacred then and there. It became an object of prostration, an eternal sign of divine proximity for the person who performs it in pure worship.

In the Old Testament, one comes across many cases of Prophets killed by the people while they exhorted them according to the Law of Moses.

[We cursed *them*] refers to the Jews

In order to explain the meaning of this verse, the Qur'ānic commentators have unanimously added the phrase *We cursed them* in reference to verse 2:88, *And they [the Jews] say: Our hearts are hardened. Nay, but Allah hath cursed them for their unbelief. Little is that which they believe.* However, is it necessary to make this addition? For the direct sequence between these two verses (4:154-155) are evident if one considers the logical continuation of the set of verses which describe the demand of the followers of Moses and of Moses himself (according to the verse 7:143 translated below) to see Allah manifestly and to bear the consequences that this attitude of theirs would provoke. This is because the strict observance of the Covenant that Allah had concluded with them and the application it implied were particularly difficult to realize. Indeed, before the divine origin of this covenant, its actualization required from the followers of Moses a total responsibility and a rigorous realization which very few can attain.

And when Moses came to Our appointed tryst and his Lord had spoken unto him, he said: My Lord! Show me [Thy Self], that I may gaze upon Thee. He said: Thou wilt not see Me, but gaze upon the mountain! If it stand still in its place, then thou wilt see Me. And when his Lord revealed [His] glory to the mountain He sent it crashing down. And Moses fell down senseless. And when he woke he said: Glory unto Thee! I turn unto Thee repentant, and I am the first of [true] believers (7:143).

Qur'ān, 4:156. *And because of their disbelief and of their speaking against Mary a tremendous calumny;*

وَبِكُفْرِهِمْ وَقَوْلِهِمْ عَلَىٰ مَرْيَمَ بُهْتَانًا عَظِيمًا

The Qur'ān recounts that certain Jews accused Mary of adultery when Jesus was born without a human father. Verses 27 and beyond of Surah 19, entitled Maryam, deal more explicitly with this negative attitude of those surrounding her. Jesus exculpated his mother who had remained virgin during this tremendous calumny. We will develop this important theme in our commentary on this Surah.

Qur'ān, 4:157. *And because of their saying: We slew the Messiah, Jesus son of Mary, Allah's messenger—they slew him not nor crucified him, but it appeared so unto them; and lo! those who disagree concerning it are in doubt thereof; they have no knowledge thereof save pursuit of a conjecture; they slew him not for certain.*

وَقَوْلِهِمْ إِنَّا قَتَلْنَا الْمَسِيحَ عِيسَى ابْنَ مَرْيَمَ رَسُولَ اللَّهِ وَمَا قَتَلُوهُ وَمَا صَلَبُوهُ وَلَكِنْ شُبِّهَ لَهُمْ ۚ وَإِنَّ الَّذِينَ اخْتَلَفُوا فِيهِ لَفِي شَكٍّ مِنْهُ ۚ مَا لَهُمْ بِهِ مِنْ عِلْمٍ إِلَّا اتِّبَاعَ الظَّنِّ ۚ وَمَا قَتَلُوهُ يَقِينًا

1. AND THEIR SAYING: WE SLEW . . .

The saying in question is that of the Jews who claimed to have slain the Anoint, Jesus, Son of Mary. If one considers the conditions of killing in Judaea during that particular era under Roman occupation and jurisdiction, then one might conclude that Jews could not have carried out themselves the killing of other human beings, as only the Romans were authorized to do it. In the New Testament, one finds that it was the Romans who, on the request of the Jews, proceeded to the slaying of Jesus on the cross. This punishment had not been practiced by the Jews. They used stoning, according to the Law promulgated by Moses. And it is because the Romans—who had the power to slay—practiced the crucifixion that they crucified him.

2. THE ANOINTED ONE, JESUS, SON OF MARY . . .

This is the full name given to Jesus in the Qur'ān. The reader may refer to our commentary on verses 2:87 and 3:52.

The complete name given to him in the Qur'ānic text, taking into account his exceptional constitution, can provide a key of interpretation for the expression *shubbiha la-hum* in this verse, upon which we are going to comment.

3. THE MESSENGER OF ALLAH

Generally speaking, as well as in the perspective of Sufism and the School of Ibn 'Arabī, the Messenger (*rasūl*) is a person sent by Allah in order to convey a form of Revelation specifically adapted to the new cyclical conditions of humanity. This function implies that such a messenger, whoever he may be, has realized the plenitude of God's Presence in God and in His supports of manifestation according to the amplitude of the possibilities which he carries in himself in order to be fully capable of transmitting the received Message and to be emulated by the faithful of his community.

In the context of this verse, the title given to Jesus "Messenger of Allah" specifies his function as transmitter. It is added to his titles and to the names given to him in the Qur'ān, such as in this verse and in 4:171. He is not only the Word of God (*kalimatu-Hu*); he is also the one who brings this word that nourishes those who are destined to it. We note that in verse 4:171 God does not say "one of the Messengers of Allah" but rather "the Messenger of Allah," as if this divine function was unique but represented by different persons whom God providentially chooses and sends to humanity in order to reaffirm, in readapted new modalities, the unity of God and of His Message.

4. They slew him not (*mā qatalū-hu*) . . .

The Jews mentioned in this passage did not kill the Anointed One, Jesus, Son of Mary, because only the Romans could kill someone, as previously mentioned.

5. Nor crucified him (*mā salabū-hu*)

The Jews did not crucify him for two reasons: firstly, under Roman occupation, they could not execute someone. Secondly, only punishment by stoning was in force among them because of the dictates of Mosaic Law. In addition, certain commentators explain that the crucifixion did not always imply death if the punished person was freed early enough.

This verb, conjugated in the accomplished form (*salabū*), comes from the root *s-l-b*. This root occurs eight times in the Qur'ān and means: to take someone to the gallows, to crucify or to put on a cross, to extract marrow from the bones, to burn, to make rotten, to be hard, rigid, robust, or resistant, to harden, or to stiffen. In the Qur'ān, the execution on the cross is inflicted by the Egyptians and the Romans (cf. 4:157, 7:124, 12:41, 20:71, 26:49). From this root the term *sulb*, pl. *aslāb*, is derived. It means spinal cord, marrow, loin, force, vigor, sclerosis, inflexible, or resistant.

6. BUT (*LAKĪN*)

This restricting word implies that certain persons who were present or non-present during the crucifixion contested it or expressed their reservations regarding what reality of Jesus had been slain or crucified. Others even expressed the hypothesis that a look-alike had been crucified instead of him.

7. IT APPEARED UNTO THEM (*SHUBBIHA LA-HUM*)

Shubbiha is the passive accomplished of the second form of the root *sh-b-h*, meaning: comparison, analogy, resemblance, symbol, similarity, ambiguity, and equivocation, a relationship of similarity, comparability, grouping, and conformity. In the second passive form, it acquires the meaning: to be similar, to look like one another, to be made uncertain, to be compared, to seem, to become analogous, to be the source of equivocation, or to be made ambiguous. The subject of this passive form can be identified as Jesus, as well as be impersonal with the neutral subject, which is why the formula at question can admit of two interpretations. In the first case this expression can be translated as: he (Jesus) was a cause of ambiguity for them. In another case it is translated: this (death or crucifixion) was a cause of ambiguity for them. The two translations may then coincide in this manner: *He was a source of equivocation for them.*

Thus one could understand that the Romans had put him to death, had actually crucified him, whereas the Jews who judged him and wanted to slay him lacked the juridical and penal power to do so. Therefore they did not put him to death or crucify him except in their intention. In addition, certain Jews of this period were convinced that their religious chiefs were responsible for this slaying which they opposed.

Nevertheless, most of the Qur'ānic commentators deduce that it was not Jesus who was crucified and who died but a look-alike who substituted him. Before the very concise character of the Qur'ānic text, people had imagined numerous possibilities of substitution concerning the presumed executed person, as well as concerning the number of individuals that may have played the role of his look-alike in order to deceive the Romans in charge of the execution, and perhaps even Jews. This reasoning often shows some incoherence.

8. Those who disagree concerning it (the matter of Jesus) are in doubt (*shakk*) thereof (or regarding him, Jesus)

The root of the active noun *shakk* is *sh-k-k* which means: confusion, incertitude, doubt, suspicion, dependence, uncertainty, or a quasi identification between two or more things due to a great proximity or affinity between them. In the Qur'ān, this active noun alone is used fifteen times.

Starting from the elements of this verse, it is difficult to discern different opinions on Jesus' fate. His complex personality and his nature must have been the cause of problems, difficulties, controversies, and discussions, given his miraculous birth and the miracles which he performed. Verses 3:50-60 clearly bring out certain attitudes which he alone possessed, both through his exceptional constitution and the resulting actions.

9. They have no knowledge (*'ilm*) thereof save pursuit of a conjecture (*dhann*)

The active noun *'ilm*, translated as knowledge, comes from the verbal root *'-l-m* meaning: to mark, to distinguish with a mark or by distinctive signs, to fix, to split, to discern, to signify, to establish a link between different signs, to know, to recognize, or to be learned. God possesses Knowledge of all realities which are gathered in Him from eternity. In the human being, science or learning generally consists of using the intellect to establish a link between the signs contained in the creation. Through knowledge about God, man becomes aware of these signs and can relate them to their ultimate principle *in divinis*. He may also have a certain approach to the divine science through pure intuition, a faculty which does not arise from rational knowledge.

The science necessarily possessed by those who entertained doubts regarding Jesus is that related to all the constituting elements of his integral, human and spiritual person. Apart from this discernment, personal conviction alone does not remove the perplexity about his reality or the miracles he performed. The term *dhann*, from the verbal root *dh-n-n*, can be translated: belief, judgment, supposition, conjecture, opinion, etc. Such an assumption can imply the intuition which leads to certitude (*yaqīn*), but initially it remains a provisory inner attitude which the spiritual realization permits to occur.

10. THEY SLEW HIM NOT FOR CERTAIN (*WA MĀ QATALŪ-HU YAQĪN[AN]*)

According to the majority of the commentators, this part of the verse allows for two interpretations and therefore two translations: (1) They are not sure of having killed him, or (2) It is certain that they did not kill him.

In light of the mystery which concerns the Person of Jesus and the willed ambiguity of the Qur'ānic text regarding his death, certain commentators, such as Ibn 'Arabī and the disciples of his school, are of the opinion that the Anoint, Jesus Son of Mary comprises two natures, one human (*nāsūt*) and another divine (*lāhūt*). Should one assert that only his human nature has suffered as a result of the punishment of the cross, and not his indestructible divine nature, despite it being intimately united with the former? See Chapter Ten of the present work in which we have given a translation of Chapter Fifteen from Ibn 'Arabī's *Fuṣūṣ al-Ḥikam*, or "The Ringstones of Wisdom."

Qur'ān, 4:158. *But Allah took him up unto Himself. Allah was ever Mighty, Wise.*

بَلْ رَفَعَهُ اللَّهُ إِلَيْهِ ۚ وَكَانَ اللَّهُ عَزِيزًا حَكِيمًا

NO BUT (*BAL*) ALLAH TOOK HIM UP UNTO HIMSELF (*ILAY-HI*)

In grammar, the particle "*bal*," or "but," indicates the refusal or revocation of the content of the negative phrase which precedes it.

This part of the verse confirms that God has called the living Jesus to Him and unto Him, body and spirit, according to the verse 3:55 which was commented upon earlier. According to certain prophetic traditions, he will come down again at the end of times, thereby showing that he continues to fulfill his function in the human cycle to which he does not cease belonging, *And lo! verily he (Jesus) will be (or is) a sign ('ilm) of the Hour. So doubt ye not concerning it, but follow me (Muḥammad). This is the right path.* (43:61)

The preposition *ilā*, translated as *unto*, is a particle which indicates the finality or the circumstance, the arriving point in space or time, the direction, the goal, and the proximity. One of the most representative verses about the divine origin and finality of all beings is the oft-cited verse: *Those who say when an adversity strikes them: Verily we are for Allah, and unto Him are we returning.* (2:156)

How can we come from other than Allah and have other than Him as an end? Does not each being appear in the manifestation, in accordance with the possibilities placed in it from eternity and which are contained in the infinite divine knowledge? Does not Allah encompass everything in His knowledge? *How! Are they still in doubt about the meeting with their Lord? Lo! Is not He surrounding all things?* (Qur'ān, 41:54). *Allah it is who hath created seven heavens, and of the earth the like thereof. The commandment cometh down among them slowly, that ye may know that Allah is Able to do all things, and that Allah surroundeth all things in knowledge* (Qur'ān, 65:12).

Although the context is different from the one we are investigating here, it is interesting to note a case in which Allah makes a person die and revives him a hundred years later. Verse 2:259 says, *Or the like of him who, passing by a township which had fallen into utter ruin, exclaimed: How shall Allah give this township life after its death? And Allah made him die a hundred years, then brought him back to life. He said: How long hast thou tarried? [The man] said: I have tarried a day or part of a day. [He] said: Nay, but thou hast tarried for a hundred years. Just look at thy food and drink which have not rotted! Look at thine ass! And, that We may make thee a token unto mankind, look at the bones, how We adjust them and then cover them with flesh! And when [the matter] became clear unto him, he said: I know now that Allah is Able to do all things.*

Most of the Muslim commentators of the Qur'ān specify that the person in question was 'Uzayr. He is similar to Esdras (Ezra) who, under divine inspiration, readapted the Mosaic tradition after the captivity of the Jews on their return to Judaea. The city in question would be Jerusalem, where the Temple built by Solomon was situated. The Persian invasion destroyed the city and the Temple had been reconstructed on the order of the Persian king Cyrus (cf. Old Testament, beginning of the Chapter of Ezra). It is interesting to note that with respect to His Divine Names, Allah makes this person who is identified with 'Uzayr/Ezra *a sign*, just like Jesus who is *a sign*, as mentioned in verses 19:21 and 43:61.

Let us also point out that this person *was* conscious of having been dead only for a day or a part of a day. In order for Allah to revive him in this world after one hundred years, he had to remain in his human condition but remain in a periphery of the human state. For this reason, the two notions of time, a day and a hundred years, are two different evaluations regarding two conditions of human existence experienced by this person.

Such is also the exceptional case of Jesus who, according to some Muslim traditions, will return at the end of time within the sacred jurisdiction of Islam. He will then establish harmony on earth for a short period. Let us also quote this verse which mentions the resurrection of certain dead people, *And when ye said: O Moses! We will not believe in thee till we see Allah plainly; and even while ye gazed the lightning seized you. Then We revived you after your extinction, that ye might give thanks* (Qur'ān, 2:55-56).

We will return to these two personalities, 'Uzayr and the Anoint (Jesus) in the commentary on verse 9:30.

Qur'ān, 4:159. *There is not one of those familiar with the Scripture but will believe in him before his death, and on the Day of Resurrection he will be a witness against them.*

وَإِنْ مِنْ أَهْلِ الْكِتَابِ إِلَّا لَيُؤْمِنَنَّ بِهِ قَبْلَ مَوْتِهِ ۦ وَيَوْمَ الْقِيَامَةِ يَكُونُ عَلَيْهِمْ شَهِيدًا

This verse comprises two principal interpretations depending on the following considerations: 1) the two pronouns *him* and *his* both apply to Jesus; or 2) the first pronoun "him" concerns Jesus, and the second "his" addresses two individuals, Jews and/or Christians called those familiar with the Scripture.

The first interpretation implies the death of Jesus at the end of times, according a large number of more or less authentic traditions. According to the Islamic statute, after his death he will return just before the general Resurrection which necessarily concerns each human being waiting for the last judgement.

The second interpretation may be formulated: "Among those familiar with the Scripture, there is not one who will die without believing in him (Jesus). On the Day of Resurrection, he (Jesus) will be a witness regarding them." This would imply that "his death" means the death of the Jews and/or the Christians, among others familiar with the Scripture who, at the time of their death, put faith in Jesus for different reasons according to the degree of their sincerity.

Qur'ān, 4:163. *Lo! We inspire thee as We inspired Noah and the prophets after him, as We inspired Abraham and Ishmael and Isaac and Jacob and the tribes, and Jesus and Job and Jonah and Aaron and Solomon, and as We imparted unto David the Psalms.*

إِنَّا أَوْحَيْنَا إِلَيْكَ كَمَا أَوْحَيْنَا إِلَىٰ نُوحٍ وَالنَّبِيِّينَ مِنْ بَعْدِهِ ۚ وَأَوْحَيْنَا إِلَىٰ إِبْرَاهِيمَ وَإِسْمَاعِيلَ وَإِسْحَاقَ وَيَعْقُوبَ وَالْأَسْبَاطِ وَعِيسَىٰ وَأَيُّوبَ وَيُونُسَ وَهَارُونَ وَسُلَيْمَانَ ۚ وَآتَيْنَا دَاوُودَ زَبُورًا

Qur'ān, 4:170. *O mankind! The messenger hath come unto you with the Truth from your Lord. Therefor believe; [it is] better for you. But if ye disbelieve, still, lo! unto Allah belongeth whatsoever is in the heavens and the earth. Allah is ever Knower, Wise.*

يَا أَيُّهَا النَّاسُ قَدْ جَاءَكُمُ الرَّسُولُ بِالْحَقِّ مِنْ رَبِّكُمْ فَآمِنُوا خَيْرًا لَكُمْ ۚ وَإِنْ تَكْفُرُوا فَإِنَّ لِلَّهِ مَا فِي السَّمَاوَاتِ وَالْأَرْضِ ۚ وَكَانَ اللَّهُ عَلِيمًا حَكِيمًا

Here as in verse 7:158, the Messenger concerned is Muḥammad, and Allah addresses all of whole humanity. The faith they must carry is the primordial, essential, and undifferentiated faith. This faith is fundamental. It is that which appeared in Abraham who is referred to as a "theotrope," a notion which we have commented upon when dealing with verse 2:135, and which is applied to the Prophet of Islam and to those who follow him.

Qur'ān, 4:171. *A) O People of the Scripture! Do not exaggerate in your religion nor utter aught concerning Allah save the truth. B) Verily, what is the Messiah, Jesus son of Mary: (1) a messenger of Allah, and (2) His word which He conveyed unto Mary, and (3) a spirit from Him. So believe in Allah and His messengers, and say not "Three"—Cease! [it is] better for you!—Allah is only One God. Far is it removed from His Transcendent Majesty that He should have a son. His is all that is in the heavens and all that is in the earth. And Allah is sufficient as Defender.*

يَا أَهْلَ الْكِتَابِ لَا تَغْلُوا فِي دِينِكُمْ وَلَا تَقُولُوا عَلَى اللَّهِ إِلَّا
الْحَقَّ إِنَّمَا الْمَسِيحُ عِيسَى ابْنُ مَرْيَمَ رَسُولُ اللَّهِ وَكَلِمَتُهُ أَلْقَاهَا
إِلَى مَرْيَمَ وَرُوحٌ مِنْهُ فَآمِنُوا بِاللَّهِ وَرُسُلِهِ وَلَا تَقُولُوا ثَلَاثَةٌ
انْتَهُوا خَيْرًا لَكُمْ إِنَّمَا اللَّهُ إِلَهٌ وَاحِدٌ سُبْحَانَهُ أَنْ يَكُونَ لَهُ
وَلَدٌ لَهُ مَا فِي السَّمَاوَاتِ وَمَا فِي الْأَرْضِ وَكَفَى بِاللَّهِ وَكِيلًا

Some linguistic aspects for introducing the meaning of the two nouns, "word" (*kalima*) and "spirit" (*rūḥ*)

This verse is essential to the understanding of the Anoint, Jesus Son of Mary, and the different aspects which his integral reality comprises. Before tackling the commentary, we would like to offer a quick analysis of what should one understand by metaphor and comparison; the figurative meaning of a term or an expression; their proper, lexical, semantic or literal meaning; their extended meaning; their levels of significations or anagogical meaning; and their spiritual and intellectual implications.

These terms or expressions, almost all of which focus on eminently concrete meanings which God presents in His Scripture brought down upon the Prophet, are adequate symbols of His Reality. In the Divine Unity, everything is contained principally and its reality is found therein from eternity. The Scripture with God, which for the human beings is hidden (*kitāb maknūn*, cf. Qur'ān, 56:78) in the divine Prototype and in the Treasure of Unity, preexists and precedes all scripture, all annunciation, all traces, and all letters, thus constituting their origin. Likewise, the Word with God is eternal. All sounds, all utterances, and all verbal expressions are but its manifestation and cannot exist without it. In addition, one cannot know the Word of God primordially and originally just by starting from our own words and modes of expression. These words must be elaborated upon under the effect of divine inspiration. This is because God has qualified Himself with all the Attributes, evoking the universal Manifestation in which we also partake and in which we participate more or less actively and consciously. We are but the receptacles of His universal and particular Functions. Is not one of the goals of spiritual realization the recognition that the human being witnesses, through all of his faculties and in all his comportments, the very Act of God and His universal Presence? The ritual recitation of the Divine Word, the Qur'ān, then reactualizes the Divine descent in him. The descent is thereby implemented and the surrounding cosmos is influenced by it; it brings down graces upon the person who meditates profoundly on the endless meanings they contain. This is the most perfected instrument for transmitting this Word. It includes numerous sounds and the rhythms in order for it to resonate in the whole being. In the divinely conceived phonetic apparatus for this purpose, each point of the transmission is a letter impregnated with multiple meanings. The Breath of the Spirit invigorates these meanings with the help of three fundamental vowels—A, U, and I—which are proper to the Qur'ānic and classical Arabic language.

The figures of style represented in rhetoric include the expressions: trope, metaphor, antonomasia, metonymy, synecdoche, etc. The Qur'ānic text incorporates all of them. The Arab rhetoricians have given to these figures of style technical names that vary from one author to another, or in accordance with the different schools. According to Merriam-Webster's dictionary,

—A trope is a word or expression used in a figurative sense.

—A metaphor is a figure of speech in which a word or phrase literally denoting one kind of object or idea is used in the place of another to suggest a likeness or analogy between them. For example, the expression "drowning in money."

—A metonymy is a figure of speech consisting of the use of the name of one thing for that of another; the second is an attribute or association of the first. For example, as "crown" in "lands belonging to the crown."

—A synecdoche is a figure of speech by which a part is substituted for the whole (*fifty sail* for *fifty ships*), the whole for a part (*society* for *high society*), the species for the genus (*cutthroat* for *assassin*), the genus for the species (as *a creature* for *a man*), or the name of the material for the thing made (as *boards* for *stage*).

'Alī ibn Muḥammad al-Jurjānī, in his *Kitāb al-ta'rifāt*, or "The Book of Definitions," defines the trope (*al-majāz*) or figure of speech (definition 1448) as: "A noun through which a thing other than the [noun's] first destination is meant in order to establish a relationship of analogy (*munāsaba*) between the two notions, like the lion in the expression, 'brave as a lion' while referring to a courageous man . . .. Metaphor is the transposition and the exceeding of the initial meaning of an expression to the benefit of another meaning, by virtue of the relation which unites them, whether it is a question of a concrete thing (*ṣūra*) or a subordinated and recognized concept (*ma'nā*), or still a relation of affinity or closeness, such as that between the lion and a courageous man, or expressions which serve as illustrations."

Al-Jurjānī defines the metaphor (*al-isti'āra*, definition 0100) as "the suggesting of the true meaning of a thing through hyperbole (*mubālagha*) in the comparison (*tashbīh*) by excluding from the context the mentioning of the compared thing. For example, when one says: I have met a lion," meaning a brave man:

> On the other hand, when the mentioning of the thing that is being compared with (*al-mushabbah bi-hi*) accompanies that of the compared thing (*qarīna*), then the metaphor is called evident (*taṣrīḥiyya*) and verifiable (*taḥqiqiyya*). For example: "I met a lion in the bathroom," or again if we specify: "the demise or death took him with its claws," which means that he was seized by its clutches. Thus we compare the demise which takes away the souls to a ferocious beast and which makes them disappear without designating in this case the advantageous or the detrimental. By personifying death, we affirm the existence of claws without which this abduction cannot be realized perfectly, thus justifying the hyperbole in the comparison.
>
> Comparing the demise to a ferocious beast reveals the metonymic (*kināya*) aspect implied in the metaphor. Explaining that the claws provoked it shows the contribution of imagination (*takhīliya*) in the metaphor.
>
> The metaphor implied in the verb denotes only that there exists a relationship of belonging or dependence (*taba'iyya*) in the metaphor, as in the expression, "the circumstance has spoken (*nataqat al-ḥāl*)."

Here are two Qur'ānic examples of metaphor through an adjective: *The good deed and the evil deed are not alike. Repel the evil deed with one which is better, then lo! he, between whom and thee no enmity [will become] as though he was a warm friend* (Qur'ān, 41:34). Here, the adjective "warm" refers first of all to a sensible quality which is transposed. *Seest thou not how Allah coineth a parable: A goodly saying, as a goodly tree, its root set firm, its branches reaching into heaven*

(Qur'ān, 14:24).

Let us also point out this remarkable metaphor concerning the prophet Joseph, whose explanation is found only at the end of Surah 12 when Joseph said unto his father: *O my father! Lo! I saw in a dream eleven planets and the sun and the moon, I saw them prostrating themselves unto me* (Qur'ān, 12:4). In verse 100 of the same chapter, Joseph tells his parents and his twelve brothers: *And he placed his parents on the dais and they fell down before him prostrate, and he said: O my father! This is the interpretation of my dream of old . . ..*

An example of synecdoche: *Ask the town . . .* (*wa s'ali-qary-ata*), is substituted for specifying *ask the inhabitants of the town* (Qur'ān, 12:82).

The language used by God in the Qur'ān is the Arabic language of the period of the Revelation. The Prophet spoke this language with a perfect mastery that he conveyed to his Companions and has been confirmed by them many times. This tongue had preserved an original purity, and that purity is found in the Qur'ānic text. The inimitability of the Qur'ān is due to the fact that it is essentially a Word of God in all its constitutive elements: in the words, in their consonance, rhythm, and morphology, in the very discourse in which they appear, in the sobriety of the means implemented by the Divine Artisan (nearly 5000 terms for 1700 consonant roots). However, the initial meaning to be given to the words and discourses employed by God at the time of the Revelation remains a major difficulty navigated by experts of Arabic. Before the rapid evolution of language shortly after the descent of the Divine word to the Prophet, the proper original meaning belonging to a particular root and to the words which depend on it through derivation remained problematic. Is the meaning of a term monosemic or polysemic, proper or figurative, and in this case does the word have a metaphorical or anagogical sense which goes back to several levels of comprehension? When does the metaphorical meaning taken by a term start to depend on the place it occupies in the divine discourse?

The reply to these questions will give rise to very diverse schools of interpretation of the Qur'ān, from those that are attached to a singularly literal or firm sense of the Qur'ānic text to those which would accord to the terms and the Qur'ānic phrase of levels of multiple meanings open to different exegetical interpretations. Occasionally, in the writings of the same commentator one may find certain inconsistencies due to preferential doctrinal positions. Let us take Fakhr al-Dīn al-Rāzī as a great representative example of *kalām*. In his work devoted to the Divine Names, he considers the word *shay'*, usually translated as "thing," masculine in Arabic (from the verbal root *sh-y-'*, which means to wish in a synthetic and primordial manner) as a divine name (cf. our translation of this work published by Editions Albouraq, Beirut, 2000, 61), in pursuant a view to two Qur'ānic verses: *Say: What thing is of most weight in testimony? Say: Allah is Witness between me and you. And this Qur'ān hath been inspired in me, that I may warn therewith you and whomsoever it may reach. Do ye in sooth bear witness that there are gods beside Allah? Say: I bear no such witness. Say: He is only One Allah. Lo! I am innocent of that which ye associate* (*with Him*) (Qur'ān, 6:19). And cry not unto any other god along with Allah. There is no Allah save Him. Everything will perish save His countenance. His is the command, and unto Him ye will be brought back.

In the primordial and essential reality represented by its face (*wajh*), the thing (*shay'*) is none other than Allah. Rāzī interprets it in this sense, without attributing a metaphorical or figurative meaning to the term "*shay'*" in the verses he quotes. In his great commentary on the Qur'ān entitled *Mafātīḥ al-ghayb*, he considers the "word" (*kalima*) in verse 4:171 to be employed in the metaphorical sense; he evades commenting on it in such a way that would give the "word" a physical meaning and thus imply that Jesus has a divine nature. The question arises as to whether this is an inconsistency, a question of method, or an opportunist doctrinal choice? Why seek for metaphors or figurative meanings when a term like *kalima* can be easily interpreted according to its operative planes of reference and the various corresponding (anagogical) meanings? A word may operate in the following planes:

a) In God Himself according to a secret which escapes us,

b) In the expression it acquires in each world and through which it is proffered or articulated in accordance with continuously and renewed and diversified modalities,

c) According to the benefits or the multiple chastisements that it provokes as a consequence of its universal action. In this case there is also no need whatsoever to consider the term "word" as a metaphor. Let us quote this verse of the Word of Allah comprising the sanction and not necessarily the benefit:

> *Lo! those for whom the word of thy Lord is realized will not believe* (Qur'ān, 10:96). This word is like the Mercy which can come with sanctions, for its universal function is two-fold: *O my father! Lo! I fear lest a punishment from the Beneficent overtake thee so that thou become a comrade of the devil* (Qur'ān, 19:45). *Shall I take gods in place of Him when, if the Beneficent should wish me any harm, their intercession will avail me naught, nor can they save?* (Qur'ān, 36:23).

This is how Ibn 'Arabī and the representatives of his School up to Amir 'Abd al-Qādir al-Jazā'irī and René Guénon envisage the Divine Word and the expression *His Word* which qualifies Jesus in the verse in question. All beings issuing from God and returning to Him, after their evolution through different phases, necessarily possess a divine nature linking them to Him. The beings constitute His Words which are never exhausted according to the two Qur'ānic verses: *Say: Though the sea became ink for the Words of my Lord, verily the sea would be used up before the words of my Lord were exhausted, even though We brought the like thereof to help* (Qur'ān, 18:109). *And if all the trees in the earth were pens, and the sea, with seven more seas to help it, [were ink], the words of Allah could not be exhausted. Lo! Allah is Mighty, Wise* (Qur'ān, 31:27).

The demonstration carried out for the word "*shay'*" can be replicated with numerous Qur'ānic terms, such as, for instance, the word *amr*, meaning order or command. We shall comment upon this term later.

This important verse lists three essential aspects of the Anoint, Jesus Son of Mary: messenger, word, and spirit. One must dissociate the two principal parts, which we divided into A) and B), and subdivided for clarity of exposition.

In the first part A), Allah informs those "familiar with the Scripture" without specifying any of them individually or collectively. At the beginning of the verse, Allah warns against extreme positions in religious matters, ranging from those involving excessive lack of conviction to fanaticism caused by a unilaterally literalist understanding of the sacred text.

To say nothing but the truth about Allah implies a profound knowledge of the divine Message—the Message conveyed to the prophets in general, and the Message conveyed to Muḥammad, the last of the prophets, in particular. This message contains the most essential knowledge about the themes concerning human beings, thus assuring their life in this world and their salvation in the afterlife in the best of conditions. The message informs humanity regarding the essentials of the different prophetic typologies, and the divine tidings brought by those typologies. In this way, revelation serves as exhortation and instruction adapted to the different phases of humanity.

Although we establish a link between the first element of the verse and the second, the phrase "familiar with the Scripture" refers primarily to Christians. However, it does not exclude other numerous "non-Christian," individuals who feel interested in this major theme.

In the second part B) of the verse, Allah establishes three essential characteristics of the Anoint, Jesus Son of Mary: He is the Messenger of Allah, His Word, and His Spirit issuing from Him.

The particle "*innamā*," which we have translated as "Verily, what is," is composed of two elements which are analyzed in the following way: 1) from *inna*, a particle of insistence, meaning certainly, verily, truly, and 2) the neutral conjunctive (which is both demonstrative and relative) *mā*, meaning "what is." In grammar, this particle is considered both with a restrictive value, meaning "only," and as signifying insistence.

1. He is the Messenger of Allah (*rasūl Allāh*)

a) The meaning of the two terms *rasūl*, messenger, and *mursal*, envoy

The two words *rasūl* and *rusūl*, the first in the singular form and the second plural, come from the root *r-s-l*. In its first form this root means: to send a messenger, to have very long hair, or to walk softly. In the second verbal form it means: to have milk in abundance, or to give it for drinking. In the fourth form it means: to send with a mission, to dispatch, to send forth, to send back, to send out, to transmit, to transport, to let go smoothly, to drop, to unravel, or to let down one's hair.

In the Qur'ānic text, words deriving from this very root *r-s-l* denote the person whose mission is to transmit the divine Message: a) *rasūl* here is in the masculine singular with an active value = the transmitting messenger; b) *mursal*, in singular, but most often employed in the plural, *mursalūn* = the envoy, or the person chosen by God to transmit a message. This last term is the passive participle of the fourth form.

a) *rasūl,* in the singular, is used 235 times; *rusūl,* in the plural, is used 96 times.

b) *mursal* is encountered twice in the singular and *mursalūn* (*mursalīn* in the direct and indirect case) occurs 33 times in the plural.

These two description signations are given to the Prophet Muḥammad:

Muḥammad Rasūl Allāh . . . Muḥammad is the Messenger of Allāh (Qur'ān, 48:29).

Ya Sin. By the wise Qur'ān, Lo! thou art of those sent on a straight path (Qur'ān, 36:1-4).

One should note the 84 Qur'ānic occurrences in which the expression *rasūlu-Hu*, His Messenger, concern only the *Prophet Muḥammad.* There exists, therefore, a notable difference between *rasūl* and *mursal*, one of which has an active sense and the other a passive sense.

These two names *rasūl* and *mursal* are not exclusive to the Prophet Muḥammad, but they are also attributed to other persons or entities mentioned in the Qur'ān:

-Angels (pl. *malā'ika,* sing. *malak*) are described as envoys (*mursalūn*).

-Other unspecified entities are also described as being sent to certain prophets, for instance: to Abraham (Qur'ān, 11:69, 15:57, 29:31, 51:31); to Loth (Qur'ān, 11:77, 15:61, 26:160, 29:33); and to Moses (Qur'ān, 27:11), etc.

-In the Qur'ānic text only five prophets received the title of envoy (*mursalūn*): Ilyās (Eliah), Lot, Moses, Jonah (Yūnus), and Muḥammad.

-The expression Messenger of Allah (*rasūl Allāh*) is reserved for the following prophets:

-Moses: only once, in the following verse*: And [remember] when Moses said unto his people: O my people! Why persecute ye me, when ye well know that I am Allah's messenger unto you? So when they went astray Allah sent their hearts astray. And Allah guideth not the evil-living folk* (Qur'ān, 61:5).

-Jesus: *And when Jesus son of Mary said: O Children of Israel! Lo! I am the messenger of Allah unto you, confirming that which was [revealed] before me in the Torah, and bringing good tidings of a messenger who cometh after me, whose name is the Praised One. Yet when he hath come unto them with clear proofs, they say: This is mere magic* (Qur'ān, 61:6; see also 4:157, 4:171).

-Muḥammad: (Qur'ān, 7:158, 9:61, 9:81, 9:120, 33:21, 33:40, 33:53, 48:29, 49:3, 49:7, 63:1, 63:5, 63:7). *Verily in the messenger of Allah ye have a good example for him who looketh unto Allah and the Last Day, and remembereth Allah much* (Qur'ān, 33:21).

-Sālih: a prophet who is not mentioned in the Old Testament, who was sent to the people of Thamud, an ancient community who lived were located in the north of Arabia on the borders of the desert of Syria. The title "Messenger of Allah" is applied to him only once in the Qur'ān: (*The tribe of*) *Thamud denied [the truth] in their rebellious pride, when the basest of them broke forth and the messenger of Allah said: It is the she-camel of Allah, so let her drink!* (91:11-13)

-Used with the universal article *al*, the noun Messenger (*al-rasūl*) is applied to the Prophet Muḥammad with the exception of three verses concerning Jesus, the Archangel Gabriel, and Moses, respectively: Our Lord! We believe in that which Thou hast revealed and we follow the Messenger (Jesus). Enroll us among those who witness (Qur'ān, 3:53). [The Sāmirī] *said: I perceived what they perceive not, so I seized a handful from the footsteps of the messenger [Gabriel], and then threw it in. Thus my soul commended to me* (Qur'ān, 20:96). *But Pharaoh rebelled against the messenger, whereupon We seized him with no gentle grip* (Qur'ān, 73:16).

-Used in an indefinite form, that is, without the universal article *al* and without the construction of the genitive case, the expression 'a messenger' is often addressed to a non-identified messenger: an emissary sent to the Prophet Joseph (Qur'ān, 12:50). When it is identified, it refers to the prophets Noah (Qur'ān, 7:61, 26:116), Lot (Qur'ān, 26:162), Hūd (Qur'ān, 26:125), Moses (Qur'ān, 7:104, 44:17-18), Sālih (Qur'ān, 26:143), Shu'ayb (Qur'ān, 26:178), Jesus (Qur'ān, 5:75), Muḥammad (Qur'ān, 9:128, 43:29, 44:13, 61:6, 69:40), and the Archangel of Revelation Gabriel (Qur'ān, 81:19).

-The expression "*rasūl Rabb*" is used in the context *rasūl Rabbi-ki* (the messenger of your Lord) in addressing Mary in Qur'ān 19:19. *Rasūl Rabb-him* (the messenger of their Lord) is mentioned in Qur'ān 69:10 as he who was sent to the Pharaoh and other rebellious people. *Rasūl Rabbi al-ʿalamīn* (the messenger of the Lord of beings of the Universe) appears in Qur'ān, 26:16 and 43:46.

b) The meaning of "Jesus is the Messenger of Allah"

Jesus, as a Messenger sent by God with a mission, is the depositary for a divine Message whose content is necessarily adapted to the human beings for whom it is destined. Verse 3:49, which we have previously commented upon, specifies that Jesus was sent to the Children of Israel. The function of the transmission of the Message of Allah is universal. Therefore each messenger, including *Jesus*, is referred to as *the Messenger of* Allah—not simply 'one of the messengers.' As we shall notice in the following discussions, in the Qur'ān this expression 'the Messenger of' is reserved for only the prophet-messengers Moses, Sālih, Jesus, and Muḥammad.

2. Jesus, the Word of Allah (*kalimatu-Hu* = His Word) which He conveyed unto Mary

a) His Word

We mentioned earlier the word *kalima*. Now we will analyze the meanings of its root and the values encompassed by its lexicon. *Kalima* comes from the ternary root *k-l-m*. In its first verbal form it has the predominant meaning of wounding; in its second verbal form *kallama* it means to wound, to pronounce, to profess a word or a saying, to speak to someone, to address the word to him; and in its fifth form *takallama* it means to speak, to utter a word, or to wound oneself. The Qur'ān uses only the second and the fifth verbal forms. The singular noun *kalām* is Qur'ānic: it means word, utterance, verb, and saying; by subsequent non-Qur'ānic grammatical extension, it took on the further meanings of phrase, discourse, proposition, theology, or science dealing with the Divine Word. Also of Qur'ānic origin are the words *kalima* (singular), *kalimāt*, and *kalim* (two plural forms, the second of which takes a collective meaning). The active noun *taklīm* from the second verbal form is also Qur'ānic. In the entry on the root *k-l-m*, Ibn Manzūr's lexicon *Lisān al-ʿarab* specifies that the first sense of this root is to wound (*kalm*). What, therefore, is the link between "wound" and "word" that has caused them to share a common root in the lexicons of our time?

Allah exteriorizes His Word (*kalām*) by emitting or uttering the infinite possibilities contained in His limitless Knowledge, just as the blood of life escapes from a body that is wounded or pierced by a sharp instrument. Is Allah not the *Splitter* (*fāṭir*) *of the heavens and the earth* (Qur'ān, 39:46), and is it not through the openings or "wounds" which He produces that the Words leak continuously? The *Qalam* (the pen, mentioned in verse 31:27), a word phonetically similar to the word *kalām* (word), is the instrument or channel which then carries the Word into the universal manifestation. The divine Word is articulated by the divine *Dhikr*, the bearer of seeds (which are all beings with their origins in God), veritable "Logos spermaticos." In another interpretation, the Pen engraves the Words composed of letters in some material, thus wounding its surface. Thus the word *kalima* acquires its meaning from the host of semantic perspectives mentioned here.

Al-Jurjānī, whom we have previously quoted, specifies in article 1287 of his Book of Definitions, *al-Qalam*: "The science of distinctiveness (*'ilm al-tafsīl*). The [ontological and formal] Letters (*hurūf*), epiphanic loci of the distinctiveness implied in them, are gathered synthetically into the Ink of the Inkwell (*midād al-dawā*), and they can never accept the distinctiveness as long as they subsist in the Inkwell. At the moment when the Ink contained therein is drawn out and penetrates the Pen, the Letters, under its effect, realize their distinctiveness on the Tablet (*lawḥ*). [Divine] Knowledge is diversified indefinitely by the letters. One can make a comparison with semen, the substance (*mādda*, a term coming from the same root as the word "ink") of man residing in the loins of Adam, as long as human forms exist synthetically in his humanity. Distinctiveness is not realized insofar as these forms remain in him. It is only when they are transferred to the Tablet of the Matrice (*lawḥ al-raḥīm*) by the human pen that man acquires a human form."

Here Jurjānī develops a symbolism of impregnation, first at the ontological degree and then at the existential degree, a symbolism which reminds us of the mythical creation of Adam and his spouse.

From the initial Semen, human being are transferred and differentiated in universal manifestation through the commanding divine Word *Be, Come to existence* (*kun*) and then they come into existence and actualize their possibilities. *And Our word unto a thing, when We intend it, is only that We say unto it: Be! and it is* (Qur'ān, 16:40).

Thus, the Word (*kalima*) or the Words (*kalimāt, kalim*) of Allah are contained in an all encompassing way in the non-manifested divine and universal Imperative (or Order, Command) (*amr*). They are actualized by the Spirit of Allah (*rūḥ Allāh*), which is non-manifested but continuously creates in order for the possibilities that it contains to manifest all the forms of the world. The Spirit invigorates these forms at each instant through the existentiating Order *Kun*, Be! *All that are in the heavens and the earth entreat Him. Every day He exerciseth [universal] power* (Qur'ān, 55:29). All the "commanded things" (*umūr*, pl. of *amr*) come into existence conditioned by the possibilities they carry within themselves from eternity, given that they have heard the Word of Allah concerning them: *But His command, when He intendeth a thing, is only that He saith unto it: Be! and it is* (Qur'ān, 36:82). Thus the divine Order, or the Imperative and the Spirit or the Breath of God, is one and the same reality envisaged in two different modalities or functions: Allah commands by His Word and invigorates and mobilizes through His Breath.

The Word of God in itself and without any modality is that through which He does not cease speaking to Himself, insofar as He is Ever-Hearing (*samiʿ*) of His Own Speech, nor does he cease to utter the "things" that are found permanently in their essential prototypical entities. This Speech whose Origin is the Silence beyond all manifestation is primordially assimilated in the original Sound. When the Prophet received the Qur'ān or the Word of God he would hear it in different modalities. The most painful was the one that was conveyed to him like the tinkling of a bell (*jaras*). This was in fact the primordial sound containing all sounds that have not yet been differentiated or developed, and ultimately all distinct words. Sometimes the divine Word was communicated to the Prophet when he was on his mount and it would bend under the pressure of the divine Descent. God Himself says: *Verily, We shall charge thee with a weighty Word* (*innā sa-Nulqī ʿalay-ka qawl*^{an} *thaqīl*^{an}) (Qur'ān, 73:5). This verse can be interpreted in several ways, all of which imply both the physical weight of the divine Descent and the density of anagogical exegeses that it comprises.

In certain cases God speaks to different beings whom He identifies. He does not specify the nature of this Word or His Words, or the manner in which they are understood by these beings depending on their receptivity and comprehension thereof. The Word of Allah can be uttered and heard in a completely inward manner, without audible sounds. However, most of us possess the average aptitude to hear through the physical organ which is conditioned for this purpose, and therefore at the most diverse levels. Let us quote some Qur'ānic verses in order to illustrate this idea:

1) In verse 3:41, previously commented upon, the elderly Zachariah asks God for a "sign" of the miracle that He will bestow upon him and his barren wife. Allah says: *The Sign unto thee [shall be] that thou shalt not speak unto mankind three days except by signals . . .* In this case, the signals represent a form of language intelligible to the persons involved.

2) What is the type of the word that Allah addresses to the human beings in the afterlife, and the word that they utter themselves? *Lo! those who hide aught of the Scripture which Allah hath revealed and purchase a small gain therewith, they eat into their bellies nothing else than fire. Allah will not speak to them on the Day of Resurrection, nor will He make them grow. Theirs will be a painful doom* (Qur'ān, 2:174). *On the day when it cometh no soul will speak except by His permission; some among them will be wretched, [others] glad* (Qur'ān, 11:105). What language will Allah and human beings speak, given that the morphology of humans will be modified and adapted to new conditions of existence after their death on earth, and given that Allah knows how to take all of this into account?

3) In the following verse, the term "word" takes on a general and almost universal meaning because it concerns all possible modes of words, in God and in His creation: *And the Word of your Lord hath been accomplished in truth and justice. There is naught that can change His words. He is the Hearer, the Knower* (Qur'ān, 6:115). It is He, Allah, who is the only Hearer par excellence who hears His Words. How, then, could one really modify them?

4) Although beings can be likened in effect to "uttered words of Allah," as indicated by verses 18:109 and 31:27 which we mentioned earlier, they depend on the annunciation of the *Kun* in order to come into existence. The Anoint, Jesus Son of Mary, is an exceptional case because he is the Word of Allah (*kalimatu-Hu*) and not a word among other words. He does not depend on the existentiating Kun through which the "things or realities willed by God" are actualized; he assumes the Func-

tion directly and without intermediary until he is incorporated into this world through Mary as intermediary. Because he is the Word of Allah, he was able to speak from the cradle, in the language of his time. With this speech he proved his mother's innocence, as God shows in verses 19:27 and others.

b) He conveyed it unto Mary

In this verse, Allah does not specify if this Word from Him is transmitted to Mary through the intermediary of His Spirit . . . *and it assumed for her the likeness of a harmonious man* (*bashar sawī*) according to verse 19:17. In this latter verse, this Spirit which takes a perfect human form is likened to Gabriel by the Tradition. It is he who will inform Mary about his action of transmitting this Word unto her by telling her: *So [will it be] for you* (Qur'ān, 19:21). Certain commentators, such as Ibn 'Arabī, have concluded that this Spirit—momentarily and in the role it had to assume in this circumstance—had the function of the "spiritual father" of Jesus. For this reason Jesus is said to be strengthened by the *Holy Spirit*.

3. Jesus, Spirit from Allah (*Rūḥ[un] min Allāh*)

In our comments on verse 2:87 we referred to the etymology of the word "*rūḥ*." Its verbal root *r-w-ḥ* connotes good odor, the movement of fresh air and breeze in the evening, doing something at night, to get wind of something, to rejoice at something, to begin, and to start doing something. In the Qur'ān, one finds the following words which derive from this root: *rūḥ*, meaning the spiritual breath of life, a spirit (from God), the spirit (of life), the spiritual principle of life, or the soul (a singular word which is applied here to Jesus); *rawḥ,* meaning a soft breeze, rest, relaxation, joy, contentment, compassion, assistance; *riḥ*, the plural of *riyāḥ*, meaning wind, breath, protection, influence, odor; *rawāḥ*, meaning evening, start of the night, rest, ease, night travel; *rayḥān*, meaning aromatic plant, strong fragrance, or subsistence. In its fourth verbal form, *arāro*, it takes on the connotation: to travel at night, to provide rest, to put at ease, to let someone rest, to sense the presence of something, and to regain one's breath.

In the Qur'ānic text, the term *rūḥ* is encountered twenty-one times, always in the singular. The themes of concern include the following:

Rūḥ al-Qudūs: Holy Spirit with respect to Jesus (Qur'ān, 2:87, 2:253, 5:110).

Rūḥ al-Qudūs: Holy Spirit with respect to the believers (Qur'ān, 16:102).

Rūḥ min-Hu: *Spirit from Him* (Qur'ān, 4:171).

Min Rūḥī: from My Spirit; *Min Rūḥī Hī*: from His (Allah's) Spirit: Regarding the creation of Adam (Qur'ān, 15:29, 32:9, 38:72).

Bi al-Rūḥ min Amri-Hi: *He sendeth down the angels with the Spirit of His command unto whom He will of His servants . . .* (Qur'ān, 16:2).

al-Rūḥ ilay-Hi: *The angels and the Spirit ascend unto Him in a Day whereof the span is fifty thousand years* (Qur'ān, 70:4).

al-Rūḥ: *On the day when the angels and the Spirit stand arrayed* (Qur'ān, 78:38).

al-Rūḥ: *The angels and the Spirit descend therein, by the permission of their Lord, with all decrees* (Qur'ān, 97:4).

al-Rūḥ min Amri-Hi: *He causeth the Spirit of His command upon whom He will of His slaves* (Qur'ān, 40:15).

Rūḥan min Amri-Nā: *And thus have We inspired in thee (Muḥammad) a Spirit of Our command* (Qur'ān, 42:52).

Bi Rūḥin min-Hu: *He hath strengthened them with a Spirit from Him* (Qur'ān, 58:22).

al-Rūḥ al-amīn: *The True Spirit hath brought down upon thy heart* (Qur'ān, 26:192-194).

al-Rūḥ min Amr Rabb-i: *They are asking thee concerning the Spirit. Say: The Spirit is by command of my Lord . . .* (Qur'ān, 17:85).

Arsāl-Nā ilay-hā Rūḥa-Nā: *Then We sent unto her Our Spirit and it assumed for her the likeness of a perfect man* (Qur'ān, 19:17).

Nafakh-Nā fī-hā min Rūḥi-Nā: *And she who was chaste, therefore We breathed into her of Our Spirit* (Qur'ān, 21:91).

Nafakh-Nā fī-hi min Rūḥi-Nā: *And Mary, daughter of 'Imrān, who guarded her the chastity of her body, therefore We breathed therein something of Our Spirit* (Qur'ān, 66:12).

In examining the expressions "His Word and Spirit from Him" (Qur'ān, 4:171) and "The Spirit is by command of my Lord" (17:85), we understand that the Word of Allah, His Spirit, and His Command proceed from the same Degree of Unity of Allah. At this already rational degree, only their functions are different. Thus they are related to each other by ontological relations that take place together for creation to come about. In none of the verses can the term *rūḥ* acquire a metaphoric sense, but only a meaning appropriate to different degrees of reality. This is because Allah mentions *rūḥ* in these twenty-one occurrences in accordance with a specific Plan. Four of these apply to Jesus, three to Mary, and three to the creation of Adam. In the case of Mary, it is interesting to note in verse 19:17 that Allah, with the totality of His Names, *sent to her His* (literally Our) *Spirit which took form*, and not from His Spirit. This is distinct from verses 21:91 and 66:12 where Allah sends *from His Spirit* which He breathed into her. In order to manifest the possibilities it contains, the Spirit must assume a quality which conforms to the world in which it must appear. The prepositional phrase "*from His Spirit*" indicates that the Spirit as such, the Spirit in itself, has acquired for Mary a form which is likened to Archangel Gabriel of the Revelation. We have already commented upon the expression "Holy Spirit" in connection with verse 2:87. In his total conformity, Adam is *formed* from the Spirit of Allah (*min Rūḥi-Hi*) and not His Spirit. We see yet again the difference between the creation of Jesus and also Mary in comparison with Adam, as we had the occasion to remark in the commentary on verse 3:59.

4. THEREFORE BELIEVE IN ALLAH AND IN HIS MESSENGERS

Whatever the value and the degree of proximity one has with Allah, he must have faith in Him and in what He has specified in His Scripture: *The messenger believeth in that which hath been revealed unto him from his Lord and [so do] believers. Each one believeth in Allah and His angels and His scriptures and His messengers—We make no distinction between any of His messengers—and they say: We hear, and we obey. [Grant us] Thy forgiveness, our Lord. Unto Thee is the journeying* (Qur'ān, 2:285). The believers therefore do not distinguish between Messengers by excluding some to the benefit of the others, even though Allah elevates some above others: *Of those messengers, some of whom We have caused to excel others, and of whom there are some unto whom Allah spake, while some of them He exalted [above others] in degree; and We gave Jesus, son of Mary, clear proofs [of Allah's Sovereignty] and We supported him with the holy Spirit . . .* (Qur'ān, 2:253). It is Allah Himself and Only He who indicates the degree of excellence of some in comparison to the others. As Messengers they are all privileged beings who Allah has sent unto humankind with an appropriate Mission so that the latter may return to Him through their mediation.

5. AND SAY NOT "THREE" (*WA LĀ TAQŪLŪ THALĀTHA*) . . . BUT ONE

The Anoint, Jesus, Son of Mary is one person. Whoever privileges one of his aspects over another does not succeed in synthesizing his complex reality which is present in the three realms—the divine, the spiritual, and the human—for he is at once Word and Spirit of Allah, Spirit embodied by the Angel Gabriel, and a true man through his mother. To acknowledge only a single aspect, or two of the three in him, amounts to concealing (*kafara*) the others. This concealing (*kufr*) is limitation and veil.

Can one say that the expression "say not Three" refers more or less implicitly to the Christian doctrine of Three Persons (*aqanīm*) of the Trinity (*tathlīth*)? Most of the commentators have envisaged it in this way, even more so since the passage that follows *Cease! [It is] better for you!—Allah is only One God . . .* insists on the worship of the One God, He who is beyond all ontological relationships of "Persons." Three, like any number, indeed implies inner relationships within the Divine Unity, but this notion of "Three" must be surpassed and integrated into the Unique One. A God who is thus described by the "Three" can also be described according to the 99 Divine Names of Islam. These names are but essential relations or Functions, and with them Allah vests all beings that come into existence. Different numbers, all of which indicate symbolically the most diverse relationships, may describe distinct existential functions and degrees without undermining divine Unity, provided one sees here relationships and functions which do not affect that Unity. Here, too, a distinction can be made between Allah and His undifferentiated Essence, and His divine Function which intervenes at all the levels because He is the Outward or the Manifest. For Allah does not cease being simultaneously the First and the Last, the Outward and the Inward:

> *He is the First and the Last, and the Outward and the Inward; and He is Knower of all things* (Qur'ān, 57:3).

Allah then warns against the temptation to relativize worship related to divine Unity to the detriment of worship related to relational or even principal aspects.

His omnipresent Glory (*subḥāna-Hu*) *excludes the possibility that a child be ascribed to Him.*

The root which forms the noun *subḥāna* is *s-b-h* which means in its first verbal form: to swim, to bathe, to be immersed, to move as if one were swimming, to evolve, to disperse in all directions, to be exempt from, and to be free. *Subḥāna* is considered by the grammarians of the Arabic language as an indeclinable active noun meaning: total and limitless glorification, exclusive omnipresence, immense praise, universal availability, or an act of glorification. Allah's Glory, at once omnipresent and transcendent, excludes all limitation. His exclusive freedom and His universal independence refuse any conditioning. His immanent Presence invigorates all things and leaves intact His transcendence, which is not attached to any particular reality: *Unto Allah belong the East and the West, and whithersoever ye turn, there is Allah's Countenance. Lo! Allah is All-Embracing, All-Knowing* (Qur'ān, 2:115). His transcendence excludes all things, while His immanence applies to all things.

Qur'ān, 4:172. *The Anoint will never scorn to be a slave unto* (or *for*) *Allah, nor will the favoured angels. Whoso scorneth His service and is proud, all such will He assemble unto Him.*

لَنْ يَسْتَنْكِفَ الْمَسِيحُ أَنْ يَكُونَ عَبْدًا لِلَّهِ وَلَا الْمَلَائِكَةُ الْمُقَرَّبُونَ ۚ
وَمَنْ يَسْتَنْكِفْ عَنْ عِبَادَتِهِ وَيَسْتَكْبِرْ فَسَيَحْشُرُهُمْ إِلَيْهِ جَمِيعًا

Our translation at the beginning of the verse takes into account the etymological meaning of existence of the verb KāNa, from the root *k-w-n*, to be, to become, or to come into existence. We have devoted a particular study to this verbal root in our work *Une approche du Qur'ân par la Grammaire et le Lexique* (Beirut: Al-Bouraq, 2002, 872 pages). See entry no. 1336 of the Lexicon.

By coming into the world of Creation, the Anoint *qua* Word and Spirit of Allah becomes His, or, more precisely, "for Allah (*lil-Lāh*)," for everything that comes to existence is for Him, Allah, and to Him, according to the end of the last verse *For Him* (or *to Him*) *is* (or *belongs*) *what is in the heavens and on earth* . . . and since everything is for Him and unto Him, it is He who answers for all things and provides sustenance for them, according to the meaning of the root *w-k-l*, meaning to entrust, to recommend something to someone, to charge someone with something, to trust, to give something for managing, to authorize a proxy, to mandate, to rely on someone, or to assign. The *wakīl*, which is a Divine Name, is the representative, the guarantor, the manager, the attorney, the bursar, or the director. Then the Anoint appeared into the world of creation. He became a servant, but an accomplished servant who only does his Lord's will in full consciousness. All aspects of his perfectly constituted being come from his mother, who is herself a perfect servant, and from the Holy Spirit which visits her. The angels brought nigh cannot but be "servants for Him" for they only do the will of their Master: *And unto Allah maketh prostration whatsoever is in the heavens and whatsoever is in the earth of living creatures, and the angels [as well] and they are not proud. They fear their Lord above them, and do what they are bidden. Allah hath said: Choose not two gods. There is only One Allah. So of Me, Me only, be in awe* (Qur'ān, 16:49-51). Whatever the beings who are servants of Allah may do, and in whichever manner they may behave, they (and we) shall all be gathered at the moment of the Day of Resurrection in order to be measured and judged.

Surah 5

Qur'ān, 5:13. *And because of their breaking their covenant, We have banished them from Our Presence and made hard their hearts. They change the literal text of the Word and forget a part of that whereof they were admonished. Thou wilt not cease to discover treachery from all save a few of them. But bear with them and pardon them. Lo! Allah loveth the kindly.*

فَبِمَا نَقْضِهِمْ مِيثَاقَهُمْ لَعَنَّاهُمْ وَجَعَلْنَا قُلُوبَهُمْ قَاسِيَةً ۖ
يُحَرِّفُونَ الْكَلِمَ عَنْ مَوَاضِعِهِ ۙ وَنَسُوا حَظًّا مِمَّا ذُكِّرُوا بِهِ
ۚ وَلَا تَزَالُ تَطَّلِعُ عَلَىٰ خَائِنَةٍ مِنْهُمْ إِلَّا قَلِيلًا مِنْهُمْ ۖ فَاعْفُ
عَنْهُمْ وَاصْفَحْ ۚ إِنَّ اللَّهَ يُحِبُّ الْمُحْسِنِينَ

The verb used in the expression "We have banished them from Our Presence" comes from the root *l-'-n*, meaning: to chase something from one's presence and to wish to banish it as far as possible. This root is also often translated as: to curse, to loathe, to reprobate, to imprecate, to condemn, launch anathema against someone, and to blame.

According to the majority of Muslim commentators, this verse and the one preceding it, which we are quote below, concern the Hebrews of the time of Moses: *Allah made a covenant of old with the Children of Israel and We raised among them twelve chieftains, and Allah said: Lo! I am with you. If ye establish worship and pay the poor-due, and believe in My messengers and support them, and lend unto Allah a kindly loan, surely I shall remit your sins, and surely I shall bring you into Gardens underneath which rivers flow. Whoso among you disbelieveth after this will go astray from a plain road* (Qur'ān, 5:12).

Muslim theologians use the technical term *taḥrīf* to refer to the alteration of scriptures. This phenomenon is dealt with in several places in the Qur'ān (cf. 2:75, 4:46, 5:41). In these verses, it concerns only the Jews.

The majority of Muslim commentators point out that the words originally uttered by Jesus in his mother tongue, Aramaic, were later written in a different language, Greek for example. These are the writings that make up what we call the Gospels, whether they are considered authentic or apocryphal. The Muslim scholars of the field are thus of the opinion that the Book given by Allah to Jesus, denoted by the Qur'ānic term *injīl*, has undergone alterations. However, one must point out that Christian authorities consider these texts as inspired and not as revealed. This belief reflects the Muslim scholars' distinction between the inspired gospel texts and the revealed Qur'ān descended from Allah to the Prophet Muḥammad. In addition, certain Muslim scholars have sometimes made the connection between the Qur'ān and Jesus Son of Mary. The Qur'ān is the uncreated Word of Allah in the "Mother of the Book" (*Umm al-Kitāb*) that took shape with the Descent of the Revelation to the Prophet Muḥammad. Jesus, Son of Mary, is the Word of Allah (according to Qur'ān, 4:171); the Spirit assumed a perfect human form with the traits of Gabriel and conveyed to Mary the form of Jesus.

The Anoint, Jesus Son of Mary, Word of Allah, conveys His Word in the form of articulated words. The first of these words, announced as it is in its language of revelation, must also come from the divine.

The Qur'ān describes its descent to the Prophet Muḥammad as the following: the fundamental nature of the Prophet as unlettered and untaught (*ummī*) enabled him to receive the divine

Word, then he heard the Word and recited in perfect and inimitable Arabic. The form of the revelation and its reception was entirely "virginal," without interference of any kind, whether individual, psychological, or spiritual. Therefore, the Prophet had no power to alter the content of the divine Message transmitted to him. Hence he may be identified with the Word which he transmitted, integrally and without deformation, to his community (*umma*, from the same root as *ummī*). This formulated Word of perfect Arabic is also of divine origin and permits the person who recites it ritually to realize all aspects of its sacred virtue. The Prophet says of the Word in the following authentic ḥadīth: "I have been given the all-comprehensive words (*ūtī jawāmiʿa al-kalimi*)," or according to other versions, "I have received the all-comprehensive words" (Bukhārī, Jihād 122; Nisā'ī, Jihād 1; Muslim, Masājid 5, 8; etc). These all-comprehensive words given to the Prophet by God constitute all the possible words of divine origin; they are manifested in the hierarchical worlds and their principle goes back to this single Word, that of Allah. Thus he always receives from Allah this synthesis, this recapitulation of all the Words of Allah, while his ever-virgin primordial nature is in a state of total availability.

The notion of *ummī*, meaning unlettered or untaught, is found in a ḥadīth quoted by Ibn Manẓūr in his dictionary *Lisān al-ʿarab*, root *ʿ-m-m*: "We are an unlettered community (*innā ummat^{un} ummiyyat^{un}*), we neither write nor count." Al-Zajjāj comments on this prophetic saying: "the name *ummī* concerns the person who has kept the same disposition that he had when his mother (*umm*) brought him into this world, that is, knowing neither reading nor writing at birth and not having received the imprint of any human knowledge."

> Qur'ān, 5:14. *And with those who say: "Lo! we are Christians," We made a covenant, but they forgot a part of that whereof they were admonished. Therefore We have stirred up enmity and hatred among them till the Day of Resurrection, when Allah will inform them of their handiwork.*

وَمِنَ الَّذِينَ قَالُوا إِنَّا نَصَارَى أَخَذْنَا مِيثَاقَهُمْ فَنَسُوا حَظًّا مِمَّا ذُكِّرُوا
بِهِ فَأَغْرَيْنَا بَيْنَهُمُ الْعَدَاوَةَ وَالْبَغْضَاءَ إِلَى يَوْمِ الْقِيَامَةِ وَسَوْفَ
يُنَبِّئُهُمُ اللَّهُ بِمَا كَانُوا يَصْنَعُونَ

We can conclude that very early after the descent of a Revelation, whichever one, this revelation acquires organized institutional forms. Human authorities generate diverse interpretations of the founding sacred texts and dogmatic positions that are far from unanimous.

This attitude generates conflicts among men, which are very often deadly, and sanctions on the part of God. Such behaviors take place both within a single revelation tradition and among different forms of revelations. This verse speaks of the Christians: it mentions the internal dissent that seized the community of believers very early after the disappearance of Jesus, dividing them frequently and often for long periods.

> Qur'ān, 5:15. *O those Familiar with the Scripture! Now hath Our messenger come unto you, expounding unto you much of that which ye used to hide in the Scripture, and forgiving much. Now hath come unto you light from Allah and plain Scripture.*

يَا أَهْلَ الْكِتَابِ قَدْ جَاءَكُمْ رَسُولُنَا يُبَيِّنُ لَكُمْ كَثِيرًا مِمَّا كُنْتُمْ تُخْفُونَ
مِنَ الْكِتَابِ وَيَعْفُوعَنْ ك ثِيرٍ قَدْ جَاءَكُمْ مِنَ اللَّهِ نُورٌ وَكِتَابٌ مُبِينٌ
اللَّهِ نُورٌ وَكِتَابٌ مُبِينٌ

This verse accommodates different interpretations according to how broadly one expands the meaning given to the expression *those Familiar with the Scripture* or *People of the Book* (*ahl al-kitāb*). See our commentary on verse 2:62 regarding this point. Taking into account the present context which concerns Jesus and the Christians, one could say that *Our Messenger* (*rasūlu-Nā*) refers to the Prophet Muḥammad invested with all the Divine Names represented by the adjective "*our*." But does the verse only concern the Prophet who is living among the people of his time, or does it refer to the Prophet since his entry into the human cycle until the Day of Resurrection, as may be implied by the following three *ḥadīth*? "I was a Prophet when Adam was between water and clay," "I am the leader of the human beings on the day of Resurrection," and "If Moses were alive, he would but follow me." Indeed, in this verse the expression *expounding unto you* is conjugated in the unaccomplished form, whereas the beginning of the Qur'ānic phrase is in the past (and accomplished form). The messenger has physically arrived in a new period of revelation but he remains witness among human beings in the past, present, and future courses of the human cycle. His universal presence is illustrated by certain verses in which it is said: *And know that the messenger of Allah is among you (fī kum). If he were to obey you in much of the government, ye would surely be in trouble; but Allah hath endeared the faith to you and hath beautified it in your hearts, and hath made disbelief and lewdness and rebellion hateful unto you. Such are they who are the rightly guided* (Qur'ān, 49:7).

Allah also shows that the Messenger of Allah is sent to all mankind: *Say: O mankind! Lo! I am the messenger of Allah to you all—[the messenger of] Him unto Whom belongeth the Sovereignty of the heavens and the earth. There is no Allah save Him. He quickeneth and He giveth death. So believe in Allah and His messenger, the Prophet who generates a community (al-nabiyy al-ummiyy) can neither read nor write, who believeth in Allah and in His Words, and follow him that haply ye may be led aright* (Qur'ān, 7:158). *We sent thee not save as a mercy for the peoples* (Qur'ān, 21:107). *There hath come unto you a messenger, [one] of yourselves, unto whom aught that ye are overburdened is grievous, full of concern for you, for the believers full of pity, merciful* (Qur'ān, 9:128).

The *Light* (*nūr*) in question at the end of verse 5:15 quoted above is juxtaposed with darkness (*dhulumāt*), a term which comes from the root *dh-l-m.* This root also includes the notion of injustice (*dhulm*), related to darkness and error due to the lack of light. Certain commentators interpret this "Light" metaphorically as being Islam or the Prophet Muḥammad. In addition, because Allah is considered *The Light of the heavens and the earth* (Qur'ān, 24:35), it may also concern the light of faith which lights up all beings that come into the world: *Is he whose bosom Allah hath expanded for al-Islam, so that he followeth a light from his Lord, [as he who disbelieveth]? Then woe unto those whose hearts are hardened against remembrance of Allah. Such are in plain error* (Qur'ān, 39:22). *He it is Who blesseth you, and His angels [bless you], that He may bring you forth from darkness unto light; and He is ever Merciful to the believers* (Qur'ān, 33:43). Here the term Islam concerns both the universal Islam, or submission to the Divine Will in accordance with the Scriptures revealed successively to mankind, as well as historical Islam, the last revelation for the whole of mankind.

Qur'ān, 5:16. *Whereby Allah guideth him who seeketh His good pleasure unto paths of peace. He bringeth them out of darkness unto light by His decree, and guideth them unto a path which demands uprightness.*

يَهْدِي بِهِ اللَّهُ مَنِ اتَّبَعَ رِضْوَانَهُ سُبُلَ السَّلَامِ وَيُخْرِجُهُمْ مِنَ الظُّلُمَاتِ إِلَى النُّورِ بِإِذْنِهِ وَيَهْدِيهِمْ إِلَى صِرَاطٍ مُسْتَقِيمٍ

Islam and peace (*salām*, which is also a Divine Name) have the same root, *s-l-m*, meaning: 1) to be safe and sound, to remain intact, to maintain a good state, to do well, to escape, or to be exempt of; and 2) to sting someone, to bite (snake), such a bite can serve as an antidote.

The expression which we have translated as *a path which demands uprightness* is often translated as "straight path." The verbal root *q-w-m* means: to get up, to dress up and to keep upright. In its tenth verbal form it acquires a desirous connotation: to search, to ask, to want, to demand for oneself, to strive for. Therefore, the active participle of the tenth verbal root *mustaqīm* that is found in this verse means: one who wants or demands straightness for oneself. According to this interpretation, the following verse takes a meaning other than "straight path," the usual translation applied to this expression: *Lo! I have put my trust in Allah, my Lord and your Lord. Not an animal but He doth grasp it by the forelock! Lo! my Lord is on a straight path* (Qur'ān, 11:56).

Qur'ān, 5:17. *They indeed have disbelieved who say: Lo! Allah (is) the Anoint, son of Mary. Say: Who then can do aught against Allah, if He had willed to destroy the Anoint son of Mary, and his mother and everyone on earth? Allah's is the Sovereignty of the heavens and the earth and all that is between them. He createth what He will. And Allah is Able to do all things.*

لَقَدْ كَفَرَ الَّذِينَ قَالُوا إِنَّ اللَّهَ هُوَ الْمَسِيحُ ابْنُ مَرْيَمَ قُلْ فَمَنْ يَمْلِكُ مِنَ اللَّهِ شَيْئًا إِنْ أَرَادَ أَنْ يُهْلِكَ الْمَسِيحَ ابْنَ مَرْيَمَ وَأُمَّهُ وَمَنْ فِي الْأَرْضِ جَمِيعًا وَلِلَّهِ مُلْكُ السَّمَاوَاتِ وَالْأَرْضِ

وَمَا بَيْنَهُمَا يَخْلُقُ مَا يَشَاءُ وَاللَّهُ عَلَى كُلِّ شَيْءٍ قَدِيرٌ

This is one of the verses of capital importance for situating an exceptional aspect of the creation of Jesus in the Qur'ānic Revelation.

We have already analyzed the verbal root *k-f-r*, meaning: to hide (*sitr*), to cover, to make disappear, to conceal, to bury, just as the farmer buries the grain (cf. Qur'ān, 57:20). The beginning of this verse can therefore be translated as: *They indeed have concealed [the truth] those who say . . .* But who are those who have said that *Allah (is) the Anoint, Son of Mary*? The creation of the Anoint, Son of Mary was exceptional due to his birth without a human father, his being the Word and Spirit of Allah, and his ability to revive the dead. Certain people must have been convinced that Allah assumed the human form of Jesus exclusively in order to perform such miracles, and therefore they limited the Divinity to this human form. It should be noted that the dogmatic Christian perspective does not hold that God is the Messiah but rather that the Messiah is the Son of God. Once again, the issue here is God in the degree of Unity which goes back to the divine Function (*ulūhiyya*) and not God free from all qualification or attributes that constitute the Divine Essence, who *begetteth not, nor is begotten* (cf. Surah 112). In this element of verse 5:17, *Allah* must be understood as the pure, transcendent Essence, beyond all relationships. Indeed, the pronoun *He* (*Huwa*) permits such an interpretation when it is applied to the absent and placed before the Name *Allah*. The consequence of this concealing (*sitr*) perpetuated by those who mistakenly liken Allah to Jesus is Allah's declaration that completes the rest of the verse. In this second part of the verse Allah demonstrates that, in respect to the human nature of Jesus including his relation to his mother and to the whole of manifested beings, Allah can make them disappear from this existence at any moment, immediately or in the future.

In Arabic, the phrase *Allah (is) the Anoint, Son of Mary* is a proposition without a doubly nominal verb. It can be rendered in English in three ways: 1) Allah (is) He, the Messiah, Son of Mary; 2) Allah, He (is) the Messiah, Son of Mary; and 3) Allah, He, the Messiah, Son of Mary, without the verb "be" in English.

Let us point out that the name given twice to the Anoint in this verse does not mention Jesus ('Isā). The second time the phrase *his mother* (*al-Masīha ibna Maryama wa umma-hu*) is added, Mary, being a virgin, guards her chastity (*farj*) according to verse 66:12, *And Mary, daughter of 'Imrān, who guarded her the chastity of her body, therefore We breathed therein something of Our Spirit. And she put faith in the words of her Lord and His scriptures, and was of the obedient.* She permanently receives the Words and the Spirit of her Lord, which are none other than Jesus, according to verse 4:171 that we have already commented upon. However, as a *mother* (*umm*) who is perfectly constituted in her whole being, she spiritually begets the beings in her universal matrix and she transmits this Word of God to human beings. One might also point out that the appellation *al-Masīh ibn Maryam wa umma-hu* exists in the Christian tradition as well. Thus in an encyclical of Pope John-Paul II on the Blessed Virgin Mary, one finds the literal statement: "the Son of Mary and his Mother with him" (page 30 of the French edition, Paris: Cerf, 1987). Although sometimes Jesus is mentioned in the Qur'ān without his mother, for example with other prophets, the Qur'ānic expression "Jesus, Son of Mary, his mother" constitutes a single and inseparable "Sign," both being united in their universal mediation: *And We made the son of Mary and his mother a Sign, and We gave them refuge on a height, a place of flocks and water springs* (Qur'ān, 23:50). We shall further comment later.

The different names attributed to Jesus in certain Qur'ānic verses evoke different aspects that his exceptional creation assumes in the three possible worlds: 1) the divine, given that he is Word and Spirit of Allah; 2) the spiritual, by Angel Gabriel who transmits Allah's Breath to Him; and 3) the physical, through his mother. His physical existence confirms at once the Words, the Breath, and the Scripture of God.

> Qur'ān, 5:18. *The Jews and Christians say: We are sons of Allah and His loved ones. Say: Why then doth He chastise you for your sins? Nay, ye are but mortals of His creating. He forgiveth whom He will, and chastiseth whom He will. Allah's is the Sovereignty of the heavens and the earth and all that is between them, and unto Him is the journeying.*

وَقَالَتِ الْيَهُودُ وَالنَّصَارَىٰ نَحْنُ أَبْنَاءُ اللَّهِ وَأَحِبَّاؤُهُ ۚ قُلْ فَلِمَ
يُعَذِّبُكُمْ بِذُنُوبِكُمْ ۖ بَلْ أَنْتُمْ بَشَرٌ مِمَّنْ خَلَقَ ۚ يَغْفِرُ لِمَنْ يَشَاءُ

وَيُعَذِّبُ مَنْ يَشَاءُ ۚ وَلِلَّهِ مُلْكُ السَّمَاوَاتِ وَالْأَرْضِ وَمَا
بَيْنَهُمَا ۖ وَإِلَيْهِ الْمَصِيرُ

The expression "*sons of Allah*" appears several times in both the Old Testament and the New Testament. Thus it is written in Genesis 6:1-4, *And it came to pass, when men began to multiply on the face of the earth, and daughters were born unto them that the sons of God saw the daughters of men that they were fair; and they took them wives of all which they chose. And the Lord said, My spirit shall not always strive with man, for that he also is flesh: yet his days shall be an hundred and twenty years. There were giants in the earth in those days; and also after that, when the sons of God came in unto the daughters of men, and they bare children to them, the same became mighty men which were of old, men of renown.* Let us also mention the Epistle to the Romans, chapter 8:13-16: *For if ye live after the flesh, ye shall die: but if ye through the Spirit do mortify the deeds of the body, ye shall live. For as many as are led by the Spirit of God, they are the sons of God. For ye have not received the spirit of bondage again to fear; but ye have received the Spirit of adoption, whereby we cry, Abba, Father. The Spirit itself beareth witness with our spirit, that we are the children of God.* The Qur'ānic expression *sons of Allah* as well as that which follows it, "*His loved ones*," prove a familiarity, proximity, and a friendship, thus implying the mercy of God and excluding His punishment. The question *Why then doth He chastise you for your sins?* could be understood as implying that those who do not transgress the divine precepts and who are described by these two expressions could be legitimately qualified in this way. But whatever the case may be, in the expression *abnā'u-Llāh*, sons of Allah, the plural "sons" here must be understood in a metaphorical sense which is highlighted by the following statement: *Nay, ye are but mortals of His creating.*

Unlike in the previous verse, the Name *Allah* cannot but have a non-absolute value; the degree of Divine Unity is at the origin of plurality and multiplicity. On the other hand, the son and the father are always in correlated relational terms. The expression *loved ones* also implies an existing correlation between 1) lover (*muḥibb*), 2) beloved, and 3) love. If one of the three terms disappears, then the other two disappear as well, love (*ḥubb*) then ceasing to exist in order to finally be reabsorbed into the Unity of the

Divine Essence.

Qur'ān, 5:19. *O ye Familiar with the Scripture! Now hath Our messenger come unto you to make things plain unto you after an interval [of cessation] of the messengers, lest ye should say: There came not unto us a messenger of cheer nor any warner. Now hath a messenger of cheer and a warner come unto you. Allah is Able to do all things.*

وَمِنَ الَّذِينَ قَالُوا إِنَّا نَصَارَى أَخَذْنَا مِيثَاقَهُمْ فَنَسُوا حَظًّا
مِّمَّا ذُكِّرُوا بِهِ فَأَغْرَيْنَا بَيْنَهُمُ الْعَدَاوَةَ وَالْبَغْضَاءَ إِلَى يَوْمِ
الْقِيَامَةِ وَسَوْفَ يُنَبِّئُهُمُ اللَّهُ بِمَا كَانُوا يَصْنَعُونَ

If the expression *Familiar with the Scripture* (*ahl al-kitāb* or People of the Book) refers to the Jews and the Christians, then Moses and Jesus sit aside the Prophet Muḥammad as the corresponding messengers of those faiths. These three are the prophets who have received the title of Messenger of Allah (*rasūl Allah*), as we mentioned earlier. But the expression above may also regard all the possible messengers who have transmitted the Revelation that God communicated to human beings in different forms, as we have shown in our commentary on verse 2:62, referring to the verses 5:65-68. According to the facts contained in this verse, after Moses and Jesus no other messenger but Muḥammad the Envoy of God has instituted a new universal Law from God that presents a universal quality concerning all of humanity. The following two verses mention the universality of the Islamic revelation as addressed to all: *Say: O mankind! Lo! I am the messenger of Allah to you all—[the messenger of] Him unto Whom belongeth the Sovereignty of the heavens and the earth. There is no Allah save Him. He quickeneth and He giveth death. So believe in Allah and His messenger, the Prophet who can neither read nor write, who believeth in Allah and in His Words, and follow him that haply ye may be led aright* (Qur'ān, 7:158). *And We have not sent thee [O Muḥammad] save as a bringer of good tidings and a warner unto all mankind; but most of mankind know not* (Qur'ān, 34:28).

Qur'ān, 5:46. *And We caused Jesus, son of Mary, to follow in their footsteps, confirming that which was [revealed] before him in the Torah, and We bestowed on him the Gospel wherein is guidance and a light, confirming that which was [revealed] before it in the Torah—a guidance and an admonition unto those who are wary.*

وَقَفَّيْنَا عَلَىٰ آثَارِهِمْ بِعِيسَى ابْنِ مَرْيَمَ مُصَدِّقًا لِمَا بَيْنَ يَدَيْهِ مِنَ التَّوْرَاةِ ۖ وَآتَيْنَاهُ الْإِنْجِيلَ فِيهِ هُدًى وَنُورٌ وَمُصَدِّقًا لِمَا بَيْنَ يَدَيْهِ مِنَ التَّوْرَاةِ وَهُدًى وَمَوْعِظَةً لِلْمُتَّقِينَ

"Their footsteps" refers to those who follow the Law revealed to Moses. This includes the prophets, the rabbis, doctors of the law, and all others who conform to it, according to verse 5:44.

In verses 3:3 and 3:50, we commented on the expression *bayna yaday-hi*, or literally "what is between our two hands." The Gospel revealed by Allah to Jesus, Son of Mary confirms in part the Law received by Moses, readjusting it in accordance with a new cycle of humanity. However, before the descent of the Gospel, Jesus freely practiced the prescriptions contained in the Torah. That was before the promulgation of the new form of revelation that he had to convey to the Children of Israel. For this reason, and no doubt for others too, Allah mentions twice the words: *confirming that which was [revealed] before him in the Torah.* The Gospel therefore contains Guidance and Light whereas the Torah brings *guidance and an admonition*: for Jesus and for the others.

Qur'ān, 5:47. *Let the People of the Gospel decide wisely by that which Allah hath revealed therein. Whoso decides not wisely by that which Allah hath revealed: such are evil-livers.*

وَلْيَحْكُمْ أَهْلُ الْإِنْجِيلِ بِمَا أَنْزَلَ اللَّهُ فِيهِ ۚ وَمَنْ لَمْ يَحْكُمْ بِمَا أَنْزَلَ اللَّهُ فَأُولَٰئِكَ هُمُ الْفَاسِقُونَ

Our translation "decide wisely" takes into account the verbal root *ḥ-k-m*. This root comprises the notions of establishing a rule of wisdom, of observing or maintaining a rule or a norm, of arbitrating, judging, deciding, resolving (a dispute), condemning, reinforcing, confirming, preserving, administrating, regulating, reigning, ruling, being prudent, having a certain judgment, muzzling a horse and putting the martingale under the chin, retaining, detaining, and preventing.

In this verse and in the following, as in numerous others, Allah settles the matter of the laws that He has promulgated and warns against eventual deviations. This is necessary because the Qur'ān is the last divine descent; therefore it recapitulates all the revelations to humanity and it addresses all of humankind.

Qur'ān, 5:48. *And unto thee have We revealed the Scripture with the truth, confirming whatever Scripture was before it, and a faithful watcher over it. So judge between them by that which Allah hath revealed, and follow not their desires away from the truth which hath come unto thee. For each of you We have appointed a divine law and a traced-out way. Had Allah willed He could have made you one community. But that He may try you by that which He hath given you. So vie one with another in good works. Unto Allah ye will all return, and He will then inform you of that wherein ye differ.*

وَأَنْزَلْنَا إِلَيْكَ الْكِتَابَ بِالْحَقِّ مُصَدِّقًا لِمَا بَيْنَ يَدَيْهِ مِنَ الْكِتَابِ
وَمُهَيْمِنًا عَلَيْهِ ۖ فَاحْكُمْ بَيْنَهُمْ بِمَا أَنْزَلَ اللَّهُ ۖ وَلَا تَتَّبِعْ أَهْوَاءَهُمْ عَمَّا
جَاءَكَ مِنَ الْحَقِّ ۚ لِكُلٍّ جَعَلْنَا مِنْكُمْ شِرْعَةً وَمِنْهَاجًا ۚ وَلَوْ شَاءَ
اللَّهُ لَجَعَلَكُمْ أُمَّةً وَاحِدَةً وَلَٰكِنْ لِيَبْلُوَكُمْ فِي مَا آتَاكُمْ ۖ فَاسْتَبِقُوا
الْخَيْرَاتِ ۚ إِلَى اللَّهِ مَرْجِعُكُمْ جَمِيعًا فَيُنَبِّئُكُمْ بِمَا كُنْتُمْ فِيهِ تَخْتَلِفُونَ

Qur'ān, 5:49. *So judge between them by that which Allah hath revealed, and follow not their desires, but beware of them lest they seduce thee from some part of that which Allah hath revealed unto thee. And if they turn away, then know that Allah's Will is to smite them for some sin of theirs. Lo! many of mankind are evil-livers.*

وَأَنِ احْكُمْ بَيْنَهُمْ بِمَا أَنْزَلَ اللَّهُ وَلَا تَتَّبِعْ أَهْوَاءَهُمْ وَاحْذَرْهُمْ أَنْ
يَفْتِنُوكَ عَنْ بَعْضِ مَا أَنْزَلَ اللَّهُ إِلَيْكَ ۖ فَإِنْ تَوَلَّوْا فَاعْلَمْ أَنَّمَا يُرِيدُ
اللَّهُ أَنْ يُصِيبَهُمْ بِبَعْضِ ذُنُوبِهِمْ ۗ وَإِنَّ كَثِيرًا مِنَ النَّاسِ لَفَاسِقُونَ

Qur'ān, 5:50. *Is it a judgment of the time of ignorance that they are seek-*

ing? Who is better than Allah for judgment to a people who have certainty?

أَفَحُكْمَ الْجَاهِلِيَّةِ يَبْغُونَ ۚ وَمَنْ أَحْسَنُ مِنَ اللَّهِ حُكْمًا لِقَوْمٍ يُوقِنُونَ

Qur'ān, 5:51. *O ye who believe! Take not the Jews and the Christians for near ones. They are near one to another. He among you who taketh them for near ones is [one] of them. Lo! Allah guideth not wrongdoing folk.*

يَا أَيُّهَا الَّذِينَ آمَنُوا لَا تَتَّخِذُوا الْيَهُودَ وَالنَّصَارَىٰ أَوْلِيَاءَ ۘ بَعْضُهُمْ أَوْلِيَاءُ بَعْضٍ ۚ وَمَنْ يَتَوَلَّهُمْ مِنْكُمْ فَإِنَّهُ مِنْهُمْ ۗ إِنَّ اللَّهَ لَا يَهْدِي الْقَوْمَ الظَّالِمِينَ

This set of four verses (5:48-51) does not present great difficulties of interpretation.

The Scripture at issue is that which came down to the Prophet Muḥammad, he who seals the legislative prophethood and marks the last of the divine descents of Scriptures. The Qur'ān, or the encompassing Recitation, confirms, *in fine*, the previous Scriptures, certain elements of which continue to have a real value in the last form of revelation. When a certain number of facts are mentioned in the Qur'ānic text concerning the previous forms taken by the perennial Revelation, these elements are thus integrated therein and can present for the Muslim believer a feature which should not to be overlooked. The Qur'ān being neither the Torah nor the Gospel, what is not mentioned in it from these two scriptures is obviously neither an omission nor an error on the part of God. On the contrary, certain supplementary notifications which one finds in the sacred text of Islam but which are absent from the Torah and the Gospel, to cite just these two Scriptures, remain true and instructive. Their content must be meditated by Muslims and others who consider the Qur'ān to be an authentic revelation. The Messengers, sent by God from Him, due to their exceptional position and spiritual and human amplitude, not completely appreciable by a believer, may have possibilities which surpass their divine mission within the framework of a given revelation. Such possibilities can nevertheless be applied within the final synthetic and all-encompassing form of the last divine descent. The Messengers, the Prophets, and human beings remain in the prolongation of the human state (*barzakh*) until the Day of Resurrection and may, up to an atemporal instant, continue to have an influence in the present human cycle in accordance with modalities that trace back to other criteria.

There is a divergence of interpretation regarding the term "*muhaymin*" which we have rendered as "faithful watcher." Its verbal root may, according to the Arab linguists, be both fourfold *h-y-m-n*, and ternary: *'-m-n*, or *h-m-n*. Its main meanings include: to flap the wings, to have an upper hand, to have a preponderant influence, to dominate, to control, to watch over, to supervise, and to guard. The noun in question, which is an active participle, should therefore be rendered as: dominating, influential, regent, vigil, watcher, guardian, and predominant. This noun form is one of the Names of Allah. Thus the Qur'ān remains the standard of perfect conformity to the Divine Norm. All the facts it includes, and notably information on the contents of certain divine Scriptures, accounts, and persons from the past, adhere to its standard.

The following divine words, *For each of you* (*min-kum*) *We have appointed a divine law and a traced-out way* (*minhājan*) highlight the uniqueness of each individual vocation which God manifests in the universe, through the totality of His Divine Names represented by the pronoun We. He manifests in accordance with appropriate conditions, a function of the possibilities in His total knowledge contained for all eternity.

In the last verse (5:51) of this sequence, the plural word *awliyā'* (sing. *walī*), which we have rendered as "those who are near," comes from the verbal root *w-l-y* meaning: to be very near, to be adjacent, to follow closely, to touch, to be within hand's reach, to be charged with, to be assigned, to be the intimate friend of someone, to govern, lead, or to administer.

Qur'ān, 5:59. *Say: O People of the Scripture! Do ye blame us for aught else than that we believe in Allah and that which is revealed unto us and that which was revealed aforetime, and because most of you are evil-livers?*

قُلْ يَا أَهْلَ الْكِتَابِ هَلْ تَنْقِمُونَ مِنَّا إِلَّا أَنْ آمَنَّا بِاللَّهِ وَمَا أُنْزِلَ إِلَيْنَا وَمَا أُنْزِلَ مِنْ قَبْلُ وَأَنَّ أَكْثَرَكُمْ فَاسِقُونَ

Qur'ān, 5:60. *Shall I tell thee of a worse [case] than theirs for retribu-*

tion with Allah? [Worse is the case of he] who Allah hath cursed, he on who His wrath hath fallen and of whose sort Allah hath turned some to apes and swine, and who serveth idols. Such are in worse plight and further astray from the plain road.

قُلْ هَلْ أُنَبِّئُكُمْ بِشَرٍّ مِنْ ذَٰلِكَ مَثُوبَةً عِنْدَ اللَّهِ ۚ مَنْ لَعَنَهُ اللَّهُ وَغَضِبَ عَلَيْهِ وَجَعَلَ مِنْهُمُ الْقِرَدَةَ وَالْخَنَازِيرَ وَعَبَدَ الطَّاغُوتَ ۚ أُولَٰئِكَ شَرٌّ مَكَانًا وَأَضَلُّ عَنْ سَوَاءِ السَّبِيلِ

How should one interpret the two nouns, "*apes*" (*qirada*, sing. *qird*) and swine (*khanāzir*, sing. *khinzir*), mentioned in the last verse?

The first term *qirada* is found three times in the Qur'ānic text, once in this verse and twice in the account of Sabbath in verses 2:65 and 7:166, *And ye know of those of you who broke the Sabbath, how We said unto them: Be ye apes, despised and hated!* (Qur'ān, 2:65).

In this verse, the human condition of transgressing individuals is distorted and perverted to the extent that it resembles the state of these two species of animals. Should one understand these words in a metaphorical sense or in a literal sense? Or should one deduce that certain humans have become apes and swine through a specific degradation, which might enable us to understand why Allah prohibits the consumption of pork? One must note that the root *kh-n-z*—which has given the word *khinzir*, pork, through the addition of the letter r—means "to be bad."

Qur'ān, 5:65. *If only those Familiar with the Scripture would believe and ward off (evil), surely We should remit their sins from them and surely We should bring them into Gardens of Delight.*

وَلَوْ أَنَّ أَهْلَ الْكِتَابِ آمَنُوا وَاتَّقَوْا لَكَفَّرْنَا عَنْهُمْ سَيِّئَاتِهِمْ وَلَأَدْخَلْنَاهُمْ جَنَّاتِ النَّعِيمِ

Qur'ān, 5:66. *If they had observed the Torah and the Gospel and that which was revealed unto them from their Lord, they would surely have been nourished from above them and from beneath their feet. Among them there are people who are moderate, but many of them are of evil conduct.*

وَلَوْ أَنَّهُمْ أَقَامُوا التَّوْرَاةَ وَالْإِنْجِيلَ وَمَا أُنْزِلَ إِلَيْهِمْ مِنْ رَبِّهِمْ
لَأَكَلُوا مِنْ فَوْقِهِمْ وَمِنْ تَحْتِ أَرْجُلِهِمْ ۚ مِنْهُمْ أُمَّةٌ مُقْتَصِدَةٌ ۖ
وَكَثِيرٌ مِنْهُمْ سَاءَ مَا يَعْمَلُونَ

Certain commentators are of the opinion that those familiar with the Scripture (or the people of the Book) who did not observe that which was revealed unto them by their Lord are those who must have had knowledge of the Qur'ān and did not accept it. One may also understand, as we have pointed out in the exegesis of verse 2:62, that this statement regards individuals other than the Jews and the Christians who received a Scripture from Allah, such as the Hindus, the Chinese, etc. It is to be noted that Surah 5 is among the last revelations, more precisely the 112th of 114; however, this Surah comprises verses which are not well-identified chronologically, including verse 5:66. These individuals are said to have benefited from the graces that enwrapped them entirely "from head to toe," to use a metaphoric expression which hopefully conveys this meaning.

The *people who are moderate* (*umma muqtaṣid*) might be that of the last revelation, Islam. The following verse may refer to them: *Thus We have appointed you a middle nation* (*ummat*^an^ *wasat*^an^)*, that ye may be witnesses against mankind, and that the messenger may be a witness against you . . .* (Qur'ān, 2:143).

Qur'ān, 5:67. *O Messenger! Make known that which hath been revealed unto thee from thy Lord, for if thou do it not, thou wilt not have conveyed His message. Allah will protect thee from mankind. Lo! Allah guideth not the disbelieving folk.*

يَا أَيُّهَا الرَّسُولُ بَلِّغْ مَا أُنْزِلَ إِلَيْكَ مِنْ رَبِّكَ ۖ وَإِنْ لَمْ تَفْعَلْ
فَمَا بَلَّغْتَ رِسَالَتَهُ ۚ وَاللَّهُ يَعْصِمُكَ مِنَ النَّاسِ ۗ إِنَّ اللَّهَ لَا
يَهْدِي الْقَوْمَ الْكَافِرِينَ

This verse implies that the Revelation is far from being complete because the Prophet-Messenger Muḥammad must convey the Message. He is immune or protected (*yu'simu-ka*) in order to fully accomplish his Mission against those who are hostile to this new form of revelation. The verbal root of concern is *'a-s-m,* meaning:

to accomplish something by overcoming obstacles, to move away, to prevent, to preserve, to keep intact, to protect, to safeguard, to immunize, and to render infallible.

> Qur'ān, 5:68. *Say O People of the Scripture! Ye have naught [of guidance] till ye observe the Torah and the Gospel and that which was revealed unto you from your Lord. That which is revealed unto thee [Muḥammad] from thy Lord is certain to increase the contumacy and disbelief of many of them. But grieve not for the disbelieving folk.*

قُلْ يَا أَهْلَ الْكِتَابِ لَسْتُمْ عَلَىٰ شَيْءٍ حَتَّىٰ تُقِيمُوا التَّوْرَاةَ وَالْإِنْجِيلَ وَمَا أُنْزِلَ إِلَيْكُمْ مِنْ رَبِّكُمْ ۗ وَلَيَزِيدَنَّ كَثِيرًا مِنْهُمْ مَا أُنْزِلَ إِلَيْكَ مِنْ رَبِّكَ طُغْيَانًا وَكُفْرًا ۖ فَلَا تَأْسَ عَلَى الْقَوْمِ الْكَافِرِينَ

> Qur'ān, 5:69. *Lo! those who believe, and those who are Jews, and Sabaeans, and Christians—Whosoever believeth in Allah and the Last Day and doeth right—there shall no fear come upon them neither shall they grieve.*

إِنَّ الَّذِينَ آمَنُوا وَالَّذِينَ هَادُوا وَالصَّابِئُونَ وَالنَّصَارَىٰ مَنْ آمَنَ بِاللَّهِ وَالْيَوْمِ الْآخِرِ وَعَمِلَ صَالِحًا فَلَا خَوْفٌ عَلَيْهِمْ وَلَا هُمْ يَحْزَنُونَ

In verse 5:68, the phrase *that which is revealed unto thee* concerns the Prophet Muḥammad. We can also understand from the expression *unto thee* (*ilay-ka*) that every believer can be called upon by this verse. If one relates the expression *that which is revealed unto thee* with the one that precedes it, *that which was revealed unto you* (*plural*), then the latter concerns the Qur'ān during its revelation. If this rapprochement does not occur, then the second phrase would concern other communities that have already received a Scripture from Allah. The commentators have been divided on the interpretation of this verse due to the polyvalence of the context's meaning.

Verse 5:69 takes up again the content of verse 2:62 in a very similar fashion.

> Qur'ān, 5:72. *They surely disbelieve who say: Lo! Allah is the Anoint, son of Mary. The Anoint [himself] said: O Children of Israel, worship*

Allah, my Lord and your Lord. Lo! whoso ascribeth partners unto Allah, for him Allah hath forbidden the garden. His abode is the Fire. For evil-doers there will be no helpers.

لَقَدْ كَفَرَ الَّذِينَ قَالُوا إِنَّ اللَّهَ هُوَ الْمَسِيحُ ابْنُ مَرْيَمَ ۖ وَقَالَ الْمَسِيحُ يَا بَنِي إِسْرَائِيلَ اعْبُدُوا اللَّهَ رَبِّي وَرَبَّكُمْ ۖ إِنَّهُ مَنْ يُشْرِكْ بِاللَّهِ فَقَدْ حَرَّمَ اللَّهُ عَلَيْهِ الْجَنَّةَ وَمَأْوَاهُ النَّارُ ۖ وَمَا لِلظَّالِمِينَ مِنْ أَنْصَارٍ

The beginning of this verse is identical to the start of verse 5:17, which we have already commented upon. The Messiah addresses the Children of Israel who expected his coming and for whom he was sent. In the second part of the verse, Allah calls him "Messiah," or the person who asks the Children of Israel to serve and worship Allah as Lord—for them, him, and for every other being. In the Qur'ān, the Lord is always placed in relation with the servant and the servant with his own Lord. The name Lord is always placed in the state of annexation with another reality, as we have already indicated: He is the Lord of the heavens and the earth, your Lord, my Lord. In the sacred text, one never finds the word "Lord" without the universal article "the Lord" (*al-Rabb*). Each servant therefore has a Lord who always represents the essential, permanent aspect of the ephemeral and serving being which is attached to Him in a relationship of reciprocity. In the expression "serve Allah," Allah is envisaged in His divine Function at the degree of Unity. He is not envisaged in His absolute Essence because that is beyond all relationships.

The term *janna*, translated as "garden," comes from the verbal root *j-n-n* which comprises the meanings: covering, wrapping, enveloping, hiding, obscuring, being possessed, becoming mad, possessing, covering oneself in plants, and taking hold of. In the Qur'ānic language, the Garden is a hidden, covered place which is inaccessible to those whom Allah has not covered with His Grace, and who have not been possessed by either His Grace or by Him. The disbeliever (*kāfir*) is he who dismisses or does not allow himself to be penetrated by the divine Presence within himself, due to his darkened individual condition that lacks the illumination of the light of the Grace. Whoever associates any other entity with Allah remains open to all the dispersing influences. These influences will progressively disintegrate his being and then will obscure it by removing its luminous centre and principle.

> Qur'ān, 5:73. *They surely disbelieve who say: Lo! Allah is the third of three; when there is no Allah save the One Allah. If they desist not from so saying a painful doom will fall on those of them who disbelieve.*

لَقَدْ كَفَرَ الَّذِينَ قَالُوا إِنَّ اللَّهَ ثَالِثُ ثَلَاثَةٍ ۘ وَمَا مِنْ إِلَٰهٍ إِلَّا إِلَٰهٌ وَاحِدٌ ۚ وَإِنْ لَمْ يَنْتَهُوا عَمَّا يَقُولُونَ لَيَمَسَّنَّ الَّذِينَ كَفَرُوا مِنْهُمْ عَذَابٌ أَلِيمٌ

Although the Christians are not mentioned in this verse, the verses before and after it denote them in particular.

Allah as absolute Essence is beyond all relationships, and consequently He cannot partake in a set of entities because that would place a condition upon Him. To assert the number three is to posit a relational set.

If one refers to Christian dogma, the "*three*" concerns the Three Persons of the Trinity: the Father, the Son, and the Holy Spirit, united threefold in one and the same Divinity, and thus forming a relational set. If one of the Persons were to disappear, then the other two would disappear as well. In certain creedal formulations, the "Father" is likened to God, while elsewhere He is presented differently. Thus, there are two main creedal formulations: 1) a tripartite creed in which God is the Father and the First of the Three: "*I believe in one God, the Father; I believe in one Lord, Jesus Christ, wholly one with the Father; I believe in the Holy Spirit, who is also Lord, one with the Father and the Son;*" and 2) a four-part creed, in which God represents the Unity of the Divine Essence. This creed does not specify whether He is the synthesis of the Three, or beyond the Three with no possible correlation amongst them: "*I believe in one God: the Father, the Son, and the Holy Spirit.*"

In the Qur'ān there are several instances of formulae in which beings are referred to as the *fourth of the three*. Lesser and greater numbers are also evoked. For example, *Hast thou not seen that Allah knoweth all that is in the heavens and all that is in the earth? There is no secret conference of three but He is their fourth, nor of five but He is their sixth, nor of less than that or more but He is with them wheresoever they may be; and afterward, on the Day of Resurrection, He will inform them of what they did. Lo! Allah is Knower of all things* (Qur'ān, 58:7). However, in this verse the Qur'ānic text does not detail the doctrinal or dogmatic content of the formula "Allah is the Third of three" (*inna Llāha thālithu thalāthatin*). The meaning of the text is extrapolated and distorted when this element is translated, as some have done: "Allah is the third of a triad," or "God is the third of a trinity," or "God is the third of the Trinity," or "Allah is the Third of *the* Three."

Surah 18, The Cave (*al-Kahf*), provides another conceptual level: *[Some] will say: They were three, their dog the fourth, and [some] say: Five, their dog the sixth, guessing at random; and [some] say: Seven, and their dog the eighth. Say: My Lord is Best Aware of their number. None knoweth them save a few. So contend not concerning them except with an outward contending, and ask not any of them to pronounce concerning them* (Qur'ān, 18:22).

In addition, let us point out that our translation of the Qur'ānic term *ilāh* as "worshiped god" takes into account its root *'a-l-h* which fundamentally means "to worship as God (or god)," and has a secondary meaning "to be in amazement, to save oneself, to take refuge, or to protect." The reader may refer to the first chapter of the present work, called "On the formula of Divine Unity," in which we have explained the distinction that must be made between Allah and *ilāh*. The reader may also consult our translation of Fakhr al-Dīn al-Rāzī's *Traité sur les Noms divins* (Beirut: Albouraq, 2000), pp. 213ff.

Qur'ān, 5:74. *Will they not rather turn unto Allah and seek forgiveness of Him? For Allah is Much-concealing, Merciful.*

أَفَلَا يَتُوبُونَ إِلَى اللَّهِ وَيَسْتَغْفِرُونَهُ ۚ وَاللَّهُ غَفُورٌ رَحِيمٌ

The Divine Name *al-Ghafūr*, which we have translated as "All Covering," comes from the verbal root *gh-f-r* connoting the following meanings: to cover (*sitr*), to conceal faults or sins, to not let something appear, to hide, to dye something, to disappear. It is very often rendered as Forgiving. The root *gh-f-r* is very close to that which forms the word *k-f-r* (hide, cover), which we have already encountered. The former differs from the latter only in its first radical, although *gh* is phonetically quite close to the letter *k*. The last two verses, 5:73 and 5:74, comprise the same root *k-f-r*. This convergence of very close meanings, both related to the notion of hiding or veiling, is remarkable in this context wherein the reality of the Anoint, Son of Mary is concealed by various abstract features, whether in isolated or group form, and thereby conducive to multiple interpretations of the reality of the Messiah, Jesus, Son of Mary.

> Qur'ān, 5:75. *The Anoint, son of Mary, was no other than a messenger, messengers [the like of whom] had passed away before him. And his mother was a saintly woman. And they both used to eat [earthly] food. See how We make the revelations clear for them, and see how they are turned away!*

مَا الْمَسِيحُ ابْنُ مَرْيَمَ إِلَّا رَسُولٌ قَدْ خَلَتْ مِنْ قَبْلِهِ الرُّسُلُ
وَأُمُّهُ صِدِّيقَةٌ ۖ كَانَا يَأْكُلَانِ الطَّعَامَ ۗ انْظُرْ كَيْفَ نُبَيِّنُ لَهُمُ
الْآيَاتِ ثُمَّ انْظُرْ أَنَّىٰ يُؤْفَكُونَ

For a more elaborated commentary on the term messenger (*rasūl*), see the commentary on verse 4:171.

In the verse *The Anoint, son of Mary, was no other than a messenger . . .* , is the name qualifying Jesus not the same as the one given to him by Allah in the verse we commented on earlier, 4:171, *Messiah, Jesus son of Mary, messenger of Allah*? In the first case, the name Jesus is mentioned in this manner only in verse 5:72, an earlier verse from the same sequence. Other differences in formulation appear in the two expressions we refer to in the following table.

For the sake of clarity, we compare the following elements of verses 5:75 and 4:171.

Verse	1	2	3	4	5	6	7
a) 5:75	mā	al-Masīh^{u}		Ibn^{u} Maryam^{a}	illā	rasūl^{un}	
	not	the Anoint		the Son of Mary	but	a messenger	
b) 4:171	innamā	al-Masīh^{u}	'Īsā	Ibn^{u} Maryam^{a}		rasūl^{u}	Allāh^{i}
	which is	the Anoint	Jesus	the Son of Mary		the Messenger	of Allah
The words in gray are common to both verses, and the flexional endings are in superscript.							

The name "*Masīh*" was given to him even before his human manifestation, as we had the occasion to explain in our commentaries on the four names attributed to him (al-Masīh, 'Īsā, Ibn, and Maryam, from verses 2:87 and 3:45). *Masīh* is a name describing function but also a name showing his dual traits, on one hand evoking his godliness in verse 3:59, and on the other hand eluding to his humanity as "Son of Mary." Thus he is one of the messengers that God Himself sent, as well as one of God's Words: *And the angels called to him as he stood praying in the sanctuary: Allah giveth thee glad tidings of [a son whose name is] John, [who cometh] to confirm a word from Allah lordly, chaste, a prophet of the righteous* (Qur'ān, 3:39). *[And remember] when the angels said: O Mary! Lo! Allah giveth thee glad tidings of a word from him, whose name is the Messiah, Jesus, son of Mary, illustrious in the world and the Hereafter, and one of those brought near [unto Allah]* (Qur'ān, 3:45).

In verse 4:171, the Anoint is designated by his full name, *the Anoint, Jesus, Son of Mary*. He is the Messenger of Allah, just as the Prophet Muḥammad is the Messenger of Allah, because the act of transmitting the Message corresponds to the acquisition of the universal character. Therefore each Messenger is the Messenger of Allah. We have shown this universality of the function of the Messenger in our commentary on the formula, *Muḥammad (is) the Messenger of Allah* (*Muḥammadun Rasūlu Allah*).

In the following table, we present the different names attributed to Jesus and to Mary. No word that God mentions is ever arbitrary, particularly in the Qur'ān, but each word always presents a necessary character. This must be remembered if one is to perform an exceptional exegesis that considers each element of a given verse. One must also take into account the mutual coherence of the verses, even though it may be difficult to reach a definitive understanding of the Divine subject merely by meditating on it. The complex Qur'ānic discourses on Jesus are obviously a case in question.

Different names attributed to Jesus and his mother

46 verses	al-Masīh	'Īsā	ibn	Maryam	Wa Ummu-hu	Ibn Allāh
2:87		'Īsā	ibn	Maryam		
2:136		'Īsā				
2:253		'Īsā	ibn	Maryam		
3:36				Maryam		

3:37				Maryam		
3:42				Maryam		
3:43				Maryam		
3:44				Maryam		
3:45				Maryam		
3:45	al-Masīh	ʻĪsā	ibn	Maryam		
3:52		ʻĪsā				
3:55		ʻĪsā				
3:59		ʻĪsā				
3:84		ʻĪsā				
4:156				Maryam		
4:157	al-Masīh	ʻĪsā	ibn	Maryam		
4:163		ʻĪsā				
4:171	al-Masīh	ʻĪsā	ibn	Maryam		
4:171				Maryam		
4:172	al-Masīh					
5:17	al-Masīh		ibn	Maryam	wa Ummu-hu	
5:17	al-Masīh		ibn	Maryam		
5:46		ʻĪsā	ibn	Maryam		
5:72	al-Masīh		ibn	Maryam		
5:72	al-Masīh					
5:75	al-Masīh		ibn	Maryam		
5:78		ʻĪsā	ibn	Maryam		
5:110		ʻĪsā	ibn	Maryam		
5:112		ʻĪsā	ibn	Maryam		
5:114		ʻĪsā	ibn	Maryam		
5:116		ʻĪsā	ibn	Maryam		
6:85		ʻĪsā				
9:30	al-Masīh					Ibn Allah
9:31	al-Masīh		ibn	Maryam		
19:16				Maryam		
19:27				Maryam		
19:34		ʻĪsā	ibn	Maryam		
23:50			ibn	Maryam	wa Ummu-hu	
33:7		ʻĪsā	ibn	Maryam		
42:13		ʻĪsā				
43:57			ibn	Maryam		
43:63		ʻĪsā				
57:27		ʻĪsā	ibn	Maryam		
61:6		ʻĪsā	ibn	Maryam		
61:14		ʻĪsā	ibn	Maryam		
66:12				Maryam		
Total	11	25	23	34	2	1

The Frequency of the Names Attributed to Jesus and Mary

Frequency and names			
3	al-Masīh	9	ʻĪsā
13	ʻĪsā Ibn Maryam	1	Ibn Maryam
1	Ibn Maryam wa Ummu-hu	3	al-Masīh Ibn Maryam
3	al-Masīh ʻĪsā ibn Maryam	1	al-Masīh Ibn Maryam wa Ummu-hu
1	al-Masīh ibn Allah	11	Maryam

Jesus Mentioned with Other Prophets
The numbers in brackets indicate chronology

2:87	(10) Moses—(20) Jesus, Son of Mary
2:136	(4) Abraham—(6) Ishmael—(7) Isaac—(8) Jacob—12 Tribes —(10) Moses—(20) Jesus—prophets
3:59	(1) Adam—(20) Jesus
3:84	(4) Abraham—(6) Ishmael—(7) Isaac—(8) Jacob—12 Tribes —(10) Moses—(20) Jesus—prophets
4:163	(2) Noah—prophets after him—(4) Abraham—(6) Ishmael —(7) Isaac—(8) Jacob—12 Tribes—(20) Jesus—(17) Job —(16) Jonas—(11) Aaron—(13) Solomon—(12) David (Zabūr)
5:78	(12) David—(20) Jesus, Son of Mary
6:85-86	(4) Abraham—(7) Isaac—(8) Jacob—(2) Noah—(12) David —(13) Solomon—(17) Job—(9) Joseph—(10) Moses —(11) Aaron—(18) Zachariah—(19) Yaḥyā (20) Jesus —(14) Eliah—(6) Ishmael—(15) Elijah—(16) Jonas—(5) Lot
33:7	(2) Noah—(4) Abraham—(10) Moses—(20) Jesus, Son of Mary
42:13	(2) Noah—(4) Abraham—(10) Moses—(20) Jesus
57:26-27	(2) Noah—(4) Abraham—prophecy/messengers —(20) Jesus, Son of Mary

In the verse 5-75 (above) Mary, the mother of Jesus is described in the superlative "very truthful" The verbal root *s-d-q* of this noun bears the idea of the spontaneous offering of oneself or of one's possessions, without reservation. Hence the meanings of: being true, sincere, truthful, genuine, loyal, frank, carry out, accomplish, increase faith in someone.

Regarding this same verse, certain Muslim commentators have suggested that Mary could be a "prophetess" (*nabiyya*). They reference the following verse from a later chapter: *And Mary, daughter of 'Imrān, guarded the chastity of her body, therefore We breathed therein something of Our Spirit. And she put faith in the words of her Lord and His scriptures, and was of the obedient* (Qur'ān, 66:12). In addition, these same commentators quote three verses in support of their likening Mary to a prophet. In these verses, the two qualities of prophetess and truthful one are directly and inseparably related. *Joseph! O thou truthful one! Expound for us the seven fat kine which seven lean were eating and the seven green ears of corn and other [seven] dry, that I may return unto the people, so that they may know* (Qur'ān, 12:46). *And make mention in the Scripture of Abraham. Lo! he was a truthful one, a prophet* (Qur'ān, 19:41). *And make mention in the Scripture of Idrīs. Lo! he was a truthful one (ṣiddīq), a prophet* (Qur'ān, 19:56).

When Allah specifies that *both* (the Messiah, Son of Mary, and Mary) *ate the food*, He wishes to show that both, and especially the Messiah, Son of Mary, partook wholly of the human nature, although they did so in exceptional conditions, given their outstanding qualities.

In *Observe how We make them discern the signs . . .* the pronoun "them" is in the plural and not in the dual, thereby referring to the Christians referenced in verse 5:73. This passage could allude to certain elements of verse 4:157, which we have commented upon earlier.

Qur'ān, 5:76. *Say: Serve ye in place of Allah that which possesseth for you neither hurt nor use? Allah it is Who is the Hearer, the Knower.*

قُلْ أَتَعْبُدُونَ مِنْ دُونِ اللَّهِ مَا لَا يَمْلِكُ لَكُمْ ضَرًّا وَلَا نَفْعًا ۚ
وَاللَّهُ هُوَ السَّمِيعُ الْعَلِيمُ

"*Say*" is addressed first of all to the Prophet Muḥammad and then to each believer. The expression "*min dūni Llāhi*," which we have translated as "*in place of Allah*," includes the noun *dūn* in the role of a preposition. The verbal root *d-w-n* means: to be inferior, to be vile, or to be contemptible. The Qur'ānic terms deriving from *dūn* have the connotation of something base or inferior. Taking into account the preposition *min*—which indicates the point of departure or origin in time and space, the relationship, or the beginning—we might conclude that the expression *min dūni* takes the following meanings: beside, below, instead of, to the exclusion of, apart from, minimizing, and smaller than. In all these meanings, the expression emphasizes that other realities are adopted beside or instead of Allah who is thereby depreciated or underestimated in favor of creatures that are taken for gods (*ilāh*, pl. *āhila*). This amounts to associating others with God and adopting idolatry. One deduces, especially in the next part of the verse, that Allah is the Supreme Actor and that His servants must be continually conscious that the Divine Author acts through His creatures in order to realize His Work.

Let us note that the two Divine Names, the All-Hearing (*al-Samī'*), and the All-Knowing (*al-'Alīm*) used here in an absolute sense stem from the divine Ipseity "Him," which is placed next to the Name *Allah.*

Qur'ān, 5:77. *Say: O ye Familiar with the Scripture! Stress not in your religion other than the truth, and follow not the vain desires of folk who erred of old and led many astray, and erred from a plain road.*

قُلْ يَا أَهْلَ الْكِتَابِ لَا تَغْلُوا فِي دِينِكُمْ غَيْرَ الْحَقِّ وَلَا تَتَّبِعُوا أَهْوَاءَ
قَوْمٍ قَدْ ضَلُّوا مِنْ قَبْلُ وَأَضَلُّوا كَثِيرًا وَضَلُّوا عَنْ سَوَاءِ السَّبِيلِ

All those who are thoroughly "Familiar with the Scripture" might certainly be representatives of the communities in possession of a Book, a Scripture, or any other verbal or written announcement of divine origin, but in this context the term refers to Jews and Christians with such bent. The Qur'ān is not addressed exclusively to individuals and communities contemporaneous to the Prophet; it also addresses all those who might nourish themselves with the Scripture until the end of the human cycle, whether they are Muslims or not. God's order that people not submit to vain desires is universal and should not be interpreted to exclude any category of persons.

Qur'ān, 5:78. *Those of the Children of Israel who covered the faith were cursed by the tongue of David, and of Jesus, son of Mary. That was because they rebelled and used to transgress.*

لُعِنَ الَّذِينَ كَفَرُوا مِنْ بَنِي إِسْرَائِيلَ عَلَىٰ لِسَانِ دَاوُودَ
وَعِيسَى ابْنِ مَرْيَمَ ۚ ذَٰلِكَ بِمَا عَصَوْا وَكَانُوا يَعْتَدُونَ

Those who have covered or concealed the faith among the children of Israel are those Hebrews and Jews who did not follow the Law revealed to Moses. This is the same law to which the prophet-king David and Jesus, Son of Mary, adhered. The Old Testament and the New Testament include several references to this attitude of disobedience.

> *Hold not thy peace, O God of my praise; for the mouth of the wicked and the mouth of the deceitful are opened against me: they have spoken against me with a lying tongue. They compassed me about also with words of hatred; and fought against me without a cause. For my love they are my adversaries: but I [give myself unto] prayer. And they have rewarded me evil for good, and hatred for my love.*

See also Matthew, Chapter 23, in which Jesus throws the anathema to the hypocritical scribes and Pharisees, and to the blind, unwise and perverted leaders.

Qur'ān, 5:79. *They restrained not one another from the wickedness they did. Verily evil was that they used to do!*

كَانُوا لَا يَتَنَاهَوْنَ عَنْ مُنْكَرٍ فَعَلُوهُ ۚ لَبِئْسَ مَا كَانُوا يَفْعَلُونَ

Qur'ān, 5:80. *Thou seest many of them making friends with those who disbelieve. Surely ill for them is that which they themselves send on before them: that Allah will be wroth with them and in the doom they will abide.*

تَرَىٰ كَثِيرًا مِنْهُمْ يَتَوَلَّوْنَ الَّذِينَ كَفَرُوا ۚ لَبِئْسَ مَا قَدَّمَتْ لَهُمْ
أَنْفُسُهُمْ أَنْ سَخِطَ اللَّهُ عَلَيْهِمْ وَفِي الْعَذَابِ هُمْ خَالِدُونَ

Qur'ān, 5:81. *If they believed in Allah and the Prophet and that which is revealed unto him, they would not choose them for their friends. But many of them are of evil conduct.*

وَلَوْ كَانُوا يُؤْمِنُونَ بِاللَّهِ وَالنَّبِيِّ وَمَا أُنْزِلَ إِلَيْهِ مَا اتَّخَذُوهُمْ أَوْلِيَاءَ وَلَٰكِنَّ كَثِيرًا مِنْهُمْ فَاسِقُونَ

In verse 5:80, the commentators share the general opinion that those "making friends" or "allying themselves" (*yutawallawna*) were the polytheists of the time of the Prophet Muḥammad who banded with the Jewish or Christian communities against him and his Companions.

These few verses summarize the hostile attitude of three communities (namely the polytheists, the Jews, and the Christians) who were established mainly in Medina and Mecca. They opposed the Prophet in order to undermine the nascent community of believers organized under the aegis of the Messenger of Allah in the city of Medina, formerly called Yathrib. This hostility was so intense and tenacious that the principal issue was the permanence or superiority of the respective communities. In verse 3:61 we noted the divine assistance that the Prophet enjoyed, surrounded by the immediate members of his noble family who assembled before the Christian delegation from Najrān.

Qur'ān, 5:82. *Thou wilt find the most vehement of mankind in hostility to those who believe [to be] the Jews and the idolaters. And thou wilt find the nearest of them in affection to those who believe [to be] those who say: Lo! We are Christians. That is because there are among them priests and monks, and because they are not proud.*

لَتَجِدَنَّ أَشَدَّ النَّاسِ عَدَاوَةً لِلَّذِينَ آمَنُوا الْيَهُودَ وَالَّذِينَ أَشْرَكُوا ۖ وَلَتَجِدَنَّ أَقْرَبَهُمْ مَوَدَّةً لِلَّذِينَ آمَنُوا الَّذِينَ قَالُوا إِنَّا نَصَارَىٰ ۚ ذَٰلِكَ بِأَنَّ مِنْهُمْ قِسِّيسِينَ وَرُهْبَانًا وَأَنَّهُمْ لَا يَسْتَكْبِرُونَ

Qur'ān, 5:83. *When they listen to that which hath been revealed unto the messengers, thou seest their eyes overflow with tears because of their recognition of the Truth. They say: Our Lord, we believe. Inscribe us as among the witnesses.*

وَإِذَا سَمِعُوا مَا أُنْزِلَ إِلَى الرَّسُولِ تَرَىٰ أَعْيُنَهُمْ تَفِيضُ مِنَ الدَّمْعِ مِمَّا عَرَفُوا مِنَ الْحَقِّ ۖ يَقُولُونَ رَبَّنَا آمَنَّا فَاكْتُبْنَا مَعَ الشَّاهِدِينَ

Qur'ān, 5:84. *How should we not believe in Allah and that which hath come unto us of the Truth. And [how should we not] hope that our Lord will bring us in along with righteous folk?*

وَمَا لَنَا لَا نُؤْمِنُ بِاللَّهِ وَمَا جَاءَنَا مِنَ الْحَقِّ وَنَطْمَعُ أَنْ يُدْخِلَنَا رَبُّنَا مَعَ الْقَوْمِ الصَّالِحِينَ

Qur'ān, 5:85. *Allah hath rewarded them for that their saying—Gardens underneath which rivers flow, wherein they will abide forever. That is the reward of the good.*

فَأَثَابَهُمُ اللَّهُ بِمَا قَالُوا جَنَّاتٍ تَجْرِي مِنْ تَحْتِهَا الْأَنْهَارُ خَالِدِينَ فِيهَا ۚ وَذَٰلِكَ جَزَاءُ الْمُحْسِنِينَ

Qur'ān, 5:86. *But those who disbelieve and deny Our revelations, they are owners of hell-fire.*

وَالَّذِينَ كَفَرُوا وَكَذَّبُوا بِآيَاتِنَا أُولَٰئِكَ أَصْحَابُ الْجَحِيمِ

According to the exegetes of the Qur'ān, certain elements in this sequence refer to the favorable and brotherly welcome extended by the Abyssinian Negus, a Christian king, to the Companions of the Prophet who had migrated to Abyssinia. They followed the Prophet's advice and traveled there to seek refuge from the persecutions suffered by the early Muslims in Mecca at the hands of polytheists hostile to the new religion. Ja'far, a cousin of the Prophet, undertook the ritual recitation of certain verses of Surah 19 (The Chapter of Maryam) before the Negus. This left a very strong and positive impression on the latter regarding the contents of this Surah and the new religion presented therein.

Qur'ān, 5:110. A. *When Allah saith: O Jesus, son of Mary! Remember My favour unto thee and unto thy engenderer;*

B: how I strengthened thee with the holy Spirit, so that thou spakest unto mankind in the cradle as in maturity;

C: and how I taught thee the Scripture and Wisdom and the Torah and the Gospel;

D: and how thou didst shape of clay as it were the likeness of a bird by My permission, and didst blow upon it and it was a bird by My permission,

E: and thou didst heal him who was born blind and the leper by My permission;

F: and how thou didst raise the dead by My permission;

G: and how I restrained the Children of Israel from [harming] thee when thou camest unto them with clear proofs,

H: and those of them who covered the faith exclaimed: This is naught else than mere magic.

إِذْ قَالَ اللَّهُ يَا عِيسَى ابْنَ مَرْيَمَ اذْكُرْ نِعْمَتِي عَلَيْكَ وَعَلَىٰ
وَالِدَتِكَ إِذْ أَيَّدْتُكَ بِرُوحِ الْقُدُسِ تُكَلِّمُ النَّاسَ فِي الْمَهْدِ
وَكَهْلًا ۖ وَإِذْ عَلَّمْتُكَ الْكِتَابَ وَالْحِكْمَةَ وَالتَّوْرَاةَ وَالْإِنْجِيلَ ۖ
وَإِذْ تَخْلُقُ مِنَ الطِّينِ كَهَيْئَةِ الطَّيْرِ بِإِذْنِي فَتَنْفُخُ فِيهَا فَتَكُونُ
طَيْرًا بِإِذْنِي ۖ وَتُبْرِئُ الْأَكْمَهَ وَالْأَبْرَصَ بِإِذْنِي ۖ وَإِذْ تُخْرِجُ
الْمَوْتَىٰ بِإِذْنِي ۖ وَإِذْ كَفَفْتُ بَنِي إِسْرَائِيلَ عَنْكَ إِذْ جِئْتَهُمْ
بِالْبَيِّنَاتِ فَقَالَ الَّذِينَ كَفَرُوا مِنْهُمْ إِنْ هَٰذَا إِلَّا سِحْرٌ مُبِينٌ

Verses 3:42-55 already point to important moments in the mission of Jesus. Certain key phases from his mission appear in the verse sequence 5:110-118. Other verses bring out essential complementary information that enables us to understand different aspects of his apostleship. We have broken down verse 5:110 into eight phrases, labelled A to H, and we shall comment on them in this order.

A: In verse 3:49, it is the *Anoint, Jesus, Son of Mary*—the complete name of Jesus mentioned in 3:45—who speaks in the first person singular. Because the Holy Spirit represented by the Archangel Gabriel strengthens the Spirit, he acts thanks to the Hearing of Allah. In the New Testament, Jesus does the Will of his Father and cannot do anything by himself, as mentioned in John 5:19, 5:30,

8:28, 12:49. For example: *Then answered Jesus and said unto them, Verily, verily, I say unto you, The Son can do nothing of himself, but what he seeth the Father do: for what things soever he doeth, these also doeth the Son likewise.*

In verse 5:110, Allah addresses Jesus, Son of Mary, in the second person singular. The complete name of Jesus is given in verse 3:45 at the moment the Angels announce to Mary the coming of the Word from Allah. Jesus is then referred to as the *Messiah* (*Masīh* or *Anoint*), even before he was conceived. In 3:45 there is a "projection" of what will be ultimately accomplished when the Anoint appears as a perfect man in the world after the intervention of an angelic being. In verses 19:17-21 this being is likened to the human shape of Gabriel, the Angel of Revelation.

Remember (*udhkur*, from the root *dh-k-r*): This root, previously analyzed in 3:37, authorizes this translation which is usually rendered "to mention." Our translation permits us to understand that this mentioning is not a simple retrospection enabling memorization, but rather the use of a faculty that initiates, revives, and activates the process of a primordial spiritual realization in the innermost conscience of the human being. When Allah says "*Remember*," He asks us to recall an essential and permanent knowledge which man must re-actualize.

In the Qur'ānic phrase "O Jesus, Son of Mary," God addresses Jesus through the vocative "O" in order to mark His intimate presence near him through "*My favor unto thee and unto thy engenderer.*" This literal translation of "*wālidati-ka*" as "thy engenderer," or the feminine active participle of the verb meaning to engender and to give birth to a child (*walada*), might mean that Jesus does not cease being engendered by his mother. Jesus, Son of Mary, and his mother (*umm*)—she who conceived, delivered, and raised him—constitute a single, inseparable sign, both standing united in their universal mediation: *And We made the son of Mary and his mother a portent, and We gave them refuge on a height, a place of flocks and water springs* (Qur'ān, 23:50). *And she who was chaste, therefore We breathed into her [something] of Our Spirit and made her and her son a token for [all] peoples* (Qur'ān, 21:91).

B: In verse 2:87 we provided an exegesis of the expression "holy Spirit" (*rūḥ al-qudūs*). From the birth of Jesus, Son of Mary, Allah strengthened or assisted (*ayyada*) him with this holy Spirit. This Spirit is His own and none other than Him, and Jesus is *His*

Word (*kalimatu-Hu*, cf. 4:171). In this element of the verse, the second part *thou spakest unto mankind*... is not separated from the first part, *I strengthened thee with the holy Spirit*, through the coordinating conjunction "and" (*wa*). This is unlike other elements of the verse, which imply that Jesus was capable of speaking from birth given that he is the Spirit of Allah (cf. 4:171) and always assisted by Him. We shall see later, in the commentary on verses 19:29-33, one of the circumstances that made Jesus speak from the cradle in order to prove the innocence of his mother, at her request. Being the Word of Allah, he could express himself like a grown up with fully developed capacities. The term "*kahl*," which we have rendered as "mature," comes from the root *k-h-l* meaning: to attain maturity, to grow fully (a plant, a human), to reach middle age, to be covered in flowers. A human being who is called by this name, *kahl*, is at his full strength.

C: This element of the verse comprises the verb "teach" (*'allama*) conjugated in the perfect tense whereas in 3:48 the same verb is conjugated in the imperfect tense form. This is because the sequence including 3:48 speaks about the annunciation of the coming of a "Word" communicated to Mary by the congregation of Angels, whereas in verse 5:110 Jesus Son of Mary is already in the course of his mission, and therefore has already received the Scripture, the Wisdom, the Torah, and the Gospel.

D: Jesus, being assisted by the Holy Spirit and himself being the Spirit of Allah, possesses the virtue of returning human beings and other creatures to life by his breath. His breath is none other than Allah's: this Spirit, initially taking the form of the Archangel Gabriel, is doubly invested in the Anoint, Jesus Son of Mary. He is the Spirit of Allah in his principal reality and he also received the Spirit from Gabriel by way of his mother Mary.

D, E, and F: In studying verse 3:49, we have briefly compared certain elements found within it. However these common elements are each made up of notable differences that should be pointed out in the following table.

In the first verse (3:49), under A: it is the Anoint, Jesus, Son of Mary—the complete name of Jesus—who speaks in the first person singular. As Spirit and strengthened by the angelic Spirit he acts through the Hearing of Allah. In the New Testament, Jesus does the will of his Father and cannot do anything by himself, as mentioned in John 5:19, 5:30, 8:28, 12:49. For example: *Then answered Jesus and*

Comparison of Certain Elements in the Two Verses	
verse 3:49	verse 5:110
A: Lo! I fashion for you out of clay the likeness of a bird, and I breathe into it and it is a bird, by Allah's leave.	D: and how thou didst shape of clay as it were the likeness of a bird by My permission, and didst blow upon it and it was a bird by My permission
B: I heal him who was born blind, and the leper,	E: and thou didst heal him who was born blind and the leper by My permission
C: and I revive (*uḥyī*) the dead, by Allah's leave.	F: and how thou didst resuscitate (*tukhriju*) the dead by My permission;

said unto them, Verily, verily, I say unto you, The Son can do nothing of himself, but what he seeth the Father do: for what things soever he doeth, these also doeth the Son likewise. In the Qur'ānic verse 5:110, it is one of the names of Jesus—Jesus Son of Mary—whom Allah addresses in the second person of the singular.

In 3:49, the form of the bird becomes a living bird by Jesus breathing into it (*nafakha*); emphasis is placed on the bird fashioned by Jesus, even though one could understand the whole phrase "form of the bird" to comply with the masculine ending in accordance with the word "*bird*," which is masculine in Arabic. In verse 5:110, labelled D, the agreement is with the word "form," which is feminine in Arabic.

In part B of verse 3:49, Jesus does not add "with the permission of Allah" as in part D of verse 5:110. One may therefore deduce that he acts either by himself—in perfect presence with Allah—or again that both elements B and C of the verse are related and must not be dissociated. The two kinds of miracles occur with the permission of Allah; Jesus, being "the Word of Allah" (cf. 4:171), is always acting with His approval.

In part C of verse 3:49, the verb conjugated in the first person singular is *ḥ-y-y*, to live, which is used here in the fourth verbal form: to revive, to invigorate, to bring back to life. In point F) of verse 5:110, the verb used in the fourth verbal form comes from the root *kh-r-j* meaning: to bring out, to expel, to withdraw, and to resuscitate. One may translate this part of the verse as "*You bring out the dead . . ."*

G: The evident proofs (*bayyināt*) are not only the miracles he accomplishes, as Allah states, but they also consist of the teachings he spreads among the Children of Israel in his role as the perfect *connoisseur* of Scriptures and holder of wisdom.

H: Those who have buried the faith or who have not recognized the true Mission of Jesus have considered his Message and the conclusive signs thereof as manifestations of an individual order that are subject to interferences from inferior forces.

Qur'ān, 5:111. *And when I inspired the disciples, [saying]: Believe in Me and in My messenger, they said: We believe. Bear witness that we have surrendered [unto Thee] "we are muslims."*

وَإِذْ أَوْحَيْتُ إِلَى الْحَوَارِيِّينَ أَنْ آمِنُوا بِي وَبِرَسُولِي قَالُوا
آمَنَّا وَاشْهَدْ بِأَنَّنَا مُسْلِمُونَ

The expression "disciples" (*ḥawāriyyūn*) was previously discussed in connection with verse 3:52. In the verse above, it is Allah Himself who inspires or reveals to those who were close to Jesus and followed him in preaching faith in Allah and His Messenger, Jesus, the Son of Mary. The quality of these individuals is illustrated by the fact that Allah Himself addresses them with the word. However, one may understand from this verse that the disciples mentioned here had been surprised by certain unusual comportments of the Messenger. He brought some modifications to the Mosaic Law and performed spectacular miracles, but their profound faith in him could not be disputed. Before whom did these disciples ask God to witness their submission to the divine Order? Certain Muslim commentators are of the opinion that they asked Jesus to testify that they submitted to him. Thus they were prepared, both in their innermost consciousness and in an act of integral faith, to ask him to perform a new capital miracle: bringing down a table-spread (*mā'ida*) from heaven.

Qur'ān, 5:112. *When the disciples said: O Jesus, son of Mary! Is thy Lord able to send down for us a table spread with food from heaven? He said: be wary of Allah, if ye are true believers.*

إِذْ قَالَ الْحَوَارِيُّونَ يَا عِيسَى ابْنَ مَرْيَمَ هَلْ يَسْتَطِيعُ رَبُّكَ أَنْ
يُنَزِّلَ عَلَيْنَا مَائِدَةً مِنَ السَّمَاءِ ۖ قَالَ اتَّقُوا اللَّهَ إِنْ كُنْتُمْ مُؤْمِنِينَ

In regards to this demand made by the disciples of Jesus, Son of Mary, it is of great importance that it specifies being wary of Allah and not of their Lord. Does this relate to the foundation of the Last Supper or the institution of the Eucharist by Jesus? Which would become the primordial sacrificial rite in the new form of Revelation? Let us emphasize that this request made of Jesus by his disciples concerns his Lord and not Allah. By "Lord" of a being one must understand the essential Principle belonging to this being and whose human aspect is to be servant. In the case of Jesus, his is a perfect servant (*'abd Allah*). The lordly reality of Jesus, which is particular to him, had to be universalized so that his immediate disciples and the members of the future Community could be nourished and realize their return to God through his mediation. With the disciples' unwavering faith in Jesus and in his Mission being beyond question, they were certain, according to most of the commentators, that their demand would be fulfilled. They possessed the profound conviction that the sending down from heaven of this Table-Spread was of utmost importance and would bring them many graces. They believed that Jesus wished for it to reach them so that they might reap its potential rewards both in the immediate future and thereafter.

The expression "be wary of Allah" can also be understood as instructing one to abstain from posing questions since Jesus has the knowledge of what he must do in accordance with the Will of his Lord at the opportune moment. It may also be that the disciples had intuition of the Divine plan in this regard. In verse 5:111, Allah had previously gratified them with the revelation of certain words to which they responded with an act of faith in God and in His Messenger.

Qur'ān, 5:113. (They said:) *We wish to eat thereof, that we may satisfy our hearts and know that thou hast spoken truth to us, and that thereof we may be witnesses.*

قَالُوا نُرِيدُ أَنْ نَأْكُلَ مِنْهَا وَتَطْمَئِنَّ قُلُوبُنَا وَنَعْلَمَ أَنْ قَدْ
صَدَقْتَنَا وَنَكُونَ عَلَيْهَا مِنَ الشَّاهِدِينَ

The disciples wished that this Table-Spread would descend from heaven, but most of all they desired to be nourished by the gift from God therein. This celestial nourishment could only bring them additional graces corresponding with the totalizing reality of the Messenger of Allah from which they had already benefited and should delight them on this occasion. There must have been unrest in the hearts of the disciples as they sensed his imminent disappearance from this world.

The Arabic expression *ṣadaqta-nā*, which we have rendered as "*thou hast spoken truth to us*," uses the first verbal form derived from the root *ṣ-d-q*, meaning: to be truthful in something, to be sincere, to say the truth, to have faith in someone's word, to fulfil, to accomplish, to acquit, to keep (one's word). For instance, it is said *ṣadaqa-a Llāhu wa'da-Hu* (God has fulfilled his promise regarding you). Such is the disciples' trust in God whose mouthpiece is Jesus, the confirmer (*musaddiq*, active participle of the second form of the same root, *ṣ-d-q*) of Scriptures. Just like every messenger of Allah (cf. 3:81, 5:46, 5:48, and 61:6), they add to the beginning of the phrase "*qad*," meaning well and good." Thus the expression *qad ṣadaqta-nā* may also be translated "*thou has fulfilled us well and good*," in addition to our first translation "thou hast spoken truth to us well and good." The polysemy of this root allows us to enrich the translation of this expression.

The importance of this Table-Spread to them and its celestial food is reinforced by the Qur'ānic expression *that thereof* (the Table-Spread) *we may be witnesses*. Indeed, the witness is one who has seen, noted, and experienced something outwardly as well as inwardly, and who communicates this knowledge to others, or who meditates on it in order to draw a lesson, or an enlightenment for himself and/or the others. It is quite clear that one cannot sincerely witness something which has no real existence or which is false. Therefore we can conclude that the coming down of this Table-Spread was an essential sign for Jesus, for the disciples immediately around him, and for the future members of the Community he founded. The following verse confirms and clarifies this reflection.

> Qur'ān, 5:114. *Jesus, son of Mary, said: O Allah, Lord of us! Send down on us a table spread with food from heaven, that it may be a festive recurrence for us, for the first of us and for the last of us, and a sign from Thee. Give us sustenance, for Thou art the Best of sustainers.*

قَالَ عِيسَى ابْنُ مَرْيَمَ اللَّهُمَّ رَبَّنَا أَنْزِلْ عَلَيْنَا مَائِدَةً مِنَ السَّمَاءِ تَكُونُ لَنَا عِيدًا لِأَوَّلِنَا وَآخِرِنَا وَآيَةً مِنْكَ ۖ وَارْزُقْنَا وَأَنْتَ خَيْرُ الرَّازِقِينَ

Jesus Son of Mary grants the request of his disciples and addresses God directly with the aid of formulae that are worthy of consideration: "*Allāhumma*" and "Lord of us" (*Rabba-nā*).

1. "Allāhumma"

This Divine Name of invocation has perplexed the Qur'ānic commentators. Although they have easily identified the first part—"Allah"—the second part has posed many problems for them. These problems are, among other things, of a linguistic order. Therefore they have divided the expression into two very distinct elements: *Allah* and *umma*. The latter term, "*umma*," is identified as originating from the verbal root *'a-m-m*: to turn towards, make for, intend, march in front, to be at the head, give one's example, to be an aid, to be a mother. "*Umma*" is therefore the imperative of this verb: turn (towards us), be (our) aid. In this interpretation, *Allāhumma* would mean: *Allah, turn* (towards us). The second part *umma* can also be understood as signifying the mother, the maternal principle, the primordial source, the prototype, the origin, the producer, and the head. *Allāhumma* would then mean "Allah-Principle," or "Allah-Producer," the mother being considered the productive principle which gives birth to beings in significant numbers, or in a limitless number when it comes to the divine Prototype. The feminine, maternal Principle is envisaged here as producing while it is "impregnated" by the masculine Principle, which then results in a whole process of manifestation and creation. Let us point out in passing that the following words deriving from the root *'a-m-m*: *umma*, meaning community or mother; and *ummiy*, meaning one who is unlettered like a newborn and projected into existence without distinctive knowledge. *Ummiy* essentially means virgin from all knowledge, just like Prophet Muḥammad was when he received the Revelation.

2. "*Rabba-nā*"

This expression means "Lord of us," or "He who concerns us," as we have already noted several times. He represents the principal aspect of the servant of God, as Lord and servant are two inseparable and correlative notions. The word *rabb* comes from a root connoting the following meanings: to master, educate, to be master, chief, lord, to have control of, exercise authority, gather, unite, arrange, elevate, possess. *Rabb* therefore means: master, lord, and educator, he who teaches with authority and competence, a possessor.

3. "SEND DOWN ON US"

The preposition "on" (*'alā*) indicates that this Table-Spread comes from on high and that it reaches each of those present at this scene (or "supper"). It means that the spread is incorporated therein and the food is celestial, as we saw earlier.

4. "A FEAST" (*'ĪD*)

The term "*'īd*" is generally translated as "feast." However, its verbal root *'a-y-d* did not initially comprise this meaning. It instead meant to come and go, or to return in a recurring way. It is related to the verbal root *'a-w-d*, meaning: come back, return, reintegrate, restart, repeat, make a habit, etc. This term has ended up signifying "feast" because the latter often connotes a regularly occurring event of commemoration. In this context, we might draw a parallel with the Eucharist instituted by the Anoint just before Allah called him to Himself, as indicated by verse 5:117 below. The Anoint is permanently present in the Eucharist, as implied by the rest of the verse: "*for the first of us and for the last of us . . . .*" Thus the feast is perpetuated in each mass by the priest who is substituted for the Messiah.

5. "FOR THE FIRST OF US AND FOR THE LAST OF US"

This expression applies to the Messiah and to the first disciples, and subsequently to all those who are part of—and those who will be part of—the Community which Jesus founded until the end of time. The pronoun "us" indicates that Jesus remains present among the Christian community and that he cannot be dissociated from it.

6. "*A SIGN FROM THEE*"

The noun "*āya*," pl. "*āyāt*," has no verbal root. It is classified differently by the lexicons. Most of them relate it to the root *'a-w-y* despite the fact that it does not derive from this etymology. The meanings of the term "*āya*" are diverse, but it can be translated as the following: a sign or indicator of something, all manifested reality, presence of God in His manifestation, celestial sign, verse of the Qur'ān, and portent. In view of the polysemy of this word and the sequence in which it appears, one may conclude that this "sign" is an epiphany of God, an exceptional divine presence which is imposed within the framework of this Community founded by the Messenger of Allah, the Anoint, Jesus, Son of Mary.

7. "GIVE US SUSTENANCE"

Although God is "*the Best of sustainers,*" He is the Sustainer par excellence and everything in existence, without exception, receives its sustenance only from Him. The spiritual provision He provides in this case comes from a privileged divine status with a view to the salvation of a certain community.

> Qur'ān, 5:115. *Allah said: Lo! I send it down for you. And whoso disbelieveth of you afterward, him surely will I punish with a punishment wherewith I have not punished any of (My) creatures.*

قَالَ اللَّهُ إِنِّي مُنَزِّلُهَا عَلَيْكُمْ ۖ فَمَنْ يَكْفُرْ بَعْدُ مِنْكُمْ فَإِنِّي
أُعَذِّبُهُ عَذَابًا لَا أُعَذِّبُهُ أَحَدًا مِنَ الْعَالَمِينَ

Allah grants the purposeful request of the disciples, thus making giving it a necessity. However, due to the considerable gravity of this request and its consequences, Allah warns those who would become ungrateful or betray this divine "sign." The sign represents a remarkable grace. Its rejection would be inevitably sanctioned by a specific punishment, although that punishment would not be inflicted upon those belonging to other forms of revelation.

> Qur'ān, 5:116. *And when Allah saith: O Jesus, son of Mary! Didst thou say unto mankind: Take me and my mother for two gods instead of Allah? he saith: Be glorified! It was not mine to utter that which did not seem as truth to me. If I used to say it, then Thou knewest it. Thou knowest what is in my soul, and I know not what is in Thy Soul. Lo! Thou, only Thou, art the Knower of Things Hidden?*

وَإِذْ قَالَ اللَّهُ يَا عِيسَى ابْنَ مَرْيَمَ أَأَنْتَ قُلْتَ لِلنَّاسِ اتَّخِذُونِي
وَأُمِّيَ إِلَٰهَيْنِ مِنْ دُونِ اللَّهِ ۖ قَالَ سُبْحَانَكَ مَا يَكُونُ لِي أَنْ
أَقُولَ مَا لَيْسَ لِي بِحَقٍّ ۚ إِنْ كُنْتُ قُلْتُهُ فَقَدْ عَلِمْتَهُ ۚ تَعْلَمُ مَا فِي
نَفْسِي وَلَا أَعْلَمُ مَا فِي نَفْسِكَ ۚ إِنَّكَ أَنْتَ عَلَّامُ الْغُيُوبِ

1. The Gospel

Revealed to Jesus, the Gospel prescribes the worship of one God to the exclusion of other divinities similar to idols. Thus, in the texts of the New Testament one does not find Jesus asking to be considered alongside his mother as two gods instead of the one Allah. Moreover, "Maryolatry" has never been a regular theological position of the Church, and whenever this attitude of worship developed it was condemned. In the Catholic and Orthodox churches, Mary is placed above other saints. For an even stronger reason she is also above other servants; worshippers nurse a cult called "hyperdulia" in her name because she is the servant *par excellence* without challenging the worship of God or substituting Him. In its eighth verbal form developed from the primitive verb *'akhadha*—meaning to take, to seize, to attribute—the verb *ittakhadha* means: to take by choosing, to opt, to choose, to adopt, etc. We have already encountered it verse 2:116 where it was translated as "to attribute."

The term "*ilāhayni*," or "two gods," has been rendered in accordance with the terminology of its root, *'a-l-h*, meaning to worship as god (or God). We have already presented this word in the study devoted to the two part profession of faith in Divine Unity included at the beginning of the present work.

The expression *instead of* (*min dūni-Hi*) has been dealt with in the commentary on verse 5:76.

2. "Be glorified!" (*subhana-Ka*)

The expression *subhana* has already been dealt with in the commentary on verse 4:171. Here, Jesus proclaims the transcendence of God as well as His immanent Presence in which everything subsists and everything bears witness to this subtle but real Presence. Through this exclamation, Jesus affirms implicitly the simultaneity of the seemingly opposed Divine Names through which God asserts His transcendence as well as His immanence. Thus Allah is the Inward while being the Outward: *All that is in the heavens and the earth glorifieth Allah; and He is the Mighty, the Wise. His is the Sovereignty of the heavens and the earth; He quickeneth and He giveth death; and He is Able to do all things. He is the First and the Last, and the Outward and the Inward; and He is Knower of all things* (Qur'ān, 57:1-3). He is the First without ceasing to be the Last, just as He is the Outward while being the Inward: these pairs of seemingly opposed Divine Names are pure relationships and cannot be envisaged without each other. This is so because the Real (*al-Ḥaqq*) comprises all reality and nothing is found outside of Him.

3. IT WAS NOT MINE TO UTTER THAT WHICH DID NOT SEEM AS TRUTH TO ME (*BI-ḤAQQI*)

According to this part of the verse, Jesus only spoke the truth and by divine necessity, for the term "*ḥaqq*"—translated here as "*truth*"—can also mean "*necessity*." It comes from the root *ḥ-q-q*, meaning to prevail by right, to owe, to make necessary, to be due, to know with certainty, to become sure of something, to be right, to realize oneself. *Ḥaqq* is therefore that which is true, real, truth, right, duty, certainty, and necessity. Al-Ḥaqq is also one of the 99 Divine Names (cf. Ar-Râzî, *Traité sur les noms divins*, pp. 497ff.). Furthermore, the Anoint, Jesus, Son of Mary, is the Word of Allah (*kalimatu-Hu*) and when he speaks, it is Allah who expresses Himself in him and through him (cf. 4:171).

4. *IF I USED TO SAY IT, THEN THOU KNEWEST IT.*

It was therefore impossible for Jesus to make such statements about himself and his mother. Moreover, nothing in the Gospels suggests that he pronounced such words.

5. *THOU KNOWEST WHAT IS IN MY SOUL, AND I KNOW NOT WHAT IS IN THY SOUL*

This part of the verse can also be translated as "*Thou knowest what is in myself, and I know not what is in Thyself*" because in Arabic the word *nafs* serves as a reflexive pronoun. In addition, Jesus Son of Mary, being subject to the conditions of the human economy, remained tributary to this soul: "*And Jesus increased in wisdom and stature, and in favour with God and man*" (Luke 2:52). He also experienced certain vicissitudes throughout his brief career. Although his miraculous engenderment conferred on him clear charisma, such as speaking from the cradle and performing miracles, he himself specifically stated his lack of knowledge about certain events such as the arrival of the Hour: "*But of that day and hour knoweth no [man], no, not the angels of heaven, but my Father only*" (Matthew 24:36 and Mark 13:32). "*O my Father, if it be possible, let this cup pass from me! . . .*" (Matthew, 26:39) He also refused to attribute certain divine qualities to himself: "*And a certain ruler asked him, saying, Good Master, what shall I do to inherit eternal life? And Jesus said unto him, Why callest thou me good? none [is] good, save one, [that is], God . . .*" (Luke 18:18-19, Mark 10:17-18).

These verses of the New Testament raise the difficult question, What is the soul? In Qur'ānic and classical Arabic, the word "*nafs*," usually translated as "soul," comes from the verbal root *n-f-s.* This root comprises the following notions: the influence one exerts on someone through breathing or looking, respiration with its four phases (inspiration, apnea, expiration, and rest), aspire, relieve, console, be precious. The term "nafs" is feminine in Arabic and means: soul (integrated or in relationship with a substrate), animated substance, spirit which takes form, or an individual being in its different modalities of expression. By extension, it also connotes the vital principle, blood (of life), and the true self of someone or oneself. In French, the word "*âme*" is related to an Indo-European root *ane* meaning "breathing" or "vital breath." In Greek *anemos* means "the wind" and in Latin *anima* means vital breath. The word "animal" comes from this word.

It is interesting to note that in the Qur'ān the notion of the soul is never a philosophical notion of the soul deprived of matter. The sacred text is concerned with the integrated soul, the soul which always evolves within a particular substance appropriate to its intrinsic quality. Several wrappings or layers envelope the soul, to in accordance with the worlds and the degrees the must take on.

Of the 298 Qur'ānic occurrences of the root *n-f-s*, only three are conjugated:

> –One is in the fifth verbal form with the meaning of respirating, exhaling a breath, opening out, being relieved, to shine, etc: *And when the pages are laid open, and when the sky is torn away, and when hell is lighted, and when the Garden is brought nigh, [then] every soul will know what it hath made ready. Oh, but I call to witness the planets, the stars which rise and set, and the close of night, and the dawn as it breathes away the darkness* (Qur'ān, 81:10-18).
>
> –Two are in the sixth form, meaning: to aspire ardently,

to enter in competition, etc: *Thou wilt know in their faces the radiance of delight. They are given to drink of a pure wine, sealed, whose seal is musk—for this let [all] the aspirers aspire (fal-yatanāfas al-mutanāfisūna)* (Qur'ān, 83:23-26).

What does the word *nafs* imply in the Qur'ān?

A—When the word nafs is determined or undetermined and it concerns the human being

I. When the word *nafs* is determined and it concerns the human being

a - *We verily created man and We know what his soul whispereth to him, and We are nearer to him than his jugular vein* (Qur'ān, 50:16).

b - *I do not exculpate myself. Lo! the* (*human*) *soul enjoineth unto evil, save that whereon my Lord hath mercy. Lo! my Lord is Forgiving, Merciful* (Qur'ān, 12:53).

c - *Nay, I swear by the self-blaming soul* (Qur'ān, 75:2). *O thou soul at peace! Return unto thy Lord, content in His good pleasure! Enter thou among My bondmen! Enter thou My Garden!* (Qur'ān, 89:27-30).

d - *He said: My Lord! Lo! I have wronged my soul, so forgive me. Then He forgave him. Lo! He is the Forgiving, the Merciful* (Qur'ān, 28:16).

The word "*nafs*" is also mentioned numerous times in the plural: the standard plural *anfus* occurs 153 times and the dual form *nufūs* occurs twice:

e - *When the souls are sorted out in couples (wa 'idhā al-nufūs zuwwijat); There hath come unto you a messenger, [one] <u>of yourselves</u>, unto whom aught that ye are overburdened is grievous, full of concern for you, for the believers full of pity, merciful* (Qur'ān, 9:128).

f - *And when thy Lord brought forth from the Children of Adam, from their reins, their seed, and made them testify of <u>themselves</u>, [saying]: Am I not your Lord? They said: Yea, verily. We testify. Lest ye should say at the Day of Resurrection: Lo! of this we were unaware* (Qur'ān, 7:172).

g - *No blame is there upon the blind nor any blame upon the lame nor any blame upon the sick nor on <u>yourselves</u> (anufi-him) if ye eat from your houses . . . But when ye enter houses, salute one another with a greeting from Allah, blessed and sweet . . .* (Qur'ān, 24:61).

In these representative Qur'ānic examples chosen from among

numerous others, the word "soul," in the singular as well as in the plural, is related to the human being himself/herself and to his/her individual nature. Moreover, the soul also corresponds to different characteristics, both positive and negative, which define it both in its psychological and corporeal individual constitution and in its numerous activities. In other words, the soul is tributary to a body that it animates. In addition, this term has acquired the connotation of a reflexive pronoun, for example: my soul, i.e. myself. In English it corresponds to the two words *soul* and *self*: *my soul, myself.*

What is the support needed by the soul after death? We find no answer to this in the numerous verses dealing with the soul in the Qur'ān.

NB. It is rather remarkable that the words designating the animate or inanimate body are limited to three in the Qur'ānic context and are rarely employed:

1. "*Jism*," pl. "*ajsām*," is mentioned twice in the Qur'ānic text and means stature, appearance, or voluminous body. This noun is related to the verbal root *j-s-m*, meaning to be or become large, voluminous, expansive, massive, or considerable:

> *Their Prophet said unto them [the children of Israel]: Lo! Allah hath raised up Saul to be a king for you. They said: How can he have kingdom over us when we are more deserving of the kingdom than he is, since he hath not been given wealth enough? He said: Lo! Allah hath chosen him above you, and hath increased him abundantly in wisdom and stature. Allah bestoweth His Sovereignty on whom He will. Allah is All-Embracing, All-Knowing* (Qur'ān, 2:247).

> *And when thou seest them their figures please thee; and if they speak thou givest ear unto their speech. [They are] as though they were blocks of wood in striped cloaks. They deem every shout to be against them. They are the enemy, so beware of them. Allah confound them! How they are perverted!* (Qur'ān, 63:4)

2. "*jasad*," sing. and pl., occurs four times in the Qur'ān and means animated body, or flesh. It comes from the verbal root *j-s-d*: to be attracted, to stick together, to give body, to incarnate:

> *And the folk of Moses, after [he left them], chose a calf [for worship], [made] out of their ornaments, of saffron hue, which gave a*

lowing sound. Saw they not that it spake not unto them nor guided them to any way? They chose it, and became wrong-doers (Qur'ān, 7:148, see also 20:88).

We gave them not bodies that would not eat food, nor were they immortals (Qur'ān, 21:8).

And verily We tried Solomon, and set upon his throne a [mere] body. Then did he repent (Qur'ān, 38:34).

3. "*badan,*" or the pl. "*budn,*" occurs twice in the Qur'ānic corpus and means body, trunk, or sacrificed corpulent victims (at Mina during the pilgrimage). This name comes from the verbal root *b-d-n*: to be/become corpulent.

But this day We save thee in thy body (badan) [of the Pharaoh] that thou mayst be a portent for those after thee. Lo! most of mankind are heedless of Our portents (Qur'ān, 10:92).

And the corpulent beasts (budn)! We have appointed them among the ceremonies of Allah. Therein ye have much good. So mention the name of Allah over them when they are drawn up in lines. Then when their flanks fall [dead], eat thereof and feed the beggar and the suppliant. Thus have We made them subject unto you, that haply ye may give thanks (Qur'ān, 22:36).

II. When the word "nafs" is undetermined and it is attributed to a designated or non designated human being in singular and/or plural

In order to situate this case, let us quote the following verses:

a - *For that cause We decreed for the Children of Israel that whosoever killeth a human being for other than manslaughter or corruption in the earth, it shall be as if he had killed all mankind, and whoso saveth the life of one, it shall be as if he had saved the life of all mankind . . .* (Qur'ān, 5:32).

b - *O my believing servants! Lo! My earth is spacious. Therefore serve Me only. Every soul will taste of death. Then unto Us ye will be returned* (Qur'ān, 29:56-57).

c - *Lo! Allah! With Him is knowledge of the Hour. He sendeth down the rain, and knoweth that which is in the wombs. No soul knoweth what it will earn to-morrow, and no soul knoweth in what land it will die. Lo! Allah is Knower, Aware* (Qur'ān, 31:34).

d - *And a soul (nafs) and Him Who perfected it and inspired it [with conscience of] what is wrong for it and right for it. He is indeed successful who causeth it to grow, and he is indeed a failure who stunteth it* (Qur'ān, 91:7-10).

B—The word "*nafs*" is associated to the epithet "*wāḥida*," unique:

The expression "*nafs wāḥida*" occurs five times in the revealed text, in verses 4:1, 6:98, 7:189, 31:28, and 39:6. It is always in the indeterminate form.

a - *O mankind! Be careful of your duty to your Lord Who created you from a single soul and from it created its mate and from them twain hath spread abroad a multitude of men and women. Be careful of your duty toward Allah in Whom ye claim [your rights] of one another, and toward the wombs [that bare you]. Lo! Allah hath been a watcher over you* (Qur'ān, 4:1).

b - *And He it is Who hath produced you from a single soul, and [hath given you] a habitation and a repository. We have detailed Our revelations for a people who have understanding* (Qur'ān, 6:98).

c - *He it is Who did create you from a single soul, and therefrom did make his mate that he might take rest in her. And when he covered her she bore a light burden, and she passed [unnoticed] with it, but when it became heavy they cried unto Allah, their Lord, saying: If thou givest unto us aright we shall be of the thankful* (Qur'ān, 7:189).

d - *Your creation and your raising [from the dead] are only as [the creation and the raising of] a single soul. Lo! Allah is Hearer, Knower* (Qur'ān, 31:28).

e - *He created you from one soul, then from that [being] He made its mate; and He hath provided for you of cattle eight kinds. He created you in the wombs of your mothers, creation after creation, in a threefold gloom. Such is Allah, your Lord. His is the Sovereignty. There is no Allah save Him. How then are ye turned away?* (Qur'ān, 39:6).

Generally, the Qur'ānic commentators have considered the expression *nafs wāḥida* to apply to Adam and the term *zawj*, or spouse, to refer to Eve (whose name is never mentioned in the Qur'ān). Although this interpretation indeed remains priority, in paragraph c (verse 7:189) some much more open exegeses remain possible. Despite the fact that the different pronouns of reminder create a real difficulty of interpretation and the names of Adam and Eve are not mentioned explicitly in the four other verses quoted, one might nevertheless consider the potential breadth of the word *nafs* and the contexts in which it is found. For example, here it occurs next to the term *wāḥida*, meaning single."

Another interpretation that is less common among many commentators but preferred among the mystics consists of considering the term *nafs* as the reality projected by the Supreme Pen (*qalam al-'alā'*). The Supreme Pen writes everything with an undifferentiated "ink" projected on the completely receptive Guarded Tablet (*lawḥ al-maḥfūẓ*). The Tablet may be likened to the term "*zawj*," meaning spouse or coupled element.

The *nafs wāḥida* is also the "indeterminate Substance" which receives all the individual souls that take shape from it in order to subsist and evolve in a determined plane of existence. All these particularized and parcelled souls are integrated into the corporeal world to form a single community (*umma wāḥida*), or joint (*zawj*) by this Single Substance: *Mankind were but one community; then they differed . . .* (Qur'ān, 10:19).

C—When "nafs" is attributed to Allah

The term *nafs* as it is applied to Allah in verse 5:116 also occurs in five other verses:

> a - *Let not the believers take disbelievers for their friends in preference to believers. Whoso doeth that hath no connection with Allah unless [it be] that ye but guard yourselves against them, taking [as it were] security. Allah biddeth you beware [only] of Himself (nafsa-Hu). Unto Allah is the journeying* (Qur'ān, 3:28).
>
> b - *On the Day when every soul (nafs) will find itself confronted with all that it hath done of good and all that it hath done of evil [every soul] will long that there might be a mighty space of distance between it and that [evil]. Allah biddeth you beware of Him (nafsa-Hu). And Allah is Full of Pity for [His] bondmen* (Qur'ān, 3:30).
>
> c - *Say: Unto whom belongeth whatsoever is in the heavens and the earth? Say: Unto Allah. He hath prescribed for Himself mercy (kataba alā nafsi-Hi ar-Raḥmata), that He may bring you all together to the Day of Resurrection whereof there is no doubt. Those who ruin their souls will not believe* (Qur'ān, 6:12).
>
> d - *And when those who believe in Our revelations come unto*

thee, say: Peace be unto you! Your Lord hath prescribed for Himself mercy, that whoso of you doeth evil through ignorance and repenteth afterward thereof and doeth right, [for him] lo! He is Forgiving, Merciful (Qur'ān, 6:54).

e - . . . *Then camest thou [hither] by [My] providence, O Moses, and I have attached thee to Myself—wa-stana'tu-ka li Nafsī* (Qur'ān, 20:40-41).

Other translations of verses 6:12 and 6:54 are possible when one interprets the terms *kataba* and *raḥma* in a more semantically technical manner:

Kataba 'alā: to write or inscribe on, to record on, to deposit on, to draft on, to register on, to impose on, to deposit on, to destin to, to prescribe to.

Nafsi-Hi: His animated Breath, His animated Substance, His essential nature, His Quintessence, His Reality, and His Active Being.

Raḥma: the root of this word is *r-ḥ-m*, which comprises the notion of the dilatable and retractable place in which the semen is deposited. This corresponds to the actualization of possibilities in accordance with a process of love, hence the notion of womb, or mercy, expansive and retractile love, radiance, and sprouting. The active noun "*raḥma*" implies all these meanings. From this root the word *raḥīm* is formed, the Qur'ānic plural of which is *arḥām*: matrix, uterus, blood relationships, blood kinship (cf. Qur'ān 4:1, *supra*).

The Soul (*nafs*) of Allah in itself, in its intrinsic reality, is identical to His Essence and can therefore have no knowledge at this "degree." The Divine Essence cannot be an object of knowledge, and cannot be qualifiable to be in any way. Knowledge as a divine quality refers to the degree of Unicity and to the Divine Name "the Unique" (*wāḥid*). It cannot be quantified by the degree of the One (*aḥad*) or of Unity in which no divine Name is distinguished, nor—for a stronger reason—by the Divine Essence which does without everything, according to the verse: *And whosoever striveth, striveth only for himself, for lo! Allah is altogether Independent of [His] creatures* (*ghaniyyun 'ani'l-'alamīn*) (Qur'ān, 29:6).

One may approach the last two terms, *nafs* and *raḥma,* with the aid of those examples found in the following prophetic tradition. It is not included in certain collections of ḥadīth but is often quoted by the masters of Sufism: "*Lo, the Breath of the All-Merciful* (*nafas ar-Raḥmān*) *is coming to me from Yemen.*" In this tradition *nafas* differs from *nafs* only by a vocalization on letter f. *Nafas* therefore means, according to one of the meanings of the root *n-f-s* (see supra), the uninterrupted relieving breath that the Prophet of Islam likens metaphorically to the assistance he received from certain Companions, known as the Anṣār. In the Qur'ān, the Prophet is thus qualified: *We sent thee not save as a mercy for the peoples* (Qur'ān, 21:107).

However, al-Raḥmān, the All-Merciful, implies all the Divine Names by virtue of the following verse: *Say [unto mankind]: Cry unto Allah, or cry unto the Beneficent, unto whichsoever ye cry [it is the same]. His are the most beautiful names . . .* (Qur'ān, 17:110). We also find the following verses which show clearly that this Divine Name encompasses even the Names of rigor: *O my father! Lo! I fear lest a punishment from the Beneficent overtake thee so that thou become a comrade of Satan* (Qur'ān, 19:45). *Shall I take [other] gods in place of Him when, if the Beneficent should wish me any harm, their intercession will avail me naught, nor can they save?* (Qur'ān, 36:23).

One must not lose sight of the fact that, first of all, the word *nafs* has the meaning of the living breath which transmits life. Therefore it is directly related to the dynamics of a living being and to its multiple faculties and actions in the domain in which the living breath is called upon.

Lo, Thou art forever Knower of Mysteries

Jesus, Son of Mary could but witness, due to his individual nature, that only God knows the limitless and mysteriously hidden realities concerning His omnipresent Being, present in all the possible corporeal, subtle, spiritual, and cosmic worlds, and whose immensity escapes the human amplitude.

> Qur'ān, 5:117. *I spake unto them only that which Thou commandedst me, [saying]: Worship Allah, my Lord and your Lord. I was a witness of them while I dwelt among them, and when Thou tookest me Thou wast the Watcher over them. Thou art Witness over all things.*

مَا قُلْتُ لَهُمْ إِلَّا مَا أَمَرْتَنِي بِهِ أَنِ اعْبُدُوا اللَّهَ رَبِّي وَرَبَّكُمْ ۚ وَكُنْتُ عَلَيْهِمْ شَهِيدًا مَا دُمْتُ فِيهِمْ ۖ فَلَمَّا تَوَفَّيْتَنِي كُنْتَ أَنْتَ الرَّقِيبَ عَلَيْهِمْ ۚ وَأَنْتَ عَلَىٰ كُلِّ شَيْءٍ شَهِيدٌ

THE ORDER TO WORSHIP ONLY ALLAH

The order of Allah to worship Him, which is addressed to Jesus Son of Mary, is universal and necessary. Two verses which were mentioned in the commentary on verse 2:138 support this assertion: *Thy Lord hath decreed, that ye worship none save Him . . .* (Qur'ān, 17:23). *I created the jinn and humankind only that they might worship Me* (Qur'ān, 51:56). Allah demands that only He be served, but according to the predispositions which reside from eternity in each being He creates. For this reason each of them devote to its Lord and Master the worship to which it is predisposed. Thereby, all beings can but worship Him without choice, and according to verse 7:172 all of them have recognized their Lord in the pre-existential world. It is beneficial and indispensable that Allah evoke this imperative concerning all the descendants of Adam.

THOU TOOKEST ME (*TAWAFFAYTA-NĪ*)

This verb, conjugated here in the accomplished form, has been analyzed in the commentary on verses 3:55 and 3:57. We could also translate it as *when Thou brought me to completion*; that is, when Thou called me to Thyself at the end of a phase of my earthly apostleship. This is why the Divine Name *Shāhid*, or Witness, is substituted by another Divine Name: *Raqīb*, the All-Watcher. *Shāhid* is mentioned in this verse, and the name is also used to qualify Jesus during his mission here-below. The All-Watcher is also the witness who guards with concentration. It is also He who watches attentively without neglecting anything and with the intention to protect. This Divine Name is also mentioned at the end of verse 4:1, translated earlier.

According to the Islamic perspective, Jesus is the last of the prophets before the apostleship of the Prophet Muḥammad, seal of prophets and messengers. Each prophet nevertheless remains present in the extension of the human state until the Day of Resurrection, so that they may always have the possibility of intervening in certain human circumstances. Allah is always omnipresent in His Work: He remains universally the vigilant Witness and the Prophet of Islam will thus be invested with this divine function. *O Prophet! Lo! We have sent thee as a witness and a bringer of good tidings and a warner. And as a summoner unto Allah by His permission, and as a lamp that giveth light* (Qur'ān, 33:45-46). . . . *That ye [mankind] may believe in Allah and His messenger, and may honour Him, and may revere Him, and may glorify Him at early dawn and at the close of day* (Qur'ān, 48:9).

Qur'ān, 5:118. *If Thou punish them, lo! they are Thy slaves, and if Thou forgive them [lo! they are Thy slaves]. Lo! Thou, only Thou, art the Mighty, the Wise.*

إِنْ تُعَذِّبْهُمْ فَإِنَّهُمْ عِبَادُكَ ۖ وَإِنْ تَغْفِرْ لَهُمْ فَإِنَّكَ أَنْتَ الْعَزِيزُ الْحَكِيمُ

In any case, whether God punishes or forgives them, they remain inexorably servants for they are destined with obedience. And if He forgives them, or more precisely, if He covers or conceals them in accordance with the meaning of the root *gh-f-r* (to cover, conceal, or veil [*satara*]), as most of the commentators interpret this word, then this veil is protection and mercy and makes the servants perpetuate in universal Existence. God, in His infinite and perfect Essence, remains beyond all qualification. In His manifestation, which maintains all things in life, He is the Wise who puts each created reality in the place it must assume in accordance with the predisposition He has wished for it.

Qur'ān, 5:119. *Allah saith: This is a day in which their truthfulness profiteth the truthful, for theirs are Gardens underneath which rivers flow, wherein they are secure for ever, Allah taking pleasure in them and they in Him. That is the great triumph.*

قَالَ اللَّهُ هَٰذَا يَوْمُ يَنْفَعُ الصَّادِقِينَ صِدْقُهُمْ ۚ لَهُمْ جَنَّاتٌ
تَجْرِي مِنْ تَحْتِهَا الْأَنْهَارُ خَالِدِينَ فِيهَا أَبَدًا ۚ رَضِيَ اللَّهُ عَنْهُمْ
وَرَضُوا عَنْهُ ۚ ذَٰلِكَ الْفَوْزُ الْعَظِيمُ

SURAH 6

Qur'ān, 6:82. *Those who believe and obscure not their belief by wrongdoing, theirs is safety; and they are rightly guided.*

الَّذِينَ آمَنُوا وَلَمْ يَلْبِسُوا إِيمَانَهُمْ بِظُلْمٍ أُولَٰئِكَ لَهُمُ الْأَمْنُ وَهُمْ مُهْتَدُونَ

Qur'ān, 6:83. *That is Our argument. We gave it unto Abraham against his folk. We raise unto degrees of wisdom whom We will. Lo! thy Lord is Wise, Aware.*

وَتِلْكَ حُجَّتُنَا آتَيْنَاهَا إِبْرَاهِيمَ عَلَىٰ قَوْمِهِ ۚ نَرْفَعُ دَرَجَاتٍ مَنْ نَشَاءُ ۗ إِنَّ رَبَّكَ حَكِيمٌ عَلِيمٌ

Qur'ān, 6:84. *And We bestowed upon him Isaac and Jacob; each of them We guided; and Noah did We guide aforetime; and of his seed [We guided] David and Solomon and Job and Joseph and Moses and Aaron. Thus do We reward the good.*

وَوَهَبْنَا لَهُ إِسْحَاقَ وَيَعْقُوبَ ۚ كُلًّا هَدَيْنَا ۚ وَنُوحًا هَدَيْنَا مِنْ قَبْلُ ۖ وَمِنْ ذُرِّيَّتِهِ دَاوُودَ وَسُلَيْمَانَ وَأَيُّوبَ وَيُوسُفَ وَمُوسَىٰ وَهَارُونَ ۚ وَكَذَٰلِكَ نَجْزِي الْمُحْسِنِينَ

Qur'ān, 6:85. *And Zachariah and John and Jesus and Elias. Each one [of them] was of the righteous.*

وَإِسْمَاعِيلَ وَالْيَسَعَ وَيُونُسَ وَلُوطًا ۚ وَكُلًّا فَضَّلْنَا عَلَى الْعَالَمِينَ

Qur'ān, 6:86. *And Ishmael and Elisha and Jonah and Lot. Each one [of them] did We prefer above [Our] creatures,*

وَإِسْمَاعِيلَ وَالْيَسَعَ وَيُونُسَ وَلُوطًا ۚ وَكُلًّا فَضَّلْنَا عَلَى الْعَالَمِينَ

Qur'ān, 6:87. *With some of their forefathers and their offspring and their brethren; and We chose them and guided them unto a straight path.*

وَمِنْ آبَائِهِمْ وَذُرِّيَّاتِهِمْ وَإِخْوَانِهِمْ ۖ وَاجْتَبَيْنَاهُمْ وَهَدَيْنَاهُمْ إِلَىٰ صِرَاطٍ مُسْتَقِيمٍ

The sequence of the prophets mentioned in these verses is neither complete nor chronological. According to these facts, the presumed historical order of the prophets whose names are found in the Qur'ānic texts would be the following. Reading from left to right, the names in bold belong to the prophets who are not mentioned in the verses above:

Prophets mentioned in the Qur'ān				
Adam	Idrīs (Enoch)	Nūḥ (Noah)	Abraham	Loth (Lūṭ)
Ishmael	Isḥāq (Isaac)	Ya'qūb (Jacob)	Yūsuf (Joseph)	Hud
Shu'ayb (Jethro)	Mūsā (Moses)	Hārūn (Aaron)	Dā'ūd (David)	Sulaymān (Solomon)
Ilyās (Elias)	Alyasa' (Elisha)	Yūnus (Jonas)	Ayyūb (Job)	Dhu al-Kifl (Ezechiel)
Ṣāliḥ	Zachariah	Yaḥyā (John the Baptist)	Jesus ('Īsā)	Muḥammad

Qur'ān, 6:101. *The Originator of the heavens and the earth! How can He have a child, when there is for Him no consort, when He created all things and is Aware of all things?*

بَدِيعُ السَّمَاوَاتِ وَالْأَرْضِ ۖ أَنَّىٰ يَكُونُ لَهُ وَلَدٌ وَلَمْ تَكُنْ لَهُ صَاحِبَةٌ ۖ وَخَلَقَ كُلَّ شَيْءٍ ۖ وَهُوَ بِكُلِّ شَيْءٍ عَلِيمٌ

A child or an engendered or begotten being (*walad*)

The term *walad* has been commented upon in verses 2:87 and 2:116, and in the commentary on the latter verse we listed all the occurrences in which the word *walad* is mentioned but as not accruing to God. Here, the appellation *walad*, or child, is wholly incompatible with the Divine Name "*al-Badī*," or "the Originator," meaning "He who produces something for the first time, without pre-existing model; He with whom none is similar or analogous; He who makes the creatures' primordial separation in an original act" (Cf. al-Rāzī, *Traité sur les Noms divins*, p. 599). The engendered or begotten being always comes from its father and mother, even though it is God Himself who, according to a common and normative process which only He knows, breathes the Spirit and gives life to all created beings.

SURAH 7

Qur'ān, 7:155. *And Moses chose of his people seventy men for Our appointed tryst and, when the trembling came on them, he said: My Lord! If Thou hadst willed Thou hadst destroyed them long before, and me with them. Wilt thou destroy us for that which the ignorant among us did? It is but Thy trial [of us]. Thou sendest whom Thou wilt astray and guidest whom Thou wilt: Thou art our protecting friend, therefore forgive us and have mercy on us, Thou, the best of all who show forgiveness.*

وَاخْتَارَ مُوسَىٰ قَوْمَهُ سَبْعِينَ رَجُلًا لِمِيقَاتِنَا ۖ فَلَمَّا أَخَذَتْهُمُ الرَّجْفَةُ
قَالَ رَبِّ لَوْ شِئْتَ أَهْلَكْتَهُمْ مِنْ قَبْلُ وَإِيَّايَ ۖ أَتُهْلِكُنَا بِمَا فَعَلَ
السُّفَهَاءُ مِنَّا ۖ إِنْ هِيَ إِلَّا فِتْنَتُكَ تُضِلُّ بِهَا مَنْ تَشَاءُ وَتَهْدِي مَنْ
تَشَاءُ ۖ أَنْتَ وَلِيُّنَا فَاغْفِرْ لَنَا وَارْحَمْنَا ۖ وَأَنْتَ خَيْرُ الْغَافِرِينَ

Qur'ān, 7:156. *And ordain for us in this world that which is good, and in the Hereafter [that which is good], Lo! We have turned unto Thee. He said: I smite with My punishment whom I will, and My mercy embraceth all things, therefore I shall ordain it for those who ward off [evil] and pay the poor-due, and those who believe Our signs.*

وَاكْتُبْ لَنَا فِي هَٰذِهِ الدُّنْيَا حَسَنَةً وَفِي الْآخِرَةِ إِنَّا هُدْنَا إِلَيْكَ
قَالَ عَذَابِي أُصِيبُ بِهِ مَنْ أَشَاءُ وَرَحْمَتِي وَسِعَتْ كُلَّ شَيْءٍ
فَسَأَكْتُبُهَا لِلَّذِينَ يَتَّقُونَ وَيُؤْتُونَ الزَّكَاةَ وَالَّذِينَ هُمْ بِآيَاتِنَا يُؤْمِنُونَ

The end of verse 7:156 can be interpreted in two ways:

1) It could be considered related to the verse that follows it, in which case it must be translated: *and who believe in Our signs, and to those who follow the messenger, the primordially-natured Prophet whom they will find described in the Torah and the Gospel* . . . until the phrase *He will enjoin on them* . . .

2) Or, just as in our translation, the intelligible content of the last part of the verse 7:156 which starts *He said: I smite with My punishment* . . . can be considered separate from the first part of the following verse (7:157).

Qur'ān, 7:157. *Those who follow the Messenger, the Prophet of primordial nature, whom they will find described in the Torah and the Gospel [which are] with them. He will enjoin on them that which is right and forbid them that which is wrong. He will make lawful for them all good things and prohibit for them only the foul; and he will relieve them of their burden and the fetters that they used to wear. Then those who believe in him, and honor him, and help him, and follow the light which is sent down with him: they are the successful.*

الَّذِينَ يَتَّبِعُونَ الرَّسُولَ النَّبِيَّ الْأُمِّيَّ الَّذِي يَجِدُونَهُ مَكْتُوبًا
عِنْدَهُمْ فِي التَّوْرَاةِ وَالْإِنْجِيلِ يَأْمُرُهُمْ بِالْمَعْرُوفِ وَيَنْهَاهُمْ عَنِ
الْمُنْكَرِ وَيُحِلُّ لَهُمُ الطَّيِّبَاتِ وَيُحَرِّمُ عَلَيْهِمُ الْخَبَائِثَ وَيَضَعُ عَنْهُمْ
إِصْرَهُمْ وَالْأَغْلَالَ الَّتِي كَانَتْ عَلَيْهِمْ ۚ فَالَّذِينَ آمَنُوا بِهِ وَعَزَّرُوهُ
وَنَصَرُوهُ وَاتَّبَعُوا النُّورَ الَّذِي أُنْزِلَ مَعَهُ ۙ أُولَٰئِكَ هُمُ الْمُفْلِحُونَ

The first mention of *the Messenger, the Prophet of primordial nature* . . . in verse 7:157 would thus refer only to the possessors of these two sacred Scriptures, the Torah and the Gospel, and therefore to those who follow the revelation made to Moses and the revelation made to Jesus, both of whom were messengers (*rasūl*) and prophets (*nabī*) just like the Messenger and Prophet of Allah, Muḥammad.

The second mention of the above expression, in verse 7:158 below, explicitly addresses all human beings without exception. Thus it is not a simple repetition but rather a step forward in the universalization of the last divine Messenger to all humanity—that is, the historical Islam meeting with universal Islam as we explained in the chapter "Universality of Islam."

> Qur'ān, 7:158. *Say: O mankind! Lo! I am the messenger of Allah to you all—[the messenger of] Him unto Whom belongeth the Sovereignty of the heavens and the earth. There is no Allah save Him. He quickeneth and He giveth death. So believe in Allah and His messenger, the Prophet who can neither read nor write, who believeth in Allah and in His Words, and follow him that haply ye may be led aright.*

قُلْ يَا أَيُّهَا النَّاسُ إِنِّي رَسُولُ اللَّهِ إِلَيْكُمْ جَمِيعًا الَّذِي لَهُ
مُلْكُ السَّمَاوَاتِ وَالْأَرْضِ ۖ لَا إِلَٰهَ إِلَّا هُوَ يُحْيِي وَيُمِيتُ ۖ
فَآمِنُوا بِاللَّهِ وَرَسُولِهِ النَّبِيِّ الْأُمِّيِّ الَّذِي يُؤْمِنُ بِاللَّهِ وَكَلِمَاتِهِ
وَاتَّبِعُوهُ لَعَلَّكُمْ تَهْتَدُونَ

Verses 7:155 through 159 are mutually related through enjambment, even though their themes differ. Verse 7:157 and the first part of verse 7:156 concern Moses and his conversation with God, his Lord.

Starting from *I smite with My punishment* (verse 7:156), God's words are no longer addressed specifically to Moses, but they concern all the creatures which are embraced without exception by God's universal mercy. The Prophet of Islam expresses the universal relevance by embodying *raḥma* (mercy), as stated by the following verses: *Whatever of good befalleth thee [O man] it is from Allah, and whatever of ill befalleth thee it is from thyself. We have sent thee [Muḥammad] as a messenger unto mankind and Allah is sufficient as Witness* (Qur'ān, 4:79). *We sent thee not save as a mercy* (*raḥmat^{an}*) *for the peoples* (Qur'ān, 21:107).

In addition, verse 7:158 announces clearly the universal mission of the Prophet: *Lo! I am the messenger of Allah to you all . . .* Yet, all messengers come from Allah Himself as He reveals in His Scripture: *And when there cometh unto them a messenger from Allah, confirming that which they possess, a party of those who have received the Scripture fling the Scripture of Allah behind their backs as if they knew not* (Qur'ān, 2:101).

Because the Messenger is sent to human beings from Allah and is therefore "truth," invested with all the Divine Names, Allah says of him: *How shall Allah guide a people who disbelieved after their belief and [after] they bore witness that the messenger is true and after clear proofs had come unto them. And Allah guideth not wrongdoing folk* (Qur'ān, 3:86). Considering the potent meaning of the word *ḥaqq* as applied to the Prophet, most of the commentators are of the opinion that the term must be uniquely interpreted in this context. In lexicons the normative meaning of *ḥaqq* is, "true, real, reality, truth" but in the case of this verse it should be understood in the sense of "truthful, sincere, loyal" (*ṣadīq*). In our opinion the Prophet is not only sincere but also truthful because he is invested with Truth.

Furthermore, in several verses Allah specifies that the Messenger is among us and in a relationship with us: *And know that the Messenger of Allah is among you. If he were to obey you in much of the government, ye would surely be in trouble; but Allah hath endeared the faith to you and hath beautified it in your hearts, and hath made disbelief and lewdness and rebellion hateful unto you. Such are they who are the rightly guided* (Qur'ān, 49:7). *Even as We have sent unto you a messenger from among you, who reciteth unto you Our revelations and causeth you to grow, and teacheth you the Scripture and wisdom, and teacheth you that which ye knew not* (Qur'ān, 2:151). See verse 23:32 regarding this issue.

In our commentary on verse 2:141 concerning the Prophet Muḥammad, we already suggested some interpretations of the term *ummī* and its relation to the root *'a-m-m* by quoting these very verses, 7:156 and 7:157. In verse 7:156, the term *raḥma* (mercy) is linked indirectly to the Prophet through the verses we just quoted, particularly verse 21:107, and the three verses 7:156-158 which encapsulate the notions of *ummī* and *raḥma*.

The connection of the terms *ummī* and *raḥma* with the Prophet Muḥammad

1. Study of the word *raḥma*.

It comes from the root *r-ḥ-m* which comprises the following meanings: the dilatable and retractable place in which the semen is deposited, which actualizes possibilities in accordance with a process of love, hence the notion of womb, or mercy, expansive and retractile love, radiance, and sprouting—radiating love, having pity, showing mercy, having compassion—and dying after childbirth. The two Divine Names *Raḥmān* and *Raḥīm*, meaning "Infinitely Good" and "All-Merciful" derive from the same root. Let us quote the verse which illustrates this fact well: *Allah knoweth that which every female beareth and that which the wombs absorb and that which they grow. And everything with Him is measured* (*kullu shay'*[in] *'inda-Hu bi-miqdar*[in]) (Qur'ān, 13:8). In another context, the Prophet is also qualified as *raḥīm*: *There hath come unto you a messenger, of yourselves, unto whom aught that ye are overburdened is grievous, full of concern for you, for the believers are full of pity, merciful* (raḥīm). *Now, if they turn away say: Allah sufficeth me. There is no Allah save Him. In Him have I put my trust, and He is Lord of the Tremendous Throne* (Qur'ān, 9:128-129). Thus, this universal mercy or radiating love illustrated by the term *raḥīm*, which is applied to the Prophet, is of the feminine, maternal type. The term *raḥīm* depends on this root: the matrix, womb, or blood relationship becomes the wholly adequate and perfect receptacle of the loving seed (*ḥubb* and *ḥubba*) deposited in the universal Matrix. Applied to realities other than the Prophet, the word *raḥīm* concerns the individual, collective, and universal, which gives rise to a being, to the Universe, to all those entities animated by divine life. For the terms semen, seed, and love are related by a common Arabic and Qur'ānic root, *ḥ-b-b*, which connotes the seed as well as love, creation, and all of creation being produced by and in Love. Thus, *ḥubb* is love and *ḥubba* is the seed or semen, the two terms being interdependent, love producing the semen and the semen containing love in a subtle way in order to develop. There is a verse which mentions both the love of Allah and the Believers and the Prophet: *Say: If ye love Allah, follow me; Allah will love you* (*yuḥibb-kum Allah*) *and forgive you your sins. Allah is Forgiving, Merciful* (*raḥīm*) (Qur'ān, 3:31). For more details on these fundamental and interrelated notions, cf. Ibn 'Arabī's *Le Traité de l'Amour*, translation and commentary by M. Gloton, published in Paris by Albin Michel.

2. Relation between *ummī* and *raḥma*

In discussing the relationship between these two words, it is more appropriate to compare the relation between their two roots *'a-m-m* and *r-ḥ-m*. The three words *raḥīm*, *lawḥ al-raḥim*, and *raḥma*—not to mention of the divine name *Raḥmān*—all derive from the last root and necessarily comprise the common meanings which we identified earlier: to spread, to extend—processes which are analogous with the two active phases of respiration, inspiration, and expiration—depending on a seed of love or a seminal love (*ḥubb* and *ḥubba*) placed in an appropriate receptacle. Yet, with respect to the term *raḥīm*, or matrix, womb, the word *umm* (deriving from the first root *'a-m-m*) means, among others, "mother,"or she who gives birth to a child or a new being, whence the idea of principle, source, and origin. In order to preserve all the very rich symbolism attached to each of the terms *raḥīm*, *umm*, *ḥubb*, and *ḥubba* and the multiple mutual relationships they maintain, we will leave to the reader to draw all the rapprochements which are adequately possible to envisage.

3. The *ummī* Messenger, Prophet in relation to the Torah and the Gospel

Verse 7:155 relates an important episode in the mission of Moses; the other verses, 7:156-158, concern the Prophet Muḥammad according to the prevailing interpretation of the Muslim exegetes; the verses which follow recall anew a few events from the prophetic career of Moses.

We have seen that the notion of *ummī* applied to the prophet Muḥammad endows him with perfect receptivity. This allowed him to be completely open to the Descent of the divine Word upon him without any individual interference which might have distorted the purity of the divine Message—the Word of Allah is weighty in itself and in its modes of transmission which he would receive in his whole being, body, soul, and spirit. For example, consider the verse, *For we shall charge thee with a word of weight* (*Innā sa-Nulqī 'alayka qawl^{an} thaqīl^{an}*) (Qur'ān, 73:5). This verse refers to: (1) the extraordinary density carried by the Divine Word in itself and in its different degrees of universal manifestation, this manifestation being the refracted expression of this Word; and (2) the countless multiplicity of meanings that this Word comprises at all levels. The Prophet, as the appropriate suitable substantiation of this perfect Word, had to possess the necessary sublimity and magnitude to receive the distinguishing qualities of this perfect Word as befitting to him and to then transmit the Word to his Community or universal Matrix (*umma*).

According to verse 7:158, the last Divine Message to date addresses all humanity through the intermediary of the *ummī* Prophet who receives the Scripture and not a scripture: *Alif. Lām. Mīm. This is the Scripture whereof there is no doubt, a guidance unto those who are wary* (Qur'ān, 2:1-2). The three letters of the first verse (*Alif. Lām. Mīm.*) also occur at the beginning of surahs 3, 29, 30, 31, 32. They are considered a divine mystery that cannot be penetrated (see p. 67 of our work *Une approache du Coran par la grammaire et le lexique*, Beirut: Albouraq). This *Kitāb* (Scripture) is that which Allah mentions: *That [this] is indeed a noble Qur'ān in a Book kept hidden which none toucheth save the purified, a revelation from the Lord of the Worlds* (Qur'ān, 56:77-80). On the other hand Allah specifies that: *Allah effaceth what He will, and establisheth [what He will], and with Him is the source of ordinance* (Qur'ān, 13:39). It is from this Hidden Scripture (*kitāb maknūn*), in the possession of Allah, that the "*Noble and generous Qur'ān*" issues. Let us note here that the expression "the Mother," which can be also translated as "the Principle" or "the Source", is related to the already studied root *'a-m-m*. This is why the Qur'ān, or the encompassing Recitation, whose root *q-r-'a* comprises the meanings of recite, read before someone, transmit, gather the scattered parts and unite them, synthesizes all the other forms of divine Revelation and contains the essence of the other revealed Books. The verse which concerns us here transmits in particular the essence of the Torah and the Gospel.

The commentators of the Qur'ān have found passages from the last two Books that allude to the Prophet Muḥammad, even though he is never named explicitly in any of the Testaments that we possess at the present. Some have considered that in verse 61:6, which we shall comment upon later, the name "*Aḥmad*," an elata meaning "very praised," (Aḥmad also being the celestial name of the Prophet) is found in the Gospel of John under the name of "Paraclete" in chapters XIV and XVI, and also in the first epistle of John in II:2 with the meaning "advocate, defender."

SURAH 9

Qur'ān, 9:29. *Fight against such of those who have been given the Scripture as believe not in Allah nor the Last Day, and forbid not that which Allah hath forbidden by His messenger, and follow not the Reli-*

gion of Truth, until they pay the tribute readily, being brought low.

قَاتِلُوا الَّذِينَ لَا يُؤْمِنُونَ بِاللَّهِ وَلَا بِالْيَوْمِ الْآخِرِ وَلَا يُحَرِّمُونَ مَا حَرَّمَ اللَّهُ وَرَسُولُهُ وَلَا يَدِينُونَ دِينَ الْحَقِّ مِنَ الَّذِينَ أُوتُوا الْكِتَابَ حَتَّىٰ يُعْطُوا الْجِزْيَةَ عَنْ يَدٍ وَهُمْ صَاغِرُونَ

This verse closes a sequence whose principal theme refers to the struggle in the path of Allah. We did not quote the last part of the verse because it concerns, *in fine*, the possessors of sacred Scriptures, in contrast to the beginning of this verse which relates to the polytheists or the idolators that were still hostile to the Prophet and to his preaching.

In the countries with a Muslim majority, the status of "non-Muslim" subjects exempts them from both the tithe (*zakāt*) and the military service expected of Muslims. These non-Muslim subjects, excluding women, minors, the elderly, and the destitute, must instead pay the "compensatory head tax" (*jizya*). This status permits them to continue practicing their religion and its respective legislation.

The juridical conditions that determine status are rather complex and vary by country. They are affected by legal rulings and customs pertaining to the contemporary and regional culture. The expression "*wa hum ṣāghirūna*," which we have translated as "*being brought low*," has been interpreted in different ways both by traditional Muslim commentators and translators of the Qur'ān.

In this context, one might ask: how should one understand, in the unitary perspective of Islam, the status of "*those who having been given the Scripture*" follow, more or less in great number, the *Religion of Truth* (din al-Ḥaqq) while keeping their religion of origin? Indeed, the expression *those who, having been given the Scripture, follow not the Religions of Truth* (*wa lā yadīnūna dīna al-Ḥaqq mina al-ladhīna 'ūtū al-kitāb*) poses several problems for the interpretation of the "compensatory head tax" which concerns them. How to distinguish them from those who are not subject to it?

On the other hand, how should one understand "*Din al-Ḥaqq*"? We have rendered it as the *Religion of Truth* but it might also be translated as "Religion of God-the Truth," *al-Ḥaqq* being a Divine Name meaning the Real, the True, the Right Truth, God-Reality, The term "*dīn*" comes from the verbal root *d-y-n*, which we have already explained in the chapter *Universality of Islam*. This root means to become indebted, to owe, to borrow and lend, obligate, subdue, remunerate. The Qur'ānic active noun "*dayn*" from the same root refers to debt, or that which is owed and which falls due. The "Dīn"—usually translated as religion, tradition, remuneration, judgment, royalty—is the worship which God institutes providentially and the subjected servants must carry out, a worship the observance of which they will have to answer toon the Day of Judgment or Remuneration (*yawm al-īn*). The acts of worship constitute channels of grace or lines of force through which divine favors are spread; they are therefore instituted in order for human beings to find, through them, the Presence of God in all His Work, in all His creatures, and to realize their primordial norm in God (*fiṭra*). This divine worship (or service) is imposed on the worshipper as God Himself specifies: *Thy Lord hath decreed, that ye worship none save Him* (Qur'ān, 17:23). *I created the jinn and humankind only that they might worship Me* (Qur'ān, 51:56). Thus, that which Allah means by "Religion of Truth" is clarified: it implies that the servant conforms himself to the sacred prescriptions that God institutes in His Scripture, brought down upon His Messengers-Prophets throughout the human cycle. The last Scripture to date, the Qur'ān, synthesizes all the Forms taken by the Revelation. Muḥammad is therefore the last of the prophets, and an excellent model: *Muḥammad is not the father of any man among you, but he is the messenger of Allah and the Seal of the Prophets; and Allah is ever Aware of all things* (Qur'ān, 33:40). *Verily in the messenger of Allah ye have a good example for him who looketh unto Allah and the Last Day, and remembereth Allah much* (Qur'ān, 33:21).

The expression "Religion of Truth" is therefore often interpreted by the Muslim commentators of the Qur'ān as referring to the historical Islam.

Qur'ān, 9:30. *And the Jews say: Ezra is the son of Allah, and the Christians say: The Messiah is the son of Allah. That is their saying with their mouths. They imitate the saying of those who veiled of old. Allah fighteth against them. How perverse are they!*

وَقَالَتِ الْيَهُودُ عُزَيْرٌ ابْنُ اللَّهِ وَقَالَتِ النَّصَارَى الْمَسِيحُ ابْنُ
اللَّهِ ذَٰلِكَ قَوْلُهُمْ بِأَفْوَاهِهِمْ يُضَاهِئُونَ قَوْلَ الَّذِينَ كَفَرُوا مِنْ

قَبْلُ قَاتَلَهُمُ اللَّهُ أَنَّى يُؤْفَكُونَ

The Qur'ānic text refers to all the Jews (*al-Yahūd* or "those who repent" according to the possible etymology of the root *y-h-d* or *h-w-d*) because it uses "*al-Yahūd*" with the universal article al ("the" in English). The same remark applies to *Naṣārā*, or the Christians. According to the prevailing interpretation, the name "*Nasārā*" can be translated as "helpers," or "those who assist," depending on the general meaning of the root n-ṣ-r. We have commented abundantly on these terms in the study of verse 2:62.

Who is "'Uzayr"?

In commenting on the verses 4:157 and 158, we have alluded incidentally to 'Uzayr. Most of the commentators of the Qur'ān identify him with Esdras according to their interpretation of the already quoted verse 2:259. The subject of the verse is the Resurrection: *Or [bethink thee of] the like of him who, passing by a township which had fallen into utter ruin, exclaimed: How shall Allah give this township life after its death? And Allah made him die a hundred years, then brought him back to life. He said: How long hast thou tarried? [The man] said: I have tarried a day or part of a day. [He] said: Nay, but thou hast tarried for a hundred years. Just look at thy food and drink which have not rotted! Look at thine ass! And, that We may make thee a sign unto mankind, look at the bones, how We adjust them and then cover them with flesh! And when [the matter] became clear unto him, he said: I know now that Allah is Able to do all things* (Qur'ān, 2:259).

According to Muslim commentators, the city in question should be Jerusalem. It was surrounded in 587 BC by the troops of the Babylonian monarch Nabuchodonosor, who destroyed the Temple that King Solomon had erected. In 550 BC, Cyrus King of Persia and later of Babylonia seized power and favored the return of the Jews in Judaea by an edict issued in 538 BC and financed the reconstruction of the Temple, which was completed in 515 BC. Cyrus received the title of "Messiah" as one can read in Isaiah 45:1, *Thus saith the Lord to his anointed, to Cyrus, whose right hand I have holden . . .* In order to further illustrate the status of King Cyrus, called "Messiah," we shall also quote this text from the Book of Ezra in the Old Testament: *Now in the first year of Cyrus king of Persia, that the word of the Lord by the mouth of Jeremiah might be fulfilled, the Lord stirred up the spirit of Cyrus king of Persia, that he made a proclama-*

tion throughout all his kingdom, and [put it] also in writing, saying: "Thus saith Cyrus king of Persia, The Lord God of heaven hath given me all the kingdoms of the earth; and he hath charged me to build him a house at Jerusalem, which [is] in Judah." (I: 1-2).

The very name of Esdras is the Hellenized form of the Hebrew word "Ezrah," or the Aramaic term "Ezra," and these words of Semitic origin comprise the same consonants '*a-z-r* as the Qur'ānic word "Uzayr." According to the Book of Ezra of the Old Testament, 'Uzayr, a priest and scribe of the temple of the Persian king Artaxerxes (465-423), was a descendant of the prophet Aaron. He was versed in the Law of Moses and a learned interpreter of the commandments of Yahve and the legislation concerning Israel. He was scribe for all Jewish matters in the court of the king. He was appointed by him to reform the religion, and to break the marriages between Jews and foreigners. One may suppose that the exceptional knowledge that 'Uzayr received from God in order to readjust the Law of Moses to the new cyclic conditions affecting the people of Israel lies at the origin of the naming of Ezra ('Uzayr) as "*son of God*" (*'Uzayr, ibn Allah*). According to this hypothesis, and in the absence of historical documents, the expression "*the son of God*" can only have a metaphorical meaning within the framework of Mosaic Law. It cannot have a literal meaning in accordance with a Christian interpretation concerning the Anoint, Jesus.

In verse 2:259, envisaged to speak of 'Uzayr by the majority of the commentators, this person to whom Allah speaks—and who is therefore considered His interlocutor—constitutes alone "a Sign unto mankind." In this way, this "Sign" must have been perceived as indubitable and extraordinary, and he must have led the people of his period to such an immediate evidence that God gratified him with an exceptional favour and the Qur'ān called him 'Uzayr ('Ezra) "*the Son of God.*" Yet, Allah blames those who call 'Uzayr "*the Son of Allah.*" The key notion is that "Son" is not legitimately applicable to God *qua* Divine Essence—which excludes all relationships and is beyond all association or modality—but rather concerns a relational "degree" which necessitates a father in order for there to be a son, and vice-versa.

Al-Masīh ibn Allāh

In the case of 'Uzayr we have only hypotheses to explain the title given to him by Allah in this verse. As for Jesus, on the other hand, we have numerous references indicating that this name was given to him in the New Testament as well as in Christian dogma. In the verse discussed here, the term "*son*" attributed to Jesus cannot have only a metaphorical meaning considering the blame that Allah attaches to these statements made by the "*Naṣārā*." However, the metaphorical expression "son of God" is found many times in the Old Testament.

In the Islamic Revelation, the term "Father" is never applied to God because the notion of fatherhood requires a necessary correlation between father and son. In this relationship one cannot exist without the other. The only exception to this rule is Adam, the first man, who was created by God without the intermediary of a father and from whom the first spouse issued forth. This observation is valid not only for God—*qua* the Divine Essence that surpasses everything and refuses any relationship in itself: *O mankind! Ye are the poor in your relation to Allah. And Allah! He is the Absolute, the Owner of Praise* (Qur'ān, 35:15). . . . *And Allah is the Rich, and ye are the poor* (Qur'ān, 47:38); *Allah is Self-sufficient, above any need of the worlds* (Qur'ān, 3:97)—but also for the divine Function at the source of all modalities of relationships. Even the most primordial modalities stem from the divine Function, and it rejects, in the Qur'ānic terminology, all notions of filiation or paternity that are applied to Him.

The term *Dhāt*, usually translated as "essence," is considered a demonstrative. In the Qur'ānic text it is encountered several times in both the masculine (*dhū*) and the feminine (*dhāt*) and means: 1) possessor, master, gifted with, who belongs to oneself; 2) he who (*dhū*), or she who (*dhāt*). In this sense, it is a word of allusive designation. To express *al-Dhāt* is to make an allusion (*ishāra*) to he who either does not want to, or is not able to, apprehend through any of the usual linguistic means. *Al-Dhāt* therefore designates the unfathomable, the indescribable, the indefinable, and the absolute Mystery. Nevertheless, we recognize that the word "essence," derived from the Latin present participle "essens" of the verb "esse = to be" and whose Indo-European origin seems to be "es" = "to be found," has acquired diverse philosophical and theological connotations in the West. These connotations do not convey the allusive value of the Arabic term *dhāt*, especially since there is no Arabic equivalent to the verb "to be," as a copula, in the Western linguistic tradition. The Arabic verb *kāna* (root *k-w-n*) means: to exist, to happen, to become, to take place, to be found, etc. In order to translate into Arabic derivatives of the verb "to be"—namely the Latin *esse* or Greek *eimi* that generates the term *oussia*, or essence—the translators from the time of the caliph al-Ma'mūn (167-218/783-833) used the active noun *wujūd* instead of the derivatives of the Arabic root *k-w-n*. *Wujūd* derives from the verbal root *w-j-d*, meaning to be found, to find, to observe, to discover, or to experience.

It is important to note that the term *ibn* in the Qur'ānic context acquires a positive meaning in contrast to the term *walad*. *Walad* denotes the child, the begotten being, or progeny, and is used both for the son and the daughter. It thus takes on a collective meaning. We have already mentioned the difference between the qualification and status of the two nouns "*ibn*" and "*walad*" in our commentary on verse 2:87.

Here, however, the term *ibn* portrays a derogatory meaning because of the fact that it is linked in a direct and real way with Allah. He discredits such a description as to specify "*Allah fighteth against them. How perverse are they!*"

Some historical points on the name "Anoint, Son of Allah"

In French, as in most Western languages of Indo-European origin, the name of God gives rise to confusion: does it refer to God, the supreme, unqualified and indescribable Essence, or God as the origin of universal creation, who is omnipresent and who therefore takes on (assumes) inner and outward relationships?

Except for this verse in which the Anoint, or the Messiah, is in a direct relationship of filiation with the Name Allah, other verses in which Jesus, Son of Mary is mentioned use the noun *ilāh*, meaning a worshiped god (or God), or God who reveals Himself. *Ilāh* is used in the following verses: 4:171, 5:73, 5:116, 9:31, and 29:46. We have given several Qur'ānic examples in which the two Names *Allah* and *ilāh* are interpreted differently in the chapter entitled "On the Formula of Divine Unity." Even though these two nouns are both applied to God in various Qur'ānic contexts, the Name "Allah" concerns the Divine Essence (*al-Dhāt*) as well as His Universal Function (*Ulūhiyya*), as we have seen many times. The same difficulty is encountered in Christian theology, where the name of "God" receives multiple meanings depending on the context. However, certain spiritual masters, such as Meister Eckhart (~1260-1327) and those belonging to his school, made a distinction between the "Deity" and "God." The Deity is an absolute Essence that is beyond the Trinitarian perspective, beyond all relationships, whereas "God" is at the degree of Divine Unicity (*wāḥidiyya*), in which the internal relationships are already envisaged. Moreover, the name *ilāh* in the Qur'ān designates God at the degree of His Unicity as well as realities which are worshiped, like the idols or even a human being *who maketh his caprice his god* (Qur'ān, 45:23).

Two readings are also possible according to the two formulations of the Christian creed, as we previously noted in the commentary on verse 5:73. The two formulations are: (1) the Symbol of the Apostles, and (2) the Symbol of Nicea-Constantinople of Roman Missal. According to this double interpretation, God is both independent of and transcends the three Persons of the Trinity and their common divine Nature.

Symbol of Apostles	Symbol of Nicea-Constantinople (Roman Missal)
(1) I believe in God the Father, All-powerful, creator of the heaven and the earth [God is the Father]	(0) I believe in only one God, [affirmation of the independent Divine nature, then the 3 Persons, in relation to their diversity, mentioned below] (1) the All-powerful Father, creator of the heaven and the earth.
(2) and in Jesus-Christ, his only Son, our Lord . . . (*Saviour*)	(2) I believe in only one Lord, Jesus-Christ, the only Son of God . . . (*Saviour*)
(3) I believe in the Holy (Sanctifying) Spirit	(3) I believe in the Holy (Sanctifying) Spirit

cf. François Bousquet, *La Trinité*, Paris: Atelier, 2000, pp. 16ff; and Jean Bezançon, *Dieu n'est pas solitaire*, Paris: Desclée de Brouwer, 1999, pp. 47ff.

"... *That is their saying with their mouths* ..."

This expression can potentially comprise several meanings. The two principal ones are:

1) These are words that, while occurring literally in the Torah and the Gospel, are interpreted to the letter.

2) These statements are but formulae with a dogmatic echo which are repeated mechanically by most of the followers.

"... THEY IMITATE THE SAYING ..."

This expression comes from both the root *d-h-'a* and the closely-related root *d-h-y*. *D-h-y* in the third verbal form is found only once in the Qur'ānic text. It means to resemble, to compare, to imitate, to be analogous, to correspond, and to forge.

Who are those who have used formulations like those of the Jews and the Christians expressed in this verse by the words *ibn Allāh*? All hypotheses are possible with none of them privileged as the definite one. Are these traditions which continued to occur in the time of the Prophet in Arabia or thereafter? The commentators express very different opinions on this subject.

"... OF THOSE WHO VEILED OF OLD ..."

We have commented several times on the verbal root *k-f-r*, particularly in relation to verse 3:52. This root means: to hide, to cover, to conceal, or to veil. Here we have translated a term deriving from *k-f-r* as "veil." This verse therefore deals with certain aspects of the Anoint, Son of Mary, that are more or less hidden—or veiled—from those who do not recognize them integrally. One must recognize these truths in all the modalities with which they are carried out in the divine Plan. But how should one understand "of old (*min qablu*)," an expression that has consistently perplexed the commentators on the Qur'ān? We shall presently observe why.

> Qur'ān, 9:31. *They have taken as lords beside Allah their rabbis and their monks and the Messiah son of Mary, when they were bidden to worship only One Allah. There is no Allah save Him. Be He Glorified from all that they ascribe as partner!*

اتَّخَذُوا أَحْبَارَهُمْ وَرُهْبَانَهُمْ أَرْبَابًا مِنْ دُونِ اللَّهِ وَالْمَسِيحَ
ابْنَ مَرْيَمَ وَمَا أُمِرُوا إِلَّا لِيَعْبُدُوا إِلَٰهًا وَاحِدًا ۖ لَا إِلَٰهَ إِلَّا هُوَ
سُبْحَانَهُ عَمَّا يُشْرِكُونَ

This verse concerns the Jews as well as the Christians who consider *'Uzayr* and the *Anoint* to be "*the Son of Allah*," respectively.

The term *'ahbār*, which we have translated as "rabbis," comes from the root *h-b-r*, meaning: to do well, to adorn, to embellish, to delight, to be cheerful, and to amuse oneself. Lexicons define the term as a Jewish doctor, a priest, or a scholar in religious matters.

The noun *ruhbān*, meaning "monks," comes from the root *r-h-b*: to fear, dread, to feel threatened, or to be afraid. The "*rāhib*," pl. "*ruhbān*" is he who dreads the world out of fear of God, or one who withdraws. The word *rahbāniyya* from the same etymology evokes the monastic life removed from the world, such as in verse 57:27.

The plural noun *arbāb*, singular *rabb*, comes from the previously discussed root *r-b-b*, meaning: to be master, chief, or lord; to have control of, to exercise authority, to gather, to unite, to raise, to educate, or to possess. The term is used in verse 12:39, *O my fellow-prisoners! Are diverse lords better, or Allah the One, Almighty? Arbāb* is also found in verses 3:64 and 3:80. It is thus mentioned in the Qur'ān four times, each instance in the plural and with identical meanings: masters, lords, teachers, professors.

In these four verses where we encounter the word *arbāb*, should we consider this plural of *Rabb* to carry the connotation of "Lord," as in the opposite of *'abd*, meaning servant or worshipper? This is how one may envisage the master with respect to his student or disciple. The first is in a position of superiority, while the other is in a condition of subordination which makes him dependent on his master. However, the end of the verse instead implies that it deals with "lords" who compete with the One and only God, who is meant to have associates that are worshiped beside Him. This would also mean that the teachings of the scholars were appreciated and considered more authentic than the prescriptions contained in the sacred Scriptures. Thus should one not conclude that the true Teacher, the ultimate Lord, is God Himself? He inspires His true servants who are completely available to receive His Word directly and intuitively. Yet, those who do not receive the Word of Allah with this perfect receptivity are not illuminated by the Divine light. They cannot accept that towards which they feel aversion; this is what verse 9:32 expresses.

> Qur'ān, 9:32. *Fain would they put out the light of Allah with their mouths, but Allah disdaineth [aught] save that He shall perfect His light, however much the disbelievers are averse.*

يُرِيدُونَ أَنْ يُطْفِئُوا نُورَ اللَّهِ بِأَفْوَاهِهِمْ وَيَأْبَى اللَّهُ إِلَّا أَنْ يُتِمَّ
نُورَهُ وَلَوْ كَرِهَ الْكَافِرُونَ

Qur'ān, 9:33. *He it is Who hath sent His messenger with the guidance and the Religion of Truth, that He may cause it to prevail over all religion, however much the idolaters may be averse.*

هُوَ الَّذِي أَرْسَلَ رَسُولَهُ بِالْهُدَىٰ وَدِينِ الْحَقِّ لِيُظْهِرَهُ عَلَى الدِّينِ كُلِّهِ وَلَوْ كَرِهَ الْمُشْرِكُونَ

The pronoun "it" (*hu*) may be also related to the word *dīn*, meaning Religion, as well as to the term *ḥaqq*, referring to the True and Real Reality of Allah. However, the majority of commentators and European translators link this pronoun to the word *dīn*. The content of this verse is found word for word in two other verses, 48:28 and 61:9. The triple occurrence of this combination of terms demonstrates their importance, in decisive religious contexts, for understanding the role of Islam and the role of the Seal of the Messengers-Prophets with respect to other revealed forms.

Several consequential interpretations have been suggested for this verse, considering the possible applications of the terms *dīn* and *ḥaqq*, as well as the pronoun "*hu*." Thus, the expression that we have translated as "over all religion" may also be translated as "over Religion in total."

The following synoptic table indicates the respective contexts of a number of verses, including verses similar to verse 9:32 and its closely related verse 61:8. It also displays the content of verse 9:33 and six verses similar to it, as well as verses 48:28 and 61:9.

One might note that verses 9:33, 48:28, and 61:9—all with identical content—assert both 1) the pre-excellence and universalism of the Message of Islam over the two forms of Jewish and Christian Revelation, and 2) the ultimate function of the Seal of the Messenger, Prophet Muḥammad. Nevertheless, the term "associaters" (*mushrikūn*) concerns the polytheists and idolaters mentioned in Surah 48 and not the Jews and Christians, as illustrated by the beginning of Surah 98: *Those who disbelieve among the People of the Scripture and the idolaters could not have left off [erring] till the clear proof came unto them, a messenger from Allah, reading purified pages containing correct scriptures. Nor were the People of the Scripture divided until after the clear proof came unto them. And they are ordered naught else than to serve Allah, keeping religion pure for Him, as men by nature upright, and to establish worship and to pay the poor-due. That is true religion. Lo! those who disbelieve, among the People of the Scripture and the idolaters, will abide in fire of hell. They are the worst of created beings* (Qur'ān, 98:1-6).

9:30	And the Jews say: Ezra is the son of Allah, and the Christians say: The Messiah is the son of Allah. That is their saying with their mouths. They imitate the saying of those who disbelieved of old. Allah fighteth against them. How perverse are they!			61:6	And when Jesus son of Mary said: O Children of Israel! Lo! I am the messenger of Allah unto you, confirming that which was (revealed) before me in the Torah, and bringing good tidings of a messenger who cometh after me, whose name is the Praised One. Yet when he hath come unto them with clear proofs, they say: This is mere magic.
9:31	They have taken as lords beside Allah their rabbis and their monks and the Messiah son of Mary, when they were bidden to worship only One Allah. There is no Allah save Him. Be He Glorified from all that they associate!	48:26	When those who disbelieve had set up in their hearts zealotry, the zealotry of the Age of Ignorance, then Allah sent down His peace of reassurance upon His messenger and upon the believers and imposed on them the word of self-restraint, for they were worthy of it and meet for it. And Allah is Aware of all things.	61:7	And who doeth greater wrong than he who inventeth a lie against Allah when he is summoned unto Al-Islam? And Allah guideth not wrongdoing folk.
9:32	Fain would they put out the light of Allah with their mouths, but Allah disdaineth (aught) save that He shall perfect His light, however much the disbelievers are averse.	48:27	Allah hath fulfilled the vision for His messenger in very truth. Ye shall indeed enter the Inviolable Place of Worship, if Allah will, secure, (having your hair) shaven and cut, not fearing. But He knoweth that which ye know not, and hath given you a near victory beforehand.	61:8	Fain would they put out the light of Allah with their mouths, but Allah will perfect His light however much the disbelievers are averse.

9:33	He it is Who hath sent His messenger with the guidance and the Religion of Truth, that He may cause it to prevail over all religion, however much the idolaters may be averse.	48:28	He it is Who hath sent His messenger with the guidance and the religion of truth, that He may cause it to prevail over all religion. And Allah sufficeth as a Witness.	61:9	He it is Who hath sent His messenger with the guidance and the religion of truth, that He may make it conqueror of all religion however much idolaters may be averse.
9:34	O ye who believe! Lo! many of the (Jewish) rabbis and the (Christian) monks devour the wealth of mankind wantonly and debar (men) from the way of Allah. They who hoard up gold and silver and spend it not in the way of Allah, unto them give tidings of a painful doom	48:29	Muḥammad is the messenger of Allah. And those with him are hard against the disbelievers and merciful among themselves. Thou (O Muḥammad) seest them bowing and falling prostrate (in worship), seeking bounty from Allah and (His) acceptance. The mark of them is on their foreheads from the traces of prostration. Such is their likeness in the Torah and their likeness in the Gospel—like as sown corn that sendeth forth its shoot and strengtheneth it and riseth firm upon its stalk, delighting the sowers—that He may enrage the disbelievers with (the sight of) them. Allah hath promised, unto such of them as believe and do good works, forgiveness and immense reward.		

Qur'ān, 9:111. *Lo! Allah hath bought from the believers their lives and their wealth because the Garden will be theirs: they shall fight in the way of Allah and shall slay and be slain. It is a promise which is binding on Him in the Torah and the Gospel and the Qur'ān. Who fulfilleth His covenant better than Allah? Rejoice then in your bargain that ye have made, for that is the supreme triumph.*

إِنَّ اللَّهَ اشْتَرَىٰ مِنَ الْمُؤْمِنِينَ أَنْفُسَهُمْ وَأَمْوَالَهُمْ بِأَنَّ لَهُمُ الْجَنَّةَ ۚ يُقَاتِلُونَ فِي سَبِيلِ اللَّهِ فَيَقْتُلُونَ وَيُقْتَلُونَ ۖ وَعْدًا عَلَيْهِ حَقًّا فِي التَّوْرَاةِ وَالْإِنْجِيلِ وَالْقُرْآنِ ۚ وَمَنْ أَوْفَىٰ بِعَهْدِهِ مِنَ اللَّهِ ۚ فَاسْتَبْشِرُوا بِبَيْعِكُمُ الَّذِي بَايَعْتُمْ بِهِ ۚ وَذَٰلِكَ هُوَ الْفَوْزُ الْعَظِيمُ

The verb *ishtarā*, translated here as "bought forth," comes from the root *sh-r-y* meaning: to conduct a trade transaction, to buy/ sell, to exchange, to negotiate, or to carry out a commercial transaction or an exchange of goods comprising of at least one buyer and one seller. The mystics often link this verse with verse 7:172 which mentions the pre-eternal covenant (*mīthāq*) established between God and the children of Adam: *And [remember] when thy Lord brought forth from the Children of Adam, from their reins, their seed, and made them testify of themselves, Am I not your Lord? They said: Yea, verily. We testify. [That was] lest ye should say at the Day of Resurrection: Lo! of this we were unaware* (Qur'ān, 7:172). The goal of the true believer is detachment from the world by orienting oneself exclusively toward Allah and by giving oneself completely to the direction of His Face. In order to reach serenity, God therefore asks the true believer to perform a continuous battle against his soul. The soul incites one to evil, as suggested by the following verses: *I do not exculpate myself. Lo! the [human] soul enjoineth unto evil, save that whereon my Lord hath mercy. Lo! my Lord is Forgiving, Merciful* (Qur'ān, 12:53). *Nay! I swear by the self-accusing soul* (Qur'ān, 75:2). *O soul that art at rest! Return to your Lord, well-pleased, well-pleasing. So enter among My servants, and enter into My garden* (Qur'ān, 87:27-30). This purifying asceticism led by the soul against its impulses begins to look like both an inward and outward battle against a multifaceted enemy. In this battle one can either succumb or triumph:

> *And strive in Allah with the endeavour which is His right. He hath chosen you and hath not laid upon you in religion any hardship; the faith of your father Abraham [is yours]. He hath named you Muslims of old time and in this [Scripture], that the messenger may be a witness against you, and that ye may be witnesses against mankind. So establish worship, pay the poor-due, and hold fast to Allah. He is your Protecting friend. A blessed Patron and a blessed Helper!* (Qur'ān, 22:78) Those who have faith confront this conflicting perspective, bearing in mind the final success with God. The respective

Scriptures expose the vicissitudes and the conflicts awaiting the Believers and which they must face.

The following verse, 9:112, lists the different categories of servants who must work with a view to the ultimate life: *[Triumphant] are those who turn repentant, those who serve, those who praise, those who fast, those who bow down, those who fall prostrate, those who enjoin the right and who forbid the wrong and those who keep the limits of Allah—And give glad tidings to believers!* (Qur'ān, 9:112)

Qur'ān, 10:68. *They say: Allah hath taken [unto Him] a son—Glorified be He! He hath no needs! His is all that is in the heavens and all that is in the earth. Ye have no warrant for this. Tell ye concerning Allah that which ye know not?*

قَالُوا اتَّخَذَ اللَّهُ وَلَدًا ۗ سُبْحَانَهُ ۖ هُوَ الْغَنِيُّ ۖ لَهُ مَا فِي السَّمَاوَاتِ وَمَا فِي الْأَرْضِ ۚ إِنْ عِنْدَكُمْ مِنْ سُلْطَانٍ بِهَٰذَا ۚ أَتَقُولُونَ عَلَى اللَّهِ مَا لَا تَعْلَمُونَ

Qur'ān, 10:69. *Say: Verily those who invent a lie concerning Allah will not succeed.*

قُلْ إِنَّ الَّذِينَ يَفْتَرُونَ عَلَى اللَّهِ الْكَذِبَ لَا يُفْلِحُونَ

Qur'ān, 16:51. *Allah hath said: Choose not two gods. There is only One Allah. So of Me, Me only, be in awe.*

وَقَالَ اللَّهُ لَا تَتَّخِذُوا إِلَٰهَيْنِ اثْنَيْنِ ۖ إِنَّمَا هُوَ إِلَٰهٌ وَاحِدٌ ۖ فَإِيَّايَ فَارْهَبُونِ

Qur'ān, 17:111. *And say: Praise be to Allah, Who hath not taken unto Himself a son, and Who hath no partner in the Sovereignty, nor hath He any protecting friend through dependence. And magnify Him with all magnificence.*

وَقُلِ الْحَمْدُ لِلَّهِ الَّذِي لَمْ يَتَّخِذْ وَلَدًا وَلَمْ يَكُنْ لَهُ شَرِيكٌ فِي

الْمُلْكِ وَلَمْ يَكُنْ لَهُ وَلِيٌّ مِنَ الذُّلِّ ۖ وَكَبِّرْهُ تَكْبِيرًا

Qur'ān, 18:1. *Praise be to Allah Who hath revealed the Scripture unto His slave, and hath not placed therein any crookedness,*

الْحَمْدُ لِلَّهِ الَّذِي أَنْزَلَ عَلَىٰ عَبْدِهِ الْكِتَابَ وَلَمْ يَجْعَلْ لَهُ عِوَجًا

Qur'ān, 18:2. *[But hath made it] straight, to give warning of stern punishment from Him, and to bring unto the believers who do good works the news that theirs will be a fair reward,*

قَيِّمًا لِيُنْذِرَ بَأْسًا شَدِيدًا مِنْ لَدُنْهُ وَيُبَشِّرَ الْمُؤْمِنِينَ الَّذِينَ يَعْمَلُونَ الصَّالِحَاتِ أَنَّ لَهُمْ أَجْرًا حَسَنًا

Qur'ān, 18:3. *Wherein they will abide for ever;*

مَاكِثِينَ فِيهِ أَبَدًا

Qur'ān, 18:4. *And to warn those who say: Allah hath chosen a son,*

وَيُنْذِرَ الَّذِينَ قَالُوا اتَّخَذَ اللَّهُ وَلَدًا

Qur'ān, 18:5. *[A thing] whereof they have no knowledge, nor [had] their fathers, Dreadful is the word that cometh out of their mouths. They speak naught but a lie.*

مَا لَهُمْ بِهِ مِنْ عِلْمٍ وَلَا لِآبَائِهِمْ ۚ كَبُرَتْ كَلِمَةً تَخْرُجُ مِنْ أَفْوَاهِهِمْ ۚ إِنْ يَقُولُونَ إِلَّا كَذِبًا

Some of these verses invalidate the belief of those claiming that Allah has a child or a son. This belief is incompatible with His Majesty and His transcendence. We have previously dealt with this theme in the commentaries on verses 2:87, 2:116, and 6:110.

SURAH 19, MARYAM

REVEALED IN MECCA, EXCEPT FOR VERSES 58 AND 71

The beginning of this Surah reproduces in part certain themes already developed in Surah 3, verses 33 to 48. The entirety of Surah 19 is articulated in accordance with the following facts. It deals with:

1) the prophet Zachariah and his posterity, represented by his son Yaḥyā (or John the Baptist), verse 2 to verse 15;

2) the Angel's encounter with Mary. She miraculously conceives Jesus, who then speaks from the cradle in order to exculpate his mother from the accusation of adultery, from verse 16 to verse 40;

3) the mentioning of certain prophets in the following order: Abraham, Isaac, Jacob, Moses, Aaron, Ishmael, Idrīs, Adam, Noah, from verse 41 to verse 59;

4) various exhortations from verse 60 to the final verse of the Surah, 98. This sequence gives priority to the divine Name *al-Raḥmān,* mentioned 11 times therein.

This Divine Name is found a total of 16 times in this Surah: verses 18, 26, 44, 58, 61, 69, 75, 78, 85, 87, 88, 91, 92, 93, and 96. In the entire sacred text it occurs 56 times, always following the preliminary formula that introduces 113 out of 114 Surahs: "*bi-ismi Llāh al-Raḥmān al-Raḥīm.*" These 56 mentions of the Name *al-Raḥmān* are distributed among the Surahs in the following manner:

The numbers of Surahs are given in ITALICS, and the number of the verses where the Name *Raḥmān* is mentioned are in the white rectangles											
1	3	*2*	163	*13*	30	*17*	110	*19*	16 times (see below)	*20*	5, 90, 108, 109
21	26, 36, 42, 112	*25*	26, 59, 60, 63	*26*	5	*27*	30	*36*	11, 15, 23, 52	*41*	2
43	17, 19, 20, 33, 36, 45, 81	*50*	33	*55*	1	*59*	22	*67*	3, 19, 20, 29	*78*	37, 38

The Divine Name *al-Raḥmān* comes from the root *r-ḥ-m*, discussed previously in the commentary on verses 5:116 and 7:158. From this root the following terms are derived: *raḥim*, meaning matrix, womb, blood kinship, and *raḥma*, meaning mercy, and universal love of the feminine and motherly kind. The significant frequency of this divine Name in this particular Surah directly relates to "Maryam," Zachariah's niece by marriage and mother of Jesus. Maryam is also the maternal first cousin of the prophet Yaḥyā, discussed below. In addition, the name *Raḥmān* acquires a capital importance here through its feminine resonance and its universal virtue. It is universal because it implies all the Divine Names except for the totalizing Name "Allah." *Say: Call unto Allah, or call unto the Beneficent, unto whichsoever ye call [it is the same]. His are the most beautiful names . . .* (Qur'ān, 17:110)

Moreover, in the three verses 19:88, 91, and 92, which are surrounded by verses which mention this same Divine Name *al-Raḥmān*, comprise the already-studied word *walad*, or child, offspring, engendered being, and therefore associated with this Divine Name: *They will have no power of intercession, save him who hath made a covenant with his Lord. And they say: The Beneficent hath taken unto Himself a son. Assuredly ye utter a disastrous thing whereby almost the heavens are torn, and the earth is split asunder and the mountains fall in ruins, that ye ascribe unto the Beneficent a son, when it is not meet for (the Majesty of) the Beneficent that He should choose a son. There is none in the heavens and the earth but cometh unto the Beneficent as a slave.*

In the case of both the name "Allah" and the name *al-Raḥmān*, their majestic Reality renders one unable to envision their attribution to a begotten being. "Allah" expresses the synthesis of all the Divine Names and *al-Raḥmān* propagates all these Names through its universal character and love. It is interesting to note that in all these verses and in other similar ones, the word *ibn*, or "son," is never used. Only the term *walad* is used and most often with a derogatory value. In the Qur'ānic text, Allah always makes a distinction between these two names. Their respective etymologies *'a-b-n* and *w-l-d* distinguish them clearly without confusing their meanings.

Sequence concerning the prophets Zachariah and Yaḥyā

Qur'ān, 19:1. *Kāf. Hā'. Yā'. 'Ain. Sād.* كهيعص

Qur'ān, 19:2. *An impregnating remembrance of the mercy of thy Lord unto His servant Zachariah.*

ذِكْرُ رَحْمَتِ رَبِّكَ عَبْدَهُۥ زَكَرِيَّا

Regarding the meaning of the five separate letters introducing this Surah, please see our work *Une approche du Coran par le grammaire et le lexique*, p. 67.

Verse 2 could also be translated "*A mention of the mercy of thy Lord unto His servant Zachariah.*"

In the commentary on verse 3:37 we have proceeded with an etymological analysis of the name Zachariah, and it is with reference to this study that we translated the term *dhikr* here as "impregnating remembrance." We have depicted a relationship between the two roots *z-k-r* and *dh-k-r*. They are very close to each other through the phonetic points of articulation, and from them the names *Zachariah* and *dhikr* are derived. Here we recall that in the same verse 3:37—to which we return—this verbal root *dh-k-r* comprises two series of principal meanings: 1) to hit at the male member, sharpen, render masculine; and 2) to remember, mention, recall, be remembered. Therefore the two Qur'ānic nouns *dhikr* and *dhakar* have a close meaning. *Dhikr* means remembrance, recall, and invocation. *Dhakar* means male, or the male member of the generation, or one which emits seeds. *Dhikr* has an eminently active, reproductive, and carrying virtue of the word and the seeds of life and of love which are introduced in beings and the worlds. In the Qur'ān, the term *dhakar* is often associated with that of the female (*unthā*) whose meaning comprises, both figuratively and properly speaking, the idea of softness, tenderness, receptivity, and the yielding of a being of the feminine gender: *Whosoever doeth right, whether male (dhakar) or female (untha), and is a believer, him verily we shall quicken with good life, and We shall pay them a recompense in proportion to the best of what they used to do* (Qur'ān, 16:97). *By the night enshrouding and the day resplendent and Him Who hath created male and female, Lo! your effort is dispersed [toward divers ends]* (Qur'ān, 92:1-4).

Zachariah, as the etymological meaning of this noun suggests and as we have seen in the commentary on verse 3:47, laid the loving seed (*habba*) of his until-then sterile spouse. This was in order to form his son Yaḥyā whose name means "he lives" and evokes his transmission of the invigorating prophetic virtue for which his father served as a depository. Yaḥyā prepares the path for his cousin Jesus, as specified by the previously analyzed verse 3:39.

Qur'ān, 19:3. *When he cried unto his Lord a cry in secret,*

إِذْ نَادَىٰ رَبَّهُ نِدَاءً خَفِيًّا

Perhaps the prophet Zachariah, affected by old age and wedded to a woman who was said to be sterile, wished to remain discrete confronting the impossibility of their producing offspring. This is what most of the commentators suggest. Then he invokes his Lord in his innermost consciousness, with the concentration of all his energies on an intense divine presence, an attitude implying a fervent aspiration and the necessity of having an offspring worthy of him, as indicated by the following Qur'ānic verses.

Qur'ān, 19:4. *Saying: My Lord! Lo! the bones of me wax feeble and my head is shining with grey hair, and I have never been unblest in prayer to Thee, my Lord.*

قَالَ رَبِّ إِنِّي وَهَنَ الْعَظْمُ مِنِّي وَاشْتَعَلَ الرَّأْسُ شَيْبًا وَلَمْ
أَكُنْ بِدُعَائِكَ رَبِّ شَقِيًّا

Qur'ān, 19:5. *Lo! I fear my kinsfolk after me, since my wife is barren. Oh, give me from Thy presence a very close person* (walī)

وَإِنِّي خِفْتُ الْمَوَالِيَ مِنْ وَرَائِي وَكَانَتِ امْرَأَتِي عَاقِرًا فَهَبْ
لِي مِنْ لَدُنْكَ وَلِيًّا

Qur'ān, 19:6. *Who shall inherit of me and inherit of the house of Jacob. And make him, my Lord, pleasing [unto Thee].*

يَرِثُنِي وَيَرِثُ مِنْ آلِ يَعْقُوبَ ۖ وَاجْعَلْهُ رَبِّ رَضِيًّا

One may deduce that this close kinship is neither disposed to nor capable of receiving or recognizing prophethood, which may only take place according to a lineage of direct descent. Such was the lineage of numerous prophets, such as Abraham with his sons Ishmael and Isaac, Isaac then becoming the father of Jacob, who was in turn the father of Joseph. Verse 19:6 goes beyond suggesting this direct descent by mentioning a successor "*who will inherit me and the house of Jacob*." We have already mentioned this heritage in the commentary on verse 3:34. The transmission of this prophetic function through blood but also through spiritual lineage occurs without interruption even if certain links of this continuous chain are not always identified or identifiable. Is this not the underlying reason for Zachariah's pressing request to have a son who would be very close (*walī*) to him and who would providentially continue this uninterrupted transmission? Furthermore, Zachariah followed this request with another just as important one, namely that this son be pleasing (*raḍiyy*[an]). In other words, that he be completely available to fulfill this prophetic function and welcome it without applying a deliberately individual will to carrying out his divine mission. This acceptance that was required of him can be interpreted in two ways. The verb paradigm "*fa'il*," according to which this qualifier is constructed, can be defined both by the passive and active meanings in the case of transitive verbs. This expression comes from the verbal root *r-ḍ-y*: to be pleased, to consent, or to approve. Therefore it can be definitively translated as approving/approved or welcoming/welcomed.

Qur'ān, 19:7. *O Zachariah! Lo! We bring thee tidings of a son whose name is John; we have given the same name to none before.*

يَا زَكَرِيَّا إِنَّا نُبَشِّرُكَ بِغُلَامٍ اسْمُهُ يَحْيَىٰ لَمْ نَجْعَلْ لَهُ مِنْ قَبْلُ سَمِيًّا

Qur'ān, 19:8. *He said: My Lord! How can I have a son when my wife is barren and I have reached infirm old age?*

قَالَ رَبِّ أَنَّىٰ يَكُونُ لِي غُلَامٌ وَكَانَتِ امْرَأَتِي عَاقِرًا وَقَدْ
بَلَغْتُ مِنَ الْكِبَرِ عِتِيًّا

Certain commentators are of the opinion that the name "Yaḥyā," which had never been given before, at least in this lineage, is related to the New Testament chapter Luke I:59-64:

> *And it came to pass, that on the eighth day they came to circumcise the child; and they called him Zacharias, after the name of his father. And his mother answered and said, Not [so]; but he shall be called John. And they said unto her, There is none of thy kindred that is called by this name. And they made signs to his father, how he would have him called. And he asked for a writing table, and wrote, saying, His name is John. And they marvelled all. And his mouth was opened immediately, and his tongue [loosed], and he spake, and praised God.*

The Hebrew form of "John" is "Yohanān," which means "Yah has done a grace," *Yah* being the abbreviation of the Divine Name "Yahveh." In Arabic, the noun *Yaḥyā* derives from the verbal root *ḥ-y-y*, meaning "to live," conjugated in the third person singular: "He lives." Thus the noun "Yaḥyā" has a certain resonance with the Hebrew word "Yohanān." In Qur'ānic verbal symbolism, the apparently strange original words have been integrated into the Arab "patrimony" and thereby acquire a meaning harmonious with the general homogeneity of the language. Such has been the case with many other Arabic words that belong to the intrinsic fund of the language but have taken on a broader meaning than that of their etymological origin. For example, the root *k-f-r*, whose lexical value has a positive connotation of to bury, cover, hide, or conceal, generates the active participle *kāfir*, plural *kuffār.* This term is one of the names given to the farmer who buries seed in the earth in order for it to blossom. In a few places in the Qur'ān, this root still corresponds to this primitive meaning, such as in verse 57:20. We previously translated that verse in our commentary on verse 3:52. However, most often the root *k-f-r* takes a negative connotation, such in the case of the words infidel, unbeliever, etc. In this usage it is juxtaposed with the root *'a-m-n* from which we derive the noun *mu'min,* meaning faithful, believer.

In verse 19:7, God directly announces to Zachariah the glad tidings of Yaḥyā's birth. Then, in verse 19:8, Zachariah directly addresses his Lord, who responds to him in the dialogue recorded in the subsequent verses. This stands in contrast to verse 3:39, where God announced glad tidings to Zachariah through the intermediary of the Angels in the intimacy of his sanctuary.

This announcement concerns all orders of reality: 1) first, it concerns the divine order through the Word of God addressed to Zachariah; 2) it concerns the angelic, through the assistance offered to him by the Angels; and finally, 3) it concerns the miraculous birth of Yaḥyā, reinforced by his name which evokes vivifying divine graces. What harmony there is in this exceptional collaboration, this convergence which will announce the birth of Jesus, Son of Mary—a birth which is just as miraculous, because Jesus is the Word of Allah and His Spirit. Some commentators are of the opinion that the first person plural used in the verse *We bring thee tidings of a son whose name is John* refers to the Angels and to all the Divine Names—in other words, God in His Majesty. These commentators refer to the Gospel of Luke, I:11-20. However, nothing in this sequence of Qur'ānic verses indicates that this is an intervention of Angels. Therefore this change of pronouns in reference to God alludes to the multiple and hierarchical Functions He exercises, this divine process evoked numerous times in the Qur'ān. Nevertheless, verse 3:49 specifies that—following the petition of Zachariah to have offspring—the Angels contact him to announce the birth of his son Yaḥyā. Then, in verses 3:40-41, a dialogue is directly established between him and his Lord, without the intervention of angels.

What does the term *ghulām* mean, referring to a young man or adolescent boy?

This term is found 13 times in the sacred text. Eleven of these occurrences are in the singular. On one occasion the term *ghulām* is used in conjunction with al-Khiḍr and Moses (in 18:82). It is used just once in the plural, in reference to the menservants in paradise (in 52:24). In the singular, it denotes Yaḥyā three times (in 3:40, 19:7, and 19:8), Jesus twice (19:19, 19:20), Isaac or Ishmael three times (in 15:53, 51:28, and 37:101), Joseph once (in 12:19), and it is mentioned twice in reference to al-Khiḍr and Moses (18:75 and 18:80).

The source of the term is the verbal root *gh-l-m,* meaning: to be in rut, in heat, to have a violent sexual penchant, to be voluptuous. *Ghulām* therefore means young man, adolescent, young adult, and boy. According to its etymological connotations, this word designates a young man who is partly in childhood and has not yet reached full maturity (*ashudd*). In verses 19:7 and 19:8, Zachariah intensely desires a child who will be gifted to him graciously, but this will be a child who will reach adult age. These verses do not suggest that he will attain his full strength (ashudd) for this latter expression is not mentioned regarding him, and neither is it used for Jesus in 19:19 and 19:20, both being called young before 40 years.

In the Qur'ān, there are verses which indicate successive phases of human life in which adolescence is included:

> *And there came a caravan, and they sent their water drawer. He let down his pail [into the pit]. He said: Good luck! Here is a youth* (*ghulām*—i.e. Joseph). *And they hid him as a treasure, and Allah was Aware of what they did. And they sold him for a low price, a number of silver coins; and they attached no value to him [. . .] And when he reached his prime* (*ashudd*) *We gave him wisdom and knowledge. Thus We reward the good* (Qur'ān, 12:19-20 and 22).

> *He it is Who created you from dust, then from a drop [of seed], then from a clot, then bringeth you forth as an infant* (*tifl*), *then [ordaineth] that ye attain full strength* (*ashudd*) *and afterward that ye become old men* (*shuyūkh*)*—though some among you die before—and that ye reach an appointed term, that haply ye may understand* (Qur'ān, 40:67).

> *And We have commended unto man kindness toward parents. His mother beareth him with reluctance, and bringeth him forth with reluctance, and the bearing of him and the weaning of him is thirty months, till, when he attaineth full strength* (*ashudd*) *and reacheth forty years, he saith: My Lord! Arouse me that I may give thanks for the favour wherewith Thou hast favoured me and my parents, and that I may do right acceptable unto Thee. And be gracious unto me in the matter of my seed. Lo! I have turned unto Thee repentant, and lo! I am of those who surrender* (Qur'ān, 46:15).

> *And when he* (Moses) *reached his full strength* (*ashudd*) *and was ripe* (*istawā*), *We gave him wisdom and knowledge. Thus do We reward the good* (Qur'ān, 28:14).

We may conclude from these verses that the terms corresponding to the different stages of a man's life are the following: the age of infancy or childhood (*tifl*), the age of adolescence or youth (*ghulām*), the age of full strength (*ashudd*), the period of life when strength is ripe (*istawā*), old age (*shuyūkhiyya*), and death (*mawt*).

Of the characters mentioned above, Yaḥyā and Jesus did not reach the age of full strength (*ashudd*) marked by forty years. On the contrary, it can be safely said that the two sons of Abraham and Joseph reached this age.

On three different occasions, the Qur'ān mentions a youth (*ghulām*) produced from exceptional conditions of divine intervention, rather than arising from the usual realm of possibility. These three examples include: 1) Abraham, in his old age, before the sterility of his wife; 2) Zachariah, owing to his old age and the sterility of his wife; and 3) Maryam, whose son Jesus was begotten without a human father.

The term *ghulām* implies that the son who is desired and/or announced will have to pass beyond the age of puberty. Puberty is the age when a human being typically becomes conscious of certain predominant dispositions that he carries within himself. Thus, at this juncture in their lives the three prophets mentioned above realized an intimate consciousness of their exceptional destiny.

Qur'ān, 19:9. *He said: So [it will be for you]. Thy Lord saith: It is easy for Me, even as I created thy norm primordially, when thou wast naught.*

قَالَ كَذَٰلِكَ قَالَ رَبُّكَ هُوَ عَلَيَّ هَيِّنٌ وَقَدْ خَلَقْتُكَ مِنْ قَبْلُ
وَلَمْ تَكُ شَيْئًا

We have translated the expression *ka-dhālika*, already mentioned in relation to verse 3:40, as "*So [it will be for you]*," but it can also be translated as "*So* (it will be)." The expression is formed by two particles: *ka*, or "like," a preposition which indicates comparison, and *dhālika*, or "this," a demonstrative of distance. In its final *ka*, *Dhālika* sometimes takes the plural ending to form *dhāli-kum* or *dhāl-kunna*. It may also take the singular feminine *ki*, such as in verses 3:47 and 19:21. These verses concern only Mary, as we noted in the commentary on verse 3:47. In the case of the elderly Zachariah and his sterile wife, this expression brings into focus the miracle that God performs in order for the prophet Yaḥyā to come into this world. This miracle enables him to fulfill his function in the framework of Mosaic revelation, and to announce the coming of the Anoint, Jesus, Son of Mary, as indicated in verse 3:39. His role was brief because he was killed around the age of twenty.

The expression "*thy Lord*" confirms yet again that the notions of "Lord" (*Rabb*) and "servant" (*'abd*) are always correlated. A servant always has a corresponding Lord who, on his own, concerns this servant, Allah being the Lord of the lords (*Rabb al-arbāb*). This notion of Lordship (*rubūbiyyah*) implies that the Lord of a being is its permanent reality in the Divine Unity, and that perfect "servitude" (*'ubūdiyya*) involves acquiring the character traits (*akhlāq*) of the Creator (*khāliq*), as well as transforming and sublimating one's individual tendencies so that one does only God's will in a fully conscious manner.

I CREATED THY NORM PRIMORDIALLY (*KHALAQTU-KA MIN QABLU*)

The verb *khalaqa*, usually translated as "created," comes from the root *kh-l-q* which means: to give something its measures, proportions, and norm; to measure something (without cutting), to render legal, polished, united, or smooth; to be used or worn out; to produce as a whole, to create, to compose, to produce; and to have a natural goodness or a nice complexion.

In the school of Ibn 'Arabī, beings come into Existence according to their predispositions towards God. Therefore they are produced from their primordial and permanent reality, not from nothingness or from a thing (*min shay^{in}*). They are in this Existence as numerous "seeds" contained in His essential knowledge and they develop the possibilities that God has placed in them from eternity. *Hath there come upon man [ever] any period of time in which he was a thing unremembered?* (Qur'ān, 76:1).

The word "knowledge" (*'ilm*) comes from the root *'-l-m*, whose primary meaning is to mark or distinguish by signs. It also means to possess knowledge. In this semantic perspective, science is a set of distinct signs (*'alamāt*) or possibilities contained in Divine Unity. It is upon these signs that the Divine Names, which are none other than God, are actualized, as well as by the particular beings emerging into existence by virtue of their permanent and eternal predispositions. It is in, and by, the Breath of the Infinitely Good (*nafas al-Raḥmān*) that the Divine Names are exhaled and propagate their effects and properties across the whole Cosmos. Their divinely-prepared receptacle is the existentiated beings. (See Ibn 'Arabî, *Le Livre de la Production des Cercles*, tr. and pr. Paul Fenton and Maurice Gloton, Paris: Eclat, 1996, introduction by Maurice Gloton, note on page xxxix).

The word *shay'*, or thing, reality, want, was previously analyzed in the commentary on verse 2:253.

> Qur'ān, 19:10. *He said: My Lord! Appoint for me some token. He said: Thy token is that thou, with no bodily defect, shalt not speak unto mankind three nights.*

قَالَ رَبِّ اجْعَل لِّي آيَةً ۚ قَالَ آيَتُكَ أَلَّا تُكَلِّمَ النَّاسَ ثَلَاثَ لَيَالٍ سَوِيًّا

Verse 3:41 mentions a "Sign" which will consist of the inability to speak and communication through *gestures* (*ramz*) *for three days.* In this verse, as in 19:10, the verb Allah uses is "*tukallim*," from the verbal root *k-l-m*: to wound someone, to make a cut or a sore; to utter, articulate, pronounce, speak, and narrate. Therefore this verb does not mean only "to speak" but also to express oneself or to be understood in one way or another. The two words *kalm* and *kalām* at first do not seem to be directly related. *Kalm* is a non-Qur'ānic term meaning "wound," while *kalām* signifies Allah's eternal Word. When a human being manifests or utters the word, this entails a release of energy or a loss of vitality. Allah, on the other hand, "externalizes" His permanent and eternal Word (*kalām*) by breathing out or uttering the infinite possibilities contained in His infinite Knowledge, just like the blood of life flowing from a wounded body, metaphorically speaking.

Unlike verse 3:41, verse 19:10 specifies "*three nights*" (*thalātha layālin*) and not "*three days*" (*thalātha ayyāmin*). Night (*layl*) symbolizes the black of non-manifestation, occultation, the period during which nothing can be seen moving, and in which nothing seems to move. Daytime (*yawm*), in contrast, expresses a total cycle representing the existential deployment and its reabsorption. In Arabic, a journey commences at the moment when the sun sets, corresponding to a complete cycle that is simultaneously nocturnal and diurnal.

This silence affecting Zachariah for only three nights and three days does not affect him as an infirmity. Its value is functional only during a determined interval of time which corresponds to both an inner state and an exceptional situation. During this period events of capital importance take place, events willed providentially by

God and about which he should not and cannot speak.

> Qur'ān, 19:11. *Then he came forth unto his people from the sanctuary, and signified to them: Glorify your Lord at break of day and fall of night.*

> فَخَرَجَ عَلَى قَوْمِهِ مِنَ الْمِحْرَابِ فَأَوْحَى إِلَيْهِمْ أَنْ سَبِّحُوا بُكْرَةً وَعَشِيًّا

Zachariah, prevented as he is from speaking or expressing himself verbally during the three nights of his secret intimacy with his Lord in the Sanctuary, goes to its tenants (*qawmi-hi*) while keeping silent. Nevertheless, he reveals to them (*'awhā 'ilay-him*) inwardly. Through the divine presence visiting him, he inspires them to immerse themselves in God's omnipresent Glory, and to sing the praises which are due to Him. The verb "inspire" is derived from the root *w-h-y*, which occurs 78 times in the Qur'ān. It is translated as: to inspire, to insufflate, to suggest, and to reveal. It occurs in connection with numerous privileged persons or creatures, prophets, disciples or apostles (5:111), the mother of Moses (20:38), the bees (16:68), the sky (41:12), and even the demons (6:121), etc.

> Qur'ān, 19:12. *O John! Hold fast the Scripture. And we gave him power of wise decision when a child,*

> يَا يَحْيَىٰ خُذِ الْكِتَابَ بِقُوَّةٍ ۖ وَآتَيْنَاهُ الْحُكْمَ صَبِيًّا

> Qur'ān, 19:13. *And compassion from Our presence, and purity; and he was devout.*

> وَحَنَانًا مِنْ لَدُنَّا وَزَكَاةً ۖ وَكَانَ تَقِيًّا

> Qur'ān, 19:14. *And kind toward his parents. And he was not arrogant, rebellious.*

> وَبَرًّا بِوَالِدَيْهِ وَلَمْ يَكُنْ جَبَّارًا عَصِيًّا

God orders the prophet Yaḥyā to attach himself to the Scripture. This certainly refers to the Torah revealed to Moses, a Book which Yaḥyā followed comprehensively without innovating anything.

This "*power of wise decision*" (*ḥukm*) is also judgment or wisdom of an innate nature. He benefitted from this power from the time of his birth, as indicated by the use of the term "*sabiyy*^{an}." This term is used only twice in the Qur'ān, once in reference to Yaḥyā in this verse and once in reference to Jesus in verse 19:29. According to its verbal root, *sabiyy*^{an} denotes a male infant, a newborn, or very young child, and therefore describes someone well before puberty.

Yaḥyā was compassionate, or possessed of a great tenderness: this is the only time in the Qur'ān where the term *hanān* is used to describe someone. The word comes from a beautiful root meaning to make a sound like the slackening bow or the affectionate cry of the camel for its young one, to sigh with love, to be moved, or to have a great tenderness.

The intensive term *jabbār*, translated here as rebellious, comes from the root *j-b-r*: of to reestablish order with constraint, to put (a broken bone) back, or to restore. In the intensive form, this word also constitutes a Divine Name: *He is Allah, than Whom there is no other Allah, the Sovereign Lord, the Holy One, Peace, the Keeper of Faith, the Guardian, the Majestic, the Compeller, the Superb. Glorified be Allah from all that they associate [unto Him]* (Qur'ān, 59:23). The name of the Archangel of the Revelation sent by God, Jibrīl (Gabriel), is formed from two distinct elements coming from 1) the root *j-b-r*, like above, and from 2) the Arabic word *'il* or *'il*, that is, God present in His creation. In Hebrew "*'El.*" Jibrīl's function is to convey a Divine Message and to establish, with constraint, a certain order to a mostly corrupt humanity distanced from God. Thus the "rebellious" is the tyrant who creates disorder and acts contrary to the instituted divine Law.

Qur'ān, 19:15. *Peace on him the day he was born, and the day he dieth and the day he shall be raised alive!*

وَسَلَامٌ عَلَيْهِ يَوْمَ وُلِدَ وَيَوْمَ يَمُوتُ وَيَوْمَ يُبْعَثُ حَيًّا

The word *salām*, meaning peace and protection, comes from a root analyzed previously in the commentary on verses 3:52 and 3:64.

Generally speaking, Peace protects the human being in himself and in his environment. From his birth until the Day of Resurrection, this peace accompanies the prophet Yaḥyā whose name, let us repeat, means "he lives," "he shall live," or "he remains in life."

Here, the word *salām* is undetermined, meaning it lacks the universal article *al*. This stands in contrast with verse 19:33 in which Jesus speaks using the first person singular and formulates al-Salām, the Peace, with the universal article. In verse 19:33, Jesus speaks about himself using his own name in three stages of his life: birth, death, and resurrection. The same is true of Yaḥyā in verse 19:15.

The Sequence concerning Mary and Jesus

Qur'ān, 19:16. *And make mention of Mary in the Scripture, when she had withdrawn from her people to a chamber looking East* (or = *illuminated*).

وَاذْكُرْ فِي الْكِتَابِ مَرْيَمَ إِذِ انْتَبَذَتْ مِنْ أَهْلِهَا مَكَانًا شَرْقِيًّا

Allah first addresses Muḥammad, as well as those who invoke Allah. Those who invoke Allah perform ritual recitation of the Qur'ān by reading its text and meditating upon the signs it contains.

This sequence, whose preamble first mentions Mary and then Jesus, highlights what verse 42 and the verses following it in Surah 3 have already stated regarding the unique and prominent role of Mary—her individual role, as well as her son's role. In the Qur'ānic text Jesus is often mentioned in conjunction with Mary. This sequence makes explicit certain aspects of their value and their function which Surah 3 did not address. Indeed, one may wonder here, 1) Why does she go into isolation? 2) What is the reason she withdraws from her people? And 3) Why does she remove herself to a place looking East (or illuminated), according to the polysemic meaning of the root *sh-r-q*? Let us try to answer these three questions:

1) Verse 3:37, revealed in Medina well after this verse dating from the Meccan period, suggests that Mary is devoted—through her exceptional vocation—to the permanent worship of her Lord in the Sanctuary, Who . . . *accepted her with full acceptance and vouchsafed to her a goodly growth* (Qur'ān, 3:37).

The Sanctuary mentioned in this sequence is the same as that mentioned in verse 3:37. This verse implies that Mary might have still been in the prime of her youth and under the charge of her maternal uncle Zachariah who, according to the tradition, died some time after this phase of his niece's youth. The verses following 3:37, such as 3:45, do not assign a precise temporal manner to the Annunciation made to Mary informing her of the miraculous coming of Jesus, her son. It is difficult to assign a determined time to these divine, spiritual, and human events. In the Qur'ān, most of them take place outside all chronology. Very often, the goal of the Divine utterance is not to convey precise events but rather to exhort the faithful through the important teachings contained in such accounts.

2) Who are her people or her family (*ahl*)? This term derives from the root *a-h-l*, encompassing the concepts of getting married, getting used, and being in the intimacy of someone. Therefore the word *ahl* means: family, the intimacy of a family in the broader sense, one's closest companions, the household, the intimate community. Were her people in the right disposition to receive the Mystery of Annunciation? The following verse might prove the contrary. Or, to pose this question once again, could the extremely important Announcement made by the Angel to Mary have been conducted in any way but in the state of most perfect intimacy? As verse 3:45 indicates, the issue here is the descent of the Spirit of Allah and of His Word. Therefore that event could only take place in the perfect and uncompromising secrecy of isolation and silence, paired with a blessed person and a pure place prepared for this event. The Spirit of God could only descend to dwell in a virgin receptacle, pure from all individual interference and away from any inadequate environment. The Angel therefore had to manifest itself in the form of a perfectly constituted being, both outwardly and inwardly. This form was necessarily in complete affinity with Mary, who was wholly available and of a virginal nature in all the constitutive elements of her being. This way the Angel could disseminate its impregnating fragrance without finding in her any resistance to receiving the divine Spirit he carried.

3) How should one understand *sharqiyy*[an], translated as either "Oriental", "Eastern" or "illuminated" according to

the various meanings comprised by the root from which it is derived? *Sh-r-q* means to split, to cut in two, to rise (the sun), to shine, to illuminate, to become red, or to pluck (fruits). *Sharqiyy* is an adjective noun meaning: relative to the east, to the east, oriental, exposed to the sun, illuminated by the light. It is therefore more appropriate to translate this term as "illuminated," given that the place whence Mary withdrew was radiating with the light of the Spirit. The following verse distinctly honors the Prophet Muḥammad and brings out the existing relationship between Spirit, Word or Command, and Light: *And thus have We inspired in thee [Muḥammad] a Spirit of Our command. Thou knewest not what the Scripture was, nor the Faith. But We have made it a light whereby We guide whom We will of Our bondmen. And lo! thou verily dost guide unto a right path* (Qur'ān, 42:52).

Qur'ān, 19:17. *And she had chosen seclusion from them (because of their inferiority) and took a protecting veil from them. Then We sent unto her Our Spirit and it assumed for her the likeness of a perfect man.*

فَاتَّخَذَتْ مِنْ دُونِهِمْ حِجَابًا فَأَرْسَلْنَا إِلَيْهَا رُوحَنَا فَتَمَثَّلَ لَهَا
بَشَرًا سَوِيًّا

THE CAUSE OF THEIR INFERIORITY OR "TO DISTANCE HERSELF FROM THEM"

We have already analyzed the Arabic expression *min dūni* in the commentary on verse 5:76. Here, the word *dūn* must be taken as a noun meaning inferior or base, and not as a particle acting as a preposition such as in verses 5:76 or 5:116. The commentators and the translators are embarrassed by this expression which has evaded commentary and translation. In this context, the people of her immediate family circle were not destined to assist in Mary's intimate and mysterious encounter with the Angel of the Annunciation.

The expression "protecting veil" is one way to translate the term *ḥijāb*, derived from the root *ḥ-j-b*. This root denotes act of hiding, as well as to mask, to protect (from looks), to prevent from being seen, to isolate, to veil, to interpose, to prevent from penetrating, or to conceal. The noun *ḥijāb* can therefore be translated as: curtain, screen, door, protecting veil, separation, interposition, and obstacle.

With all His Names, Allah intervenes through the intermediary of *His Spirit. His spirit* took on a form in order to manifest itself unto Mary. The Spirit of Allah, which is formless in its principle, is identified with Him and takes on countless forms suiting the most diverse circumstances following the principal Order of Allah or His Word.

Unlike the content of verse 3:45, in which the Angels announce to Mary a Word from Allah, here Allah sends *His Spirit* unto Mary. Through His excellent Names represented by the plural pronoun *We*, He sends his spirit without specifying the nature of he who assumes a human form for her. The tradition teaches that he was Gabriel (*Jibrīl*) the Archangel of the Revelation, a human form taken by the Spirit of Allah in order to give Mary, a human being, the exceptional opportunity to conceive Jesus. Jesus thus issued from his relationship with the Spirit.

> Qur'ān, 19:18. *She said: Lo! I seek refuge in the Beneficent One from thee, if thou art God-fearing.*

قَالَتْ إِنِّي أَعُوذُ بِالرَّحْمَٰنِ مِنْكَ إِنْ كُنْتَ تَقِيًّا

The apparently unusual encounter between Mary and the Angel who assumes a human form of great beauty permits us to imagine the implicit transition between this verse and the preceding one. We are able to feel the worry Mary was caused by this sudden, surprising, face-to-face encounter between two scrupulous youths of opposite sexes, as such an encounter did not conform to the cultural norms of that time. Mary's first reaction is to be on her guard before such an apparition. The annunciation that the Angels made to her in verse 3:45 had to be etched forever into her whole being and also into her memory. Nevertheless, the modalities of the occurrence of this event were not unveiled to her at that moment. They were unveiled only during this unforeseen encounter when the Angel explained to her the "motive" of his visitation (these modalities are revealed in the following verse). This is why Mary protected herself, or took refuge with the Infinitely Good (*al-Raḥmān*), This Divine Name has a universal function and characterizes Surah 19. It must be distinguished from the synthetic Name *Allah*, as we have pointed out in the introduction to this Surah. Verse 19:18 thus underlines the direct relationship between the Virgin Mary and the Name *al-Raḥmān*: the feminine resonance of the etymology *r-ḥ-m* generates the word "raḥim," meaning womb, uterus, or blood relationship.

Qur'ān, 19:19. *He said: I am only a messenger of thy Lord, that I may bestow on thee a pure boy.*

قَالَ إِنَّمَا أَنَا رَسُولُ رَبِّكِ لِأَهَبَ لَكِ غُلَامًا زَكِيًّا

Qur'ān, 19:20. *She said: How can I have a boy when no mortal hath touched me, neither have I been unchaste?*

قَالَتْ أَنَّىٰ يَكُونُ لِي غُلَامٌ وَلَمْ يَمْسَسْنِي بَشَرٌ وَلَمْ أَكُ بَغِيًّا

Qur'ān, 19:21. *He said: So [it will be]. Thy Lord saith: It is easy for Me. And [it will be] that We may make of him a sign for mankind and a mercy from Us, and it is a thing ordained.*

قَالَ كَذَٰلِكِ قَالَ رَبُّكِ هُوَ عَلَيَّ هَيِّنٌ ۖ وَلِنَجْعَلَهُ آيَةً لِلنَّاسِ
وَرَحْمَةً مِنَّا ۚ وَكَانَ أَمْرًا مَقْضِيًّا

These three verses expose the Annunciation and the miraculous Conception through the expression "*so [it will be] for you*," encountered previously in verse 3:45. This expression was included in a sequence that only mentioned the Annunciation made to Mary by the Angels and the Lord and not the Conception, as is the case with 19:21. It is easy to note the differences between Annunciation and Conception by comparing the elements shown in the synoptic table. The table regroups the two different sequences of verses 3:45-47 and those of the present Surah. The term "*youth*" (ghulām) has been previously explained in the commentary on verse 19:7.

This angelic being who presents himself to Mary in the most beautiful human form is said to be "*the Messenger*" of Mary's Lord. This role implies the communication of a divine Message, in this case being "*. . . The Anoint, Jesus son of Mary, the Messenger of Allah, and His Word and Spirit . . .*" as in 4:171. Indeed, like every messenger, the Angel and the Anoint both carry the divine Word with themselves and in themselves. One must conclude that Mary therefore carries two divine messages: the one she receives from the Angel and the message which Jesus himself constitutes. But Allah knows best.

3:45	*When the angels said: "O Mary! Lo! Allah giveth thee glad tidings of a word from him, whose name is the Anoint, Jesus, son of Mary, illustrious in the world and the Hereafter, and one of those brought near.*	19:18	*She said: Lo! I seek refuge in the Beneficent One from thee, if thou art God-fearing.*
3:46	*He will speak unto mankind in his cradle and in his manhood, and he is of the righteous.*	19:19	*He said: I am only a messenger of thy Lord, that I may bestow on thee a pure boy.*
3:47	*She said: "My Lord! How can I have a child (walad) when no mortal hath touched me?"*	19:20	*She said: How can I have a boy (ghulām) when no mortal hath touched me, neither have I been unchaste?*
3:47	*He said: "So (it will be)." Allah createth what He will. If He decreeth a thing, He saith unto it only: Be! and it is.*	19:21	*He said: So (it will be). Thy Lord saith: It is easy for Me. And (it will be) that We may make of him a sign for mankind and a mercy from Us, and it is a thing ordained.*

The expression: *And it is a thing ordained* (*wa kāna 'amr^{an} maqdiyy^{an}*) will be commented upon later in the context of verse 19:35.

When we follow the order of the Surahs according to the codex of the Caliph 'Uthmān, and not in the presumed chronological order of the Revelation, we notice the Annunciation made to Mary about the coming of Jesus in Surah 3. This Surah was revealed eighty-ninth in Medina and precedes Surah 19 in a way that is not arbitrary but rather providential. Surah 19 was revealed forty-fourth in Mecca and announces certain essential modalities of "After Annunciation" through the act of the Spirit of Allah that assumes the form of a perfect human being.

It is appropriate to recall here that this part of Surah Maryam, revealed in Mecca, was recited to the Negus of Abyssinia by Jaʿfar ibn Abī Ṭālib, one of the most eloquent of the some twenty-four Muslim immigrants. The immigrants traveled to Abyssinian on the advice of the Prophet: during the first five years of his Mission, the newly converted Muslims were subjected to severe persecutions.

Qur'ān, 19:22. *And she conceived him, and she withdrew with him to a far place.*

فَحَمَلَتْهُ فَانْتَبَذَتْ بِهِ مَكَانًا قَصِيًّا

The conception of Jesus, Son of Mary took place through the intervention of the Spirit, which assumed a human form. Mary was penetrated by the spirit in a unique manner. The text mentions curiously that *she withdrew with him*. This goes without saying, for she was heavily pregnant and could not but carry him and withdraw with him. Should one therefore refrain from concluding that there was already a great intimacy of spiritual presence between mother and child, even before Jesus was born? Moreover, her knowledge that she would soon be a mother without the intervention of a known father—a condition that would have certainly been considered an attack on good morals and therefore religiously unacceptable and reprehensible—forced her to withdraw in order to temporarily avoid the blame of her environment. However, as shown by verses 19:27-29, this blame occurred in any case.

Qur'ān, 19:23. *And the pangs of childbirth drove her unto the trunk of the palm-tree. She said: Oh, would that I had died before this and had become a thing of naught, forgotten!*

فَأَجَاءَهَا الْمَخَاضُ إِلَىٰ جِذْعِ النَّخْلَةِ قَالَتْ يَا لَيْتَنِي مِتُّ
قَبْلَ هَٰذَا وَكُنْتُ نَسْيًا مَنْسِيًّا

Why does Mary utter this enigmatic sentence: "*Oh, would that I had died before this*!" Were the birth pains so overwhelming that they drove her to exclaim these harsh words? Or did she become aware, at that moment, of the great responsibility associated with the role that God reserved for her and the great suffering attached to it, as well as the role of her son to whom she is intimately linked? The latter hypothesis would be subsequently corroborated by the other supplication that she utters: *and had become a thing of naught, forgotten!* In this phrase Mary evokes an ordinary life, without fame, and most readily forgettable—the type of life lived by the overwhelming majority of people who live and die without being mentioned by their posterity.

Qur'ān, 19:24. *Then (one) cried unto her from below her, saying: Grieve not! Thy Lord hath placed a spreading source beneath thee,*

فَنَادَاهَا مِنْ تَحْتِهَا أَلَّا تَحْزَنِي قَدْ جَعَلَ رَبُّكِ تَحْتَكِ سَرِيًّا

Qur'ān, 19:25. *And shake the trunk of the palm-tree toward thee, thou wilt cause ripe dates to fall upon thee.*

وَهُزِّي إِلَيْكِ بِجِذْعِ النَّخْلَةِ تُسَاقِطْ عَلَيْكِ رُطَبًا جَنِيًّا

In general, the commentators wonder who cried unto her from below. Was it an angel, Jesus, or "God," given that Allah often speaks of Himself in the Qur'ān by changing the subject mid-verse and different pronouns to refer to Himself. For example, Allah uses Me or I, We, He, etc. Certain scholars belonging to the schools of Basra and Kufa used to read *man tahti-hā*, or "he who was below her." This reading implies it was Jesus who cried out, in contrast to reading that word as *min*, meaning "from": (one) *cried unto her from below her*.

We are of the opinion that Mary has just given birth and that Jesus spoke unto her amidst her enduring pain. This makes sense considering the reassurance that Jesus addresses to his mother, *Grieve not*! The interpretation we suggest is further justified by the fact that later in verses 19:29-23 Jesus speaks from the cradle in order to exculpate his mother and to free her from the fundamental ignorance of her situation held by the people around her. The expression *Grieve not*! might also reference Mary's foreknowledge of the trials awaiting her sooner or later because of her son.

What is this spreading source that Mary's Lord placed beneath her? The word *sariyy*[an], translated here as "a spreading source," comes from the root *s-r-y*: to travel on the night, to traverse, to extend, to spread, to propagate, to flow, etc. The noun *sariyy*^{an} thus means: a source that flows and spreads, or a hollow rivulet beside a (palm) tree that brings water to it. The source mentioned in the verse serves to refresh Mary and the palm-tree to nourish her after childbirth. One might also conclude that Jesus will be first for her, and for those destined to follow him—a living source of water and spiritual nourishment that spreads in order to invigorate the bodies and the hearts.

According to this interpretation, this double provision constitutes the first miracle performed by the *Anoint, Jesus, Son of Mary*. In verse 3:45, Jesus is already called by this complete name from the moment the choir of Angels informs Mary of the Annunciation. This composite noun, given to him by Allah in verse 3:45, highlights the exceptional destiny that was reserved for him in the Plan of Divine Wisdom.

> Qur'ān, 19:26. *So eat and drink and be consoled. And if thou meetest any mortal, say: Lo! I have vowed a fast unto the Beneficent, and may not speak this day to any mortal.*

فَكُلِي وَاشْرَبِي وَقَرِّي عَيْنًا ۖ فَإِمَّا تَرَيِنَّ مِنَ الْبَشَرِ أَحَدًا فَقُولِي
إِنِّي نَذَرْتُ لِلرَّحْمَٰنِ صَوْمًا فَلَنْ أُكَلِّمَ الْيَوْمَ إِنْسِيًّا

Drink and food were placed at Mary's disposal in order to comfort her: At this point she is ordered to eat and drink and she is told that her whole being, in all of its components, must be consoled. Indeed, the expression *wa qarrī 'ayn*^{an} is imperative. We have translated this phrase as "*be consoled*," and it is made up of two symbolic elements:

1) *Qarrī* comes from a verb derived from the root *q-r-r*. This root is very rich in related meanings, among them: a) to remain calm, persist, to settle, to fix some part; b) to become calm, to relieve; c) to be cold, to refresh (the eyes), to console someone, to conceive of joy after grief, to rejoice, to comfort, to reassure;

2) *'Ayn* derives from the root '-y-n which connotes several important meanings: a) to flow, to drip, to seep out, to reach a

source; b) to touch or wound the eye, or to have a large pupil. The noun *'ayn* therefore means: source, fountain, or the point where the water seeps out; an eye or a look (through which light shines forth); the central aspect of a thing, its essence or nature; a hole or an opening.

In accordance with this verse and with 19:29, there are three ways to understand the phrase "*if thou meetest any mortal*":

1) One may consider this phrase independently from the preceding one and interpret the fast that Mary is ordered to accomplish as being a pure abstention from food and drink;

2) One may consider this fasting to have a comprehensive meaning, including abstention from food and drink as well as speech;

3) One may directly relate the phrase to the preceding phrase, in which case Mary's fast must be silent. This would have prevented her from speaking to the people around her about her unusual and unexpected situation.

Let us note that the root *s-w-m* of the word *sawm*, or "fasting," means not only "to fast," but also to abstain, to keep silent, to wait for the hour of zenith, or to become calm.

Just as in verse 19:18, the divine Name in verse 19:26 is "*al-Raḥmān*," *the Infinitely Good.*

On the other hand, one may establish a partial comparison between the abstention from speaking mentioned in both verses 19:10 and 19:26. The first verse concerns Zachariah and the silence of three days his Lord imposed on him with respect to the miraculous conception of Yaḥyā. The second verse speaks of Mary and the "more" miraculous birth of Jesus without a human father. Mary abstains from speaking during the day when Jesus is presented to the people around her. The following table highlights the comparison and the difference between the two situations.

19:10	*He said: "My Lord! Appoint for me some Sign." He said: "Thy sign is that thou, with no bodily defect, shalt not speak unto mankind three nights."*	19:26	*So eat and drink and be consoled. And if thou meetest any mortal, say: Lo! I have vowed a fast unto the Beneficent, and may not speak this day to any mortal.*

Let us point out once again the ambivalence of the root *k-l-m*, which includes the double meaning of *wounding* and *speaking*, or uttering, as we pointed out in the commentary on verse 19:10. All the words that Mary could have pronounced would have been taken by the people around her as a hurtful attack and a blasphemous incomprehension of the Law that Moses promulgated on God's Command. Fasting, meaning pure abstention, permitted Mary to not act or react to the malicious statements formulated by the people around her a few verses later.

Qur'ān, 19:27. *Then she brought him to her own folk, carrying him. They said: O Mary! Thou hast come with an amazing thing.*

فَأَتَتْ بِهِ قَوْمَهَا تَحْمِلُهُۥ قَالُوا يَا مَرْيَمُ لَقَدْ جِئْتِ شَيْئًا فَرِيًّا

Qur'ān, 19:28. *O sister [descendent] of Aaron! Thy father was not a wicked man nor was thy mother a harlot.*

يَا أُخْتَ هَارُونَ مَا كَانَ أَبُوكِ امْرَأَ سَوْءٍ وَمَا كَانَتْ أُمُّكِ
بَغِيًّا

When baby Jesus is born, Mary shows him to the people. They cry out when faced with the arrival of a child whose father they do not know, and they easily imagine Mary committing the worst sin: fornication. Only her son can exculpate her, which he does in the verses that follow. His mother gives way to the word of her son, her son who is also the Word of Allah according to the verse 4:171.

The Muslim commentators and the translators of the Qur'ān have not failed to point out the puzzling expression: *O sister of Aaron*. In commenting on verse 3:34, we have demonstrated the affiliation, still alive in the time of the Family of 'Imrān, stretching back to Aaron in a well-known or discrete lineage in which the prophetic virtue continued without interruption. Thus, when the word *sister* in the expression "*O sister of Aaron*" is interpreted according to the Semitic tradition, this expression refers to a descendent of the spiritual lineage of Aaron.

Mary had received in her family an education that predisposed her to behave in the best manner in harmony with the Mosaic Law. It is undoubtedly for this reason that the people around her were disconcerted by her case. They were unable to situate her state of affairs. They could not help but ask themselves: how could Mary bring a child into the world without the involvement of a human father?

> Qur'ān, 19:29. *Then she pointed to him. They said: How can we talk to one who is in the cradle, a young boy?*

فَأَشَارَتْ إِلَيْهِ ۖ قَالُوا كَيْفَ نُكَلِّمُ مَنْ كَانَ فِي الْمَهْدِ صَبِيًّا

The Lord of Mary had instructed her not to speak on that day, so she pointed to the child to reply instead of her. This was also because the Anoint, Jesus, Son of Mary is the Word of Allah and also possesses of his Spirit from Him, according to the verse 4:171. Therefore he was perfectly qualified to exculpate his mother and to state his own miraculous case before the concerned people.

> Qur'ān, 19:30. *He spake: Lo! I am the slave of Allah. He hath given me the Scripture and hath appointed me a Prophet,*

قَالَ إِنِّي عَبْدُ اللَّهِ آتَانِيَ الْكِتَابَ وَجَعَلَنِي نَبِيًّا

Jesus describes his case up until verse 19:33. In this verse, he calls himself "*servant of Allah*" (*'abd Allah*) for he knew with certitude that he only does the will of His Lord and that he is entirely imbued with His character traits. The qualifier *'abd Allah* is mentioned twice in this form in the Qur'ānic text, the other instance in reference to the Prophet Muḥammad: . . . *And when the slave of Allah stood up in prayer to Him, they crowded on him, almost stifling* (Qur'ān, 72:19). In verse 4:172, Allah clarifies that *The Anoint will never scorn to be a slave unto Allah* (*'abdan li-Llāhi*), according to a literal translation.

The Qur'ān attributes the term *'abdu-Hu*, or "His servant," to the Prophet several times. God refers to him this way in verse 17:1 when He succinctly describes the Prophet's nocturnal journey through non-time from Mecca to Jerusalem. In verses 53:1-18, on the other hand, He describes in a very symbolic and elusive manner the Prophet's atemporal Ascension (*mi'rāj*) to His Lord and beyond, in Allah, and his re-descent to Mecca on the other.

> *Glorified be He Who carried His servant by night from the Inviolable Place of Worship to the Far distant place of worship the neighborhood whereof We have blessed, that We might show him of Our tokens! Lo! He, only He, is the All-hearing, the All-seeing* (Qur'ān, 17:1).

> *By the Star when it setteth, your comrade erreth not, nor is deceived; nor doth he speak of [his own] desire. It is naught save an inspiration that is inspired, which one of mighty powers hath taught him, one vigorous; and he grew clear to view when he was on the uppermost horizon. Then he drew nigh and came down till he was [distant] two bows' length or even nearer, and He revealed unto His slave that which He revealed. The heart lied not [in seeing] what it saw. Will ye then dispute with him concerning what he seeth? And verily he saw him yet another time by the lote-tree of the utmost boundary, nigh unto which is the Garden of Abode. When that which shroudeth did enshroud the lote-tree, the eye turned not aside nor yet was overbold. Verily he saw one of the greater revelations of his Lord* (Qur'ān, 53:1-18).

To read more about the nocturnal journey of the Prophet—performed with his whole being that was reabsorbed completely, his Ascension to Allah, and his re-descent into this world, see our translation of Ibn 'Arabī's *l'Arbre du Monde* (Paris: Les Deux Océans). This work is dedicated to the integral reality of the Prophet Muḥammad.

Allah, Who gives the Scripture to Jesus, does not specify the particular nature of the Scripture. It might be the Scripture that has accompanied Allah from eternity in His "*Mother of the Book*" (*Umm al-Kitāb*) (cf. Qur'ān, 3:16, 13:39, 43:4), the Gospel being just one of its manifestations. Jesus already knew this Scripture at his birth just as he was Prophet before coming into this world, as mentioned in this verse. Not only did Allah grant him the Scripture, but He also taught him its content, as implied in verses 3:48 and 5:110.

Qur'ān, 19:31. *And hath made me blessed wheresoever I may be, and hath enjoined upon me prayer and almsgiving so long as I remain alive,*

وَجَعَلَنِي مُبَارَكًا أَيْنَ مَا كُنْتُ وَأَوْصَانِي بِالصَّلَاةِ وَالزَّكَاةِ مَا دُمْتُ حَيًّا

Qur'ān, 19:32. *And [hath made me] kind toward her who bore me, and hath not made me arrogant, unblest.*

وَبَرًّا بِوَالِدَتِي وَلَمْ يَجْعَلْنِي جَبَّارًا شَقِيًّا

The word "*blessed*" is the translation of the passive participle of the third verbal form of the root *b-r-k.* In its unbound form this root means: to kneel (like the camel), to bend the knees and lie down, to stand still, to apply to something, or to drop water. In its third verbal form, this root takes the following meanings: to bless, or to place one's beneficial presence on someone or something, e.g. a place. This passive participle also forms nouns of time and place. Jesus therefore received spiritual influences (graces) wherever he went and he transmitted them through his word, which is one and the same as God's word.

In the Qur'ān, *ṣalāt* and *zakāt* are very frequently associated with each other (23 times) because of their complementary virtues. The term "*ṣalāt*," translated here as "action of unifying grace," was previously analyzed in the chapter "The *ṣalāt* on the Prophet." The word "*zakāt*" comes from the root *z-k-w* meaning: 1) to be pure, spotless; 2) to increase, grow, or augment; 3) to live in well-being, to thrive in an environment. The *zakāt* has a universal religious and ethical value by way of its etymology and by what it prescribes. It corresponds to the necessity of removing, through deduction, the excess of idle goods unnecessary to the person possessing them. These goods are therefore meant for the destitute in general. Prayer, or the action of unitive grace, is firstly an acquisition of personal grace bringing nearness to God. The purifying deduction, on the other hand, is distributed by certain affluent persons to the needy. This payment can be envisaged in several ways: it consists of donating extra money possessed by those who have been gratified by God. By extension, the notion of *zakāt* may consist of the contribution that the individual brings to his community through his diverse gifts. Such gifts include one's intellectual, artistic, and professional capacities, and could therefore take the form of teaching, social services, and charitable aid. This universal meaning of the *zakāt* is found in the following verse: *Who believe in the Unseen, and establish worship, and spend of that We have bestowed upon them* (Qur'ān, 2:3).

After mentioning certain traits that characterize his relationship with God, Jesus knows what he owes his mother in the context of the intimate filial relationship linking him to her. God bestowed this relationship upon him as an inalienable spiritual and natural gift.

It is only after listing certain dispositions specific to him that the Qur'ān calls Jesus not "*arrogant,*" or "*unblest,*" in reference to his function as transmitter of the divine Law. The text does not specify here what the rest of his life will be like.

With the help of the following table, one may compare verse 19:32 on Jesus to verse 19:14 on John. These two prophets were both granted certain cardinal comportments, and thus they are both qualified as "reformers."

19:14	*And kind toward his parents. And he was not a rebellious reformer.*	19:32	*And (hath made me) kind toward her who bore me, and hath not made me an unblest reformer.*

In verse 19:14, the prophet Yaḥyā is not a "rebellious reformer" of the Mosaic Law that he follows, as we pointed out earlier. He is not a "messenger" (*rasūl*). Therefore he does not bring a new Message to the continuation of the universal Revelation, unlike Jesus who is at once servant of God, a prophet, a messenger, the Word of Allah and a Spirit from Him. Jesus brings and carries an actualized divine Message that will apply to new conditions as the historical human cycle unfolds. In this cycle and in his function willed by God, he will not be "*an unblest reformer.*"

In verse 5:110, under point (A), we have commented on the expression "thy mother (engenderer)" (*wālidati-ka*). This is another example of Allah using this expression, through the word of Jesus, with the possessive adjective "mine." *Wālidat-ī* means "my mother" or "my engenderer," literally "she who gives birth to me," or "she who is about to engender me." In this context the act of engendering never ceases. Mary continues manifesting Jesus, who is the divine Word contained in Mary herself.

Qur'ān, 19:33. *Peace on me the day I was born, and the day I die, and the day I shall be raised alive!*

وَالسَّلَامُ عَلَيَّ يَوْمَ وُلِدْتُ وَيَوْمَ أَمُوتُ وَيَوْمَ أُبْعَثُ حَيًّا

From verse 19:30 until the verse above, Jesus, Son of Mary speaks about his role in the first person singular. In verse 19:15, a similar formula is applied to the prophet Yaḥyā but used in the third person singular. Here, Jesus is the Word of Allah and he is aware of his condition, therefore he can speak about his own case. It is Allah Himself who speaks through him and Who formulates the situation.

When Allah speaks of Yaḥyā by saying "*a peace on him*," the undetermined term "*salām*" is not considered a divine name. On the contrary, when Jesus Son of Mary is qualified by this Name it takes the universal article *al*: *al-Salām* is one of the excellent Names of Allah mentioned in the Qur'ān (verse 59:23) and in the prophetic tradition. This divine Name can be translated as the Peace, the Protection, the Intact, and the Unscathed. It applies particularly to the three essential dispositions of his exceptional vocation mentioned in this verse.

The word *hayy*^{an}, meaning living, or animated by the spirit, acts as a circumstantial complement: "*qua* living." One can interpret it as applying to each of the three cyclic dispositions concerning Yaḥyā in 19:15 and Jesus in verse 19:33. It could also be related only to the last element of the verse, according to the nearly unanimous opinion of the Muslim commentators: "*the Day I shall be raised alive*." According to this interpretation, life and death must be understood as being simultaneous; death is succeeded immediately by a new life. Verse 6:95 illustrates this point of view: *Lo! Allah [it is] Who splitteth the grain of corn and the date-stone [for sprouting]. He bringeth forth the living from the dead, and is the bringer-forth of the dead from the living. Such is Allah. How then are ye perverted?*

It is interesting to note that in the Qur'ānic text the expression "*al-salām 'alā . . .*" (peace on . . .), including the universal article, is mentioned only twice. It is mentioned in connection with Jesus in the present verse (19:33), and used to refer to both Moses and his brother Aaron—who were sent by God to the Pharaoh—in verse 20:47: *So go ye unto him and say: Lo! we are two messengers of thy Lord. So let the children of Israel go with us, and torment them not. We bring thee a token from thy Lord. And peace will be for him who followeth right guidance.*

Qur'ān, 19:34. *Such was Jesus, son of Mary: [this is] a statement of the truth concerning which they doubt.*

ذَٰلِكَ عِيسَى ابْنُ مَرْيَمَ ۚ قَوْلَ الْحَقِّ الَّذِي فِيهِ يَمْتَرُونَ

Here is Jesus as he presents himself and as Allah compels him to speak. Jesus himself thus clarifies his intimate experience of his exceptional constitution, according to the miraculous dispositions that only he possesses. He is the Word; the Word which expresses itself and which God expresses in His omnipresent reality that is at once transcendent and immanent: He who is *the First and the Last, the Outward and the Inward* (cf. 57:3). Here He is qualified by relational Names that are mutually inseparable, in a correlative and paradoxical way: if one exists, then so does the other. They cannot but coexist. This correlation challenges beings which are left in the greatest perplexity since there is none but Him in Existence, He who is the only real Being. All other beings partake in Him and are attached to Him as their unique and permanent Principle; all of them, without exception, come from Him and return unto Him. This is why the person of Jesus who is the *Expression of the Real* (*qawl al-Ḥaqq*) serves as an example of faithful tributes of interrelational realities which can only be reached beyond the partial intelligence of the mental plane and penetrate intuitively into some aspects of the mystery of the integral constitution of Jesus. Jesus is the *Expression of the Real* in creation just as he is the Word of Allah (*kalimat Allah*) in the primordial and principal reality itself.

Qur'ān, 19:35. *a) It befitteth not [the Majesty of] Allah b) that He should attribute Himself with c) some son. d) Glory be to Him! e) When He decreeth f) an order, g) He saith unto it only: Be! and it is.*

مَا كَانَ لِلَّهِ أَنْ يَتَّخِذَ مِنْ وَلَدٍ ۖ سُبْحَانَهُ ۚ إِذَا قَضَىٰ أَمْرًا
فَإِنَّمَا يَقُولُ لَهُ كُنْ فَيَكُونُ

This verse is difficult to translate. Its profound meaning does not permit easy interpretation. The translators of the Qur'ān have indeed sensed this and have proposed various interpretations.

An analysis of this verse according to the above division (a to g)

a) It befitteth not Allah (*mā kāna li-Llāhi*)

The verb *kāna* is the perfect form of the verbal root *k-w-n*. *K-w-n* has numerous meanings; despite its variation in context-dependent nuance, it mostly retains its original meaning "to be," in the sense of existing. It can therefore be translated: to exist, to be found, to become, should, to have to, to be able to, to have the nature of, to belong to, to befit, to be capable, to take place, to become, to present oneself, to rest, to assume, to behave, to comprise, to be realized, to reveal oneself, to establish oneself, or to show oneself to be, and so on. (cf. our *Une Approche du Qur'ân par la grammaire et le lexique*, entry 1336 and chapters 8 and 9, Beirut: Albouraq, 2002).

b) that He should attribute Himself with (*an yattakhidha*)

The root *'-kh-dh* in its eighth form means: to take unto oneself, to attribute oneself with, to appropriate, to try to take hold of, etc. In certain contexts, it may be translated: to adopt, to opt, to put, or to take. All of these are unsuitable meanings when talking about a divine disposition; indeed, how could Allah adopt or take a child (*walad*)! This expression is found in verses 10:68, 17:111, and 18:4, all of which have been previously translated.

c) some son (*min walad*^{in})

In verses 2:87, 2:116, and 6:101, we have commented on the term "*walad*." In the Qur'ān this term often appears in negative contexts. We have indicated the difference between *walad* and *ibn*, a term that always has a positive meaning.

The partitive particle *min* (some) must be accurately rendered in the translation, for it carries a very specific definition that must be retained.

d) Glory be to Him! (*subḥāna-Hu*)

This expression has already been analyzed in verse 4:171. In the Qur'ān, *subḥāna-Hu* always expresses Allah's transcendence and also His presence in His universal Act. It occurs following contexts that do not befit His majesty in any way; therefore it is used to deny a shortcoming, a deficiency, or a lack which creatures might be apt to attribute to Him.

e) When He decreeth (*idhā qaḍā*)

In verse 2:253 we have highlighted the distinction between the two aspects of the Divine Will: the *Mashī'a* and the *Irāda*. Both are attributed to Him and to the existing correspondence between these two nouns the terms "*qaḍā*" and "*qadar*." "*Qaḍā*" is a non-Qur'ānic term which expresses the Decree of Allah which is pre-established in itself, and not its actualization which is called "*Qadar*," in the existentiated beings.

The term *qaḍā* comes from the root *q-ḍ-y*, meaning: to prescribe, to decree, to measure out, to decide, to determine, to judge, to accomplish, to complete, to pronounce, etc. The issue here is a decision in the Divine Knowledge pre-decreed from eternity, and the fact that the Divine Command or Order (*amr*) is expressed through His authoritative and existentiating Word "*kun*." By virtue of his existentiating Word, all creatures come into existence and are invigorated by the Holy Spirit, depending on their innate predispositions in God and their actualization of the "Qadar."

In his "Book of Definitions" (*Kitāb al-ta'rīfāt*, op. cit.), entry 1253, Jurjānī defines these two terms in the following way:

> The *Qadar* is the passing of the possibilities from non-existence or potentiality into existence, progressively, in conformity with the immutable decree (*qaḍā*). The *Qaḍā* is found in pre-eternity just as *Qadar*, determination, is situated in that which does not cease. The difference between *qadar* and *qaḍā* is that the latter includes in synthesis the reality of all things existing in the Guarded Tablet (*lawḥ al-maḥfūẓ*), whereas *qadar* comprises their reality in the determined entities when the conditions for their actualization are fulfilled.

f) an order or command

We have already dealt indirectly with the reality of *amr* in the discussion of verses 2:87 (5), 4:171 (c), and 3:47. This term comes from the verbal root *a-m-r*: to order, to command, to decide, to prescribe, to enjoin, and to exercise authority. Therefore its primary meanings are: order, command, ordainment, edict, ruling, imperative, injunction, motivation, decision, prescription, function, situation, condition, status, a thing or reality in the world of Creation envisaged from the aspect of order or of command, or even injunction.

The divine Command or Order, which is uncreated and

decreed, takes place continuously and permanently. It is similar to the creating Word *kun*, another uncreated element that exercises, through the Spirit its authority and influence in all degrees and through all created beings. The Divine Command and the Spirit cannot be dissociated in the permanent process of the spread and invigoration of the realities that are present in the universal Manifestation: *The Exalter of Ranks, the Lord of the Throne. He causeth the Spirit of His command upon whom He will of His slaves, that He may warn of the Day of Meeting, the day when they come forth, nothing of them being hidden from Allah. Whose is the Sovereignty this day? It is Allah's, the One, the Almighty* (Qur'ān, 40:15-16).

Allah decrees a command which is not existentiated yet will become existentiated when He utters authoritatively: "*Come to existence.*" This is a specific command that must come to be: "*and it comes about.*" This command (*amr*[an]) that Allah has decreed even before its existence, and that He accomplishes, is contained in the synthetic and universal divine Order, or in His Command expressed in verse 40:15 above. This command gives effective existence to the multitude of commanded or ordered realities: the realities are envisaged with respect to things that have received the injunction of manifesting themselves and which become the locus whereby manifestation takes place. The order to exist, received primordially, cannot be dissociated from Hearing at the atemporal instant in which the ordained thing must hear the Word uttered by God in order for that thing to actualize its possibilities. To encourage this actualization within all of creation, the divine Order must include all the Divine Names and thus exercise its authoritative function in its plenitude.

In order to enable the reader to better comprehend the various meanings indicated by the term *amr* in certain Qur'ānic contexts, we shall quote a few more representative verses. In these verses *amr* comprises anagogical and not metaphorical meanings; the word retains its original etymological resonance in its occurrences of the sacred text.

> *The Originator of the heavens and the earth! When He decreeth a thing, He saith unto it only: Be! and it is* (Qur'ān, 2:117).

> *She said: My Lord! How can I have a child when no mortal hath touched me? He said: So (it will be). Allah createth what He will. If He decreeth a thing, He saith unto it only: Be! and it is* (Qur'ān, 3:47).

But His command, when He intendeth ('arāda) *a thing* (shay'), *is only that He saith unto it: Be! and it is* (Qur'ān, 36:82).

He it is Who quickeneth and giveth death. When He ordaineth a thing, He saith unto it only: Be! and it is (Qur'ān, 40:68).

And thou seest those in whose heart is a disease race toward them, saying: We fear lest a change of fortune befall us. And it may happen that Allah will vouchsafe [unto thee] the victory, or a commandment from His presence. Then will they repent them of their secret thoughts (Qur'ān, 5:52).

Wait they for naught else than that Allah should come unto them in the shadows of the clouds with the angels? Then the command would be already accomplished. All commands go back to Allah [for judgment] (Qur'ān, 2:210).

Lo! your Lord is Allah Who created the heavens and the earth in six Days, then mounted He the Throne. He covereth the night with the day, which is in haste to follow it, and hath made the sun and the moon and the stars subservient by His command. His verily is all creation and commandment. Blessed be Allah, the Lord of the Worlds! (Qur'ān, 7:54)

And Allah's is the Invisible of the heavens and the earth, and unto Him the whole Command will be returned. So worship Him and put thy trust in Him. Lo! thy Lord is not unaware of what ye [mortals] do (Qur'ān, 11:123).

Allah's is the command in the former case and in the latter—and in that day believers will rejoice (Qur'ān, 30:4).

And Our commandment is but one, as the twinkling of an eye (Qur'ān, 54:50).

Allah it is who hath created seven heavens, and of the earth the like thereof. The commandment cometh down among them slowly, that ye may know that Allah is Able to do all things, and that Allah surroundeth all things in knowledge (Qur'ān, 65:12).

The commandment of Allah will come to pass, so seek not ye to hasten it. Glorified and Exalted be He above all that they associate. He sendeth down the angels with the Spirit of His command unto whom He will of His bondmen, [saying]: Warn mankind that there is no Allah save Me, so keep your duty unto Me (Qur'ān, 16:1-2).

And of His signs is this: The heavens and the earth stand fast by His command, and afterward, when He calleth you, lo! from the earth ye will emerge (Qur'ān, 30:25).

And thus have We inspired in thee [Muḥammad] a Spirit of Our command. Thou knewest not what the Scripture was, nor what the Faith. But We have made it a light whereby We guide whom We will of Our bondmen. And lo! thou verily dost guide unto a right path, the path of Allah, unto Whom belongeth whatsoever is in the heavens and whatsoever is in the earth. Do not all things reach Allah at last? (Qur'ān, 42:52-53).

g) He saith unto it only: Be! and it is (*fa-innamā yaqūlu la-hu: kun fa-yakunu*).

The last part of this verse is the completion of the primordial and essential process which is carried out by the Word of Allah. This process brings into existence the realities arising from the Order that He universally decrees of His Creation. This recurring and ceaseless process might perhaps be simplified in the following way:

1) The pre-established decree of Allah → 2) His Command, or reality in itself, with respect to the Order, at the "Divine Level" → the existentiating non-created divine Word → the coming into existence of the thing commanded by the divine Word.

It is in the last phase that generation appears with its dual and multiple deployments in order to ceaselessly produce all the possible beings which arise from the Order (*umūr*, meaning "ordained realities"): father, mother, and child, or genitor, mother, and progeny.

Qur'ān, 19:36. *And lo! Allah is my Lord and your Lord. So serve Him. That is the right path.*

وَإِنَّ اللَّهَ رَبِّي وَرَبُّكُمْ فَاعْبُدُوهُ ۚ هَٰذَا صِرَاطٌ مُسْتَقِيمٌ

Qur'ān, 19:37. *The sects among them differ: but woe unto the disbelievers from the meeting of an awful Day.*

فَاخْتَلَفَ الْأَحْزَابُ مِنْ بَيْنِهِمْ ۖ فَوَيْلٌ لِلَّذِينَ كَفَرُوا مِنْ
مَشْهَدِ يَوْمٍ عَظِيمٍ

Qur'ān, 19:38. *See and hear them on the Day they come unto Us! yet the evil-doers are to-day in error manifest.*

أَسْمِعْ بِهِمْ وَأَبْصِرْ يَوْمَ يَأْتُونَنَا ۖ لَٰكِنِ الظَّالِمُونَ الْيَوْمَ فِي ضَلَالٍ مُبِينٍ

Qur'ān, 19:39. *And warn them of the Day of anguish when the case hath been decided. Now they are in a state of carelessness, and they believe not.*

وَأَنْذِرْهُمْ يَوْمَ الْحَسْرَةِ إِذْ قُضِيَ الْأَمْرُ وَهُمْ فِي غَفْلَةٍ وَهُمْ لَا يُؤْمِنُونَ

Qur'ān, 19:40. *Lo! We, only We, inherit the earth and all who are thereon, and unto Us they are returned.*

إِنَّا نَحْنُ نَرِثُ الْأَرْضَ وَمَنْ عَلَيْهَا وَإِلَيْنَا يُرْجَعُونَ

SURAHS 21 TO 112

Qur'ān, 21:89. *And Zachariah, when he cried unto his Lord: My Lord! Leave me not childless, though Thou art the Best of inheritors.*

وَزَكَرِيَّا إِذْ نَادَىٰ رَبَّهُ رَبِّ لَا تَذَرْنِي فَرْدًا وَأَنْتَ خَيْرُ الْوَارِثِينَ

Qur'ān, 21:90. *Then We heard his prayer, and bestowed upon him John, and cured his wife's barrenness Lo! they used to vie one with the other in good deeds, and they cried unto Us in longing and in fear, and were submissive unto Us.*

فَاسْتَجَبْنَا لَهُ وَوَهَبْنَا لَهُ يَحْيَىٰ وَأَصْلَحْنَا لَهُ زَوْجَهُ إِنَّهُمْ كَانُوا يُسَارِعُونَ فِي الْخَيْرَاتِ وَيَدْعُونَنَا رَغَبًا وَرَهَبًا وَكَانُوا لَنَا خَاشِعِينَ

These two verses, previously commented upon in relation to verses 3:37-3:41 and 19:2-15, summarize the two long sequences concerning Zachariah, his wife, and Yaḥyā. Here, the Divine Author mentions Zachariah in a Surah called al-Anbiyā' (the Prophets). Zachariah's name appears after a series of prophets who are listed in the following non-chronological order: Moses, Aaron, Abraham, Lot, Isaac, Jacob, Noah, David, Solomon, Ishmael, Idrīs, Dhu al-Kifl (Ezekiel), Jonas, Zachariah, and Yaḥyā.

Mary is mentioned after them in verse 21:92. In the last verses of the Surah, from 21:107-112, and particularly in the first of this set, the Divine Author alludes to the Prophet (Muḥammad) without mentioning his name: *We sent thee not save as a mercy for the peoples* (Qur'ān, 21:107).

> Qur'ān, 21:91. *And she who was chaste, therefore We breathed into her (something) of Our Spirit and made her and her son a Sign for (all) peoples.*

وَالَّتِي أَحْصَنَتْ فَرْجَهَا فَنَفَخْنَا فِيهَا مِنْ رُوحِنَا وَجَعَلْنَاهَا
وَابْنَهَا آيَةً لِلْعَالَمِينَ

Although the name of Mary is not mentioned, unlike verse 66:12 which contains two elements characterizing her (see parts a) and b) in the comparative table below), this verse about Mary follows two preceding verses (21:89-90) concerning figures who are similar to her both through blood relationships and an exceptional spiritual height.

Literal translation			
21:91	*And she a) who kept her chastity (farj), therefore b) We breathed into her (something) of Our Spirit and made her and her son a Sign for (all) peoples.*	66:12	*And Mary, daughter of 'Imrān, a) whose body was chaste, b) therefore We breathed therein (fī hi) something of Our Spirit. And she confirmed the words of her Lord and His scriptures, and was of the obedient.*

The expression that we have translated as *kept* comes from the Qur'ānic root *h-ṣ-n* conjugated in the fourth verbal form. This form means: to be strong, to fortify, to be inaccessible, or to remain intact. The word *farj* derives from the root *f-r-j*, meaning to split, open, widen, spread, make room, console, relieve, or liberate (from pain). The noun *farj* therefore means: slit, fissure, tear, sexual organ, or consolation. This term is often interpreted by the traditional commentators and the French translators as "sexual organ." From this perspective, which is both Islamic and Christian, Mary is corporeally and spiritually virgin at the moment when God breathes into her from His Spirit, and she will remain such, for this breath is of the spiritual order. It is this spiritual Breath that will form the "body" of Jesus in a mysterious way. Thanks to this angelic intervention and this divine breath, Jesus Son of Mary will have an angelic and spiritual nature and, through his mother, he will take an animated corporeal form.

Let us note that, in these two verses, God breathes from His Spirit in two ways: 1) in Mary (*fī-hā*)—that is, by penetrating her entirely, and 2) into the "sexual organ" (*fī-hi*) of she who remained a virgin. The verse does not specify if the woman referred to is Mary, but this can be deduced by comparing the two verses in question. In the expressions *Mary* or in *she who kept her chastity*, the Spirit of Allah conveys the Word which is Jesus and, through this intimate communication, they both become a single "Sign" for all the beings of the world.

Jesus will therefore be perfectly formed by his mother who was herself formed in complete harmony, according to verse 3:37: . . . *And her Lord accepted her with full acceptance and vouchsafed to her a goodly growth* . . . He will also be perfectly shaped by the Angel of the Revelation, according to verse 19:17: . . . *Then We sent unto her Our Spirit and it assumed for her the likeness of a perfect man.*

In this verse, it is the uncreated Spirit of Allah which assumes a form for her in the likeness of an Angel. In verse 21:91, on the other hand, Allah breathes—through His Names—in her *from* His Spirit and not "*His Spirit.*" This is the Spirit that takes shape in order to act in Mary, and the Angel will transmit to her the Word of Allah (*kalimatu-Hu*). The complete name of this Word is the Anoint, Jesus, Son of Mary, according to verses 3:45 and 4:171. *She confirms the words of her Lord and His scriptures* because she receives mysteriously, in all her being, Jesus—Jesus, Word of Allah and a Prophet, and Jesus whom Allah has given the Scripture according to a verse we examined previously, 19:30: *He spake: Lo! I am the slave of Allah. He hath given me the Scripture and hath appointed me a Prophet.*

The encounter between the Angel and Mary could only take

place through and in a perfect providential affinity and harmony existing between them. In the context of this mystery, the Son who is born is made in the perfect likeness of these two "co-operators." Mary therefore had to be completely reverential and was prepared to receive this Word in all the components of her being, whence the expression "*she was of the obedient*," as mentioned in the previously explained verse 3:43. This perfect affinity and harmony between the Angel and Mary implies that the Son of Mary himself has great affinity and harmony with his mother to the extent of constituting a single "*Sign*" which concerns all "*beings of the world*."

Let us mention here that the word *'alamīn* is used to designate human beings and that the verbal root from which it is formed, *'-l-m*, means: to distinguish by a mark or a sign, to mark, discern, signify, to establish a link between different signs, or to know how to distinguish one thing from another. The term *'alamīn* can therefore be translated as "beings-signs." We shall find this same expression "a Sign" attributed to the Son of Mary and his mother in verse 23:50, as we have already found in the previously discussed verse 5:17.

> Qur'ān, 22:17. *Lo! those who believe, and those who are Jews, and the Sabaeans and the Christians and the Magians and the idolaters—Lo! Allah will decide between them on the Day of Resurrection. Lo! Allah is Witness over all things.*

إِنَّ الَّذِينَ آمَنُوا وَالَّذِينَ هَادُوا وَالصَّابِئِينَ وَالنَّصَارَى
وَالْمَجُوسَ وَالَّذِينَ أَشْرَكُوا إِنَّ اللَّهَ يَفْصِلُ بَيْنَهُمْ يَوْمَ الْقِيَامَةِ
إِنَّ اللَّهَ عَلَى كُلِّ شَيْءٍ شَهِيدٌ

This verse contains elements that are also found in verses 2:62 and 5:69. In order to better note the different sequences of these three verses, we present them in the following synoptic table:

Surahs according to their presumed order of revelation		
2:62 (Medinite, 87th)	22:17 (Medinite, 103rd)	5:69 (Medinite, 112th)
1) Lo! Those who believe, and	1) Lo! those who believe, and	1) Lo! those who believe, and
2) those who are Jews, and	2) those who are Jews, and	2) those who are Jews, and
3) Christians, and		
4) Sabaeans—	4) the Sabaeans and	4) Sabaeans, and
	3) the Christians and	3) Christians—
	5) the Magians and	
	6) the polytheists—	
7) whoever believeth in Allah and the Last Day and doeth right—	Lo! Allah will decide between them on the Day of Resurrection. Lo!	7) Whosoever believeth in Allah and the Last Day and doeth right—
8) surely their reward is with their Lord,		
9) and there shall no fear come upon them neither shall they grieve.		9) there shall no fear come upon them neither shall they grieve.
	10) Allah is Witness over all things.	

The common elements shared by the three Surahs are found in numbers 1, 2, 3, and 4; those which are shared by just two Surahs are found in numbers 7 and 9; those which are found only once are in numbers 5, 6, 8, and 10. In these contexts, the commentators liken those who believe to Muslim men and women. One may also consider them as believers who have reached the end of the Straight Path (*ṣirāt mustaqīm*) and who have met their Lord, regardless of what may have been their original affiliation: Muslim, Jewish, Christian, etc. These believers may also be considered pure "theotropes" (*ḥanīf*, pl. *ḥunafā*), like Abraham. In our commentary on verse 2:62 we quoted verses 2:135 and 3:67 in which Abraham is qualified as a theotrope. Certain commentators, especially mystics, have asserted that each of the denominations of those who received a scripture previously had an etymological meaning which describes them in accordance with specific spiritual categories.

Qur'ān, 23:50. *And We made the son of Mary and his mother a portent, and 1) We gave them refuge on 2) a height, 3) a place of flocks and 4) springs.*

وَجَعَلْنَا ابْنَ مَرْيَمَ وَأُمَّهُ آيَةً وَآوَيْنَاهُمَا إِلَى رَبْوَةٍ ذَاتِ قَرَارٍ وَمَعِينٍ

In verse 21:91, we have already mentioned the existing affinity between Mary and Jesus to the extent of them constituting a single "*Sign*." This intimacy connecting them to each other permits them to be received into one and the same highly qualitative "place" given their exceptional constitution.

In verse 5:17 we have commented on each of the words composing the expression "*the Anoint, son of Mary and his mother*" which does not include a mentioning of "*Jesus*"; in verse 23:50, the term "*Anoint*" is not mentioned, nor is the name "*Jesus*."

The four terms from the end of this verse deserve to be analyzed etymologically in detail:

1)*We gave them refuge* The Qur'ānic root '-*w*-*y* making up this expression has the peculiarity of containing three radicals which are not mutually connected. This root means: to withdraw in order to take shelter (especially during the night), to take refuge, to look after, or to be moved by tenderness. Here it is conjugated in its fourth verbal form whose meaning is: to give shelter, to provide refuge, to receive someone inside as a host, to be hospitalized.

2) *a height* (*rabwat*^{in}). The root *r*-*b*-*w* from which the word *rabwat* is constructed means: augment, mount, climb up, increase, be elevated, inflate, and lend with interest. *Rabwat* therefore means a height, an elevated place, and an eminence.

3) *a resting place* (*qarār*^{in}). The term "*qarār*," meaning a fixed stay or place, stability, rest, tranquillity, firmness, or constancy, comes from the root *q*-*r*-*r*. This root is very rich in meanings, including: to stop, to rest, keep calm, persist, set in, settle, to ease, to be fresh and rested, to be consoled, feel joy after grief, etc. This term can therefore be translated as: a fresh and constant stay of permanent tranquillity and joy.

4) *and springs* (*ma'īn*^{in}). The noun *ma'īn* comes from the root '*a*-*w*-*n* which is also very rich in meaning: to flow, drip, and seep out, to have an essential nature, to touch or wound the

> eye, or to have a large eye pupil. *Ma'īn* therefore means: place where the water comes out from a source, spouting spring, stream, and limpid and pure flowing water. One can therefore translate it as *springs*.

This withdrawn, elevated, permanent, fresh, primordial, and essential "place" where Jesus and his mother are intimately received comes from the divine secret in everything related to it, from the origin of mother and child up to their withdrawal from this world.

> Qur'ān, 23:51. *O ye messengers! Eat of the good things, and do right. Lo! I am Aware of what ye do.*

يَا أَيُّهَا الرُّسُلُ كُلُوا مِنَ الطَّيِّبَاتِ وَاعْمَلُوا صَالِحًا إِنِّي بِمَا تَعْمَلُونَ عَلِيمٌ

An enigmatic verse! Does it concern all the messengers (*rusūl*) sent by God, up to Muḥammad? If such is the case, the vocative used here—"O ye messengers!"—by necessity addresses persons who are present, like every vocative. Although they have disappeared from this world, they remain in the subtle prolongations (*barzakh*) of the human state until the Day of Resurrection and continue to subtly hear the perennial divine Words contained in the Scripture (*kitāb*) that is actualized, the cosmic *Qur'ān* or Recitation. In this domain, it is possible to experience various forms of interferences from planes and beings found in this world and in the posthumous states after the bodily death. For example, the jinn heard the Qur'ān (sacred recitation) that the Prophet recited when he was returning from Taif to Mecca, at the time when he was persecuted by the inhabitants of these two towns: . . . *It hath been revealed unto me that a company of the jinn gave ear, and then said: Verily we have heard a wondrous recitation* (qur'ān)*which guideth unto rightness, and we believe in it* (Qur'ān, 72:1-2). *And when We inclined toward thee* (Muḥammad) *certain of the jinn, who wished to hear the Qur'ān and, when they were in its presence, said: Give ear! and, when it was finished, turned back to their people, warning. They said: O our people! Lo! we have heard a scripture* (kitāb)*which hath been revealed after Moses, confirming that which was before it, guiding unto the Truth and a right path* (Qur'ān, 46:29-30).

It is to be noted that this Scripture is not a simple piece of writing, but a complex act, a dynamic texture that evolves and is renewed continuously according to the Divine Plan and Wisdom. As such, it is inseparable from its recitation because of God's clarification, in verse 46:30, that the jinn heard the scripture in the form of recitation. On the other hand, the Prophet's recitation to the jinn had to affect those beings which were prepared to receive it.

What are the tasted realities experienced in a new way for these messengers in this world, presumed to be intermediary, through which God told them how to comport themselves correctly? The plural feminine noun *ṭayyibāt*, which we have rendered as "tasted realities," comes from the verbal root *t-y-b* which is rich in meanings: to be good, of good quality, pleasant, welcoming, excellent, and delightful; to have a good taste, to smell nice, etc. During the nocturnal ascension of the Prophet, his Lord inspired him with these words which are repeated at the end of daily ritual prayers: "The invigorating realities belong to Allah, the purifying realities belong to Allah, the delightful realities and the graces of nearness (or prayers) belong to Allah." The term *ṭayyibāt* therefore lends itself to numerous interpretations concerning the subsistence of beings in the posthumous life, as well as the religiously permitted foods that nourish the body in the here-below. Several verses mention the good foods which can be consumed in this world and the food that shall be bestowed upon believers in the Hereafter: *O ye who believe! Eat of the good things wherewith We have provided you, and render thanks to Allah if it is He Whom ye worship* (Qur'ān, 2:172). *Lo! those who kept their duty are amid shade and fountains, and fruits such as they desire.[Unto them it is said:]Eat, drink and welcome, O ye blessed, in return for what ye did. Thus do We reward the good* (Qur'ān, 77:41-44). *O Children of Adam! Look to your adornment at every place of worship, and eat and drink, but be not prodigal. Lo! He loveth not the prodigals. Say: Who hath forbidden the adornment of Allah which He hath brought forth for His bondmen, and the good things of His providing? Say: Such, on the Day of Resurrection, will be only for those who believed during the life of the world. Thus do we detail Our signs for people who have knowledge* (Qur'ān, 7:31-32).

Like most Qur'ānic words, the term *ṭayyibāt* comprises a number of superposed, polysemic, and anagogical meanings, as we have pointed out in the commentary on verse 4:172. One word may, to a certain extent, apply to hierarchical planes or degrees of reference that include a plurality of analogical, but never identical, meanings. The following verse shows an application thereof: *And give glad tidings unto those who believe and do good works; that theirs are Gardens underneath which rivers flow; as often as they are regaled with food of the fruit thereof, they say: this is what was given us aforetime; and it is given to them in resemblance. There for them are pure spouses* (*azwāj*)*; there forever they abide* (Qur'ān, 2:25).

Qur'ān, 23:52. *And lo! this your community is one community and I am your Lord, so keep your duty unto Me.*

وَإِنَّ هَٰذِهِۦٓ أُمَّتُكُمْ أُمَّةً وَٰحِدَةً وَأَنَا۠ رَبُّكُمْ فَٱتَّقُونِ

Whom does the word "your" address in this verse which follows the interpellation of the messengers in the previous verse?

For most of the commentators of the sacred text, the inner economy of this sequence shows that the verse refers to the community arising from the last Revelation, namely that which was established by the Seal of the Prophets, Muḥammad.

In our opinion, it could concern the community composed of all the communities, each of which comprises a messenger and his community to whom he is sent by Allah. In this perspective, this "community" can only be "one," for it represents the whole of mankind taken in its globality. Without exception, Allah remains the Lord of all messengers as well as the Lord of all beings, which submit to Him whether they recognize Him or not. For Allah has said: *Seek they other than the religion of Allah, when unto Him submitteth whosoever is in the heavens and the earth, willingly or unwillingly, and unto Him they will be returned* (Qur'ān, 3:83). Human kind, in its oneness, does not prevent the differentiation of communities, as God expresses it very clearly in the sacred text: *Mankind were one community, and Allah sent [unto them] prophets as bearers of good tidings and as warners, and revealed therewith the Scripture with the truth that it might judge between mankind concerning that wherein they differed . . .* (Qur'ān, 2:213).

Nonetheless, just as the Qur'ān sums up the previously revealed Scriptures, so does the Prophet of Islam synthesize all the previous prophetic types. This interpretation permits one to better understand the verse below:

Qur'ān, 23:53. *But they* (mankind)*cut off their affair, among them, into sects, each group rejoicing in that which is with itself.*

فَتَقَطَّعُوا أَمْرَهُم بَيْنَهُمْ زُبُرًا كُلُّ حِزْبٍ بِمَا لَدَيْهِمْ فَرِحُونَ

This verse indicates clearly that each community stands united at the beginning of each revelation but is then progressively divided, for several reasons. Each community is also disorganized, eventually ruining its own legitimate authority. What is one to make of the various authentic revelations that presently exist in the world, often clashing, each of which considers itself to hold exclusive authority and simply basks with satisfaction in what it possesses!?

The following synoptic table allows us to compare sequences of verses in which certain elements are common across different contexts:

<table>
<tr><td rowspan="2">21:91</td><td rowspan="2">And she kept her chastity (farj), therefore We breathed into her of Our Spirit and made her and her son a token for (all) peoples.</td><td>66:12</td><td>And Mary, daughter of 'Imrān, her body was chaste, therefore We breathed therein something of Our Spirit. And she put faith in the words of her Lord and His scriptures, and was of the obedient.</td></tr>
<tr><td>23:51</td><td>O ye messengers! Eat of the good things, and do right. Lo! I am Aware of what ye do.</td></tr>
<tr><td>21:92</td><td>Lo! this, your community, is one community, and I am your Lord, so worship Me.</td><td>23:52</td><td>And lo! this your community is one community and I am your Lord, so keep your duty unto Me.</td></tr>
<tr><td>21:93</td><td>And they have broken their religion (into fragments) among them, (yet) all are returning unto Us.</td><td>23:53</td><td>But they (mankind) cut off their affair, among them, into sects, each group rejoicing in that which is with itself.</td></tr>
</table>

21:94	Then whoso doeth some good works and is a believer, there will be no rejection of his effort. Lo! We record (it) for him.	23:54	So leave them in their error till a time.

The comparison focuses on the two verses 21:91 and 66:12, which we have commented on earlier. These verses include only a few differences that were mentioned in the commentary on 21:91. They both concern Mary, although verse 21:91 does not mention her name.

When we compare the two continuous sequences, 21:91-94 and 23:51-54, each of which is made up of four verses, we note that verse 21:91 concerning "*she who kept her chastity*"—presumed to be Mary, the daughter of 'Imrān and Mother of Jesus—corresponds to verse 23:51 of the other sequence which is indicated by "*O ye messengers!*"

When one considers the two nouns MaRYaM and RuSuL, one notes that the sum of the consonants forming each of them has the same arithmetic value. Maryam is composed of the letters *m-r-y-m*, or 40+200+10+40=290, and Rusul is composed of the letters r-s-l, or 200+60+30=290. According to this procedure, there is a certain correspondence between Mary and the Messengers as a whole. Indeed, Mary *confirms the Words of her Lord and His Scriptures.* Such a confirmation of the Scriptures and the lordly Words, and what is forever pertinent in them no matter the evolution of the human cycle of revelation, is also part of the function of the Messengers. One can therefore conclude that, just like in verse 21:91, Mary—without her name being mentioned—is portrayed as a perfect servant who receives in her wholly virgin and divinely predisposed being a universal function. This universal function is equally necessary for Messengers to bear, within themselves and to others, this divine Word and the sacred Scriptures until the end of time. The revealed text, in its subtlety, its symbolism and its conciseness, never ceases to permit us to discover treasures and secrets, so long as we meditate on them attentively and open ourselves to all its components.

Qur'ān, 29:46. *And dispute not with the People of the Scripture unless it be in [a way]that is better, save with such of them as do wrong; and say: We believe in that which hath been revealed unto us and revealed unto you; our Allah and your Allah is One, and unto Him we surrender.*

وَلَا تُجَادِلُوا أَهْلَ الْكِتَابِ إِلَّا بِالَّتِي هِيَ أَحْسَنُ إِلَّا الَّذِينَ ظَلَمُوا مِنْهُمْ وَقُولُوا آمَنَّا بِالَّذِي أُنْزِلَ إِلَيْنَا وَأُنْزِلَ إِلَيْكُمْ وَإِلَٰهُنَا وَإِلَٰهُكُمْ وَاحِدٌ وَنَحْنُ لَهُ مُسْلِمُونَ

The word *tujādilū*, which we have translated as the imperative "*dispute*," comes from the root *j-d-l*. In its first verbal form it means to: plait strongly, strengthen, and throw someone on the ground. Here, in its third conjugated form, it connotes the verbs: to dispute, argue, discuss, joust, engage in dialogue, use dialectics, polemicize, and contest. This divine imperative opens the verse and offers the possibility of the best kind of dialogue with the believers of other Revelations and Divine descents, though it does not specify modalities. Must this dialogue focus on apologetic questions, or rather must it be initiated within different topics whatever these may be, and with all the People of the Book, whoever they might be? The next part of the verse implies that there is agreement, on both sides, that God is the only object of exclusive worship. The People of the Book, or those Familiar with the Scripture (*ahl al-kitāb*), are those who are mentioned in verse 5:48, which we have already quoted when studying verse 2:62: *Say O People of the Scripture! Ye have naught [of guidance] till ye observe the Torah and the Gospel and that which was revealed unto you from your Lord. That which is revealed unto thee* (Muḥammad) *from thy Lord is certain to increase the contumacy and disbelief of many of them. But grieve not for the disbelieving folk* (Qur'ān, 5:68). As maintained by the majority of the Muslim commentators, "the People of the Book" are not only the Jews and the Christians but also all those who have received Scriptures in one form or another. They are all included in the "*you*" of the expression "*that which was revealed unto you.*" However, it is stipulated here to avoid initiating such dialogue with those who do wrong and whose intention is to denigrate the authentic religious values of the other.

Qur'ān, 29:47. *In like manner We have revealed unto thee the Scrip-*

ture, and those unto whom We gave the Scripture aforetime will believe therein; and of these [also] there are some who believe therein. And none deny Our revelations save the disbelievers.

وَكَذَٰلِكَ أَنْزَلْنَا إِلَيْكَ الْكِتَابَ فَالَّذِينَ آتَيْنَاهُمُ الْكِتَابَ يُؤْمِنُونَ بِهِ وَمِنْ هَٰؤُلَاءِ مَنْ يُؤْمِنُ بِهِ وَمَا يَجْحَدُ بِآيَاتِنَا إِلَّا الْكَافِرُونَ

The *unto thee* (*'ilay-ka*) first addresses the Prophet Muḥammad, then those who have adhered to Islam with him during his lifetime. Only the form taken by the Revelation differs in accordance with the evolution of the human cycle. The historical Islam transmitted by Muḥammad, Seal of the prophets and Messenger of Allah, only confirms that which remains forever pertinent to the divine prescriptions included in the universal Message communicated to each messenger that the One God has sent to humanity.

How should one understand "*those unto whom We gave the Scripture*?" They are those who, adhering to the historical or universal Islam, have been nourished by the Qur'ān through reciting it ritually and by meditating upon it profoundly. They are also those whom Allah has favoured with His Grace: only therein will they secure themselves through this Scripture (*yu'minūna bi-hi*). This expression is derived from the verbal root *'a-m-n* and conjugated in the fourth form with the preposition *bi*, meaning "by." The expression thus translates: to bring security by, to give confidence, to reassure by, to adhere to, to secure through, and to give shelter. In accordance with these meanings, the Divine Name al-Mu'min—a passive participle of the same verbal form—has the meaning of "the Giver of Security." In religious contexts, the last verbal root is often juxtaposed to the root *k-f-r*. We have encountered this root in the commentary on verses 3:52 and 5:17. Etymologically speaking, this root sometimes maintains some eminently positive meanings: to hide, conceal, or to make disappear like the farmer who sows as in the already quoted verse 57:20.

Qur'ān, 29:48. *And thou [O Muḥammad] wast not a transmitter of any scripture before it, nor didst thou trace it with thy right hand, for then might those have doubted, who follow falsehood.*

وَمَا كُنتَ تَتْلُو مِن قَبْلِهِ مِن كِتَابٍ وَلاَ تَخُطُّهُ بِيَمِينِكَ إِذاً لاَّرْتَابَ ٱلْمُبْطِلُونَ

Prior to the Prophet receiving the Revelation on Mount Ḥirā' near Mecca at the age of forty, he did not transmit or communicate any revealed scripture. He did not know any scripture and he did not know what faith was, according to the verses 42:52-53 that we quoted while commenting on verses 2:141, 19:16, and 19:35. Therefore the Prophet's primordial and innate knowledge of Allah was of a synthetic order. According to the tradition and certain verses (7:156-158), he was "unlettered" (*ummī*); we have dealt with this question in the commentary on verse 2:141.

In accordance with these references, we have interpreted the syntax of this verse (29:48) in the following way: we have considered the verb "*takhuttu*" (you trace) in the imperfect tense. The root of this verb, *kh-t-t*, means: to trace, to draw lines, to draw characters, or to write. In the imperfect tense, the verb has not been acted upon by a verb of existence *k-w-n* (*kunta* here) as is the verb "*tatlū*" (you transmit—*kunta tatlū*). This perfectly grammatical way of giving a certain independence to the components of the proposition in question allows us to translate *takhuttu* in the present and not in the imperfect tense, and therefore to affirm that the Prophet remained "unlettered" during all his life. If we admit that the verb *kunta* acts on the other two verbs *tatlū* and *takhattu*, we must translate the phrase which includes them in the following way: "*And thou wast not a transmitter of any scripture before it, nor didst thou trace it with thy right hand,*" and the imperfect tense could then imply, as certain authors have maintained, that the author had not been unlettered after receiving the Revelation.

Had the Prophet communicated revealed scriptures other than the Qur'ān, which was transmitted orally by the Archangel Gabriel, or written the Scripture in question with his hand, his deniers would have expressed doubts. They would have doubted his manner of receiving the Scripture, revealed in the form of the divine Dictation and thus recited orally, or doubted his sincerity.

Qur'ān, 33:7. *And when We exacted a covenant from the prophets, and from thee and from Noah and Abraham and Moses and Jesus son of Mary. We took from them a solemn covenant.*

وَإِذْ أَخَذْنَا مِنَ النَّبِيِّينَ مِيثَاقَهُمْ وَمِنْكَ وَمِنْ نُوحٍ وَإِبْرَاهِيمَ وَمُوسَى وَعِيسَى ابْنِ مَرْيَمَ وَأَخَذْنَا مِنْهُمْ مِيثَاقًا غَلِيظًا

Qur'ān, 33:8. *That He may ask the loyal of their loyalty. And He hath prepared a painful doom for the unbelievers.*

لِيَسْأَلَ الصَّادِقِينَ عَنْ صِدْقِهِمْ وَأَعَدَّ لِلْكَافِرِينَ عَذَابًا أَلِيمًا

This sequence first concerns all the prophets more generally, although they are not identified. The prophetic tradition states that there were 124,000 of them. It then deals with the prophets who articulate the important cyclical phases of humanity. "Thee" represents Muḥammad, who is placed at the forefront as the seal of the prophets who synthesized all the prophetic types. Then follow the major prophetic figures whose names are often mentioned in the Qur'ān, including Noah, Abraham, Moses, and Jesus, Son of Mary.

Let us note that here Jesus is mentioned with Mary, his mother, and not alone, thus confirming once again that Jesus and Mary are but a single, inseparable "Sign" in the function that they assume together, as we pointed out several times already.

What is this *covenant* that engages the prophets towards God? They must, with integrity, bring to their people the permanent Message that God communicates to them. This transmission comprises the veritable and constant worship due to the One God and the different prescriptions to be realized in order to achieve it. The forms taken by this message vary depending on the fruition of human beings within the shorter or longer cycles.

Qur'ān, 42:13. *He hath established for you that religion which He commended unto Noah, and that which We inspire in thee* (Muḥammad), *and that which We commended unto Abraham and Moses and Jesus, saying: Establish the religion, and be not divided therein. Dreadful for the idolaters is that unto which thou callest them. Allah chooseth for Himself whom He will, and guideth unto Himself him who turneth [toward Him].*

شَرَعَ لَكُمْ مِنَ الدِّينِ مَا وَصَّى بِهِ نُوحًا وَالَّذِي أَوْحَيْنَا إِلَيْكَ

وَمَا وَصَّيْنَا بِهِ إِبْرَاهِيمَ وَمُوسَى وَعِيسَى أَنْ أَقِيمُوا الدِّينَ وَلَا تَتَفَرَّقُوا فِيهِ كَبُرَ عَلَى الْمُشْرِكِينَ مَا تَدْعُوهُمْ إِلَيْهِ اللَّهُ يَجْتَبِي إِلَيْهِ مَنْ يَشَاءُ وَيَهْدِي إِلَيْهِ مَنْ يُنِيبُ

In the chapter on the universality of Islam, we have dealt with the theme of religion and its relationship with the etymology of the Qur'ānic term *dīn*. This is why we have translated *dīn* as "worship due." As we remarked in the same chapter, the prophetic tradition stipulates that the *dīn* comprises not only the ritual practices (*islām*) but also the foundations of faith (*īmān*) prescribed in the Qur'ān and the prophetic Sunna. It also involves the perfect inward and outward comportment of a person in sincere worship who is completely directed towards his Lord (*iḥsān*). These three prescriptions have been recognized all the way from Noah down to the last of the prophets, Muḥammad. The prophets mentioned in this verse—Noah, Abraham, Moses, Jesus, and Muḥammad whose name is not mentioned here—are those who have inaugurated distinct and progressive transitional phases of the traditional human cycle. The universal content of this "worship due" includes first and foremost the Unity of God and the exclusive worship due to Him, as well as other prescriptions. This worship should necessarily concern human beings to avoid them becoming divided and to remain united around these essential themes. However, this unity should occur without alienating individual vocations within the context of normative modalities of worship, which are lived individually in markedly varied ways. Indeed, each individual is unique and thus is a reflection of this divine Unity that is universally diversified in countless facets of creation. These fundamental divine injunctions which seem so evident to many individuals, and which unite them on the essentials, are contested or rejected by others who disperse their energies, their virtue, and their gifts in the multiplicity of the conditions of existence without recognizing the Principle of unity which gives us life. *O mankind! Lo! We have created you male and female, and have made you nations and tribes that ye may know one another. Lo! the noblest of you, in the sight of Allah, is the best in conduct. Lo! Allah is Knower, Aware* (Qur'ān, 49:13).

Qur'ān, 43:57. *And when the son of Mary is held as an example, behold, thy people raise a clamor thereat [in ridicule]!*

وَلَمَّا ضُرِبَ ابْنُ مَرْيَمَ مَثَلًا إِذَا قَوْمُكَ مِنْهُ يَصِدُّونَ

Surah 43 was revealed in Mecca, the 63rd in order of revelation.

The expression "the Son of Mary" is used in this verse only to qualify Jesus in this way. This name suffices to identify him without confusing him with another person, for since it is impossible that he had a human father, he is known by the name of his mother and not by the name of his father, as is the custom among the Jews and also Arabs. In addition, the complete name of Jesus—"*the Anoint, Jesus, Son of Mary*"—is announced to Mary by the angels in verse 3:45. This verse was revealed in Medina as the 89th Surah, at the moment that the angels make their Annunciation to Mary about the coming of Jesus. It is with the name "Son of Mary" that he is introduced as an *example* (*mathal*) to those mostly polytheist persons who stood by the Prophet and who refused to consider Jesus as *model*. The term *mathal* has been discussed in the commentary on verse 3:59.

Qur'ān, 43:58. *And say: Are our gods better, or is he? They raise not the objection save for argument. Nay! but they are a contentious folk.*

وَقَالُوا أَآلِهَتُنَا خَيْرٌ أَمْ هُوَ مَا ضَرَبُوهُ لَكَ إِلَّا جَدَلًا بَلْ هُمْ قَوْمٌ خَصِمُونَ

These Meccan polytheists who worshiped idols liken their worship to that which certain Christians devoted to the Son of Mary. The question arises as to whether their idols were better than Jesus. But were those who posed such questions sincere? The end of this verse leaves no doubt about this subject. These people were only interested in dispute, lacking as they did consciousness of the worship due exclusively to God, and also the intuition of the reality of the person of Jesus whom they identified as being just "*the Son of Mary*" and not "*the Anoint, Jesus Son of Mary.*" They disputed his case without having certain knowledge thereof, and this rendered them incapable of speaking about him in a satisfactory way.

Qur'ān, 43:59. *He is nothing but a slave on whom We bestowed favour, and We made him a pattern for the Children of Israel.*

إِنْ هُوَ إِلَّا عَبْدٌ أَنْعَمْنَا عَلَيْهِ وَجَعَلْنَاهُ مَثَلًا لِبَنِي إِسْرَائِيلَ

Jesus is but a servant (*'abd* = worshipper, servant)—entirely and perfectly. His will is that of his Lord, and he is fully conscious that it is God who acts in him. For this fundamental reason, Allah has accorded him His grace and has made him a model to be emulated by those who have recognized his value. The same is true for the Prophet Muḥammad who is an "excellent model" to be emulated: *Verily in the messenger of Allah ye have an excellent model for him who looketh unto Allah and the Last Day, and remembereth Allah much.* (Qur'ān, 33:21). Here the term model is *uswat* and not *mathal* as in 43:57 and 43:59. It comes from the root *'-s-w*: to treat, heal, console, aid, and to return to the normal state. *Uswat* is then the emulation, the model, the consolation, the remedy, and the support.

Qur'ān, 43:60. *And had We willed We could have set among you angels to be viceroys in the earth.*

وَلَوْ نَشَاءُ لَجَعَلْنَا مِنْكُمْ مَلَائِكَةً فِي الْأَرْضِ يَخْلُفُونَ

This verse, which is inserted between two others referring to Jesus, causes difficulty regarding the way in which it should be related to the other two. The exegetes of the Qur'ān comment on it without situating it and therefore without referring to Jesus. The case of Jesus was contested during his apostleship and after his ascent by many individuals, including Jews, Christians, idolaters, and the Arabs during the time of the Prophet. Does that mean that Allah could have replaced human beings in order to maintain peace and assure the function of Vicegerency? *And when thy Lord said unto the angels: Lo! I am about to place a viceroy in the earth, they said: Wilt thou place therein one who will do harm therein and will shed blood, while we hymn Thy praise and sanctify Thee? He said: Surely I know that which ye know not* (Qur'ān, 2:30). *He it is Who hath placed you as viceroys of the earth and hath exalted some of you in rank above others, that He may try you by (the test of) that which He hath given you. Lo! Thy Lord is swift in prosecution, and Lo! He verily is Forgiving, Merciful* (Qur'ān, 6:165).

Qur'ān, 43:61. *And [Jesus] shall be a Sign [of recognition for] the*

Hour [of Judgment]: therefore have no doubt about the [Hour], but follow ye Me: this is a Straight Way.

وَإِنَّهُ لَعِلْمٌ لِلسَّاعَةِ فَلَا تَمْتَرُنَّ بِهَا وَاتَّبِعُونِ هَذَا صِرَاطٌ مُسْتَقِيمٌ

The term which we have translated as a "Sign [of recognition]" is *'ilm* in the present version. Certain traditionalists used to read it *'alam*, meaning token or sign. In this context, sign indicates the limit of two or more things. Like *'ilm*, this term also comes from the verbal root *'-l-m*, which is rich in meanings: to mark, to distinguish by a sign or token, to know how to distinguish a thing from another, etc. This word could be also, and more justifiably, be translated as "limit sign."

This verse has confirmed numerous traditions, some of which go back to the Prophet, regarding the second coming of Jesus under the jurisdiction and the form of Islam, before the end of times. During his nocturnal ascension, the Messenger of Allah met several messengers, one of whom was Jesus. He asked Jesus about the Hour. He specified: ". . . The knowledge of the premises of its coming has been given to me and only Allah knows its advent . . ." (Nasā'ī, *Sunan*, I, 77).

The Hour (*sā'a*) is mentioned forty-eight times in the sacred text. Let us quote some verses wherein this term is found:

> *Men ask thee of the Hour. Say: The knowledge of it is with Allah only. What can convey [the knowledge] unto thee? It may be that the Hour is nigh* (Qur'ān, 33:63).

> *To Allah belongeth the Mystery of the heavens and the earth. And the Decision of the Hour [of Judgment] is as the twinkling of an eye, or even quicker: for Allah hath power over all things* (Qur'ān, 16:77).

> *Lo! the knowledge of the Hour is with Allah [alone]. It is He Who sends down rain, and He Who knows what is in the wombs. Nor does any one know what it is that he will earn on the morrow: Nor does any one know in what land he is to die. Lo! Allah is Knower, Aware* (Qur'ān, 31:34).

There are numerous works in French concerning the second coming of Jesus at the end of time. The traditions that they quote do not always converge, nor are they mutually consistent. Therefore they must be consulted with discernment. A critical work on this important subject is yet to be written.

> Qur'ān, 43:62. *And let not Satan turn you aside. Lo! he is an open enemy for you.*

وَلَا يَصُدَّنَّكُمُ الشَّيْطَانُ إِنَّهُ لَكُمْ عَدُوٌّ مُبِينٌ

This verse warns against the most disparate interpretations of the preceding verse and echoes in a certain way the words of the Gospel mentioned in Matthew 24:23-25, *Then if any man shall say unto you, Lo, here [is] Christ, or there; believe [it] not. For there shall arise false Christs, and false prophets, and shall shew great signs and wonders; insomuch that, if [it were] possible, they shall deceive the very elect. Behold, I have told you before.*

> Qur'ān, 43:63. *When Jesus came with clear proofs, he said: I have come unto you with wisdom, and to make plain some of that concerning which ye differ. So keep your duty to Allah, and obey me.*

وَلَمَّا جَاءَ عِيسَى بِالْبَيِّنَاتِ قَالَ قَدْ جِئْتُكُمْ بِالْحِكْمَةِ وَلِأُبَيِّنَ
لَكُمْ بَعْضَ الَّذِي تَخْتَلِفُونَ فِيهِ فَاتَّقُوا اللَّهَ وَأَطِيعُونِ

Certain commentators, such as Ibn 'Abbās, are of the opinion that the *bayyināt*, translated as *the clear proofs*, refer only to those miracles performed by Jesus that are mentioned in the Qur'ānic text. These miracles include: bringing the dead back to life, curing those who were born blind, healing the lepers, giving life to birds created from clay, and bringing down the Table-Spread. Others, such as Qatāda, assert that it refers to the Gospel (*Injīl*). The term *bayyināt* has been discussed in the commentary on verses 2:87 and 5:110.

The term *ḥikma*, translated as "wisdom," has already been commented upon when dealing with verse 3:48.

The clarification in question refers to, according to the commentators, certain prescriptions, exhortations, and rules of wisdom contained in both the Torah and in the Gospel. Both scriptures were, or are, an object of controversy due to the difficulties arising from the way they should be interpreted or understood.

Qur'ān, 43:64. *Lo! Allah, He is my Lord and your Lord. So worship Him. This is a right path.*

إِنَّ اللَّهَ هُوَ رَبِّي وَرَبُّكُمْ فَاعْبُدُوهُ هَذَا صِرَاطٌ مُسْتَقِيمٌ

We have already encountered the expression *my Lord* and *your Lord* in verse 5:117. The distinction that Jesus makes between *my* and *your* is one of the proofs of the wisdom which he demonstrates, for everyone worships their Lord, He who concern each worshipper in accordance with possibilities that are not those of another worshipper. Indeed, the Lord of each person is unique, just as the worship dedicated to Him is unique, Allah being the 'summation of Lords. It is a *straight path* that concerns everyone. It is also individual, for the basic differences between individuals lead them onto different paths, different trajectories just like arrows shot by several archers at the same target, or the attraction of pieces of metal around a magnet.

Qur'ān, 43:65. *But the factions among them differed. Then woe unto those who do wrong from the doom of a painful day.*

فَاخْتَلَفَ الْأَحْزَابُ مِنْ بَيْنِهِمْ فَوَيْلٌ لِلَّذِينَ ظَلَمُوا مِنْ عَذَابِ يَوْمٍ أَلِيمٍ

Qur'ān, 43:66. *Await they aught save the Hour, that it shall come upon them suddenly, when they know not?*

هَلْ يَنْظُرُونَ إِلَّا السَّاعَةَ أَنْ تَأْتِيَهُمْ بَغْتَةً وَهُمْ لَا يَشْعُرُونَ

According to certain commentators, the factions (*aḥzāb*) at issue here represent different schools of interpretation that diverge mainly on the question of divine Unity, the "Three Persons" of the Trinity, and the question of Jesus in particular. Allah therefore warns them against closed dogmatic positions and against their controversial attitudes; these mentalities make them forget the presence of God both in the present moment and at the unpredictable time of the Hour. For each person, each passing moment is already a prelude to one's passing on to the limits of this world; this concept is evoked by the Islamic belief in "the renewal of creation at each instant." The verses on the Hour—previously discussed in relation to verse 43:61—bring out the instantaneity of the Hour, situated as it is outside of measured time. Allah thus reminds us that everyone must urgently cultivate an awareness and concern that permeates every instant.

Qur'ān, 48:29. *Muḥammad is the messenger of Allah. And those with him are hard against the disbelievers and merciful among themselves. Thou [O Muḥammad] seest them bowing and falling prostrate, seeking bounty from Allah and [His] acceptance. The mark of them is on their foreheads from the traces of prostration.*

Such is their likeness in the Torah and their likeness in the Gospel—like as sown corn that sendeth forth its shoot and strengtheneth it and riseth firm upon its stalk, delighting the sowers—that He may anger the disbelievers with (the sight of) them. Allah hath promised, unto such of them as believe and do good works, forgiveness and immense reward.

مُّحَمَّدٌ رَّسُولُ اللَّهِ وَالَّذِينَ مَعَهُ أَشِدَّاءُ عَلَى الْكُفَّارِ رُحَمَاءُ بَيْنَهُمْ
تَرَاهُمْ رُكَّعًا سُجَّدًا يَبْتَغُونَ فَضْلًا مِّنَ اللَّهِ وَرِضْوَانًا سِيمَاهُمْ فِي
وُجُوهِهِم مِّنْ أَثَرِ السُّجُودِ ذَٰلِكَ مَثَلُهُمْ فِي التَّوْرَاةِ وَمَثَلُهُمْ فِي
الْإِنجِيلِ كَزَرْعٍ أَخْرَجَ شَطْأَهُ فَآزَرَهُ فَاسْتَغْلَظَ فَاسْتَوَىٰ عَلَىٰ
سُوقِهِ يُعْجِبُ الزُّرَّاعَ لِيَغِيظَ بِهِمُ الْكُفَّارَ وَعَدَ اللَّهُ الَّذِينَ آمَنُوا
وَعَمِلُوا الصَّالِحَاتِ مِنْهُم مَّغْفِرَةً وَأَجْرًا عَظِيمًا

The name "Muḥammad" has been commented upon in detail at the beginning of this work, in the chapter entitled "Muḥammad is the Messenger of Allah."

Although the Gospels presently available to us do not mention it literally, this parable takes on great symbolic and metaphorical meaning in the Qur'ānic text. The sowers in question hope, thanks to their effort and for their own good, to see the grains that God has created grow and develop. They draw a lesson for themselves from this concrete parable and thus increases their faith, whereas those who do not believe in God are irritated by this parable.

Qur'ān, 57:26. *And We verily sent Noah and Abraham and placed the prophethood and the scripture among their seed, and among them there is he who goeth right, but many of them are evil-livers.*

وَلَقَدْ أَرْسَلْنَا نُوحًا وَإِبْرَاهِيمَ وَجَعَلْنَا فِي ذُرِّيَّتِهِمَا النُّبُوَّةَ وَالْكِتَابَ فَمِنْهُمْ مُهْتَدٍ وَكَثِيرٌ مِنْهُمْ فَاسِقُونَ

Qur'ān, 57:27. *Then We caused Our messengers to follow in their footsteps; and We caused Jesus, son of Mary, to follow, and gave him the Gospel, and placed compassion and mercy in the hearts of those who followed him. But monasticism they invented—We ordained it not for them—only seeking Allah's pleasure, and they observed it not with right observance. So We give those of them who believe their reward, but many of them are evil-livers.*

ثُمَّ قَفَّيْنَا عَلَى آثَارِهِمْ بِرُسُلِنَا وَقَفَّيْنَا بِعِيسَى ابْنِ مَرْيَمَ وَآتَيْنَاهُ الْإِنْجِيلَ وَجَعَلْنَا فِي قُلُوبِ الَّذِينَ اتَّبَعُوهُ رَأْفَةً وَرَحْمَةً وَرَهْبَانِيَّةً ابْتَدَعُوهَا مَا كَتَبْنَاهَا عَلَيْهِمْ إِلَّا ابْتِغَاءَ رِضْوَانِ اللَّهِ فَمَا رَعَوْهَا حَقَّ رِعَايَتِهَا فَآتَيْنَا الَّذِينَ آمَنُوا مِنْهُمْ أَجْرَهُمْ وَكَثِيرٌ مِنْهُمْ فَاسِقُونَ

The expression "their footsteps" refers to Noah and Abraham, in whose posterity prophethood was established. This descent comprises messenger-prophets, others who are only prophets, and those who follow them with diverse inner and outer dispositions that they carry in themselves according to the divine Plan. These dispositions make the followers rightly guided or corrupt. Jesus Son of Mary is one of these messenger-prophets, and Allah has given the Gospel to him.

Allah has placed compassion and mercy in those who follow Him, but what are the comportments of those who do not follow Him? What do those who are indifferent to Him, and who do not recognize Him in His reality and His role? The Qur'ānic text specifies only that they become corrupt; that is, they destroy themselves by damaging their own primordial nature (*fiṭra*) and wronging themselves.

On the other hand, what is the meaning of *monasticism*

(*rahbāniyya*)? This descriptive noun comes from the verbal root *r-h-b*, previously encountered in verse 9:31 and meaning: to fear, dread, to be afraid, and to feel threatened. It is linked to those who fear the life of this world and desire intensely to distance themselves from its perils and temptations, in order to draw near to God and please Him by taking Jesus Son of Mary and his lifestyle as their model. Does living in this way not imply escaping the world and shirking the difficulties of the straight path? Does this verse thus imply a condemnation of the excesses associated with monasticism?

> Qur'ān, 61:6. *And when Jesus son of Mary said: O Children of Israel! Lo! I am the messenger of Allah unto you, confirming that which was (revealed) before me in the Torah, and bringing good tidings of a messenger who cometh after me, whose name is the Praised One. Yet when he hath come unto them with clear proofs, they say: This is mere magic.*

وَإِذْ قَالَ عِيسَى ابْنُ مَرْيَمَ يَا بَنِي إِسْرَائِيلَ إِنِّي رَسُولُ اللَّهِ إِلَيْكُمْ
مُصَدِّقًا لِمَا بَيْنَ يَدَيَّ مِنَ التَّوْرَاةِ وَمُبَشِّرًا بِرَسُولٍ يَأْتِي مِنْ
بَعْدِي اسْمُهُ أَحْمَدُ فَلَمَّا جَاءَهُمْ بِالْبَيِّنَاتِ قَالُوا هَذَا سِحْرٌ مُبِينٌ

In verse 3:49, we have commented on the expression "*Children of Israel*." It was to the Children of Israel that Jesus, Son of Mary was sent as a Messenger of Allah.

On the other hand, in verse 5:46 we commented on the expression *bayna yadayya*, translated here as *between my two hands* or *which is always current for me*. Jesus Son of Mary, as the Messenger of Allah, brings a Law confirming that the prescriptions of the Torah can always be applied to the new cycle of revelation. The Messenger of Allah inaugurates the new cycle without however abrogating the Mosaic Law, for this verse does not imply abrogation. The difficult question of confirmation and/or abrogation has been the object of numerous interpretations. In Islam, it explains in part the "compensatory head tax" (*jizya*) that we have mentioned in the commentary on verse 9:29.

In this verse, Jesus Son of Mary is responsible for announcing the glad tidings of a Messenger arriving after him. According to the teachings of Islam, no messenger was sent between Jesus and Muḥammad, and therefore this verse could only refer to the Prophet of Islam. He is called Aḥmad, a heavenly name of the Prophet meaning "the most praised, the most praiseworthy," according to both the etymology *ḥ-m-d* of this noun and the paradigm according to which this elative is constructed.

On the other hand—and this is essential for the understanding of this verse that cannot be doubted, for it is the word of God revealed to the Prophet like every other verse contained in the Qur'ān—God does not tell Jesus that the name of the Messenger who will come after him is mentioned in the Gospel. According to this verse, during his apostleship Jesus merely announced the coming of the Prophet Muḥammad whose heavenly name is Aḥmad. Again according to the verse, he did not say that this name appears in the Gospel he transmitted. It is the Qur'ānic commentators who envisaged that the name of the Messenger in question who would come after him was mentioned in the Gospel.

In addition, in the authenticated texts of the different gospels in our possession, there is no explicit, convincing, or allusive indication to this matter. One must exclude from these gospels those that are openly recognized as later forgeries seeking to support certain polemical theses.

Certain contemporary Muslim commentators and some Western scholars assert that elements of chapters XIV, XV, and XVI of the Gospel of John, which mentions the Greek noun *parakletos* in its Anglicized form "Paraclete," would seem to designate the Prophet Muḥammad. This Greek noun means: comforter, adviser, intercessor, mediator, advocate, and revealer. Certain modern polemists think that this Greek word has been misinterpreted and that it should have been read as "periklitos," with the meaning of "praised" or glorified." Only the two vowels of these two Greek words differ whereas their consonants, or consonant framework, are the same: PRKLTS. This explanation arises from a gratuitous hypothesis that seems forced, in order to justify the assertion that the three chapters of the Gospel of John concern the Prophet Muḥammad. Let us quote certain passages from these three chapters, as well as the first epistle of John referred to by the commentators:

Ch.	vs.	Gospel of John
XIV	15	If ye love me, keep my commandments.
XIV	16	And I will pray the Father, and he shall give you another Paraclete, that he may abide with you for ever;

XIV	17	[Even] the Spirit of truth; whom the world cannot receive, because it seeth him not, neither knoweth him: but ye know him; for he dwelleth with you, and shall be in you.
XIV	26	But the Paraclete, the Holy Ghost, whom the Father will send in my name, he shall teach you all things, and bring all things to your remembrance, whatsoever I have said unto you.

XV	26	But when the Paraclete is come, whom I will send unto you from the Father, [even] the Spirit of truth, which proceedeth from the Father, he shall testify of me:
XV	27	And ye also shall bear witness, because ye have been with me from the beginning.

XVI	5	But now I go my way to him that sent me; and none of you asketh me, Whither goest thou?
XVI	6	But because I have said these things unto you, sorrow hath filled your heart.
XVI	7	Nevertheless I tell you the truth; It is expedient for you that I go away: for if I go not away, the Comforter will not come unto you; but if I depart, I will send him unto you.
XVI	8	And when he is come, he will reprove the world of sin, and of righteousness, and of judgment:
XVI	9	Of sin, because they believe not on me;
XVI	10	Of righteousness, because I go to my Father, and ye see me no more;
XVI	11	Of judgment, because the prince of this world is judged.
XVI	12	I have yet many things to say unto you, but ye cannot bear them now.
XVI	13	Howbeit when he, the Spirit of truth, is come, he will guide you into all truth: for he shall not speak of himself; but whatsoever he shall hear, [that] shall he speak: and he will shew you things to come.
XVI	14	He shall glorify me: for he shall receive of mine, and shall shew [it] unto you.
XVI	15	All things that the Father hath are mine: therefore said I, that he shall take of mine, and shall shew [it] unto you.

Ch.	vs.	FIRST EPISTLE OF JOHN
II	1	My little children, these things write I unto you, that ye sin not. And if any man sin, we have an advocate (*paraclete*) with the Father, Jesus Christ the righteous

In the first epistle of John, Jesus Christ is also called "paraclete" (advocate), thus confirming the content of verse XIV:16 in which Jesus speaks of himself as also being a paraclete. He refers to himself as a paraclete that the Father will give, but who is not the Holy Spirit mentioned in XIV:26. This term is therefore significant as a qualifier, as specified by verse XIV:16: in verse XVI:13 the Paraclete, or the Holy Spirit, is likened to the Spirit of Truth that assumes all possible forms in exercising this function.

If, as some have maintained, the Prophet Muḥammad, through the name Aḥmad ("very praised" in Arabic) was indeed the "person" whom Jesus calls *paraclete* in the Gospel, then how should one interpret the fact that in the Gospel Jesus could ask God, his Father, to send Muḥammad? It is thus impossible to admit that the demand Jesus makes to his Father in verses XIV:26 and XV:26 of the Gospel of John should concern the Prophet of Islam. The only convincing lesson for understanding the word that Jesus pronounces in this Qur'ānic verse is that which we have advanced: Jesus did utter it, but we have not yet discovered the gospel so at the present we have no scriptural proof of this declaration.

There is an additional issue of fundamental importance for Christians: in these three chapters of John, Jesus directly addresses his immediate disciples, who become concerned by his predictions when he announces the advent and the "rule" of the "Paraclete" as being imminent. He tells them that this change will occur on the Pentecost, fifty days after the disappearance of Christ, when the Spirit is manifested unexpectedly to the disciples who had gathered in the same place. Yet, after these statements by Jesus Christ, the coming of the Prophet Muḥammad would not take place until six centuries had passed.

On the other hand, if the Paraclete is not only a man but also a divine reality—that is, the Holy Spirit or the Spirit of Truth, as the text from the gospel of John makes clear—then he will be expressed in other countless aspects and forms befitting the countless circumstances, but not necessarily in the form of words.

In the Qur'ān, the Messenger of Allah—whoever he may be—is invested by God Himself with the Function of transmitting the divine Message in different personified forms called, for example, Muḥammad, or Jesus. This Messenger may also be of an angelic nature like Gabriel, the permanent Archangel of the Revelation, who manifested himself in several aspects throughout the apostleship of the Prophet of Islam.

Qur'ān, 61:14. *O ye who believe! Be Allah's helpers, even as Jesus son of Mary said unto the disciples: Who are my helpers for Allah? They said: We are Allah's helpers. And a party of the Children of Israel believed, while a party disbelieved. Then We strengthened those who believed against their foe, and they became the uppermost.*

يَا أَيُّهَا الَّذِينَ آمَنُوا كُونُوا أَنْصَارَ اللَّهِ كَمَا قَالَ عِيسَى ابْنُ مَرْيَمَ لِلْحَوَارِيِّينَ مَنْ أَنْصَارِي إِلَى اللَّهِ قَالَ الْحَوَارِيُّونَ نَحْنُ أَنْصَارُ اللَّهِ فَآمَنَتْ طَائِفَةٌ مِنْ بَنِي إِسْرَائِيلَ وَكَفَرَتْ طَائِفَةٌ فَأَيَّدْنَا الَّذِينَ آمَنُوا عَلَى عَدُوِّهِمْ

In verses 3:52 and 5:111, we have already studied the terms *ḥawāriyyūn*, meaning disciples, and *anṣār*, meaning helpers.

This verse—which is the one before the last in the Qur'ān that simultaneously evokes Jesus, his mission, the disciples who strengthened him, and the children of Israel to whom he was sent and who followed or contested him—recapitulates the important elements of his apostleship.

Qur'ān, 66:12. *And Mary, daughter of 'Imrān, whose body was chaste, therefore We breathed therein something of Our Spirit. And she put faith in the words of her Lord and His scriptures, and was of the obedient.*

وَمَرْيَمَ ابْنَتَ عِمْرَانَ الَّتِي أَحْصَنَتْ فَرْجَهَا فَنَفَخْنَا فِيهِ مِنْ رُوحِنَا وَصَدَّقَتْ بِكَلِمَاتِ رَبِّهَا وَكُتُبِهِ وَكَانَتْ مِنَ الْقَانِتِينَ

In commenting on the verses 3:42, 3:43, 21:91, and 23:53, we have highlighted certain aspects concerning Mary's perfect constitution. Now we wish to quickly explain the characteristic elements of Mary that structure this verse.

The name of Jesus is not mentioned here, and Mary is called "daughter of 'Imrān," the 'Imrān whose name refers to that of Amran, father of Aaron, as we have explained in the commentary on verses 3:33-34. On the other hand, Mary is closely linked to a line of prophets who *descend one from another*, according to verse 3:34.

Not only is she a virgin, but she also maintains her virginal nature. Then Allah, with all of His Names, breathes His Spirit into the totality of her being. Thus she could welcome and receive the Word that the Spirit conveyed unto her, and thereby conceive—in all her amplitude—Jesus who is the Word of Allah and "Spirit from Him." It is the Spirit of Allah that assumed, in the form of the Archangel, the likeness of a perfect man carrying this Word. Since Mary carries it, she can confer the Word in its countless modes of expression, as well as confirm the Scriptures that Allah reveals to His messenger-prophets in the most diverse forms. Mary's whole being therefore had to be perfectly receptive and possessing of a total concentration on maintaining full mastery of the environment in which she had been called to grow.

It is remarkable that this verse, which shows Mary's perfection as being capable of confirming divine Words and Scriptures, closes the group of verses dealing with her and her son. Once more, we wish to point out that the order of the presentation of surahs and verses in the codex of Caliph 'Uthmān is not arbitrary, but rather results from an ordering inspired by God Himself.

Chapter VIII

Conclusion of Chapter VII

We have devoted Chapter VII to commentary on the verses regarding Jesus, Mary, Zachariah, and Yaḥyā. These verses represent the perspective of Islam, the last historical Revelation, as received by the seal of the Prophets, Muḥammad. Among other important themes, this chapter has enabled us to depict the personality of the Anoint, Jesus, Son of his virgin mother Mary, and to show how Zachariah and Yaḥyā are closely linked by congenital and spiritual kinship.

In this conclusion, we will regroup and list the verses on the Divine interrelations between Allah, the Lord, His Command, His Spirit, and the created entities or beings directly related to those realities, be they angels, the Spirit which appears in several forms, Gabriel, the Archangel of Revelation, the Prophet Muḥammad, Jesus, Mary, Adam, or the Believers. All of these entities are concerned with the Spirit of Allah who manifests its countless possibilities.

The schema shown below will permit us to better situate the principal realities and the beings upon which they are applied, according to relationships resulting from pertinent verses translated below. In order to facilitate commentary of the verses, we have included the table below. The numbers are determined according to a certain order that we have adopted, but this scheme could be different, instead counting from zero to nine on a representative and pedagogic basis. This would involve ten divisions, without the need to see allusions to a dogmatic Christian perspective both with respect to the "Trinity" and to "Filiation." Let us see therefore what these ten numbers correspond to.

***

The table below and those that follow, as well as the verses illustrating these schematic presentations, allow us to show new aspects that previous exegetes have not fully emphasized. They will justify in a more concrete way the relationships which govern the realities thus exposed: divine (numbers 1, 2, and 3), angelic (number 5), and human (numbers 4, 6, 7, 8, and 9), and the atemporal and temporal relationships existing between them.

Table I

Divine, angelic, and human realities (from 1 to 9) concerning Adam, Mary, the Anoint Jesus Son of Mary, the Prophet, and the Believers

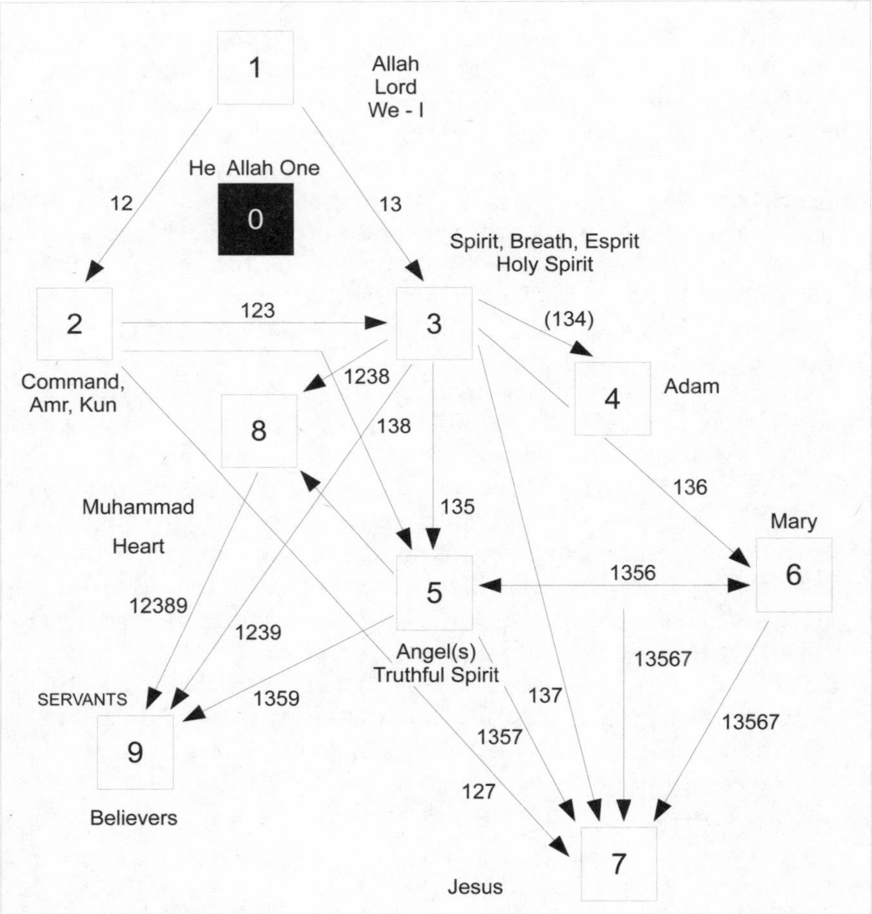

-0-
ALLAH AS ESSENCE

Our focus is the name Allah and that to which it alludes in certain verses. It is a pure designation of the Infinite, the Absolute, the Ineffable, the Inexpressible, the inexplicable, and the unqualifiable: the absolute Mystery which is spoken of only in negative terms. It alludes to the unconditioned Essence (*Dhāt*), as He Himself states in verse 3:97, 29:6, and 112:1 for instance. He is beyond all determination. It is the Mystery of the Mystery (*ghayb al-ghayb*), the absolute Silence, and the unfathomable Void.

In verse 112:1, the phrase "*Say, He, Allah,[is]One*" designates the mysterious and unfathomable Essence. The Divine Name *Aḥad*, meaning "One," posits the indivisible and undifferentiated Unity, the Non-Duality of this Essence, and the absence of even essential relationships. In the unqualifiable, non-qualified divine Unity, the beautiful Divine Names (*al-asmā' al-ḥusnā*) which are primordial relationships at the Degree of the Unicity (*waḥdaniyya*) or of the divine Function which they qualify, are not distinguished from each other; they are in potentiality "within" this Unity and synthetically hidden within It.

1
ALLAH, IN HIS FUNCTION OF DIVINITY

When Allah is envisaged in His divine Function (*ulūhiyya*), He is subtly present in all Degrees of the universal Manifestation. He is then perceived as a worshiped God (*ilāh*).

The divine Function comprises countless relational and hierarchical aspects, some of which are mentioned in the Qur'ānic text. In this function, Allah is qualified by pronouns: I (*anā*), Thou (*anta*), We (*nahnu*), and Lord (*Rabb*). He also possesses the most beautiful Names (*al-asmā' al-ḥusnā'*) (cf. Qur'ān 7:180, 10:16, 17:110, 20:8, and 59:24) whose number is 99 according to the tradition.

2 AND 3
TWO PRINCIPAL DIVINE FUNCTIONS: THE COMMAND (AMR) AND THE SPIRIT (RŪḤ)

In addition, Allah possesses essential, principal, uncreated, and necessary Functions in order for the universal Manifestation to occur: these Functions include the Command (*amr*), the existentiating Word (*Kun, Kalima, qawl*), the Spirit (*rūḥ*), and the Holy Spirit (*rūḥ al-qudūs*). The latter takes forms that are adapted to the situation and listed in the Qur'ān in numerous places. The Holy Spirit is mentioned four times in three verses concerning Jesus, Son of Mary, as we shall see below, and in one verse concerning the Prophet Muḥammad (16:102).

These essential functions are not considered as divine Names and must therefore be differentiated. They are excluded from the list of ninety-nine Names that qualify God according to the Tradition. Hence, the Divine Name *al-'Alīm*, meaning "the Omniscient," is not identifiable with the function of the Command (*al-amr*) even though the latter is in a direct and inseparable relationship with Divine Knowledge (*'ilm*). The Divine Name *al-Ḥayy*, the Living, is not identifiable with the function of the Spirit (*al-Rūḥ*), even though the latter is animated by divine Life and even though It invigorates everything.

Through His Principal Order (*amr*) which is expressed by the imperative in the second person *kun*, come to existence!, become!, be!, the divine Words are disseminated and are exteriorized by the supreme function of the Spirit—or of the divine Breath (*rūḥ*)—which brings into play the universal divine Name *al-Raḥmān*, the Infinitely Good This happens through the Breath (*nafas raḥmān*) of which all the realities are "breathed out" and therefore come to existence. Or they are "breathed in" and therefore reabsorbed into their single divine Principle.

Although they are not always mentioned together in the same verse, the two essential and principal functions of the Command and the Spirit are not conceivable without each other; they are both in necessary and inseparable relationships in order for universal Manifestation to take place.

Let us quote some verses in which Allah mentions His Command and His Spirit:

> *They ask thee concerning the Spirit. Say: The Spirit is by command of my Lord (al-Rūḥ min 'Amri Rabb), and of knowledge ye have been vouchsafed but little* (Qur'ān, 17:85).

In this verse, the Command and the Spirit are envisaged in themselves, in a universal manner, in the Divine Principle and without any qualifier which would inflect or specify what their essential reality consists in. This contrasts with what is presented in the verses that follow, in which the same Spirit is considered with respect to various realities and/or persons.

In two occurrences, this universal Spirit is mentioned in certain of its manifestations in the following designations: *a Spirit of Our command* (*rūḥ min 'Amri-Nā*) (Qur'ān, 42:52), *a Spirit from Him* (*rūḥ min 'Amri-Hi*) (Qur'ān, 58:22). In other cases, it is Allah who communicates or breathes *From Our Spirit* (*min Rūḥi-Nā*), as in Qur'ān 21:91 and 66:12 and with regards to Mary, and in 15:29, 32:9, and 38:72 regarding Adam. We shall illustrate this below in the commentary on the related verses.

> *Of those messengers, some of whom We have caused to excel others, and of whom there are some unto whom Allah spake, while some of them He exalted [above others]in degree; and We gave Jesus, son of Mary, clear proofs [of Allah's Sovereignty] and We assisted him with the holy Spirit. And if Allah had so willed it, those who followed after them would not have fought one with another after the clear proofs had come unto them. But they differed, some of them believing and some disbelieving. And if Allah had so willed it, they would not have fought one with another; but Allah doeth what He will* (Qur'ān, 2:253).

> *When Allah saith: O Jesus, son of Mary! Remember My favour unto thee and unto thy mother; how I strengthened thee with the holy Spirit, so that thou spakest unto mankind in the cradle as in maturity . . .* (Qur'ān, 5:110).

> *Say: The holy Spirit hath delivered it from thy Lord with truth, that it may confirm [the faith of]those who believe, and as guidance and good tidings for those who have surrendered [to Allah]* (Qur'ān, 16:102).

The uncreated Spirit of Allah, as such, arises from the divine Function and is inseparable from it; when the Spirit intervenes or disseminates into universal manifestation, the Spirit assumes the most diversified, suitable forms which are always in conform with the receptacle receiving it. It invigorates, consolidates, and assists these receptacles; it proceeds from the divine Command which is indefinitely diversified, through the act of the Divine Spirit, into universal Manifestation. Therefore, the Divine Spirit receives the same name in the Qur'ānic text: *'amr* in the singular and *'umūr* in the plural. In other words, these are the created realities envisaged with respect to the command or the injunction: *Wait they for naught else than that Allah should come unto them in the shadows of the clouds with the angels? Then the case would be already judged. All cases go back to Allah [for judgment]*(Qur'ān, 2:210). *But His command, when He intendeth a thing, is only that He saith unto it: Be! and it is* (Qur'ān, 36:82). These two inseparable or correlated divine functions are therefore the original cause of the realities (*'umūr*) found in the universal Existence.

The Spirit is also called the *Trustworthy Spirit* (*al-rūḥ al-amīn*) when it descends to the heart of the Prophet. It is mentioned in verses 26:193-194, as we shall note below. In the prophetic tradition (*Ḥadīth*), it is Gabriel—the Archangel of the Revelation—who realizes this principal function of the Divine Spirit with the Prophet and other prophets. In the Qur'ān, however, the name of the Archangel Gabriel is never mentioned in the sequences concerning the Prophet Muḥammad, Jesus, Mary, Zachariah, and Yaḥyā, and even Muslim Qur'ān commentators recognize in him the Archangel Gabriel, as we have discussed in certain previous verses.

4
Adam, or the Primordial Man, and the Spirit of Allah

The integral creation and constitution of Adam are mentioned in several verses, some of which concern the direct breathing into him of the Spirit of Allah. In this formation process, and at this level, the Archangel of Revelation, Gabriel, perfect manifestation of the universal Spirit, does not play a role, even though in the two verses quoted below God addresses the Angels—who are distinguished from Archangel Gabriel—in order to announce to them the creation of the primordial man.

> *Verily We created man of potter's clay of black mud altered, and the jinn did We create aforetime of essential fire. And [remember] when thy Lord said unto the angels: Lo! I am creating a mortal out of potter's clay of black mud altered, so, when I have made him and have breathed into him of My Spirit, do ye fall down, prostrating yourselves unto him* (Qur'ān, 15:26-29).

> *Who made all things good which He created, and He began the creation of man from clay; then He made his seed from a draught of despised fluid; then He fashioned him and breathed into him of His*

> *Spirit; and appointed for you hearing and sight and hearts. Small thanks give ye! And they say: When we are lost in the earth, how can we then be re-created? Nay but they are disbelievers in the meeting with their Lord* (Qur'ān, 32:7-10)
>
> *When thy Lord said unto the angels: Lo! I am about to create a mortal out of mire, and when I have fashioned him and breathed into him of My Spirit, then fall down before him prostrate* (Qur'ān, 38:71-72).

The body of the original Human is formed integrally before something is breathed into it from (*min*) the Spirit of Allah. This human or Adamic prototype, through the divine Spirit, is comprised of an organized human body that is vivified without the intermediary of the Archangel of Revelation, Gabriel. Therefore Adam has a double origin: an individual one through his vivified body, and a divine one through the Spirit of Allah that is breathed into him. It is easy to conclude that the Human always possesses the possibility of drawing near to Allah and recognizing Him through His Spirit or again through his/her spirit; that is, through that which Allah has breathed into him or her and which is ultimately the Spirit of Allah.

Note that human beings, the posterity of Adam, are originally made from a drop of semen. Adam, having been made primordially androgynous before the creation of his spouse (*zawj*)—whose name is never mentioned in the Qur'ānic text—is neither masculine nor feminine. To be more precise, intrinsically and at his origin, Adam comprises these two indivisible and inseparable elements, without division or differentiation, as one may deduce from different Qur'ānic accounts mentioning the creation of Adam, his fall provoked by his disobedience to the Order of Allah not to taste from the tree of distinction (*shajarat*), and his rehabilitation after his return to God (cf. Qur'ān, 2:30-38, 7:11-23, 15:26-44, 20:115-124, and 38:71-85).

5
The Truthful, DEPOSITORY Spirit, the angel or angels, the Angel Gabriel

The Spirit, which assumes the most diversified forms in order to exercise its function through creatures, receives different names. In the Qur'ān, it is identified by the following names in which it occurs: angel in the singular or plural, an entity which takes on a human appearance traditionally likened to Gabriel, and an unidentified spirit which is breathed or "inhaled" (*waḥyī*) into Mary, Jesus, Muḥammad, or the believers, as we shall see in the following verses. Although it is never designated by this name in the context of the Spirit, in the Qur'ānic text, the Angel, when identified with Gabriel (*Jibrīl*), is a bearer of the Word and of the Spirit of Allah. The Angel transmits the Word and the Spirit to beings which are its predisposed receptacles.

The name of the Archangel Gabriel (*Jibrīl*) is mentioned three times in the Qur'ānic text, namely in 2:97-98 and 66:4:

> *Say: Who is an enemy to Gabriel! For he it is who hath revealed [this Scripture] to thy (Muḥammad's) heart by Allah's leave, confirming that which was [revealed] before it, and a guidance and glad tidings to believers; who is an enemy to Allah, and His angels and His messengers, and Gabriel and Michael! Then, lo! Allah [Himself] is an enemy to the disbelievers* (Qur'ān, 2:97-98).

> *If ye twain turn unto Allah repentant, [ye have cause to do so]for your hearts desired [the ban]; and if ye aid one another against him (Muḥammad) then lo! Allah, even He, is his Protecting Friend, and Gabriel and the righteous among the believers; and furthermore the angels are his helpers* (Qur'ān, 66:4).

6
Mary in Her Relationship to the Spirit, the Words, and the Scriptures

Three Qur'ānic verses that mention the Spirit concern Mary directly. These are verses 19:17, 21:91, and 66:12, which we have already discussed in chapter VII. Here, we wish to emphasize the two manners in which the Spirit functions with Mary.

In verse 19:17, Allah with all His Divine Names is represented by the pronoun *We*. Allah transmits (*arsāl-Nā*) the Spirit (*Rūḥa-Nā*) to Mary, this Spirit which presented itself to her in the form of a perfect human being: . . . *Then We sent unto her Our Spirit and it assumed for her the likeness of a perfect man*. Mary therefore receives the Spirit of Allah (or *Our Spirit*), thanks to the Angel of Revelation. This Angel is traditionally likened to Gabriel and here takes on *the form of a perfect human being*. In verse 19:17, the preposition (*min*) is not used in the phrase "from Our Spirit," whereas the two other verses (21:91 and 66:12) make use of the particle *min*: *And she who was chaste, therefor We breathed into her [something] of Our Spirit and made her and her son a token for [all] peoples* (Qur'ān, 21:91). *And Mary, daughter of 'Imrān, whose body was chaste, therefor We breathed therein something of Our Spirit. And she put faith in the words of her Lord and His scriptures, and was of the obedient* (Qur'ān, 66:12).

There is a notable difference between the act of sending to Mary the Spirit (Our Spirit) that takes a formal human appearance likened to the Angel of Revelation, and the act of breathing into her from the Spirit. The expression "Our Spirit" suggests that all the Divine Names participate universally in this Sending to Mary, the Elect, who is thus penetrated by the Spirit in all the degrees of her perfect constitution. The breathing of the Spirit takes place in her, and the Word of Allah—which is the Anointed, Jesus, Son of Mary—that the Angels announced to her in verse 3:45 is projected into her, as described in verse 4:171. Thus she is able to confirm and to verify the Words and the Scriptures of God. Indeed, the Angel brings the divine Word that he confers upon Mary. She bears it within herself, and this Word takes the human form of Jesus through Mary his mother. The Word also takes on a spiritual form through the intervention of the Angel of Revelation with her. This Word remains the same as it has been in God from eternity: His Word is identical to His very Being.

7
The Anoint, Jesus, Son of Mary, His Word and Spirit from Him

In the exceptional constitution of Jesus, four verses mention the term "spirit," three of which occur in the compound form "the Holy Spirit" (*Rūḥ al-Qudūs*) in verses 2:87, 2:253, and 5:110. We have already commented on these verses in earlier chapters and other parts of chapter VII. The fourth verse using the word "spirit" is 4:171. In this verses Allah specifies: *The Messiah, Jesus son of Mary: the messenger of Allah, and His word which He conveyed unto Mary, and a spirit from Him* (Qur'ān, 4:171).

The preposition *min*, like all prepositions in any language, has several meanings. In classical and Qur'ānic Arabic, it means: the starting point or origin, the relation, the dependence, the comparison, the means, the part with respect to the whole, the distancing, the cause, and so on.

The complete Qur'ānic name of *The Anointed One, Jesus, Son of Mary* consists of four elements, including the Word of Allah and Spirit from Him as follows from verse 4:171 quoted above. In two other verses discussed here, 3:39 and 3:45, Jesus is considered "*a Word from Allah.*" In the former, only the name of Yaḥyā—that is, John the Baptist—is mentioned. He confirms the coming of a Word which the Islamic tradition will consider to be Jesus. In the four gospels of the New Testament—considered canonical by ecclesiastic authorities (cf. Matthew 3, Mark 1, Luke 1 and John 1)—John the Baptist (identified with Yaḥyā by the Muslim commentators of the Qur'ān) announces the coming of Jesus. In the Qur'ānic text, Allah says: *Allah giveth thee glad tidings of [a son whose name is] John, [who cometh] to confirm a Word from Allah lordly, chaste, a prophet of the righteous* (Qur'ān, 3:39). Here Jesus, whose name is not mentioned, is announced as *a Word from Allah*, in contrast with the expression *the Word of Allah* used in verse 4:171. This is because, although the Command of Allah concerning Yaḥyā has been decreed and announced to Zachariah, it is not yet accomplished. Thus Jesus, not having been born into his humanity at this moment, is not considered the Word of Allah. For seemingly the same reason, in verse 3:45 the Angels communicate these divine words to Mary: . . . *Allah giveth thee glad tidings of a Word from Him, whose name [is] the Anoint, Jesus, son of Mary* . . . Here, Jesus is mentioned using his complete name in which Mary's name is included, but the Angels only announce the coming of the Anoint, Jesus, Son of Mary envisaged as an individual, not as an eventual conception by Mary. In this preliminary phase, which comes after the one mentioned in 3:39, a being is individualized by his mother but has already received his complete name. Each individual as such is generally considered as one of the Words of Allah. However, in the case of Jesus, once he was born in this world he was identified as being the very Word of Allah, according to verse 4:171. With this in mind, the term "word"—deployed by Allah in verses 3:39 and 3:45—expresses a progression in the linear chronology in order to engender a comprehension of the term "Word." "Word" is finally applied to the Anoint, Jesus, Son of Mary, beyond time as counted in a pre-eternal perspective, even before the existentiating of the divine Command represented by the Qur'ānic expression *kun* (cf. 3:59). It is at once a word and the Word. After studying the Qur'ānic text, one notes two natures of the person of the Anointed, Jesus, Son of Mary: the human one represented in verses 3:39 and 3:45, and a divine one in 4:171. One may understand why the exceptional and complex constitution of Jesus gave rise, and continues to give rise, to numerous interpretations that are far from being congruous. This is the way in which Ibn 'Arabī and the masters of his school understood the polyvalent, specific, and unique constitution of the Anoint, Jesus Son of Mary in accordance with an open and detailed exegesis of the verses concerning him (cf. Chapter X). Moreover, the body of Jesus is formed directly from the Spirit of the Angel and from Mary, and not starting from clay as in the case of Adam and human beings who spring from a human father and a human mother according to the usual and natural order. Let us note, incidentally, that Jesus is never called "*bashar*" in the Qur'ānic text, unlike Adam who had a large posterity, Jesus did not have offspring,

8
The Prophet Muḥammad in relation to the Command and the Spirit

The following verses concern the Prophet Muḥammad in relation to the Command, the Word, and the Spirit:

> 1. *Say: The holy Spirit hath delivered it from thy Lord with truth, that it may confirm* [the faith of]*those who believe, and as guidance and good tidings for those who have surrendered* [to Allah] (Qur'ān, 16:102).
>
> 2. *Which the True Spirit hath brought down upon thy heart, that thou mayst be (one) of the warners, in plain Arabic speech* (Qur'ān, 26:193-196).
>
> 3. *And it was not [vouchsafed]to any mortal that Allah should speak to him unless [it be]by revelation or from behind a veil, or [that] He sendeth a messenger to reveal what He will by His leave. Lo! He is Exalted, Wise. And thus have We inspired in thee (Muḥammad) a Spirit of Our command. Thou knewest not what the Scripture was, nor what the Faith. But We have made it a light whereby We guide whom We will of Our bondmen. And lo! thou verily dost guide unto a right path* (Qur'ān, 42:51-52).

In verse 16:102, the Holy Spirit proceeds directly from the Lord of Prophet Muḥammad to whom it is sent, and this "Spirit" is likened to the Archangel of Revelation, Gabriel, just as in verse 2:97 quoted in section 5 of this chapter, *Say: Who is an enemy to Gabriel! For he it is who hath revealed [this Scripture] to thy heart by Allah's leave, confirming that which was [revealed]before it, and a guidance and glad tidings to believers* (Qur'ān, 2:97).

In the case of Jesus, Son of Mary, God strengthens or assists him through the same Holy Spirit, according to the three already quoted verses 2:87, 2:253, and 5:110. In verse 16:102, the Lord (*Rabb*) of the Prophet Muḥammad also concerns every believer who is thus confirmed by the Holy Spirit, formally likened to Gabriel. The Qur'ān, or the Word of Allah, will be the means of grace *par excellence* so that the Believers receive the Holy Spirit. The Holy Spirit is also the Truthful Spirit (*rūḥ amīn*) that the Prophet received in his universal heart, as mentioned in verses 26:193-194. In the human being who is wholly realized in God, the heart (*qalb*) is the central "organ" which understands all physical, psychological, spiritual, or angelic realities and their corresponding degrees. This perfect constitution of the Prophet, as mentioned in verse 16:102, is described in Sufism as the Universal Man (*al-insān al-kāmil*) who receives the summation of the Divine Words comprising the Qur'ān. This is why the Prophet of Islam includes all the believers and is amongst them: *And know that the messenger of Allah is amongst you* (Qur'ān, 49:7; cf. also 8:33 and 23:22).

9
The servants, the Believers

Three verses mention the Spirit in a direct relationship with the believers, the servants, and those who submit or guard themselves (*muslimūn*):

> 1. *He sendeth down the angels with the Spirit of His command unto whom He will of His bondmen, [saying]: Warn mankind that there is no Allah save Me, so keep your duty unto Me* (Qur'ān, 16:2).
>
> 2. *Say: The holy Spirit hath delivered it from thy Lord with truth, that it may confirm* [the faith of]*those who believe, and as guidance and good tidings for those who have surrendered* [to Allah] (Qur'ān, 16:102).

3. *The Exalter of Ranks, the Lord of the Throne. He causeth the Spirit of His command upon whom He will of His slaves, that He may warn of the Day of Meeting* (Qur'ān, 40:15).

1. In verse 16:2, the Spirit of Allah, proceeding from His Command, and therefore from His Word, receives the Angels that take on forms. This strengthens the servants of God who submit to His Will so that they become worthy of witnessing His Unity in the realms they evolve. They must, therefore, be protected by God in order to take on with discernment, in universal Manifestation, the conflicting tendencies governed by the antinomic Divine Names, such as "He who abases" and "He who elevates,""the Beneficent" and "the Avenger,"and so on. Human beings are necessarily submitted to the influence of the Divine Names at random. It is to be noted that, although the Divine Spirit and Command co-act in agreement, the Qur'ānic text asserts that the Spirit comes from the Command or from the Lord, but never that the Divine Command comes from the Spirit.

2. In verse 16:102, the Spirit, proceeding directly from God and taking form in order to disseminate and exercise its influence, is called the Holy Spirit (*Rūḥ al-Qudūs*): the one that sends down the Divine Word (the Qur'ān) so that the believers may be confirmed by it. The Divine Word that penetrates the believers is guidance and glad tidings for those who implement the instruments of grace instituted by God through the mediation of His Prophet. These instruments of grace include, for example: prayer, fasting, and the tithe (*zakāt*). And in this, the believers submit.

3. The Throne, the Master of which is Allah, acquires different names in the Qur'ānic text depending on the function it occupies in the Divine economy as a whole, and in relation to distinct phases of the process of differentiation of the divine possibilities. In the Qur'ān, five names are applied to the Throne:

a) the immense Throne (*al-'arsh al-'aẓīm*), in 9:129, 23:82, 27:23, and 27:26;
b) the noble Throne (*al-'arsh al-karīm*) in 23:116;
c) the bearing Throne (*al-'arsh al-makīn*) in 81:20;
d) the glorious Throne (*al-'arsh al-majīd*) in 85:15;
e) the Throne of the All-merciful (*al-'arsh al-raḥmān*) in 20:5 and 25:59.

The Throne designated with this name has been established on the primordial waters (cf. Qur'ān, 11:7) from which all living things emerged (cf. Qur'ān, 25:32),"within" which different "degrees" are present, and within which beings evolve.

And it is always by virtue of God's Command that His Spirit is transmitted to certain of His servants so that Allah warns about the Day in which they encounter Him face to face (*yawm al-talāqi* = the Day of the mutual Encounter, or confluence). The servants (*'ibād*) who receive the Spirit of Allah are those in whom the individual tendencies have been transformed into lordly character traits and who are therefore with their Lord in order to facilitate His Will. In Sufism this process is called "assuming the character traits of God" (*al-takhalluq bi akhlāq Allāh*).

Outside the Table

Of the 21 verses that contain the term Spirit, the last three (70:4, 78:38, and 97:4) mention both the Spirit and the Angels:

> *The angels and the Spirit ascend unto Him in a Day whereof the span is fifty thousand years* (Qur'ān, 70:4).
>
> *On the day when the angels and the Spirit stand arrayed, they speak not, saving him whom the Beneficent alloweth and who speaketh right* (Qur'ān, 78:38).
>
> *The angels and the Spirit descend therein, by the permission of their Lord, with all decrees* (Qur'ān, 97:4).

The Muslim commentators are almost unanimous in their understanding of "spirit" as the Archangel of Revelation: Gabriel (Jibrīl), an Angel that occupies a central position in the context of the revelation and who represents the intervention of God's universal Spirit in creation by assuming the most diverse forms. In these three Qur'ānic contexts, the Angels are specific, purely spiritual "entities" whose function is to look after the management of the world.

Table II

God	Amr Word Qur'ān	Breath Spirit or Holy Spirit	Adam	The Spirit that takes form Angels Gabriel	Mary	Jesus	Muḥammad	Believers	verses
0									29:6, 112
1	2			5	6	7			3:45
1	2					7			19:29-34
1	2	3							17:85
1	2	3		5			8		42:52
1	2	3		5				9	16:2, 40:15
1	2	3			6	7			4:171
1	2	3					8		17:85
1	2	3					8	9	40:15
1		3	4						15:29, 32:9, 38:72
1		3		5	6				19:17, 21:91, 66:12
1		3		5	6	7			19:17-21
1		3		5		7			2:87, 2:253, 5:110
1		3		5			8		26:193, 194
1		3		5			8	9	16:102
1		3				7			2:87, 2:253, 5:110
1		3					8		16:102

Translation of the corresponding verses

The numbers in brackets correspond to those in table I, page 310, and on table II, page 323. They represent the relationships between the divine, angelic, and human realities, identified by numbers 1 to 9.

2:87 (137) (1357)	And verily We gave unto Moses the Scripture and We caused a series of messengers to follow after him, and We gave unto Jesus, son of Mary, clear proofs, and We supported him with the Holy spirit. Is it ever so, that, when there cometh unto you a messenger with that which ye yourselves desire not, ye grow arrogant, and some ye disbelieve and some ye slay?
2:253 (137) (1357)	Of those messengers, some of whom We have caused to excel others, and of whom there are some unto whom Allah spake, while some of them He exalted in degree; and We gave Jesus, son of Mary, clear proofs and We supported him with the holy Spirit. And if Allah had so wiled it, those who followed after them would not have fought one with another after the clear proofs had come unto them. But they differed, some of them believing and some disbelieving. And if Allah had so willed it, they would not have fought one with another; but Allah doeth what He will.

3:45 (12567)	(And remember) when the angels said: O Mary! Lo! Allah giveth thee glad tidings of a word from him, whose name is the Messiah, Jesus, son of Mary, illustrious in the world and the Hereafter, and one of those brought near (unto Allah).
4:171 (12367)	O People of the Scripture! Do not exaggerate in your religion nor utter aught concerning Allah save the truth. The Messiah, Jesus son of Mary, was only a messenger of Allah, and His word which He conveyed unto Mary, and a spirit from Him. So believe in Allah and His messengers, and say not "Three" - Cease! (it is) better for you! - Allah is only One God. Far is it removed from His Transcendent Majesty that He should have a son. His is all that is in the heavens and all that is in the earth. And Allah is sufficient as Defender.

5:110 (137) (1357)	When Allah saith: O Jesus, son of Mary! Remember My favour unto thee and unto thy mother; how I strengthened thee with the holy Spirit, so that thou spakest unto mankind in the cradle as in maturity; and how I taught thee the Scripture and Wisdom and the Torah and the Gospel; and how thou didst shape of clay as it were the likeness of a bird by My permission, and didst blow upon it and it was a bird by My permission, and thou didst heal him who was born blind and the leper by My permission; and how thou didst raise the dead by My permission; and how I restrained the Children of Israel from (harming) thee when thou camest unto them with clear proofs, and those of them who disbelieved exclaimed: This is naught else than mere magic;
15:29 (134)	So, when I have made him and have breathed into him of My Spirit, do ye fall down, prostrating yourselves unto him.
16:2 (12359)	He sendeth down the angels with the Spirit of His command unto whom He will of His bondmen, (saying): Warn mankind that there is no Allah save Me, so keep your duty unto Me.
16:102 (13589)	Say: The holy Spirit hath delivered it from thy Lord with truth, that it may confirm (the faith of) those who believe, and as guidance and good tidings for those who have surrendered
17:85 (123) (1238)	They are asking thee concerning the Spirit. Say: The Spirit is by command of my Lord, and of knowledge ye have been vouchsafed but little.

19:17 -21 (13567)	And had chosen seclusion from them. Then We sent unto her Our Spirit and it assumed for her the likeness of a perfect man. She said: Lo! I seek refuge in the Beneficent One from thee, if thou art Allah-fearing. He said: I am only a messenger of thy Lord, that I may bestow on thee a faultless son. She said: How can I have a son when no mortal hath touched me, neither have I been unchaste? He said: So (it will be). Thy Lord saith: It is easy for Me. And (it will be) that We may make of him a revelation for mankind and a mercy from Us, and it is a thing ordained.

19:29 -34 (127)	Then she pointed to him. They said: How can we talk to one who is in the cradle, a young boy? He spake: Lo! I am the slave of Allah. He hath given me the Scripture and hath appointed me a Prophet, And hath made me blessed wheresoever I may be, and hath enjoined upon me prayer and almsgiving so long as I remain alive, And (hath made me) dutiful toward her who bore me, and hath not made me arrogant, unblest. Peace on me the day I was born, and the day I die, and the day I shall be raised alive! Such was Jesus, son of Mary: (this is) a statement of the truth concerning which they doubt.

21:91 (1356)	And she who was chaste, therefore We breathed into her (something) of Our Spirit and made her and her son a token for (all) peoples.
26:193 -194	Which the Truthful Spirit (*rūḥ amīn*) hath brought down Upon thy heart, that thou mayst be (one) of the warners,
29:6 (0)	And whosoever striveth, striveth only for himself, for lo! Allah is altogether Independent of (His) creatures.
32:9 (134)	And whosoever striveth, striveth only for himself, for lo! Allah is altogether Independent of (His) creatures.

38:72 (134)	And when I have fashioned him and breathed into him of My Spirit, then fall down before him prostrate.
40:15 (12389) (1239)	The Exalter of Ranks, the Lord of the Throne. He causeth the Spirit of His command upon whom He will of His slaves, that He may warn of the Day of mutual Meeting,
42:52 (12358)	And thus have We inspired in thee (Muḥammad) a Spirit of Our command. Thou knewest not what the Scripture was, nor what the Faith. But We have made it a light whereby We guide whom We will of Our bondmen. And lo! thou verily dost guide unto a right path,

66:12 (1356)	And Mary, daughter of 'Imrān, whose body was chaste, therefor We breathed therein something of Our Spirit. And she put faith in the words of her Lord and His scriptures, and was of the obedient.
112 (0)	Say: He, Allah, (is) One! Allah, the eternally Besought of all! He begetteth not nor was begotten. And there is none comparable unto Him.

Summary of the 21 verses on the Spirit (*rūḥ*) contained in the commentaries above, the Spirit of God, its unfolding, and its universal vivifying action:

- Jesus, Son of Mary strengthened by the Holy Spirit: 2:87, 2:253, 5:110.
- the Anoint, Jesus, Son of Mary, the Messenger of Allah, His Word conveyed unto Mary, and Spirit from Him: 4:171.
- of the Spirit of God on Adam: 15:29, 32:9, 38:72.
- the Spirit of God by His Command (17:85) and by the angels on certain servants (16:2): 16:2, 17:85, 40:15.
- the Holy Spirit comes from the Rabb and confirms the believers: 16:102.
- the Spirit of God sent unto Mary (19:17)—from His Spirit unto Mary (21:91) (66:12): 19:17, 21:91, 66:12.
- the Truthful Spirit (*rūḥ amīn*) on the heart of the Prophet: 26:192ff. a Spirit by Our Command on the Prophet: 42:52.
- the Believers strengthened by a Spirit from God: 58:22.
- the Angels and the Spirit—their active presence: 70:4, 78:38, 97:4

His Spirit unto	Jesus, Son of Mary (2:87, 2:253, 5:110) Mary (19:17) the Believers (16:102, 40:15) the Believers by the Angels (16:2)
From His Spirit unto	Jesus, Spirit of Allah (4:171) Adam (15:29, 32:9, 38:72) Mary (21:91, 66:12) Muḥammad (42:52) the Believers (58:22)

Introduction to The Translations of Ibn 'Arabī

The translations presented below have been taken from the two main works of the Master:

Fuṣūṣ al-Ḥikam (The Ringstones of Wisdom)
al-Futūḥāt al-Makkiyya (The Meccan Openings)

From the first work we have translated three out of the twenty-seven chapters which Ibn 'Arabī devotes to the prophets and sages recognized by the Qur'ān and Tradition. These are chapters fifteen, twenty, and twenty-one, entitled "Ringstone of the Wisdom of Prophethood in the Word of Jesus,""Ringstone of the Wisdom of Prophethood in the Word of Yaḥyā (John the Baptist)," and "Ringstone of the Wisdom of Prophethood in the Word of Zachariah."

From the second work, we have selected the passages in which Ibn 'Arabī comments on Qur'ānic verses and prophetic sayings, exposing certain doctrinal positions which deal very particularly with the Prophet Muḥammad, Jesus, and Mary. The passages that we have selected concerning the Prophet of Islam are few, given that most of our work is related to Jesus and to his family: Mary, Zachariah, and Yaḥyā. Nevertheless we had to situate Jesus within the framework of the Islamic Revelation and therefore in relation with Prophet Muḥammad. In this immense work of the Master, the Muḥammadan Reality occupies a primary place: firstly, because he is the Seal of the prophets, and secondly, because he is invested with the characteristics of the Qur'ān, a synthesis of previous Revelations.

In addition, we have retained most of the passages that Ibn 'Arabī dedicates to Jesus and to Mary in the *al-Futūḥāt al-Makkiyya* so long as they did not constitute repetitions, although these passages are found in doctrinal contexts and contents which are often different. However, we did not intend to translate *in extensio* the chapters in which Jesus and Mary are mentioned, as they often appear on the margins of a main theme.

The Master's commentaries on Jesus and Mary bring out subtle, penetrating, and often unknown aspects of their reality, which most of the exegetes of the Qur'ān very often pass over in silence. The original interpretations of the author demand a sustained effort on the part of the reader in order for him to draw greater intellectual and spiritual benefit.

***

Our translations are based on the following Arabic texts:

1. For the *Fuṣūṣ al-Ḥikam*: the critical edition by A. E. Afīfī, 1365 A.H./1946
2. For the *al-Futūḥāt al-Makkiyya*: the new Arabic edition of 1420 A.H./1999 in nine volumes (Beirut: Dar al-Kutub al'Ilmiyyah).

Chapter IX

Extracts from the *Fuṣūṣ al-Ḥikam*

RINGSTONE OF THE WISDOM OF PROPHETHOOD IN THE WORD OF JESUS (CHAPTER 15)

Was it from the water of Mary, or the inbreathing of Gabriel
In the form of a man that came to exist out of clay?
The spirit took on existence in a purified essence
Out of the nature you call Sijjīn
That is why he was destined to reside
Therein over a thousand years
A spirit from God, not another, and because of this
Did he give life to the dead and make birds from clay
That his relationship to his Lord would hold true
And by which he would affect the high and the lowly
God purified him bodily, and made him untouched in spirit
And made him a likeness of bringing into being

Know that one of the qualities particular to spirits is that they do not tread upon a thing without giving life to that thing. Life then flows within it. For this reason the Sāmirī [cf. Qur'ān, 20:85] took in hand some of the traces left by the messenger–who was Gabriel, upon him be peace, the spirit. The Sāmirī had knowledge of this matter. Since he knew it was Gabriel, he knew that life flowed in whatever he had trodden upon. So, he took in hand some of the traces left by the messenger, a handful or [just a scoop] with his fingertips, and cast it into the calf, which then lowed, since the sound of a cow is that of lowing. Had he made it another form, the name of the sound proper to that form would have been attributed to it–for example the braying of a camel, the bleating of rams and sheep, or the voice, words, and discourse of man.

That measure of life flowing in things is called *lāhūt*, and *nāsūt* is the locus where that spirit resides. Nāsūt is called spirit by virtue of what resides in it. When the *trusted spirit*–that is, Gabriel–appeared to Mary, peace be upon them both, as *a man without fault*, she imagined that he was a man intent on lying with her, so she sought refuge from him in God with all she had, knowing as she did that such a thing was forbidden. She attained complete presence with God, which is the spirit and meaning. Had he breathed into her at that moment, in that state, Jesus would have emerged such that no one could bear the sullenness of his character, which would have stemmed from the state of his mother. When he said to her, *I am but a messenger come from thy Lord*, having come, *to give thee a boy most pure* [Qur'ān, 19:17-21], she found expansion after contraction, and became glad. At that moment he inbreathed Jesus. Gabriel conveyed the Word of God to Mary just as the Messenger conveyed the Word of God to his community. This is spoken of in His Words, *His Word that He committed to Mary, and a Spirit from Him* [Qur'ān, 4:171].

Desire flowed in Mary. The body of Jesus was created from the real water of Mary and the imaginary water of Gabriel. Moisture flowed within that breath, for the breath of an animal body is moist due to what is contained therein of the pillar of water. Thus Jesus was existentiated from real water and from imaginational water, and emerged in the form of a mortal man, so that exitentiation would take place for the species of man in only the usual way.

Jesus emerged and quickened the dead, for he was the Spirit of God. The quickening was that of God, while the inbreathing belonged to Jesus, just as the inbreathing belonged to Gabriel while the Word was God's. Jesus' quickening of the dead was a real quickening with respect to what manifested from his inbreathing, as was the case when he became manifest out of the form of his mother. However, his quickening was also imaginational with respect to its coming from him, for it was naught but God's. He brought them together by virtue of the reality he was created to be. As we have said, he was created from imaginational water and real water, so quickening is attributed to him in a real way from one point of view and in an imaginary way from another [point of view].

It is said of him regarding this real way, *And he quickeneth the dead* [Qur'ān, 3:49, and 42:9], while it is said of him regarding the imaginational way, *He breathed into it, and it became a bird by the leave of God* [Qur'ān, 5:110]. The action belonging to the prepositional phrase is *it became* and not His words he breathed, or it can be that the action is *he breathed*, in which case it became a bird by virtue of his corporeal, sensorial form. Such is also the case with, *And thou healed the blind and the leper* [Qur'ān, 5:110]; and all else that is attributed to him and to *the leave of God*, as well as to the leave alluded to in His Words such as, *By My leave* [Qur'ān, 5:110], and, *By the leave of God* [Qur'ān, 3:49]. If the prepositional phrase is attached to *he breathed*, then the one who breathes is given leave in breathing, and the bird comes to be because of the one who breathes by the leave of God. If the one who breathes does so without leave, then it is the bird's being brought into being that takes place by the leave of God, in which case the action is *it became*.

If it were not for the fact that there is imagination, and true reality in the matter, this form would not allow of these two aspects. Nay, it has these two aspects because it is so accorded by the makeup of Jesus. Jesus emerged out of humility, so much so that it is prescribed for his community that, *They shall pay the tax, humbling themselves* [Qur'ān, 9:29], and that when one amongst them is struck on the cheek that they should offer the other to the one who struck him and not rise up against him or seek revenge against him. This aspect stems from his mother, for lowliness belongs to woman, as does humility; she is below man both legally and physically. Any power he possessed to give life or to heal came from the aspect of Gabriel's breath into the form of a mortal. Jesus gave life to the dead in the form of a mortal man. Had Gabriel not come in the form of a mortal man, but in another form from among the other elemental beings–animal, vegetable, or mineral–Jesus would not have given life until he took on that form and became manifest in it. Moreover, had Gabriel come in his luminous form, which lies outside of the elements and pillars (and since he does not come out of his nature), Jesus would not have given life to the dead until after he became manifest in that natural, luminous non-elemental form together with the form of mortal man which came from the side of his mother. It used to be said upon his quickening of the dead, "it is he, it is not he." Bewilderment occurred when one looked upon him, as will happen for any intelligent being in his discursive reasoning upon seeing an individual mortal give life to the dead, since it is a special prerogative of the Divine to give life to reason, though it is not in the case of animals. The onlooker is left bewildered when he sees divine effects coming from a mortal man.

This has led some to hold the position of incarnation, and to hold, by virtue of the dead he brought to life, that he is God. For this reason they have been associated with disbelief, which is a covering, for they cover God, who gives life to the dead, with the mortal form of Jesus. He, most high, said, *They disbelieve, those who say that God is Christ the son of Mary* [Qur'ān, 5:17]. They bring together both error and disbelief when they say all of these words, because they do not do so in saying that he is God, nor in saying that he is the son of Mary. With respect to the dead being brought to life, they turned from God—while enclosing Him—to a *nāsūt* mortal form with their words, "the son of Mary," for indeed he was the son of Mary. One who hears this might imagine that they attribute divinity to him, making it identical with the form, but this is not what they do. Rather, they begin by placing the Divine Selfhood in the mortal form that is the son of Mary, thus making a distinction between the form and the object of their judgment. Remember the case of Gabriel, who, while in the form of a mortal man, did not breathe and then *did* breathe, a distinction being made between the form and the breathing. The breath came from that form, which was when the breath was not; thus the breath is not part of its essential definition.

Differences of opinion arose among the sects as to what Jesus was. There are those who argue in favour of his mortal, human form, saying that he is the son of Mary. There are those who argue from the represented mortal nature and associate him with Gabriel. Some make an argument based on the quickening of the dead which became manifest from him, and associate him with God through the aspect of spirit, saying that he is the Spirit of God, meaning that by him life manifests from those in whom he breathes. Sometimes God is imagined to be in him, sometimes the angel is imagined to be in him, and sometimes the human and mortal aspects are imagined to be in him.[1] For the proponents of these positions, he will be determined by what predominates over them: he is the Word of God, and he is the Spirit of God, and he is the slave of God. This is the case for no other in the domain of sensorial form. Indeed, all individuals are related to their form-

1. These three supposed aspects are in principle inseparable in the integral person of Jesus.

possessing father, and not to one who breathed his spirit while in the form of a mortal man. When God fashioned the body of man, of which He spoke when He said, *And when We fashioned him* [Qur'ān, 15:29],[2] He breathed into him, transcendent is He, of His Spirit. Thus the spirit, as far as his being and his identity are concerned, is associated with Him, transcendent is He. Jesus was not so, for the inbreathing of the spirit was incorporated into the fashioning of his body and mortal form. As we have already mentioned, this was the case for no other.

* * *

All existent things are the inexhaustible Words of God; all come from *Be!* and *Be!* is a Word of God. Is the Word related to God with respect to what He *is*, its quiddity thus being unknown, or does He descend, transcendent is He, into the form of the one who says, *Be!*, the utterance *Be!* being the reality of that form into which He descends and in which He is manifest? Some knowers hold the first view, and some the other, while others experience bewilderment in the matter and know not. This matter can only be know through taste, as when Abū Yazīd breathed into an ant he had killed, giving it life. Upon that he knew who breathed, and so breathed. He was Christic in his locus of witnessing.

As for the spiritual (principle) quickening that takes place through knowledge, this is the divine, everlasting, exalted and luminous life of which God spoke saying, *Who was dead, and we gave him life, and appointed him a light to walk among the people* (Qur'ān, 6:122). Whose gives life to a dead soul with the life of knowledge, in a special matter connected to one's knowledge of God, does so possessing *a light to walk among the people*, that is, amidst their outward appearances in form.

If not for Him, and if not for us
What it would not yet be
We worship truly
And indeed God is our Master

---

2. Let us quote the following verses in which Allah mentions the different phases of the creation of Adam, in body and spirit: *Verily We created man of potter's clay of black mud altered, and the jinn did We create aforetime of essential fire. And [remember] when thy Lord said unto the angels: Lo! I am creating a mortal out of potter's clay of black mud altered, so, when I have made him and have breathed into him of My Spirit, do ye fall down, prostrating yourselves unto him* (Qur'ān, 15:26-29).

And we are identical with Him
So know, when you say 'man'
Do not veil using 'man'
For He hath given thee a proof
Be thou the Real or be thou creation
Thou wilt be, through God, All-Merciful
Feed thou this creation of His
And be spirit and bounty
We accord Him that by which He
Appears in us, and He accords us
And the matter becomes divided up into
What is His, and what is ours
He who knoweth my heart gave it life
When he gave us life
In Him we were beings,
Identities, and moments
'Tis not perpetual in us
But only sometimes

Something that points to what we have spoken of, concerning the matter of the spiritual breath together with the form of elemental mortal man, is that the Real described Himself as possessing the *Breath of the All-Merciful.* For everything described by some quality, it must be that everything that entailed that quality followed that quality, and you know that the breath of a breather is entailed by him. That is why the Divine Breath receives the forms of the world, being to them like the hylic substance, and is none other than nature itself. The elements are one of the forms of nature. That which is above the elements and that which it begets—the exalted spirits above the seven heavens—are also forms of nature. As for the seven heavens and their identities, they are elemental, and consist of the smoke of the elements, which is begotten of those elements. The angels that are brought into being from each heaven come from them, and so they are "elementals" while those who are above them are 'naturals.' For this reason God described them as being disputatious–I refer here to the supreme plenum–for nature consists of opposition, and the opposition between the Divine Names, which are relationships, is only granted by the Breath. Do you not see how the Essence, which lies outside of this determination, is narrated to us as being *Beyond Need of the worlds* [cf. Qur'ān, 3:97 and 29:6]? By virtue of the heat therein, it rises. By virtue of the coldness and humidity therein, it descends. By virtue of the dryness therein it stays fixed and does not quake. Sedimentation is proper to coldness and humidity. Do you not see that when a physician wishes to deliver medicine to someone, he looks at his urine in a bottle, and that when he sees sedimentation he knows that the maturation is complete, and so delivers the medicine to accelerate the good progress? The sedimentation takes place through none other than its natural humidity and coldness.

The clay of this human person was kneaded by His *two Hands* [cf. Qur'ān, 38:75], which stand opposite one another even though both His hands are right. There is no hiddenness in the difference between the two of them, even though it only consists in there being two of them, that is, being two Hands. Nothing can affect nature except that which has a correspondence with it, and nature consists of opposition, so He used two Hands. Because he existentiated him with two Hands, He called him mortal, owing to the contact—in a manner befitting the Divine–of the two Hands which are attributed to Him. He made this part of His solicitude for this species of man, and said to the one who refused to prostrate to him, *What prevented thee to bow thyself before what I created with My two Hands? Has thou waxed proud*, before one like you, that is, elemental, *or art thou one of the exalted ones?*[Qur'ān, 38:75], that is, exalted above the elements, for you are not so. What is meant by exalted ones are those who are transcendent, in their essences, above being elemental in their luminous makeup, though they are 'natural.' Man is only superior to other elemental species due to his being a mortal[3] made of clay. He is superior to the species created from the elements without that contact. Man is at a degree above the angels of the earth and heavens, although the exalted angels are better than the human species, according to Divine Writ. Let he who desires to know the Divine Breath know the world, for indeed whose knoweth himself knoweth his Lord who manifests therein. That is to say, the world becomes manifest in the Breath of the All-Merciful which God breathes for the Divine Names,

3. The two terms *bashar* and *mubāshara* come from the same root *b-sh-r*: to remove the skin, to peel, to rejoice from a tiding, to live with a spouse. The *bashar* is therefore the being with human appearance whose formal aspect expresses its belonging to a species. The word *bashara*, meaning skin or epiderm, comes from the same root.

which find it from out of the absence of their effects' manifestation. He bestowed upon Himself through what He existentiated by His Breath. The Breath's first effect takes place *in divinis*, and then the affair keeps descending through the universal breathing to the end of what exists.

All things are in that very Breath
Like light in the darkness before dawn
Knowledge by demonstration is in
The day's end for one who slumbers
And sees what we have said
In a vision showing the Breath
Which relieves him of all the sadness
Of his reciting He frowned [cf. Qur'ān, 80:1]
He discloses Himself to the one
Who comes searching out the firebrand
He sees it as fire, but it is a light
For kings and centurions
If you understand my words
You will know that you are needful
Had he been seeking after other than that
He would have seen Him in it without being turning away

When the real confronted this Christic word in the station of *That we may know* [Qur'ān, 47:31]–and he does know—He asked it whether what had been attributed to it was true or not, although he already knew whether or not this thing had happened. He said, *Didst thou say unto men, "Take me and my mother as divinities apart from God?"* [Qur'ān, 5:116] Now, it is necessary to have *adab* in responding to this questioner, for, since he disclosed Himself to him in this station and in this form, it demands wisdom of response, in separation while in union itself. He spoke to Him, beginning with the assertion of incomparability, "*To Thee be glory!*" He delimited it with the pronoun, which necessitates there being an encounter as well as an address. "*It is not mine,*" insofar as I am mine and not Thine, "*to say what I have no right to,*" that is, it is required neither by my selfhood nor my essence. "*If I indeed said it, Thou knowest it,*" for Thou art the tongue by which I speak. Recall that the Messenger, may God bless him and grant him peace, told us in the divine narration that, "I am the tongue by which he speaketh." He thus made His Selfhood the very tongue of the speaker, and related the speech to His slave. Then the righteous slave finished his response by saying, "*Thou knowest what is in my soul*–the speaker is the Real–*and I know not what it within it.*" He denied knowledge to the Jesus' selfhood as such, though not with respect to his being a speaker or producer of effects. "*Thou Thyself*" using distinction and emphasis, reinforcing the explanation and relying upon it, since only God knows the invisible. He divided and unified, made one and made many, widened and constricted, and then said, completing his response, "*I spoke not to them except what Thou didst command me.*" [Qur'ān, 5:117] He first used negation, indicating that he was not. Then he responded to His words, having *adab* with the Questioner. Had he not done so one could have attributed ignorance of the realities to him, and far be it from him that this should be so. He said, except what *Thou didst command me*, that is, Thou speakest with my tongue, and Thou *art* my tongue. Contemplate how subtle and precise is this divine, spiritual news-giving! *Worship Allah*, using the name 'Allah' because of the diversity of slaves and because of the diversity of laws. He did not specify a particular Name to the exclusion of another Name. Rather, he used the Name that gathers them all together. Then he said, *My Lord and your Lord.* It is known that His relationship to a given existent through His being Lord is not identical with the relationship He has with another, which is why he said, My Lord and your Lord, indicating both the speaker and those addressed.

. . . *Except that thou didst command me*, thus establishing his soul as being subject to command. This is none other than his slavehood, since one is not commanded unless it is conceivable that he will obey, even if he does not do so. Now, the command descends as determined by hierarchy, so whoever manifests in some level will be colored by what is accorded by the reality of that level. The level of the commanded has a determination appearing in everything commanded, while the level of the Command has a determination appearing in every command. The Real says, *Establish the Prayer* [Qur'ān, 2:43], and is the one who commands, the one charged with responsibility, and the one commanded. The slave says, *My Lord, forgive me* [Qur'ān, 23:108], and is the one who commands while the Real is the one who is commanded. What the real seeks of the slave through His Command is the very thing the slave seeks of the Real through his command. For this reason every supplication is answered. This must be so, even though it may be delayed, just as some of those who are burdened with responsibility, addressed to stand and establish the Prayer, do not pray at that time but delay their compliance and pray at another time, though they were capable of doing so. There must need to be an answer, if only through intention.

"*I was a witness over them, while I remained among them*," not saying over myself *with* them as when he said, "*My Lord and your Lord*," for indeed the prophets are witnesses over their communities while they remain among them. "*When Thou didst take me to Thyself*," that is, Thou didst raise me to Thyself, veiling them from me and from them, "*Thou wast Thyself the watcher over them*," not in my matter, but in their matter when Thou wast their sight, making necessary this watchfulness. Man's witnessing of himself is the Real's witnessing of him. He used the Name the Watcher because he used "witness" for himself, and wished to distinguish between himself and his Lord, in order for it to be known that he was what he was due to his being a slave, and that the Real is the Real due to His being Lord over him. Therefore he used "witness" for himself and "Watcher" for the Real. He placed them before himself, saying, "*I was over them as a witness while I remained among them*," showing adab and preferring them to come first, but placed them after the Real when it came to Him, saying, the *Watcher over them*, since the Lord deserves precedence of degree. Then he showed that the Real, the Watcher, is also possessed of the name Jesus employed for himself, the witness, in his words, *over them as a witness*. He said, "Thou Thyself art witness over everything." He used "every" due to the generality of "thing", for the latter is the most non-specific of things. He used the Name the Witness, for He is the Witness of every witnessed thins in accordance with what is necessitated by the reality of that witnessed thing. He thus points out that He, transcendent is He, is the Witness over the people of Jesus when he says, *I was over them as a witness while I remained among them*. This is the Real's witnessing in the matter of Jesus. Remember that it has been established that He is his tongue, his hearing, and his sight.

Then he spoke a Muḥammadan Word and a Christic Word; as for its being Christic, this is because it is an utterance of Jesus, spoken of by God about him in His Book. As for its being Muḥammadan, this is due to its coming from Muḥammad, may God bless him and grant him peace, in a certain place. He stood repeating it an entire night, turning to nothing else until the coming of dawn: *If Thou chastisest them, they are Thy slaves; if Thou forgives them, Thou art the Mighty, the Wise* [Qur'ān, 5:118]. 'Them' is a pronoun of what is absent, just as 'he' is a pronoun of what is absent, as in His Words, *It is they who disbelieve*, using a pronoun of what is absent. The absentness veils them from what is intended by the witnessed and present. He said, *If Thou chastisest them*, using the pronoun of what is absent, which is the very veil in which they find themselves and which keeps them from God. God reminded them before their being present, so that when they *were* present the yeast would have determined the dough, making it like itself. *They are Thy slaves*, making his address in the singular, because of the doctrine of unity to which he held. There is no greater servility than that of slaves, for they cannot dispose on their own. They are determined by what their masters want, and who share them with no one. Thus he said, *The slaves*, making it singular. What is meant by the chastisement is their abasement, and there are none more abased than them, due to their being slaves. *If Thou fogivest them*: that is, cover them from the onset of the chastisement they deserve on account of their disobedience. This is to say: make for them a cover to veil them from it and to block it from them. Then Thou art the Mighty, that is, the Preventor and Protector. When the Real grants this name to a slave, He is called the Giver of Might, and the one who is given the name is called 'mighty.' He is the Preventor and Protector against the chastisement and vengeance desired by the Chastiser and the Avenger. He used distinction and emphasis, again to reinforce the explanation and so that the verse would follow one mode, in His Words, *Thou Thyself knowest the things invisible* [Qur'ān, 5:109], and also, Thou art Thyself the Mighty, the Wise.

This was a question and an earnest solicitation that the Prophet, may God bless him and grant him peace, put to his Lord, in that entire night where he repeated it until the coming of dawn, seeking a response. Had he heard an answer at the beginning of his questioning he would have not repeated it. The Real set out to him, one by one, the kinds of things for which they merited punishment. At each example set out and each thing specified he said to him, *If Thou chastisest them, they are Thy slaves; if Thou forgives them, Thou art Thyself the Mighty, the Wise*. If he saw, in what was set out to him, something that demanded he give the Real precedence and prefer His side, he would offer supplication against them, not for them. All that was set out to him was that by which they merited what it bestowed upon this verse, namely surrender to God and exposure to His forgiveness. It is related that the Real, when he loves the voice of His slave in his supplication to Him, delays the answer so that it may be repeated–out of love, not out of reluctance. For this reason He used the Name the Wise. The Wise is He who puts things in their places, deviating not from what is demanded and sought after by their realities and qualities. The Wise is He who knows the ordering of things.

The Prophet, may God bless him and grant him peace, was wont to repeat this verse, being possessed of a great knowledge from God most high. Let he who recites recite it this way, otherwise silence is better. When God graces a slave to speak of some matter, He does so only after having willed it response as well as the fulfilment of his need, so let no one believe that for which they have been graced is slow in coming. Rather, let them persevere as the Prophet persevered over this verse, in all his states, that they may hear with their ears or hearing—however you like, or however it is that God lets you hear the response. If he allows you to ask with your tongue, He will have you hear with your ears, and if He allows you to do so as meaning, then He will have you hear with your hearing.

QĀSHĀNĪ, *SHARḤ ʿALĀ FUṢŪṢ AL-ḤIKAM*, PAGE 208, 1386/1966 EDITION

Qāshānī's commentary on Ibn ʿArabī's first four verses of the first poem

A spirit from God, not another, and because of this
Did he give life to the dead and make birds from clay.

". . . He [Jesus] is perfect Spirit, locus of manifestation for the Name of Allah. Allah, and none other than Him, (is) He who, in the form of Gabriel, breathed him (unto Mary). Thus, he [Jesus] comes from a Name of the Essence and not by a derived name, without there being numerous intermediaries between him and Allah as is the case for the spirit of other prophets. These spirits, although they have issued from the dignity of the Name of Allah, exist only through the mediation of numerous theophanies stemming from all the dignities of the Names. Jesus had the privilege of stemming from the intimacy of the synthetic Unity which is proper to the divine Dignity. This is why He (God) named him His Spirit and His Word (*kalima*), and his apostleship was to invite to the inner approach and to the spiritual world for the Word proceeds from the intimacy of Allah. Also his mysterious ipseity proceeds from Allah and from His Name through the intermediary of Gabriel. Therefore, he is the servant of Allah and His locus of manifestation. Allah made [some of] His prerogative (*ṣifāta-Hu*) appear in him: quickening the dead, making birds come to life from clay, healing the mute, etc."

RINGSTONE OF WISDOM OF MAJESTY IN THE WORD OF JOHN (CHAPTER 20)

This is the Wisdom of firstness as it concerns [Divine] Names. God gave him the name John, which is to say that the memory of Zachariah lives through him: *No namesake have We given him aforetime* [Qur'ān, 19:7]. He took the actualization of that quality, which was possessed by those who came before and left children, and joined it to the name belonging to it. And thus He named him John, and his name lives on as does the knowledge of taste. The memory of Adam lived through Shem, and so it was for other prophets. Before John, God had not brought together one's proper name with its quality for anyone. He only did so for Zachariah, in solicitude of Him, since he said, So give me, from Thee, a kinsman [Qur'ān, 19:5]. He placed the Real before the mention of his son, just as Asiyah placed the mention of the Neighbor before the Abode in her words, "*. . . with Thee a house in Paradise.*" [Qur'ān, 66:11] God honoured him by fulfilling his need. He gave him the name of his quality, so that his name might be a reminder of what His prophet had sought of Him, because he preferred, upon him be peace, that the remembrance of God should abide in his progeny, for the son is the secret of his father. Thus he said, *who shall be my inheritor and the inheritor of the House of Jacob* [Qur'ān, 19:6]. For these men there is no inheritance other than the station of the Remembrance of God and that of calling Him.

He then offered him glad-tidings of the peace He had given him, *the day he was born, and the day he dies, and the day he is raised up alive* [cf. Qur'ān, 19:15]. He used the quality of Life, which is his name, and told of the peace He had given him. His words are truthful and certain. Even though the words of the Spirit, *Peace be upon me, the day I was born, and the day I die, and the day I am raised up alive* [Qur'ān, 19:33], are more perfect in terms of union *and* creed, and better in terms of exegesis. For Jesus, the miracle lay only in his speaking; his intellect was enabled and perfected at that moment in which God made him speak. It does not necessarily follow that one who is made able to speak–whatever be his state–be truthful in what he says, as opposed to one who witnesses it, as was the case with John. From this point of view, since Divine solicitude accompanied it, the real's greeting of peace upon John was more exalted than was Jesus' greeting of peace upon himself, even though the context shows his nearness to God and his veracity in it, having spoken in the cradle for the purpose of exculpating his mother. It was one of two testimonies, the other testimony being the dried palm dropping dates without a male and without pollination, just as Mary gave birth to Jesus without a male, without the usual union with man as normally expected. If a prophet were to say, "My sign and my miracle is that this wall shall speak," and if the wall were to speak and say in its speaking, "You have lied. You are not the messenger of God," then the sign would still be valid, and thus it would be confirmed that such a one is the Messenger of God, and one would not take into account what the wall had said. Now, since this possibility is contained in the words of Jesus, which were prompted by his mother's act of gesturing to him while he was in the cradle, God's greeting of peace upon John is more exalted in this respect. The purpose was to prove that he was God's slave, because there are those who say he is the Son of God and there are those who side with prophethood and say he is God's slave; the fact of speaking alone carried out this proof. Whatever was left of that theoretical possibility remained until his truthfulness became manifest in the future, concerning everything of which he had spoken in the cradle. That to which we have alluded has now been affirmed.

RINGSTONE OF THE WISDOM OF POSSESSING IN THE WORD OF ZACHARIAH (CHAPTER 21)

Know that God's Mercy accompanies everything in existence and in determination, and that the existence of anger stems from God's mercy upon anger. His Mercy surpasses His Anger, which is to say that mercy's attribution to Him surpasses anger's attribution to Him. Now, since every identity has an existence that it seeks from God, His Mercy applies universally to each identity. Through His Mercy, by which He shows mercy upon each, He accepts their desire for the existence of their identities, and so existentiates them. For this reason we say that God's Mercy encompasses everything in existence and determination.

The Divine Names are things, and come from a single identity. What is first encompassed by God's Mercy is the thingness of that identity which exitentiates Mercy through Mercy. So the first thing encompassed by Mercy is itself; then the thingness indicated; then the thingness of all existents that exist, which have no end, neither in this lower world nor in the Hereafter, neither in accident nor in substance, neither in the compounded nor in the simple. The attainment of some purpose or agreeability with one's nature are not taken into account as far as it is concerned; indeed, what is agreeable and what is not are all encompassed by the Divine Mercy in existence.

We have said in *al-Futūḥāt* that effects belong only to non-existents, not to existents, and that if they do belong to existents it is through the determination of a non-existent. This is a rare knowledge and an uncommon matter, and only the men of imagination know how to realize it, and in their sight it is based on taste. As for those for whom imagination has no effect, they remain far removed from this matter.

God's Mercy flows in beings
And runs its course through essences and identities
Mercy's superior rank, if thou comest to know it
By witnessing with meditation, is exalted

Anything Mercy remembers is happy, and there is nothing that is not remembered by Mercy. Mercy's remembrance of things is its very existentiation of them. Every existent is an object of mercy. Do not allow what you see of an afflicted person and what you believe regarding the torment of the Hereafter–which allows those who reside with it no outward glimpse–to veil you, my friend, from grasping what we have spoken of. Firstly, know that Mercy, as it concerns existentiation, applies universally. Through showing Mercy upon torments He existentiates torments.

Moreover, Mercy has an effect in two ways. There is its effect in itself, which consists of its existentiating every identity into an existent thing. It does not look to purpose or to the absence of purpose, nor to what is agreeable or what is disagreeable; it looks to the identity of every existent thing before its existence. Indeed, it sees each in its very immutability. Thus, it saw the real created in belief as immutable identity among the immutable identities, and with itself showed it mercy through existentiation. This is why we say that the Real created in belief is the first thing shown mercy after its showing mercy through itself in the existentiation of the receivers of mercy.

It also has another effect, one based on request. Veiled persons ask the Real to show them mercy in their belief, while the Folk of Unveiling ask God's Mercy to reside in them. They ask with the Name *Allah*, saying, "O Allah, have Mercy upon us." Nothing shows them Mercy save Mercy's residing in them. It owns its determination, for indeed in reality the determination belongs to the meaning residing in a locus. In reality, *it* is what is merciful. God, who is solicitous to His slaves, is merciful to them only through Mercy. When it resides in them they taste its determination. Whosoever is remembered by Mercy is merciful, though the agent is named "merciful" or "giver of mercy." Determination does not possess the quality of being created, for it is something necessitated by meanings in themselves. States are neither existent nor non-existent, which is to say that they have no identity in existence because they are attributions, but neither are they non-existent in terms of determination, because that within which knowledge resides is called a knower and this is the state. The knower is an essence described as possessing knowledge. It is neither that very essence nor that very knowledge: there is nothing more than knowledge in an essence wherein there resides this knowledge. Being a knower is a state of this essence by virtue of its having taken on that meaning as quality. The attribution of knowledge to it comes to be, and so it is referred to as 'knower.' In reality, mercy is an attribution of that which is merciful. *It* necessitates the determination, and it is the giver of mercy. He who existentiated it in the object of mercy did not existentiate it in order that He show mercy to the latter; He only existentiated the former so that he in whom it resides would be merciful. He, glorified be He, is not a locus for becoming, and is not a locus in which mercy can be existentiated in His giving mercy. Any giver of mercy can only be so by mercy residing in him. It is established that He is identical with Mercy.

There are those who have no taste in this, nor have they set foot in it. They venture to say that He is identical with Mercy, or identical with a Quality, and they also say that He is not identical with that Quality nor with any other. In their view the Real's Qualities are neither He nor other than Him, because they are not able to deny them, nor are they able to make them identical with Him. They thus assume this manner of speaking, which is a good thing. However, something else would have been more true to this affair and more exalted in its form: namely, to deny that the identities of the Qualities have an existence residing in the essence that is said to possess them. They are only attributions and relations between that which possesses them as quality and their intelligible identities.

Even though Mercy is all-encompassing, it is differentiated in relation to each Divine Name. It is because of this that he is asked to show Mercy through every Divine Name, glorified be He. God's Mercy and the allusion are what encompass everything. Moreover it has many ramifications, which are as numerous as the Divine Names. It is not universal in relation to that specific Divine Name in the petitioner's saying, "My Lord, grant me Mercy," and the same is true for the other Names, even in the case of the Avenger when one says, "O Avenger, grant me Mercy." This is so because these Names, by their realities, indicate the named Essence according to differentiated meanings. One calls by them for the sake of Mercy, and with respect to their indicating none other than the Essence named by that Name. One does not do so with respect to what it is granted by that which this Name indicates, which is that by which it is separated and distinguished from what is other than itself, and, so far as he is concerned, it indicates the Essence. What distinguishes it in itself is its essence, since no matter what terminology one chooses there is a reality which, in its essence, is distinguished from what is other than itself, even though all are used to indicate a single named Identity. There is no disagreement as to each Name's having a determination not possessed by another, and this should be taken into account, just as one takes into account the fact of their indicating the named Essence. This is why Abū al-Qāsim ibn al-Qasī said of the Divine Names, "Indeed each Divine Name, standing alone, is named by the totality of the Divine Names, all of them." When you offer it in remembrance, you qualify it with all the Names, all of them." When you offer it in remembrance, you qualify it with all the Names, and this is because they indicate a single Identity, even if the Names are multiple, and their realities variegated–that is, the realities of these Names.

Mercy is obtained in two ways. There is the way of obligation, spoken in His Words, *We shall write it for those who are wary and offer alms* [Qur'ān, 7:156], and who offer the qualities of knowledge and works which He has enjoined upon them. The other way by which Mercy is obtained is the way of Divine free-giving, which is not reached through action. His Words said, *And My Mercy encompasseth everything* [Qur'ān, 7:156]. Of this it is also said, *That God may forgive thy sins which came before and those that come after* [Qur'ān, 48:2]. In addition are His words, "Do as thou wilt, I have forgiven thee." Know this.

Chapter X

Extracts from *al-Futūḥāt al-Makkiyya*

The Prophet Muḥammad In al-Futūḥāt al-Makiyya

Chapter 10—vol. I, pp. 207ff.

On the knowledge of the Cycle of the Kingdom and of the Command which appeared in him.

1. If the existence of the Kingdom (*mulk*) were not, the possessor (*malik*) would have not been known.
   He cannot be described by any qualification (*ṣifāt*).
2. But the Cycle of the Kingdom is a proof thereof.
   Therefore it has united the two extremities. Thus it (the Kingdom) has been unveiled.
3. Its end is like its beginning
   and its beginning precedes all beginning.
4. When it is concluded by its seal (the Prophet Muḥammad), its Possessor governs it as a prince thankful to Allah.
5. As a favor, his Creator has accorded him the knowledge of this cycle:
   that which is, that which has been, and that which will be.

Know—may Allah strengthen you—that in two traditions the Prophet—Allah's blessing and peace be on him—has said: "I am the Prince of the children of Adam and [I say it] without pretense." Now, pretense [here] would consist in bragging in vain. The second tradition is found in the collection of Muslim: "I shall be the Prince of all human beings on the Day of Resurrection." The primacy (*siyāsa*) and the eminence (*sharaf*) of the children of his species among the human kind (*bashar*) are recognized for him. He has said: "I was a Prophet when Adam was between water and clay." This means that he knew it well. Allah—Exalted is He—has therefore informed him of his station—which is the Spirit—even before He existentiated the human bodies, just as He made the covenant (*mīthāq*) with the children of Adam before creating their bodies [cf. 7:172]. Allah has attached us to His Prophets for He bore witness before them with respect to their communities when He raised from each community a witness—and they are the Messengers. Thus, the Messengers are his deputies in the world from Adam to the last of the Messengers—Allah's blessing and peace be upon him.

The Prophet—Allah's blessing and peace be upon him—has informed us about this dignified station (*maqām*) in several ways; one of them is his saying, "By Allah! Had Moses been alive, he would have no other possibility but to follow me." Another is his saying concerning the coming of Jesus, Son of Mary, before the end of times: "His aim will be to follow me"—that is, he will be placed among us (*fi-nā*) according to the tradition of our Prophet—Allah's blessing and peace be upon him—"he will break the cross and slay the pig."

Had Muḥammad—Allah's blessing and peace be upon him—arisen [corporeally] at the time of Adam, the prophets and all the human beings would have been under the authority of his Law (*sharī'a*) until the Day of Resurrection. For this reason, he was not created (in this world) universally but only in a particular (*khāṣṣatan*) manner. Thus, he is the sovereign (*malik*) and the prince (*sayyid*). Each messenger save him has been sent to a particular community and none of their messages was able to spread universally except his—Allah's blessing and peace be upon him. Hence, since the time of Adam—Allah's peace be upon him—to the Day of Resurrection, his Kingdom and his precellence were established in the future life on all the messengers. His primacy is clearly mentioned in the *ḥadīth* collections.

His spirituality—Allah's blessing and peace be upon him—is effective (*mawjūda*) just like that of each of the prophets and messengers. Divine assistance (*imdād*) has invested them, from this pure Spirit, with legal dispositions (*sharā'ī*) and sciences that they would expose during their lives as messengers. Examples of his establishing legislative prescriptions were also those of 'Alī, Mu'ādh, and other [Companions] in their role and his own; and also that of Ilyās and Khiḍr—Allah's peace be upon them. Such will also be the case of Jesus—Allah's peace be upon him—during his manifestation in the end of times as one invested with authority (*ḥākim*) under the Law (*shar'*) of Muḥammad—upon whom Allah's blessing and peace—in the latter's community and as a confirmer (*muqarrir*) outwardly. Nonetheless, due to the fact that his individual being did not come into the sensible world before since the beginning [of the cycle], each Law has been attributed to he whom it had been sent to; but in reality, it is the Law of Muḥammad—upon whom Allah's blessing and peace—even though this has been unconsciously lost sight of, as is the case at the present and when Jesus—Allah's peace be upon him—returns under the authority of his Law.

Through his Law, Allah has abrogated all the Laws, but this abrogation (*naskh*) does not exclude the Laws which have preceded it and which are found to be part of his Law. Allah has presented this abrogation to us in the outward Law which has been promulgated, that is, in the Qur'ān and the Sunna. This takes place with the full consensus of our community (*ma'a ijmā'i-nā*) and with our assent (*ittifāq-nā*) before the fact that what has been abrogated (is part) of the Law with which he has been sent to us. What precedes is therefore abrogated by what follows.

This abrogation formulated in the Qur'ān and the Sunna is for us a lesson, namely that all the previous Laws have not been excluded from being a law for Him. At the end of the temporal cycle, Jesus—Allah's blessing and peace be upon him—will return invested with an authority which is different from his Law or certain disposition it included at the time of his Mission (*risāla*). His statute (*ḥukm*) will therefore will be according to the Muḥammadan Law established (*muqarrir*) today. This argument shows that no other statute legally established before (Islam) by the prophets could interfere with the Law that Muḥammad—Allah's blessing and peace be upon him—has promulgated. These considerations include those under protection (*ahl al-dhimma*) among the people of the Book insofar as they will pay the compensatory head tax (*jizya*) readily and with deference (cf. Qur'ān, 9:29).

CHAPTER 73/73—VOLUME III, PP. 129FF.

What is the praiseworthy station (*maqām maḥmūd*)?

It is the station where all stations end up, the one for which all the

Divine names belonging to the stations are intended.

It belongs to the Envoy of Allah—Allah's blessing and peace be upon him—and that will be apparent to all creatures on the Day of Resurrection. Because of that, primacy (*siyāda*) over all creatures will return to him on the day of their Presentation (*yawm al-'arḍ*). The Envoy of Allah has said: I am the Prince (*sayyid*) of the humankind (*al-nās*).

This is the station in which Adam dwelt when the angels prostrated before him. It belonged to him here below, and in the life to come it belongs to Muḥammad—Allah's blessing and peace be upon him. It consists in the Perfection of the Divine Presence.

The father of Humankind (*abū al-bashar*, i.e. Adam) only appeared there because his body included the formal aspect (*bashariyya*) of Muḥammad—Allah's blessing and peace be upon him. Adam is therefore the supreme father (*ab a'ẓam*) with respect to the corporeal entity (*jismiyya*), the one drawn near (*muqarrab*) unto Allah and the first of this human constitution to have been made of clay. All the stations are manifested in him including that of opposition (*mukhālafa*) because he gathers the two deposits (lit. "fists"—*qabḍatān*): that of accord (*wifāq*) and that of opposition (*khilāf*). Only the vital breath (*nasama*) of Adam is put in motion by his opposition to the [divine] interdiction [to not approach the Tree]. His opposition was relative to the interdiction that Allah has placed on him to put this vital breath in movement, which was contained in his loins (*ẓahr*, or outward being). The station of Adam required this disposition. I asked our master Abū 'l-'Abbās on this matter and he told me: "Only those descendants of Adam who are in contestation in their reins disobey."

It accrued to Muḥammad—Allah's blessing and peace be upon him—to reach this station made of praises in the Abode of the Hereafter.

In this station the Door of intercession (*shafā'a*) will be opened. He (the Prophet) will first intercede with God in favour of those who in their turn have the ability to intercede: angels, messengers, prophets, saints, animals, plants, and minerals. The Envoy of Allah will intercede for them all so that then they may themselves intercede in favour of other men. For this reason, Muḥammad will be praised (*maḥmūd*) in every language and with every word. Allah will then say [according to a *ḥadīth qudsī*]: "The angels have interceded, the prophets have interceded, and the faithful have interceded. There remains only the Most Merciful of the Merciful (*arḥām al-rāḥimīn*)." The sequence of words in this ḥadīth involves the intercession of the Most Merciful of the Merciful. Now it is absolutely necessary that He intercede with someone, even though only He subsists.

Know then that Allah will intercede through the relationship of His names: His name "the Most Merciful of the Merciful" will intercede with the names "the All-Conqueror" (*al-Qahhār*) and "He whose punishment is terrible" (*shadīd al-'iqāb*) so that the punishment which oppressed those beings subjected to these names will be taken away, so that those who never did any good will be taken out of the fire. Allah has clearly drawn the attention on this by saying: *On the day when We shall gather those who are wary* (*muttaqīn*) *unto the Beneficent, a goodly company. And drive the guilty unto hell, a weary herd, they will have no power of intercession, save him who hath made a covenant with his Lord* (Qur'ān, 19:85-87).

He who is wary (*muttaqī*) takes refuge in the Divine Name which engenders fear (*khawf*) in the heart of servants. This is how Allah leads the one who is wary from this Name (of vigor) to the Divine Name which procures him security (*amān*) from the One who engenders fear in him. And it is precisely the Infinitely Good in accord with the verse above: *On the day when We shall gather those who are wary* (*muttaqīn*)*unto the Beneficent, a goodly company.* This means that they shall be secure from what they fear. And this is why the Prophet—Allah's blessing and peace be upon him—has said regarding intercession, in the *ḥadīth* mentioned above: 'There remains only the Most Merciful of the Merciful (*arḥām al-rāḥimīn*).' It is through this relation that the intercession is brought back to the True having proceeded from the True from the effects of His Names. This is how the Gnostics from among the saints understand it.

Thus, on the Day of Resurrection, all the praises (*maḥāmid*) will be gathered by Muḥammad: this is what is designated by the "praiseworthy station."

Regarding this station, the Prophet—Allah's blessing and peace be upon him—has said: "I will praise Him then by praises which I do not know at the present." This is a proof that has been granted to you [regarding the fact] that the knowledge which the prophets and the saints have been invested with comes from the direct experiences (*adhwāq*, lit. tastes) and that they are obtained neither by meditation (*fikr*) nor by rational speculation (*naẓar*). That abode (*mawtin*) implies, through effects that are proper to it, Divine Names through which Allah is praised and that the abode of the here below cannot comprise. For this reason, the Prophet—Allah's blessing and peace be upon him—has said: ". . . which I do not know at the present."

This station is [also] that of the degree of mediation (*wasīla*) for it is from this that he supplicates to Allah in favor of what solicits the opening of the gate of intercession, and this is the intercession of Muḥammad—Allah's blessing and peace be upon him—for all. Have you not seen what he has said regarding the station of mediation (*wasīla*): "There is a station in the Garden suited only for one of God's servants, and I hope to be that one. If anyone asks that I be given the mediation (*wasīla*), my intercession (*shafā'a*) for him will become lawful." He (Allah) has therefore made intercession the recompense for he who solicits it. And this is why the station of praises has been called "*wasīla*," or mediation. The recompense that shall be given to them by this demand will permit them to intercede. What is at issue here is a universal divine function (*mansib*) coming from the King of the Kingdom Himself (*'ayn malik al-mulk*). Allah—exalted is He—has said: *Do not all affairs reach Allah at last?* (Qur'ān, 42:53). He has also said, *unto Him is returned the whole of the affair* (Qur'ān, 11:123). Therefore, the "place" of reintegration (*marji'*) is in Him, and this is how all the stations and the Names reintegrate this station made of praises for the Prophet—Allah's peace and blessings be upon him—has said: "I have been given the all-encompassing word (*'ūtitu jawāmi'a al-kalim*)."

Chapter 73/74

By virtue of what did he obtain it?

The Prophet—Allah's blessing and peace be upon him—has said: "Each prophet has a fulfilled supplication and each of them asks for it to be answered promptly; but I have deferred my petition in order to intercede on behalf of the great sinners (*li-ahli al-kabā'ir*) of my Community." This is so because his knowledge of the Abode of the Hereafter is greater than that of the other prophets.

Know this. All stations refer to this station made of praise which totalizes them. It does not befit the one who possesses it to be other than he who has "received the all-encompassing word" for the modalities of praise (*maḥāmid*) are related to the [divine] attribute of Speech (*ṣifāt al-kalām*). Since the Prophet has been sent to all of us, the Law he promulgated has encompassed all the other laws and it also implies the whole of the comportments that may be made lawful. [. . .]

Jesus and Mary In al-Futūḥāt al-Makkiyya

Chapter 5—vol. I, p. 172—extracts

The Mother of the Book, the Book and the relations, Mary and Jesus

[. . .] The Book (*al-kitāb*) includes the Fātiḥa and other elements since they are part of it. The name of Fātiḥa (the Opener) is adequate for it is the one that opens the Book of Existence in the beginning. It is interpreted as being the incomparable (*munazzah*) Model or Likeness (*mithl*) in reference to the verse: *Naught is as His likeness* (*ka-mithli*) . . . (Qur'ān, 42:11) since, in the expression *ka-mithli*, the letter *kāf* is considered as qualifying the term *mithl*. It has existentiated the Book after having existentiated the *mithl*, which is the Fātiḥa, and which He has placed as a key for it. Pay heed to this!

The Fātiḥa is the Mother (or = engendering maternal prototype) of the Qur'ān, for the Mother is the locus in which existentiation takes place, and the Qur'ān is that which is existentiated in her; the Existentiater is the Author or the Agent (*Fā'il*) who acts through the Mother (*fī al-'umm*). Thus, the Mother is the perfect synthesis and the Fātiḥa is the Mother of the Book which is with Him according to the word of God: *And with Him is the Mother of the Book* (Qur'ān, 13:39).

Consider therefore the case of Jesus and of Mary and the Agent of existentiation, it will appear to you as the opposite (through symbolic inversion) of what is manifested to your sensible perception. The Mother is then Jesus, and the Son which is the Book in Him or the Qur'ān is Mary. Understand this!

The same is true for the Spirit (*rūḥ*) which couples with the Soul (*nafs*) through the intermediary of the Intellect (*'aql*). The Soul becomes thus the locus of existentiation from the sensible aspect. The Spirit is manifested only by the Soul and the latter is therefore the Father (*ab*). This Soul is therefore "a Book inscribed" (*kitāb marqūm*—Qur'ān 83:9 and 20) to complete the imagery. There appeared in the Son (*ibn*) that which the Pen inscribes onto the

Mother (*umm*), and this constitutes the Qur'ān reaching the World of the Concrete (*'ālam al-shahāda*).

The Mother is also interpreted as being the existence of Likeness (*mithl*), the locus of the Secrets (*maḥall al-asrār*) which is "*a parchment unrolled*" (*raqq manshūr*—Qur'ān, 52:3) in which "*a book inscribed*" (*kitāb mastūr*—Qur'ān, 52:2) is deposited (and) its divine secrets are contained in him. In this case, the Book is more excellent than the Fātiḥa for she is a proof (*dalīl*) and the Book is that to which it leads (*madlūl-hā*) . . .

Chapter 7—vol. I, p. 192—extracts

The four modalities of the creation of the human body

1) The body of Adam—2) the body of Eve—3) the body of Jesus—4) the bodies of the children of Adam.

[. . .] Each of these four categories of the body concern a production (*nash'a*) which differs from the others in causality (*sababiyya*) when considering both aspects together, corporeal and spiritual. We expound on this in order to draw attention on this point so that a person of weak intelligence may not imagine that the Divine Power or the essential Realities accomplish this human production only starting from a single cause whose nature would provoke this production.

Allah removes this ambiguity (*shubha*) by making the human production of Adam appear according to a manner which is different from that which the body of Eve manifests, and the latter was manifested in a way which differs from that of the children of Adam. On the other hand, the body of the children of Adam is manifested differently from that of Jesus. However, the name "man" has been given to each of these four categories of bodies through its definition and its reality so that it be known . . . *that God has knowledge of everything* (Qur'ān, 8:75) and that He is *Powerful over every thing* (Qur'ān, 22:6).

In addition, Allah has gathered these four types of created beings in verse 49:13 of the Qur'ān: *O mankind, We have created you* (i.e. Adam) *from a male* (i.e. Eve) *and from a female* (i.e. Jesus), and from the union of a male and a female, i.e. the children of Adam by way of marriage (*nikāh*) and engendering children (*tawālud*). This verse is to be related to the *all-encompassing word* and the *discernment of the book* (*fasl al-kitāb*) that have been given to Muḥammad. [. . .]

[. . .] Physiologists affirm that the female liquid is not at the origin of the constitution of a human being. [They say that] the embryo that exists in the mother comes from man's semen. For this reason, we say that the making of the body of Jesus comes from another nature. The development (*tabdīr*) of this body in the womb is similar to that of the body of all children. The making of the body of Jesus proceeds from the female liquid due to the fact that the *Spirit presented himself to her* (Mary) *a man without fault* (*bashar sawiyy*) (Qur'ān, 19:17) or from an insufflation without water. In any case, this is a fourth category of the making of other bodies from the same species. For this reason, Allah has said (Qur'ān, 3:59): *Lo, the likeness of Jesus, in God's sight, is as Adam's likeness; He created him of dust . . .* Here the pronoun him (*hu*) refers to *Adam*. This similitude appeared in his (Jesus') creation due to the fact that he had no father (like Adam), that is, the condition of his (Jesus') making is like Adam' creation, except that he was created from dust (and not like Jesus who was created directly from the insufflation of Gabriel unto Mary). *Then He said unto him* (Adam) *be! and he was* (*kun fa yakun*).

Moreover, Jesus, according to what is being said about him, did not remain in the womb of his mother for the usual time of gestation, as it was faster for him. For Allah wanted to make of him *a sign* [for mankind]. This conception contradicts the position of the physiologists who rule according to nature as it presents itself to them usually and not according to what it entails in relation with the secrets and extraordinary makings which Allah casts in it. An expert in this field will rightly speak of this natural formation by saying: "We only know of nature what it shows to us, and there remains in it what we do not know." [. . .]

CHAPTER 9—VOL. I, P. 202—EXTRACTS

[. . .] As for the human being, his creation differs in accordance with four modalities: the creation of Adam is not similar to that of Eve—the creation of Eve does not resemble the creation of the other children of Adam—the creation of Jesus is not of the same nature as the creation which starts from a male (*dhakar*). [. . .]

[. . .] He created Adam from dust, Eve from a rib (or curve—*dila'*), Jesus from the insufflation of the Spirit, and the children of Adam from simple semen. [. . .]

Chapter 10—vol. I, pp. 207ff.—Extracts

At the end of time, Jesus will descend according to the Muḥammadan Law

[. . .] Ḥadīth: "I am the master of the children of Adam and I do not boast about it." "I am the master of the human beings on the Day of Resurrection." "I was Prophet when Adam was between water and clay." "Had Moses been alive, he would have no choice but to follow me."

The first human body that came into existence was that of Adam. He is the first Father of mankind and of other fathers of this species. [. . .] He is therefore the first of those who appeared according to the ruling (*ḥukm*) that Allah gave to this human gender (*jins*), but in the aspect we specified before.

In addition, starting from him, Allah has extracted a second father for us, which is called "Mother" (*umm*) over which this first Father rightly possesses a degree (*daraja*), for he is her root (*aṣl*). Through him (Muḥammad), Allah has completed the substitutes (*nuwwāb*) belonging to the cycle of the Kingdom (*dawra al-mulk*), in the same way in which He had inaugurated it, in order to warn that the favor is in His Hand and that in itself this process has necessitated this first Father.

He existentiated Jesus starting from Mary. Mary is likened to Adam in the generation of Jesus (fatherless) and of Eve (motherless). Just as a female (Eve) comes from a male (Adam, without the intervention of a woman), so does a male (Jesus) issue from a female (Mary, without the intervention of a father). Allah stopped (this particular mode of generating) just like He had started it, by giving existence to a fatherless son (for Jesus), just like He had done initially for Eve without a mother. Jesus and Eve are therefore like two siblings and Adam and Mary like two fathers for the two of them (Adam for Eve, and Mary for Jesus). [. . .]

[. . .]*Truly, the likeness of Jesus, in God's sight, is as Adam's likeness; He created him of dust, then said He unto him, 'Be,' and he is* (Qur'ān, 3:59). Here, the comparison (*tashbīh*) is established in the absence of paternity by the male. For this reason, this verse constitutes a proof (*dalīl*) concerning Jesus for the innocence of his mother, whereas the comparison could not be established with Eve—although it is possible to envisage it—for woman can give place to suspicion (*tumha*, for adultery) before the state of pregnancy (*haml*), since she is so constituted as to conceive the child whereas man is not made for it. These proofs must serve to remove the doubt. In the case of Eve issuing from Adam, there can be no ambiguity, for Adam has not been constituted to give birth. This is a proof only for those who maintain the existence of Adam, his formation (*takwīn*), and that which comes from him (*takwīn min-hu*). Just like a son cannot be conceived without a father, he cannot be conceived without a mother either.

According to an interpretative approach, the term *mathal*, likeness (used in 3:59) means that Jesus is like Eve (from the aspect of generation). However, while doubt on this matter has seized the disputants regarding woman who is formed with a view to childbearing, as we just mentioned, and here lies the doubt; the comparison with Adam is made in order to exculpate Mary from the usual process [of nature regarding childbearing]. Jesus is formed from Mary without a [human] father just like Eve was manifested from Adam without mother. And he is the second father. [. . .]

CHAPTER 20—VOL. I, PP. 255-257—EXTRACTS

On the Christic knowledge

Where from did it come? What is its outcome? What are its modalities? Is it related to the "height" (*tūl*: lit. length) of the universe or to its "width" (*'arḍ*) or both?

1. The knowledge of Jesus is that
   whose value is ignored by the creatures.
2. Through it he gave life
   to a being whose tomb was the earth.
3. The insufflation of Him in which he was concealed
   coincided with the permission (*idhn*) and the Command (*amr*).
4. His hidden divine aspect (*lāhūt*)
   was his family link (*siḥr*),
5. An integrated Spirit,
   whose secret was made manifest by Allah.
6. He came out of occultation from a Presence.
   Allah had hidden his splendor.
7. He became creature while being Spirit.
   Then Allah illuminated him.
8. His Command was accomplished in him,
   It fulfilled him and rejoiced him.
9. Allah has already glorified the reward

Know, may Allah strengthen you, that knowledge concerning Jesus is that of the letters (*'ilm al-hurūf*), and for this reason he received the insufflation (*nafkh*) which is the air coming from within the heart and which is the Spirit of Life. Therefore, when this air is interrupted in its process of coming out at the mouth of the body, the places in which its stoppings are produced are called 'letters' and these points of emission manifest the essential entities of the letters (*a'yān al-hurūf*). When these letters enter into compositions, sensory life is produced under the effect of intelligible realities. This process constitutes the commencement of the appearance of the divine Presence in the universe.

In the condition of non-manifestation (*'adam*) of these essential entities, there is no other mode of relationship apart from hearing. In themselves, these essential entities in their state of non-manifestation are predisposed to receive the Divine Command (*amr ilāhī*) when it appears in them in order to give them their existence. Allah thereby formulates this imperative: Exist (*kun*). Then, they become existent and manifest themselves qua determined entities. Also, when He intends to bestow existence to them, the first "thing" (*shay'* or reality) which they understand is the Divine Word (*al-kalām al-ilāhī*) coming from Allah through this Word, which befits Him, Glory be to Him.

The first organized word was therefore *Kun*, which is composed [from a root] comprising three letters: *kāf* (k), *wāw* (w), and *nūn* (n), and each of these three letters are composed of three letters. So the number nine appears whose square root (*jidhr*) is three, that is, the first odd number (*afrād*). The simple numbers cease with the existence of the number nine whose origin is the *Kun* which thereby cause the number to appear as well as that which is counted.

This is why the foundation of the composition of the two premises [of a syllogism] proceeds from three, even if, seemingly four terms are concerned. Indeed, one of these is repeated in the two premises so that there are only three terms at question. The generation (*kawn*) comes from the odd (*fard*) and not from the one (*al-wāḥid*).

God has already made known to us that the cause of Life in the forms of being is the divine Insufflation expressed in the verse: *When I have shaped him* (the human being: *bashar*), *and breathed My spirit in him . . .* (Qur'ān, 15:29). It is the Breath (*nafas*) through which Allah invigorates Faith by making it manifest. The Prophet has said: "The Breath of the All-Merciful comes to me from Yemen." Obviously, the form that faith takes in the heart of those who carry it is living as well as the form of the legislative rulings (*aḥkām mashrū'a*).

Jesus had received the knowledge of this divine Insufflation and that which it implied. Thus, he breathed unto the (human) form, which was in the tomb or unto the form of the bird that he had fashioned out of clay. Each of them became living by the divine permission (*idhn*) which spread by means of this insufflation and this air (*hawā'*). Had there been no spreading (*sarayān*) of the divine permission, life would have never appeared in any form whatsoever. It is therefore from the Breath of the All-Merciful that the specific knowledge of Jesus comes. Thus he could revive the dead by his finalized insufflation in the forms it was instilled. This process which concerns all existentiated beings comes from Allah and permits to lead to Him, for all returns to Him.

During the human being's ascension to his Lord, when he is absorbed and he is freed in its course from all condition of existence related to him, there remains only this "secret" (*sirr*) which resides in him and which comes from Allah. Thus, he sees Him only through it and understands His Word only through it. Such is the sublime nature and the sanctity of Allah that He can only be attained through it. When the individual returns from this "locus" of contemplation, his form which has been absorbed during his ascension is recomposed and each plane of existence (*'ālam*) restores to him all that which is related to him and which he was deprived of, for no degree of existence can go beyond his nature (*jins*, lit. gender). This ensemble is thereby reunited in accordance with this divine secret and encompasses it, and through it the form [of this being] sings His praises and proclaims the perfection of its Lord, which is impossible for other than this [secret]. Had the form praised him in accordance with itself and not with this secret, the divine grace would have not manifested itself within this form. However, the divine grace proves to be concerned with all creatures as it is well established that the glorification and praise of Allah by the creature comes only from this divine secret and all things come from His Spirit, whereas no [created] thing is in [this secret]. Thus, God is He who praises and glorifies Himself and the divine Good that returns in this form during the praise and the glorification comes from the grace and not from existential merit.

In effect, God has attributed Himself with the merit to the extent that He obligates Himself with it.

The words (*kalimāt*) then stem from the letters, and the letters issue from the air, and the air stems from the Breath of the All-Merciful (*nafas al-raḥmān*). The effects (*āthār*) are manifested in generated beings through the Names. It is from this whole that the knowledge proper to Jesus finds its completion. In addition, through these words the human being establishes the presence of the All-Merciful (*Raḥmān*) which accords to him, under the effect of His Breath, that through which the life entailed by these words is maintained. Thus, the process is developed cyclically and uninterruptedly.

Know that the life of the spirits is an essential life. Thereby, every possessor of spirit is living through his own spirit. The Sāmirī (= Samaritan from the time of Moses) knew this at the moment when he perceived Gabriel and he knew that the latter's spirit was his very essence. He (Gabriel) does not appear in a place without invigorating it through the direct contact of his form. The Sāmirī took a handful [of dust] in the trace left by Gabriel, according to what Allah says about the Sāmirī: *'I beheld what they beheld not,' he said, 'and I seized a handful of dust from the messenger's track, and cast it into the thing. So my soul prompted me.'* (Qur'ān, 20:96). When he had shaped the form of the veal, he threw this handful of dust on him and the calf lowed.

[In verse 4:171] Allah qualifies Jesus as Spirit (*rūḥ*), but He constituted him as Spirit in the definitive form of a man [unlike] Gabriel to whom He had given the provisory form of a Bedouin. This is why Jesus could revive the dead only through Insufflation. Moreover, Allah confirmed him through the Holy Spirit. He is therefore a spirit confirmed by a spirit, purified from the taint of engendered beings. The foundation of all this is the Living without beginning, the endless essential source of Life. The distinction between these two extremes, the Begininglessness and Endlessness is solely based on the existence of the living world and its contingent character.

This knowledge is in relation to the "height" (*tūl*) of the universe, I mean a spiritual world, the world of the intelligible principles (*ma'ānī*) and of the Command. It also concerns the "width" (*'arḍ*) of the universe, of the world of creation, of nature, and of the bodies. All is Allah's: *Verily, His are the creation and the command*

(Qur'ān, 7:54). *The Spirit is of the Command of my Lord* (Qur'ān, 17:85). *Blessed be God, the Lord of all Being* (Qur'ān, 7:54).

[. . .] Among the people of spiritual realization, he who knows the reality of the *Kun* possesses the knowledge proper to Jesus, and he who gives existence to beings generated by his spiritual energy (*himma*) does so thanks to this knowledge.

CHAPTER 54—VOL. I, PP. 420FF.—*AL-ISHĀRĀT*

The knowledge of allusion is rapprochement (taqrīb) and distancing (ibād).
Its process in yourself is repetition (ta'wīb) and illness (is'ād).
So scrutinize this knowledge, for Allah has transferred it
To he through which lies and deviation can come about.
Information of immunity for he to whom God said: "Be!"
Then he became established as an existent and the initiates are spectators.

The absence of the vision of the Face of God in things

Know—may Allah assist you through a spirit from Him—that, for the people of Allah's path, allusion implies distance (*bu'd*) or even assistance from another (*hudūr al-ghayr*). In his work *Maḥāsin al-majālis*[1], a certain master has said: "Allusion is an appeal (*nidā'*) especially in accordance with distancing, and a manner of communicating (*bawh*) due to an imperfection (*'illa*)." He meant that this is the observation (*taṣrīḥ*) of the existence (*ḥusūl*) of deficiency or sickness (*marad*) for the imperfection (*'illa*) is deficiency (*marad*), and this is the meaning of the expression "[with] help from another." By the term "imperfection" (*'illa*), this author did not mean "the cause" (*sabab*)[2], as the speculative intellectuals define this term.

For those who proceed from allusion, the form taken by this shortcoming consists of the aspect of truth (*wajh al-ḥaqq*) that is hidden in the other (mentioned above). Thus, the allegation (*da'wā*) takes hold of him for whom the aspect of the truth is hidden in things. This is the reason why allegation constitutes deficiency. For the realizers of the truth (*muḥaqqiqūn*), it is certain that

1. This treaty by Ibn al-'Ārif (Abū al-'Abbās Aḥmad, Ibn Muḥammad, ibn Mūsā, ibn 'Atā' Allah) was translated by Asin Palacios. This Sufi lived from 481/1088 to 536/1141 and was buried in Marrakesh.

2. In Aristotelian logic, in a classical syllogism, the terms "*'illa*" and "*sabab*" are defined as the middle term which unites the two premises.

throughout the universal Existence (*wujūd*) there is naught but Allah, and although we are existentiated beings (*mawjūdīn*), our existence is only through Him. This is the reason why he whose existence would be through another beside Him would fall within the status of non-existence (*'adam*).

Allusion is well and truly affirmed and its status is evident, no doubt, in accordance with the explication provided above.

The doctors of the law and the Sufis—outward knowledge and inner knowledge

Know that when Allah created the creatures, He created the humans in contrast (*aṭwāran*, to one another). Among us are found the knowledgeable and the ignorant, the just and the unjust, the restrictive and the restricted, the ruling and the ruled, the dominating and the dominated, the superior and the inferior, the commander and the commanded, the sovereign and the populace, the envied and the envier. He did not create beings that are tougher and more rigorous than the literalist scholars (*'ulamā al-rusūm*) who are hostile to the folk of Allah who devote themselves to His service and who know Him in the path of the divine Gift, the same ones He has bestowed with His secrets and whom He has taught the meanings of His Book and the allusions (*ishārāt*) of His Speech. And for these initiates (*al-ṭā'ifa*), such literalist scholars are like the tyrants for the messengers—peace be upon them.

When, as we mentioned, this circumstance presents itself in Existence, in accordance with what the pre-existing knowledge has determined, our companions turn to allusions in the same way that Mary—Peace be upon her—turned to allusion due to the people of calumnies and deviation. Their word regarding the exegesis (*sharḥ*) of the precious Book of Allah—which contains nothing futile—are allusions, even though they constitute a truth and a commentary on the beneficial meanings it contains. They give their proper interpretation by establishing for everything and that which it was revealed for, as the linguists teach with their language in which they have received this Book. Thus Allah applies these two aspects to them, as He has said: *We shall show them Our signs in the horizons and in themselves . . .* (Qur'ān, 41:53), that is, the signs that have descended in the horizons and in themselves.

Commentary on allusion and the Sufi interpretation thereof

All revealed signs comprise two aspects: one aspect which they see in themselves and another which they see as outward to themselves. They call allusion that which they see in themselves so that the literalist (*ṣāḥib al-rusūm*) doctor of the law (*faqīh*) gets used to it, but they do not say that it is a commentary (*tafsīr*) in order to protect themselves against the evil of these scholars and of their charges of disbelief regarding the matter due to their ignorance about the scope of the divine word. Thus, they conform to the established use in the matter of guidance. Yet Allah would have been perfectly capable of specifying in His Book how the folk of Allah should interpret His text. In spite of this, He did not do so, but he makes them penetrate into these divine words which are revealed in accordance with the common language of chosen significant sciences which He has taught His servants at the moment when he He enables the understanding of what He has given them.

Had the literalists been fair-minded, they would take account of what is in themselves when they envisage the signs according to the outward aspect (*wajh*) which they aspect among themselves. They would consequently see that they seek to compete with the others in this, and that some are better than others in the interpretation of the meaning of the verse. He who is lacking recognizes the superiority enjoyed by he who is not, in the interpretation of this verse. All of them go in the same direction!

Despite their recognized superiority in this domain, they impugn the folk of Allah when they bring something which escapes their comprehension due to the fact that they assess that the former are not scholars and that knowledge can only be obtained by the usual teaching according to the tradition. And they are right in this! For our companions do not realize this [outward] science but through teaching (*ta'allum*) and such is indeed the information (*i'lām*) which the merciful Lord bestows. Allah has said: *Recite: In the Name of thy Lord who created Man of a blood-clot. Recite: And thy Lord is the Most Generous, who taught by the Pen, taught Man that he knew not . . .* (Qur'ān, 96:1-5). *And it is Allah who brought you forth from your mothers' wombs knowing nothing, and He appointed for you hearing, and sight, and hearts, that haply so you will be thankful* (Qur'ān, 16:78). *He created man and He has taught him the Explanation* (Qur'ān, 55:3-4). Hence, He—glorified is He—is the Teacher (*mu'allim*) of the human being.

The folk of Allah are the heirs to the prophets in knowledge, guidance, and wisdom

We have no doubt that the folk of Allah are the heirs to the prophets—peace be upon them—as Allah has said of the Messenger: *[Allah] teacheth thee that which thou knewest not* (Qur'ān, 4:113). Regarding Jesus, He has said: *We taught him the Scripture and Wisdom, the Torah and the Gospel . . .* (Qur'ān, 3:48). The literalist scholars are right when they say: "There is no knowledge without teaching," but they are wrong in their conviction which consists in saying that Allah does not instruct him who is not a prophet or a messenger. Allah has said: *He grants wisdom to whom He pleaseth* (Qur'ān, 2:269), a wisdom which means knowledge. He means by the expression "to whom" those who do not have this knowledge.

But when the literalist scholars prefer this immediate way to the ultimate way and when they give priority to the creature and not to God, they are inclined to take knowledge from Scriptures as well as the mouth of these men who have the same tendency. In their allegation, they are convinced to be the folk of Allah due to the fact that they possess the [outward] knowledge and that therefore they are distinguished from the common people, which actually prevents them from knowing that Allah has worshippers whose teaching in their intimate secrets He undertakes in accordance with what He reveals in His Scriptures and with the language of His messengers. Such is the authentic knowledge coming from the Knowing Teacher the perfection of whose knowledge no believer or disbeliever disputes.

Those who maintain that Allah does not know the particular realities, however, do not mean to deny that He has this knowledge. Instead they envisage that the knowledge of Allah is not renewed for Him due to each [individual] thing [that He makes], but rather that He knows the particular realities as being included in His knowledge of the universal realities. They affirm therefore that He possesses this knowledge—Praised is He—even though they are not the folk of faith. They maintain His transcendence—Praised is He—although they are wrong in how they express it.

Thanks to the assistance He grants to certain of His servants, Allah takes responsibility of teaching them about Himself by communicating them intuition (*ilhām*) and comprehension (*ifhām*): *and inspired it to lewdness and Godfearing* (Qur'ān, 91:8). In the verse preceding this one, Allah says: *By a soul and Him who fashioned it . . .* (Qur'ān, 91.7). He has enabled the soul to clearly distinguish lewdness from God-fearing through an intuition that it feels as coming from Him in order for it to avoid lewdness and act in god-fearing.

The sending down of the Scripture on the Prophet and the comprehension in the heart of the saints

Just like the principle (*aṣl*) of the sending down of the Scripture on the prophets comes from Allah, so is the comprehension that comes from Him produced in the heart of certain believers. The prophets—peace be upon them—do not utter anything regarding Allah without Him inspiring their hearts. They are conscious that this does not come from them, and that it does not result from their comprehension. They do not exert themselves at all, but they reach it as coming from Allah, for He has said: *a sending down from One All-wise, All-laudable. Falsehood comes not to it from before it nor from behind it* (Qur'ān, 41:42). The principle (*aṣl*) we are speaking about comes from Allah and not from human cogitation or from its modalities of expression. But the literalist scholars know this well! It therefore suits the folk of Allah, who apply the givens of the Scripture, to be more qualified than the literalist scholars for the elucidation (*sharḥ*) thereof and the explication (*bayān*) of what Allah has sent down. The comprehension concerning this domain will also come from a divine intervention in the heart of the folk of Allah, according to the demand of the divine principle.

'Alī ibn Abī Ṭālib could say regarding this: "On the matter of the comprehension of the text of the Qur'ān, there is but what Allah grants to whomever He wills among His servants." He considered this disposition as a gift (*'atā'*) from Allah, which he interpreted as being the comprehension coming from Allah. Yet the folk of Allah are more capable of receiving it than all others.

The hold of the folk of the outward with respect to the literalist scholars in this life

In addition, the folk of Allah see that He has clearly conferred, in this life, the power (*dawla*) to persons among the literalist scholars (*'ulamā' al-rusūm*) motivated by the outward meaning (*al-ẓāhir*), and that He has granted them the exercise of power (*tahakkum*) over the creatures due to the statements they make. He likens them to those who *know an outward part of the present life, but of the Hereafter they are heedless* (Qur'ān, 30:7). The latter, in their disavowal of the folk of Allah, *think that they are working good deeds* (Qur'ān, 18:104). Thus, the folk of Allah protect their states from them for they know to which extent they can express themselves! This is why they guard themselves from them by calling the profound realities (*ḥaqā'iq*) "allusions" (*ishārāt*). For the literalist scholars do not deny the allusions. Later, on the Day of Resurrection, it shall be as they say:

Once the dust settles, you shall see
Whether under you lies a horse or a donkey

Similarly, on the Day of Resurrection (*yawm al-qiyāma*), the realizer of the truth (*muḥaqqiq*) among the folk of Allah will be clearly distinguished from the one who claims (*mudda'ī*) to be competent. Someone has said:

When the tears spread over the cheeks
The crying person is clearly distinguished from the pretender

What is the position of the literalist scholar regarding the following saying of 'Alī ibn Abī Ṭālib: "If I were to comment on the Surah al-Fātiḥa, it would have loaded seventy camels." Would this derive from other than the comprehension of the Qur'ān that Allah granted him?

The noun perspicacious (*faqīh*)[3] is more suitable for the initiated (*ṭā'ifa*) than for the literalist scholar, for Allah has said regarding this matter: *to become learned in religion, and to warn their people when they return to them, that haply they may beware* (Qur'ān, 9:122). God places them in the same situation as the Messenger in order to obtain perspicacity (*tafaqquh*) in religion and warning. He who aspires to Allah in accordance with an intuitive look (*baṣīra*) resembles the Messenger of Allah—blessings and peace upon him—who aspires [to Him] according to an intuitive look and not by virtue of a predominantly individual conviction (*ẓann*), as the literalist scholar thinks. What a difference between he who gives new commentaries and who speaks thereof according to an intuitive view which follows from his aspiration towards Allah, and who acts in accordance with a proof from his Lord, versus he who gives commentaries in religious matters from a

3. This term comes from a root which means: to be gifted with a penetrating intelligence, and terminological meaning is to be knowledgeable in Islamic jurisprudence.

simple, predominantly individual conviction.

Knowledge taken from a dead one versus knowledge taken from the Living who never dies

Furthermore, part of the condition of the literalist scholar who is left to himself is his failure to account for what he says; he asserts "My Lord has made me understand," for he feels superior and thinks of himself as possessing knowledge. He who is of the folk of Allah says: "Certainly, Allah has introduced his breath into my innermost consciousness through this wisdom contained in such and such verse." Or he expresses himself in the following manner: "I have seen the Messenger of Allah—upon whom be blessings and peace—in a spiritual event which concerns me (*wāqi'at-ī*) and he has taught me on the validity of this tradition which is related from him and its authority with me." Regarding what the literalist scholar Abū Yazīd al-Basṭāmī[4] has said on this issue and its validity: "You take your knowledge dead from the dead, but I take my knowledge from the Living who does not die." Those who resemble us say: "My heart has given me news from my Lord," whereas you say: "Such and such has related to me . . ." But where is he? They reply: "He is dead." And you continue, ". . . from such and such." But where is he? "He is dead!" you say.

When the Shaykh Abū Madyan[5] was told: "[A report has been related] from such and such from such and such," he said: "We do not wish to eat withered meat, bring us fresh meat." In this way he wanted to increase the aspirations of his companions. He continued, "This is the statement of such and such. What do *you* say? Which gift from Allah coming from the knowledge of with Him has He granted you?" He wanted to say: "Relate reports [directly] from your Lord and stop saying such and such. They will be eating fresh meat for He who gives has not died since." *He is closer to you than your jugular vein* (Qur'ān, 50:16).

The divine favor endures and the glad tidings are part of prophethood

The divine favor is permanent and the bringing of glad tidings

4. A famous Persian Sufi, 184/800–234/848.

5. Born in the vicinity of Seville in 520/1126, he died close to Tlemcen in 594/1198. About these two figures who were considered as saints, cf. Cyril Glassé, *Dictionnaire encyclopédique de l'Islam*, Paris, Bordas, 1991.

(*mubashshirāt*) is not closed, "they constitute a part of prophethood." The way is clear, the door is open, and the comportment [of people] is determined by the Law. Allah is oft-returning in meeting the one who comes to him in haste. *Three men conspire not secretly together, but He is the fourth of them . . . but He is with them, wherever they may be* (Qur'ān, 58:7). He is with you by virtue of this encounter due to the proximity, despite your pretension of possessing science and faith in this matter. Why do you neglect learning with Him and having a close relationship with Him for, instead of learning from others than Him and not from Him, you would then have a new knowledge [or new rain] from your Lord? [Even] rain (*matar*) is above your rank, for when the Messenger of Allah—upon whom be blessings and peace—exposed himself to it when it was falling, he uncovered his head in order for it to touch him. When asked about this, he replied that this rain was a new knowledge obtained from his Lord in order to teach us and inform us.

Sufi allusions in the interpretation of the Scripture of Allah

You must know moreover that our companions use the technical term "allusion," which they employ to the exclusion of other words, to interpret the Book of Allah, only when they must expose a divine teaching (*ta'līm ilāhī*) that the literalist scholars do not know. This is so because allusion only appears in accordance with the intention of he who uses this manner and not in relation to what he alludes to. If you ask them about the interpretation they intend to give to the term allusion, [they will say] that they use it with he who poses questions from among the literalist scholars according to the method of premonition (*fa'l*). For example, a man feels anxiety regarding a matter that worries him. Or a person calls someone whose name is Faraj (which means consolation) by saying to him: "O Faraj!" Then, hearing this call, the anxious person rejoices and says to himself: "May Allah console me, if He so wills!" He refers to being saved from the oppression which has seized him, and he is relieved.

This is how the Messenger of Allah acted—peace and blessings be upon him—in his conciliation with the idolaters when they prevented him from entering the Sanctuary [of the Ka'ba]. An idolater with the name of Suhayl (from the root *s-h-l* which means to be easy) arrived and the Messenger of Allah said: *Sahula-l-amr* = the affair has become easy! He took this name as a premonitory sign, and everything happened as the Messenger of Allah had anticipated. The affair had a happy outcome thanks to Suhayl. However, his father who had named him thus had not done so with this precise goal in mind. He had considered it only as a proper noun in order for this individual to be recognized among other persons, and his father did not have any other intention apart from the good of giving a beautiful name to his son.

The technical language of the folk of Allah concerning words which only they understand

When the folk of Allah see that the Prophet took into consideration allusion, they make use of it among themselves, but then they clarify its meaning, place, and moment. They employ it in their sessions and for themselves only when persons sit with them who are not from them and when the situation demands it.

The folk of Allah employ terms unknown to others except those who have learned the meanings from them, thus following an approach of which the outward persons are not of aware. In the same way the Arabs in their speech proceed with analogies (*tashbīhāt*) and metaphors (*isti'ārāt*) in such a way that they understand each other. When they withdraw with those who are affiliated with them, they discuss a subject according to the suitable language. However, when someone who is not of them is present, they speak among themselves according to terms agreed among them, so that the stranger who sits with them cannot understand what is at issue and what they say.

One of the most remarkable things in this domain—and which is not found in others—is that each category of scholars who master a science, whether logicians, grammarians, geometricians, mathematicians, astronomers, theologians, or philosophers, use technical terms whose meaning the non-affiliated can grasp only through a master or a person who is close to them, and necessarily familiar with this kind of knowledge. However, the folk of this path in particular do not proceed in this way.

When the sincere aspirant is introduced into the circle of the initiates, his sincerity is recognized with them even though he has no information (*khabar*) regarding the technical vocabulary they use.

When Allah opens the sincere person's eye of comprehension, he learns from his Lord, in the beginning from his intuitive experience, without having information on the technical language they use, for [before] he did not know that initiates (*qawm*) among the folk of Allah had particular conventions of language. When this sincere aspirant sits with them and they discuss in their technical terms, using expressions that only they know or that he who has learned from them, he understands everything about which they speak as if he had established this language by himself. In addition, he encounters the related knowledge without being able to dismiss it. It is as if he did not cease understanding without knowing how this knowledge is realized for him. As for the stranger to this initiated folk, someone who is outside of the circle of the affiliates, he will understand this only with a competent interpreter (*muwaqqif*).

This is the meaning of allusion with the initiates (*qawm*), and they express themselves in this way only in the presence of he who is not of their group, or in their works and products, and not elsewhere!

Allah speaks the truth and guides on the way (Qur'ān, 33:4).

Chapter 63—vol. I, p. 461—extract

On the intermediary world (*barzakh*)

[. . .] When Allah mentioned the act which produced the form of the complete man, He said: . . . *I breathed my spirit in him* . . . (Qur'ān, 15:29, and 38:72). He said this regarding Jesus before he created his form: . . . *We breathed into her of Our spirit* . . . (Qur'ān, 21:91 and 66:12). The form therefore appeared together with perplexity (*hayra*): What is the Origin (*aṣl*)? Is the form—origin or principle—included in the Insufflation (*nafkh*) or is Insufflation—origin or principle—included in the form (*ṣūra*)? There is no significant proof on this matter. Thus, in the verse above, *We breathed into her of Our spirit*, the angel Gabriel assumed the likeness of a man and Mary imagined that he was well and truly a man. Did she therefore perceive by the sensory sight or by the eye of the imagination? And was she among those who perceive imagination through imagination? [. . .]

Chapter 69—vol. II, p. 147—extracts

On prayer

[. . .] Jesus was in the presence of his Lord all the time. When he insufflated (*nafkhu-hu*) the Spirit into [the form of] the bird (cf. Qur'ān, 5:110 and 3:49), this presence did not cease. His insufflation was produced with the leave of his Lord, and how could it be otherwise seeing that he was in His presence; for he, like other creatures, strived to ceaselessly keep God present in his innermost consciousness because He does not cease being by Himself. This is what they seek.

He who interprets the Qur'ānic references to the act of insufflating as replacing the imperative *Be!* (*kun*, cf. 16:40) considers it as a word (*kalām*), and he who does not interpret it in this sense interprets it only as a means (*sabab*) and not as a word (*kalām*). Thus he deems that the divine statement *by My leave* (Qur'ān, 5:110) and not *and thou insufflatest into it* (*fatanfukhu fi-hi*, Qur'ān, 5:110) which concludes the statement . . . *and it became* (*fa-yakūn*, the form of) *a bird* (*tā'ira*) . . . (Qur'ān, 3:49). [. . .]

CHAPTER 69—VOL. II, P. 228—EXTRACTS

On prayer

[. . .] Women are the locus where the forming or generation (*maḥall al-takwīn*) is produced; thus they are closer to their Form-giver of Generator (*mukawwin*) and more disposed to the essential orientation (*qibla*) than men, this process being the dominant principle. In the case of men (*rijāl*), formation or generation is [initially] presented only once, and that is the forming of Eve issuing from Adam.

More particularly, one could compare (*muqābala*) the forming of Eve [without a mother]to that of Jesus in Mary, who was born without the intervention of a male being (*fahl*). However, generally women are always the locus wherein the forming takes place. Thus they are more concerned with the essential orientation, in order that each child is born in accordance with the primordial predisposition (*fiṭra*). When the child is born he comes to us and becomes "news from his Lord," such as the rain (*ghawth*), as it has been related by the Messenger of Allah when he said that it was "a new knowledge coming from [his] Lord." [. . .]

CHAPTER 70—VOL. II, P. 291—EXTRACTS

On *Zakāt*

[. . .] The individual or particular soul (*nafs juz'iyya*), that which governs the soul of the human being and his faculties, is [from a certain point of view] the child of his natural body which is [like] the mother of this soul and the divine Spirit (*rūḥ ilāhī*) is [like] his father. That is why she said in her intimate discussion: "Our Lord and the Lord of our fathers above and our mothers below."

Regarding Adam, Allah has said, *When I have shaped him, and breathed My spirit in him* (Qur'ān, 15:29 and 38:72). [As for Mary, Allah says]: *And Mary, 'Imrān's daughter, who guarded her virginity, so We breathed into her of Our Spirit . . .* (Qur'ān, 66:12). Jesus was thus his child and she his mother.

The well-fashioned body is that in which the Spirit as Breath (*nafas*) was insufflated. This body is therefore [like a] mother and that which is insufflated into him [like] a father. The difference is that this child [resulting from this encounter] is like the orphan (*yatīm*) who has no father, for his intellect (*'aql*) has not been consolidated by the consideration (*naẓhar*) he would have had for his father; it is as if he has no link (*'aql*, or intellect). Thus, he is like the child who has no father to teach him and train him. His vegetative soul (*nafs nabātiyya*)—reigning over his body—governs that which Allah has created in it as a wholesome complexion (*ṣalāḥ al-mizāj*), the inner and outer forces being utterly pure and in full equilibrium.

Chapter 71—vol. II, p. 401—extracts

On fasting

[. . .] Some say, *God is the Anoint, Mary's son . . .* (Qur'ān, 5:72), while this has not been said for any other prophet before him.

The most that was said about 'Uzayr (cf. Qur'ān, 9:30) was that he was the Son of Allah (*Ibn Allāhi*) but they have not said: he [is] Allah (*huwa Allah*). Pay attention to the implication of the last statement coming from behind the veil of Mystery (*min khalfi ḥijāb al-ghayb*), into the hearts of people who are veiled from among the folk of unveiling to the extent that they said: *God is the Anoint, Mary's son.* For this, God attributed them with unbelief (*kufr*) by according them an excuse. Indeed, they were not polytheists (*ashrakū*). Quite the opposite, they said: *he [is]Allah* (*huwa Allāhu*). But the polytheist (*mushrik*) is he who places another worshiped god beside Allah. For this reason, they were concealers of faith or unbelievers (*kāfirūn*) and not polytheists. Allah has said, *They are unbelievers who say, 'God is the Messiah, Mary's son.'* (Qur'ān, 5:72). He attributed them the veil (*sitr*). They made of the human nature of Jesus a theophanic "locus" (*majallā*), and Jesus exhorted them in this manner, as Allah mentions in the same verse: *the Anoint said, 'Children of Israel, serve God, my Lord and your Lord* . . . They replied, "This is exactly our course of action in serving Allah from our perspective." Jesus specified to them, *Verily whoso associates with God anything, God shall prohibit him entrance to Paradise* . . . This means that Allah refuses His assistance to such a person by veiling him.

This is why Allah attributed them the veil (*sitr*) when He describes them with covering (or "disbelief," *kufr*). This is a verse whose immediate meaning permits to understand the order contained therein and whose interpretation entails blame. This verse enables us to understand what we have already mentioned and it introduces an immense sea which never delivers one from drowning for it is the Sea of endless Eternity (*baḥr al-abad*). How judicious is the Word of Allah for whoever ponders over it, is attentive, and receives his intuition from Him! [. . .]

CHAPTER 72—VOL. II, PP. 439FF.—EXTRACTS

[. . .] Woman has been created receptive (*munfa'ila*) in relation to man so that he may be attracted to her (*li-yahinna ilayhā*) by means of the affection (*hanīn*) of he whose primacy (*siyāda*) is manifested to her, and he loves her with the love of He who has conferred to him this degree of primacy (*daraja al-siyāda*). She is attracted by him and she loves him by the attraction that the part feels for the whole which is the attraction for the origin (*al-watan*), for man is indeed the origin of woman, despite their mutual dependence in desire (*shahwa*) and pleasure (*iltidhādh*).

However, woman can attain perfection (*kamāl*) in the same respect as man. But in imperfection he can descend to a degree of imperfection inferior to that of woman. On the contrary, they can both meet or differ in certain modalities governing the works of worship. Nevertheless more often, in his use of reason man outstrips woman for he uses his reason on subjects dealing with Allah before woman, for he preceded her in his coming to existence. Yet, divine Order does not repeat itself. Thus, that which takes place for he who comes first is realized for that who comes second, as we stated in speaking of God who does not manifest Himself twice in the same form, nor in a single form in two individuals due to the divine Infinity (*tawassu' ilāhī*). Such is the degree by which man surpasses woman. What is the whole with respect to the part, even if the latter is inseparable from him in perfection? It is therefore a particular perfection (*kamāl khāṣṣī*). This is so also for certain limbs of man when he is amputated for blood money (*diyya*), by being damaged integrally or more or less partially in certain limbs. Each part depends on the whole in different possible domains [. . .]

[. . .] Furthermore, man (*rijāl*), that is Adam, has been created in His Form whereas Eve has been created in the form of Adam. On the other hand, the children (*banūn*) have been created from the fusion (*intizāj*) of the two parents (*abawayn* : lit. two fathers) and not from just one of them, but from their union (*majmū'*) through sense (*hiss*) and conception (*wahm*). Yet the aptitudes (*isti'dād*) of the children (*abnā*) are more important than those of the parents for the child combines the aptitudes of them both. Thus the perfection (*kamāl*) of the perfect son is greater than that of the father. For this reason, Muḥammad—upon whom be blessings and peace—was gratified by an unsurpassable perfection as a son. Each son, in his original constitution (*nasha'a*) possesses this perfection, however with the difference that certain sons, in relation to this perfection, are more excellent than others due to sublime motions (*harakāt 'ulūwiyya*), luminous elevations (*tawāli' nūrāniyya*), and beneficial unions (*iqtirānāt sa'ādiyya*). Not all sons attain the latter perfection which is added to his original constitution. What is at issue here is another subtlety that the characteristic divine Face (*wajh khāṣṣ ilāhī*) confers to him in theophany (*tajallī*), due to that which the son receives from it. A divine Name is assigned to this Face, a Name which, in its encompassing perfection, is more perfect than certain other Names, such as the Knower which is more universal or encompassing (*iḥāṭa*) than the other Names which are not likened to it. Whoever among the sons possesses a father, a mother, and a particular encompassing (*iḥāṭī khāṣṣ*) divine Name elevated in degrees (*rafī' darajāt*) is more perfect than he who has a father, a mother, and an inferior divine Name in encompassing and degree.

Among the sons, he who stems from a [human] mother and a non-human father (*mutawahhum*: lit. imaginal) takes therefore the form of a human likeness (*mithālī*) and is similar (*ashbaha*) to his ancestor (Adam) through his mother for he has no [corporeal] father like Jesus—peace be upon him—whose particularity is that which his ancestor Adam comprised, who came from the [divine]

Command (*'amr*). It is because of this disposition that the following divine news was uttered: *Truly, the likeness of Jesus, in God's sight, is as Adam's likeness; He created him of dust, then said He unto him, 'Be,' and he is* (Qur'ān, 3:59), that is, the divine Name by virtue of which Adam was existentiated (*wujida*) is that which Jesus was existentiated [too]; *He created him of dust.* The pronoun "him" refers to Adam. Jesus is therefore [like] a brother of Eve, and he is the son of a daughter of Eve.

Among the sons, he who stems from a [human] father without a [human] mother is diminished (*qaṣara*) with respect to the degree of his father, like Eve who was created from the shortest rib (*qusayra*) was lessened (*qaṣarat*) and her curvity (*'iwāj* = or bending) constitutes her normal form (*istiqāma*). Her inclination (*inhinā'*) is her compassion (*hunuww*) towards her sons and towards her husband (*māl*), who constitute her treasures (*khazā'in*), similar to the bending of ribs (*idlā'*) in the cavity where the womb and the bowels are stored for the smooth functioning of she who possesses them. Thus the curvity of Eve is also the rectitude (*istiqāma*) which is required for him [Adam]. It is for this reason that the curving of the arch (*i'wijāj al-qaws*) is its normal form (*istiqāma*). If you bend this arch in trying to conform it to a rectitude which is clearly against nature, you shall break it and you will not obtain the rectitude which you expected from it, that is, the goal you hoped, due to your ignorance of the appropriate rectitude in this matter [. . .]

CHAPTER 73—VOL. III, P. 6—EXTRACTS

Response to the questionnaire of Ḥakīm Tirmidhī

[. . .] Know—may Allah strengthen you and us with a Spirit from Him—that this chapter enumerates the different kinds of men (*rijāl*) whose number is limited and against whom you should take no protection. This chapter also includes questions that are known only by the greatest among the servants of Allah, who are to their contemporaries like the prophets in the time of prophethood, that is, the general prophethood (*nubuwwa 'āmma*). For the prophethood which has ceased with the coming of the Messenger of Allah—upon whom be blessing and peace—is only the legislative prophethood (*nubuwwa al-tashrī'*) which can no longer occur: no Law (*shar'*) will come to abrogate the Law which he conveyed and no other Law is added to his statute (*ḥukm*). This is the meaning of the prophetic saying: "The Message (*risāla*) and Prophethood have now ceased. There is no Messenger or Prophet after me." That is, there will be no Prophet after me who will come with a Law succeeding mine. On the contrary, while it exists, it comes under the status of the legislation that I transmit (*tashrīʿatī*). "No Messenger . . ." means that no messenger will come after me who will be one of the creatures of Allah that would bring a law to which he would invite. This has ended, and access to it has been closed. Therefore, there is no more place for (legislative) prophethood.

There is no disagreement about the fact that Jesus—peace be upon him—remains a Prophet and a Messenger, or about the fact that he will descend at the end of times as a fair and just arbiter (*ḥakam*) according to our Law and not another Law, not even the Law by virtue of which the children of Israel worshipped Allah and with which he was sent. On the contrary, what is explicit in this matter is that which the Law of Muḥammad has confirmed and which the prophethood of Jesus corroborates truly in his favor, namely the affirming of the coming of a Prophet and a Messenger after him (Jesus, cf. Qur'ān, 61:6). Muḥammad is truthful in his word: "No Prophet after me." We therefore know without any doubt that he meant specifically the legislative prophethood and this is way in which the matter is interpreted by the folk of reflection (*ahl al-naẓhar*) who use the term "election" (*ikhtiṣāṣ*), thus implying that prophethood is not acquired. [. . .]

Chapter 73—vol. III, p. 10—extracts

[. . .] After the coming of the Messenger of Allah—blessings and peace be upon him—Allah has left corporeally in life, in this world, three Messengers: Idrīs in the fourth heaven . . . He has left Ilyās and Jesus in life, both of whom assume their function according to the original religion (*dīn ḥanīfī*) with which Muḥammad has been sent . . . As for al-Khiḍr, he is the fourth messenger, and he is disputed by some but not by all [. . .]

Chapter 73, vol. III, p. 15—extracts

[. . .] It is among this type of saints that the seal (*khatm*) through which Allah seals the Muḥammadan sanctity is found. He is unique not with respect to an epoch, but unique in the world. Among the Muḥammadan saints there is none greater than him. In addition, there is another seal through which Allah seals the universal sanctity (*wilāya 'āmma*) from Adam up to the last saint. It is Jesus—peace be upon him—who is the seal of the saints (*khatm al-awliyā'*), as he will be the Seal of the Cycle of the Kingdom (*dawra al-mulk*). On the Day of Resurrection, he will participate in two gatherings (*hashrān*). He will be introduced to the Community of Muḥammad and he will be introduced as a messenger with the messengers [. . .].

Chapter 73—vol. III, p. 48—extracts

[. . .] Among the saints, there are those men and women who make the invocation (*dhikr*) of Allah abundantly. Allah has invested them by inspiring them with the *dhikr* (*tawallā-hum bi-ilhām al-dhikr*) in order for them to make His *Dhikr* and for Him to make their *dhikr*. This process is related to the Name *al-'Ākhir*, the Last. Such is the *ṣalāt al-Ḥaqq*, the "Prayer" of God on His servant. Thus, the servant is forward (*sābiq*) and God is the second in the prayer (*musallī*) for this disposition (*maqām*) demands it.

Allah has said: *Therefore remember Me* (lit. make My *dhikr*), *I will remember you* (lit. make your *dhikr*) . . . (Qur'ān, 2:152). He has deferred the mentioning of His Dhikr by them in favor of their *dhikr* by Him. He has also said (in a *ḥadīth qudsī*): "He who makes My *dhikr* in himself I make his *dhikr* in Myself. He who makes My *dhikr* in an assembly, I make his *dhikr* in an assembly that is better than his." "He who draws near to me by a span, I draw near him by a cubit." Allah has said: *If ye love Allah, follow me* (*the Prophet*), *Allah will love you* . . . (Qur'ān, 3:31)

Each divine station (*maqām ilāhī*) is attached (*tata'akhkhara*) to an existential station (*maqām kawnī*) which depends on the Name *al-'Ākhir*, the Last. The following verse illustrates this point: *He it is who prays on you* (Qur'ān, 33:43). Reality therefore oscillates between two divine Names: *the First* (*al-awwal*) and *the Last* (*al-ākhir*), the very essence of the servant being the locus of manifestation (*maẓhar*) unto which the function (*ḥukm*) of these two Names is exercised. [. . .]

[. . .] Without the dependence of the entity of the servant (*'ayn al-'abd*), the power (*sulṭān*) of these two Names would have not been manifested, given that, in the case of God, the essence (*'ayn*) is simple (*wāḥida*) and has not to be unified (*lā muttahida*) contrary to the case of the servant whose entity is unified for it is not simple. Thus Unity (*aḥadiyya*) concerns Allah, whereas unification (*ittiḥād*) concerns the servant and not Unity (as such). Indeed, the servant can only be envisaged as coming from another but him and not from himself. Thus, the created being will never realize the perfume of Unity, although it can conceive of the notion of unity regarding God, for the concept of relation (*iḍāfa*) is intelligible given that everything belongs to Him. Even more! He is the All in itself (*'ayn al-kullī*) and not the totalization of a sum (*lā kulliyyata jam'in*) but rather the intrinsic reality of a unity (*bal ḥaqīqatu aḥadiyyatin*) wherefrom multiplicity (*kathra*) proceeds. This is carried out only by the Truth (*al-Ḥaqq*).

Reason (*'aql*)[6] cannot conceive of there proceeding from one other than one, but it can never conceive of the Unicity of God, for multiplicity (*kathra*) proceeds from unity (*aḥadiyya*). Indeed, God's Unity does not follow from the judgment of the intellect (*ḥukm al-'aql*) or from its capacity. The judgment elaborated by reason will bear only in the Unity of God. Yet the Unity of God is beyond this judgment (*ḥukm*). How could He be grasped by reason, who has a once created the judgment and the person carrying it (*ḥākim*)? No god but Him, the Inaccessible (*al-'Azīz*), the Wise (*al-Ḥakīm*).

Dhikr is the most elevated of all spiritual stations (*maqāmāt*). The invoker is the man (*rajul*) who possesses a degree (*daraja*) superior to the others who are in stations. It is of the same order of ideas as the one mentioned by Allah: *and man a degree above them . . .* (Qur'ān, 2:228). From the root *dh-k-r* two terms derived: *dhikr* (invocation, remembrance, recollection), and *dhakar* (male, hard, consistent), the latter being the opposite of *unth* (female, soft, tender). The first, active (*fā'il*) term is opposed to the second, receptive (*munfa'ila*) term, like Adam with respect to Eve. I have already underlined the *dhikr* of God in relation to your *dhikr* as He (God) is the *musalli*, the second, the approaching one.

Eve was manifested from a male (*dhakar*) of human formal and divine likeness (*bashar suwarī ilāhī*) whereas Jesus appeared from a spiritual and angelic male (*dhakar rūḥī malakī*) in the form of a human likeness. That is why the *dhikr* of Eve is more perfect due to its [individual] form (*ṣūra*), whereas the *dhikr* of Jesus is more perfect due to the angelic form manifesting itself in the human individual form, created in accordance with divine dignity (*hadra*

6. The term "'*aql*," intellect, reason, intelligence, comes from the root '*-q-l* which means: attach, keep linked, connect two or more things, understand, conceive of, to "intellect", to reason. Considering these concordant different meanings, this term cannot apply to Allah as Ibn 'Arabī shows in this passage.

ilāhiyya). Thus, Jesus unites the individual form and the Spirit. He was made in a perfect constitution (*nash'at tamāmiyya*), his outward reality being human likeness and his inner reality an angel. He is therefore . . . *the Spirit of Allah and His Word* . . . (cf. 4:171). God has said, *The Anoint will not disdain to be a servant of God, neither the angels who are near stationed to Him* (Qur'ān, 4:172): that is, for Allah and in favor of the creatures manifested by the divine Power. They were therefore humble towards the creatures under the effect of the divine Irresistibility for humility is authentic only through the manifestation of this Irresistibility. Irresistible beings are such by virtue of innate dispositions (*min al-khalā'iq*): they are the locus of manifestation of divine irresistibility. The humble (*mutawādi'*) is he who submits under the constraint (*jabarūt*) of the creatures and the destitute (*faqīr*) is he who is in need of rich creatures (*aghniyā'*). Indeed, richness (*ghinā*) of the creature consists in its being the locus of manifestation for the divine attributes. Thus, the poor needs this attribute that the locus of manifestation does not veil from him. The same is true for each sublime divine attribute that accrues only to Allah, its locus of manifestation being in the created beings. The knowers through Allah remain humble under the authority of Allah and they alone know this disposition [. . .]

CHAPTER 73, NO. 13—VOL. III, P. 75—EXTRACTS

If you ask: "Who is he that has a right to the title of the seal of saints like Muḥammad—upon him be blessings and peace—has a right to the title of the seal of the prophets?" we will respond:

There are two seals: that through which Allah seals the universal sanctity and the seal through which Allah seals the Muḥammadan Sanctity.

The first seal concerns expressively Jesus—peace be upon him—who is the saint according to the universal prophethood (*nubuwwa mutlaqa*) during the time of this community. His function is therefore distinguished from the legislative prophethood (*nubuwwa al-tashrī'*) and from the revealed Message (*risāla*). He (Jesus) will descend at the end of times as the Inheritor (*wārith*) and the sealer (*khāṭim*), and after him there shall be no more saints according to the universal prophethood, just like—Muḥammad being the Seal of the prophets—there will be no more legislative prophethood after him, even though after him (Muḥammad) there is the example of Jesus who is one of the messengers and the elite of the prophets who possess the firm resolution (*ūlā al-'aẓm*). Nevertheless, starting from his second coming, his legislative function (*ḥukm*), by virtue of [new] modalities (*ḥukm*) of the times, will not be possible to be applied. Jesus will then descend as Saint invested with a universal prophethood to which the Muḥammadan saints will be associated. He will be of us and our Prince (*sayyid*). There has been at the beginning of this cycle (*amr*) a prophet who is Adam and there shall be in the end a prophet who is Jesus. I am going to speak here about the prophethood of election (*nubuwwa al-ikhtiṣāṣ*). Hence there will be two gatherings for him on the Day of Resurrection: one with us and another with the Messengers and the Prophets [. . .]

CHAPTER 73, NO. 14, VOL. III, P. 75—EXTRACTS

What is the quality of he who has the right of this dignity [of being the seal of universal sanctity]? The response is the following:

It is invested from the qualification of the entrusted (*amāna*) Storehouse. In his hand are the keys of the breaths (*mafātīḥ al-anfās*, or the means of liberating the breaths). Its disposition consists in being in detachment (*tajrīd*) and movement (*ḥaraka*). This is a characteristic of Jesus—peace be upon him—who revived the dead through the insufflation (*nafakh*) of the spirit and who was among the ascetic messengers (*zuhhād al-rusūl*) . . .

CHAPTER 73, NO. 17—VOL. III, P. 79—EXTRACTS

[. . .] The Messenger of Allah—upon whom be blessings and peace—has been distinguished by the following favor which he has mentioned: "I have received the all-encompassing Word (*ūtī jawāmi'a al-kalimi*)." Jesus has been distinguished *qua* Spirit. Insufflation has been attributed to him when he created from clay (the birds) whereas Insufflation for giving life anew has been attributed only to Jesus, or even better, to Allah himself, by using both the pronoun "thou" (which represents Jesus) and the pronoun which is reserved to he who speaks (*mutakallim*) about himself (cf. Qur'ān, 3:49 and 5:110) [. . .]

CHAPTER 73, NO. 44—VOL. III, PP. 106FF.

On the notion of "*bashar*"

Why did He name man *bashar*? Our response is:

Allah has said: . . . *what prevented thee to bow thyself before that I created with My two hands? Hast thou waxed proud, or art thou of the lofty ones?*(Qur'ān, 38:75) This verse is related to the ennobling of man by God. The context here alludes to the direct contact (*mubāshara*) with his creation by means of His *two Hands* as it befits His Majesty (*jalāl*). For this reason, He named him "*bashar*" (from the same root *b-sh-r* as *mubāshara*). Thus the term "*yad*" (hand, directed active force, etc.) when it means power (*qudra*) does not confer an additional dignity (*sharaf*) to the person invested with it. The same is true when the term "*yad*" means blessing (*ni'ma*). Indeed, blessing and power extend to all existentiated realities. Thus, the expression "with My two Hands" must comprise a proper intelligible meaning which is different from these two qualifiers as they are understood in the Arabic language in which the Qur'ān was sent down. Thus, when the Arabic linguist says: "He did that with his hand," he means to say that no intermediary (*raf' al-wasā'iṭ*) was involved.

Adam's relationship with the human bodies is like that of the first Intellect (*'aql al-awwal*) with the intelligences (*'uqūl*). The bodies being composed, they require the two hands in order for the composition to take place, whereas this is not said for the first Intellect which is not composed. These two realities (Adam and the first Intellect) are therefore similar in the suppression of intermediaries (*raf' al-wasā'iṭ*). In generation or conformation (*takwīn*), after this suppression of intermediaries and the mentioning of the *two hands*, there is but one entity (*amr*) named for this reason "*bashar,*" this reality (*ḥaqīqa*) being transmitted to the children and no one amongst them is existentiated without a direct intimate coupling (*mubāshara*) (with the "two divine hands").

Did you not notice that, for the existence of Jesus—upon whom be peace—the Spirit assumed for Mary *the likeness of a perfect bashar* (cf. Qur'ān, 19:17) and that God made him an intermediary (*wāsiṭa*) between Him and Mary in order to give existence to Jesus, thus drawing attention to a direct coupling (*mubāshara*) illustrated by His word "*a perfect bashar*." Allah said: . . . *and do not lie with them* (*wa lā tubāshirū humma*) *while you cleave to the mosques* . . . (Qur'ān, 2:187). On the other hand, the skin (*bashara*, from the same root as *bashar*) of an individual and his appearance is the *bushrā*, a glad tiding (also from the same root as *bashar*) which makes a mark (*'alama*) appear on the skin (*iẓhār 'alamati ḥusūli-ha fi al-bashara*).

The term *Kun*, expressed in the Word that Allah addresses to a thing: "*Be and it is*" (*kun fa-yakūnu*), comprises the two letters *kāf* (*k*) and *nūn* (*n*). The term *Kun* therefore comprises a correspondence with the expression "the two Hands" in the creation of Adam [by God]. In the verse, *The only words We say to a thing, when We desire it, is that We say to it 'Be,' and it is* (Qur'ān, 16:40), the Word He addresses to the thing is of the same order as the notion of the direct coupling (*mubāshara*). The *k* and the *n* constitute an equivalent to the "*two Hands*." The *w* (of the non-conjugated verbal root *k-w-n*) which disappears in order to avoid the meeting of two silent letters (which is impossible in the Qur'ānic Arabic) is of the same order as the space which disappears between the *two Hands* during their union (*jāmi'*) during the creation of Adam, its mentioning being hidden like the *w* is hidden in the imperative *Kun*, with the difference that its ellipse of space in the Kun implies an occasional reality (*amr 'āriḍ*). The disappearing of space between the "*two Hands*" is necessitated by the reality of the [divine] Action (*ḥaqīqat al-fi'l*) according to the verse *I made them not witnesses of the creation of the heavens and earth, neither of the creation of themselves . . .* (Qur'ān, 18:51). This is the mode of the [divine] Action, for in realities (*ḥaqā'iq*) other than Allah, no one can bear such witness. None other than Allah acts and no action proceeding from a choice (*ikhtiyār*) is produced in existence. Indeed, the choices determined in the world come from constraint itself (*min 'ayn al-jabar*). Thus, the letters are constrained in their choice, but the veritable act is neither constrained nor free for the divine Essence (*dhāt*) requires it to be so. Understand this.

Hence, the "direct or intimate coupling" (*mubāshara*) of the absolute Existence (*wujūd muṭlaq*) with the permanent essences (*a'yān thābita*) entails the manifestation of the conditioned existence (*wujūd muqayyad*) that is called "*bashar*" characterizing man (*insān*), for he is, qua creature, the most perfect of the existentiated realities, all other kinds of existentiated realities lacking this perfection in Existence. Thus, man (*insān*) is the most complete locus of manifestation and has therefore full right to the title of "*bashar*" to the exclusion of other creatures (*a'yān*).

Allah has said, *It belongs not to any mortal* (*bashar*)*that God should speak to him, except by inspiration, or from behind a veil, or that He should send a messenger and he reveal whatsoever He will, by His leave; surely He is All-high, All-wise* (Qur'ān, 42:51). Thus, he that Allah is speaking about (*mutakallam*) has been called "*bashar*" here in accordance with these different kinds of language [mentioned in the verse], due to the specific dispositions which are intimately related to him (*yubāshiru-hu*) and which prevent him from attaining the degree of the Spirit inherent in his spiritual capacity. If the one concerned by this divine word surpasses the degree which is proper to *bashar*, Allah speaks to him as He does to the spirits, the latter having more possibilities than him due to their nature which does not admit spatialization (*tuhayyuz*) or divisibility (*inqisām*). They are manifested in forms which comprise neither interior nor exterior; they have no other lineage (*nisba wāḥida*) than that of their essence (*dhāt*), and this lineage constitutes their very essence (*wa hiya 'ayn al-dhāti-hā*).

The "*bashar*" is not formed in this manner for he is made entirely according to the form of the world. In him are found the necessity of cohabitation (*mubāshara*), of spatialization, and divisibility. And that is why he has been called *bashar*. He possesses the Spirit which has been insufflated into him and which does not require these [three] dispositions. It is in function of his quality of *bashar* (*bashariyya*) that the *two Hands* are orientated and that the notion of duality (*shaf'iyya*) appears with the *two Hands* implied in the constitution (*nash'a*). Qua *bashar*, he understands the Word of God only according to the modalities which were just mentioned or through only one of them.

As long as he ceases to consider (*naẓhar*) his quality of *bashar* and he realizes himself by contemplating his spirit, Allah speaks to him as He does to the spirits emptied of matter, as He did with Muḥammad—upon whom be blessings and peace—and the Bedouin: *And if any of the idolaters seeks of thee protection, grant him protection till he hears the Word* (*Kalam*) *of Allah* (Qur'ān, 9:6). This Word has been transmitted to him only by the tongue of Muḥammad who has been manifested in this form (of *bashar*) according to the degree taken by the truthful Spirit (*rūḥ amīn*, i.e. Gabriel) who came down with the Word of Allah onto the heart of Muḥammad (cf. Qur'ān, 26:193 et passim).

In verse 42:51, Allah says: . . . *or that He should send a messenger* . . ., that is, for this *bashar*, . . . *except by inspiring* . . . in him *whatsoever He will, by His leave* . . ., that is, Allah inspires him with this by virtue of what He expresses [in this verse]. With His Word . . . *except by inspiration* . . . He means an intuition (*ilhām*) obtained by a token (*'alama*) through which he discerns that His Lord speaks to him in order for that which is expressed not to be ambiguous to him. By . . . *or from behind a veil* . . . He means that He makes him understand [these words] either by the interposition (*ḥijāb*) of the isolated letters (*hurūf muqaṭṭa'a*) and sounds, just like the Bedouin had understood the Qur'ān thus transmitted, which is the Word of Allah, or by the interposition of the call to prayer for the hearer, or still by the interposition of his *nature as bashar* (*bashariyya*) in a general manner. Allah speaks to him through things as He spoke to Moses from the bush which was found on the right side of the Mountain in the blessed place: *Moses, Lo, I am Allah . . .* (Qur'ān, 28:30). The limit (*ḥadd*) in direction (*jiha*) and in the determination of the place (*ta'yīn al-buq'a*) appeared so that Moses would engage in looking for the fire requires by his *bashariyya*. Thus, he was called in accordance with the need he had for fire. Allah informed him well and truly that the human being (*nās*) is poor before Allah. In this verse, Allah designates Himself by the name that suits all that which in need of Him, namely Divine Jealousy (*ghayra ilāhiyya*) of the fear of being in need of other than Him. Thus Allah revealed Himself to Moses in the very form of his need. When Moses approached the fire, Allah called him, and then he truly felt the need for Allah and the interposition appeared according to the form in which theophany is produced. Had Allah not called him in this manner, he would have not recognized Him. According to a similar perspective, the theophany takes place in the hereafter where it is not recognized (*inkār*) (Allah revealing Himself in a diversified manner in accordance with convictions) [. . .]

[. . .] Therefore [now] you know the meaning of the term "*bashar*" which we wanted to clarify to you in accordance with the meaning that this word takes in the Arabic language.

Chapter 73, no. 145—vol. III, p. 186—extracts

[. . .] It is known that Jesus is of a greater excellence than Abū Bakr who was part of the Community of Muḥammad and followed him. We have only mentioned this in order for the disputant to know that he (Jesus) must reappear in this Community at the end of times and that he shall judge according to the Tradition of Muḥammad. He will break the Cross and kill the pig. Thus many from among the People of the Book shall embrace Islam under him. [. . .]

Chapter 74—vol. III, p. 214—extracts

On *al-tawba*

. . . And it is a bird by My leave . . . (Qur'ān, 5:110). The Insufflation

proceeds from Jesus in order for the animal spirit (*rūḥ hayawānī*) to appear for Insufflation—I mean the air (*hawā'*) coming out of Jesus—is the very animal spirit which penetrates the body of the bird and acts upon it, for the bird is predisposed to receive life through this animated breath, as was the case with the calf who received life and on which the Samaritan threw [a handful of dust trodden by the Spirit]. Thus the bird flew with the leave of Allah. A similar phenomenon took place with the calf that the Samaritan made to low with Allah's leave [. . .].

CHAPTER 188—VOL. IV, P. 11—EXTRACTS

On *Ru'yā*

[. . .] If you want to become familiar with what we mentioned, pay attention to the knowledge of the natural world (*'ilm al-ṭabī'a*). When a pregnant woman has cravings and she is preoccupied with something, the child that will be born will have a certain correspondence with that thing. If during the sexual union she imagines something or if the man imagines a form at the moment of the carnal act and ejaculation, the child will be in accordance with the form engendered from that which has been imagined [at that moment]. For this reason, the greatest physicians (*ḥukamā'*) in this field recommend the imagining of the most excellent forms at the moment of the union, for if the woman and the man imagine this form, it is engraved in the imagination and affects the child who is constituted from this semen. This is an astonishing secret of the natural science (*'ilm al-ṭabī'a*).

Consider the structure of Jesus—upon whom be peace—who was constituted according to the contemplation (*mushāhada*) that Mary had had of Gabriel appearing in the form of a *bashar* (a being in human likeness) and how he united the Spirit by means of which he revived the natural bodies (*ajsām ṭabī'a*). The peak of this is what the Samaritan did with a handful [of dust which he threw on the golden calf], a dust which was taken from the trace left by Gabriel. The Samaritan knew that life is linked to the Spirit where the latter is located. He therefore threw this handful of dust on the calf which lowed under the effect of the dust taken from the tread of the Spirit. Had he thrown it unto the form of a horse, it would have neighed, and had it been a man, he would have talked.

The predisposition that appears in life is therefore dependent on the receptacle (*qābil*). It results from this that you know the form that is exteriorized in the loci of manifestation. You know that the latter, through the predispositions that appear in them, accept the forms carrying the possibilities and receive them. For this reason, Allah makes this wisdom appear in order for you to consider this disposition as it is.

In addition, the Prophet—upon whom be blessing and peace—has given this disposition the following two names: *bushrā* and *mubāshara* (glad tiding) due to the trace it leaves on the skin of the human being (*bashara al-insān*). For the appearance of the *bashar* is modified under the effect of that which is produced within in relation to the form seen in the imagination or the word understood both in sadness and in joy. A trace is necessarily left on the skin (*bashara*). That is a natural *property* (*ḥukm*) that Allah has placed in nature, which only exists in this mode [. . .].

Chapter 195—vol. IV, pp. 24-26

Al-shaṭḥ = ecstatic statement, outrageous utterance, inebriation, raving, extravagance

Know—may God strengthen you—that an ecstatic utterance is a statement of claim (*kalima da'wā*) which truthfully indicates, to the one uttering it, the degree granted to him by God in relation to his spiritual aptitude (*makāna*). It indicates through this ecstatic utterance that it is not a divine command. For those present (*rā'*), such utterances are considered to stem from an vane attitude (*fakhr*). However, if one is commanded to enunciate such words through which knowledge of a divine order is expressed, the person cannot be said to be a seeker of vanity. The Prophet said: "*I am the lord (sayyid) of the children of Adam and I do not seek glory (fakhr) from this.*" *Then he continued: "I do not seek to boast before you through this declaration (ta'rīf) but I inform you about this subject for your own good so that you may know, through the grace of God upon you, the measure of your Prophet with God.*"

The *shaṭḥ* is a shortcoming for the realizer of truth (*muḥaqqiq*) when he does not receive the command to express himself in this way. He must behave as the Prophet did. For this reason the latter expressed himself thus: "*and I do not lay claim to glory*" for I know that I am the servant of God just as you are. Now a servant does not claim glory for his being a servant because there is only one Prince (*sayyid*).

This is the manner in which Jesus expresses himself when, in verse 19:30 of the Qur'ān he begins by mentioning servant hood in a phrase equivalent to that of the Prophet, "*and I do not lay claim to glory*." In fact, Jesus acknowledges his servitude in order to exonerate his mother. When he knew, through the light of prophesy which was his nature, that they said of him that he was undoubtedly the son of God (*ibn li-Llāhi*), he said: *I am the servant of God . . .* (Qur'ān, 19:30).

From the outset of his announcement and his testimony (in favor of his mother), he began to express himself in an unusual manner, namely: "I am not the son of someone (i.e. of a man, *fa mā ana ibnu li-aḥadin*), for my mother is chaste and a virgin: therefore, I am not the son of God. Just as God admits of no associate, neither does He admit having a child and I am therefore the servant of God like all of you."

He has given me the Scripture and made me a prophet (Qur'ān, 19:30). Thus, for those present, he spoke of his prophethood (*nubuwwati-hi*) during its time and at other times. In fact, as a necessity, during the time in which he carried out his mission (*risālati-hi*), he necessarily knew the mission of his prophethood, (to make it known) in keeping with God's wont with the prophets that came before him (to make their missions known). They received the command of all that was revealed to them, or came from them, through authentic claims (*da'āwāṣādiqa*). These claims demonstrate dignity because of their great nearness to God (*makānazulfā*) as well as the discernment (*tamayyuz*) of similitudes (*amthâl*) and formal resemblances (*ashkāl*) in accordance with the highest level (*martabamuthlā*) with God.

In the same chapter, Jesus specifies: *He has made me blessed . . .* (Qur'ān, 19:31), that is, the place (*maḥallā*) and the distinctive mark (*'alāma*), making possible the increase of bounties amongst you.

. . . wherever I may be . . . (Qur'ān, 19:31), in any state (*ḥāl*) in which blessings are bestowed upon you because of me, in any circumstance whatsoever. He mentions all of this using the past tense (*māḍī*) in order to indicate the present (*hāl*) and the future (*istiqbāl*). The condition in which he finds himself at this moment enables him to bear witness to the innocence of his mother and to warn and give knowledge to the one who wanted him to say that he was the *Son of God* (*IbnuAllāhi*). Thus he proclaimed God's transcendence as well as the innocence of his mother regarding what

had been reported about her. With respect to God, this is a declaration of transcendence (*tanzīh*), and with respect to his mother it is an exoneration (*tabri'a*).

Therefore, he used the past tense to describe it: . . . *wherever I may be* (*aynamākuntu*) . . . , in order for this to be an announcement by God regarding him, as it was for Muḥammad when he said: "*I was a prophet when Adam (was) between water and clay*." He knew his rank (*martaba*) with God when Adam's corporeal form was not yet manifest.

By using the past tense, God informed Jesus that He had given him the Scripture (*kitāb*) and had enjoined him to (maintain) prayer (*ṣalāh*) and give alms (*zakā*) as long as he remained in the domain of legal charge (*taklīf*) and legislation (*tashrī'*)as per the divine word *as long as I live* (Qur'ān, 19:31), that is, as long as I remain in the life bound to the legal charge of the outward command of those present. In our view, this is what he wanted to make clear. God also wanted to express in verse 4:117 another aspect related to Jesus: his being the Word of God (*kalimatu Allāh*), the Word being composed of a series of letters. This science shall be dealt with in Chapter 198 dedicated to the breath (*nafas*). God has also made it known that Jesus received the Scripture, that is, the Gospel (*injīl*), and He meant that this is the support of his existence, given that he is Word. Now Scripture is composed of traced letters (*ḥurūfraqmiya*) in order to engender the word and combine the meaning with the form of the letters expressing the Word, necessarily through combination (*min tarkīb*). For this reason Jesus mentioned that God had given him the Scripture, in the manner of the word: *He gave everything its norm* (*khalqa-hu*, lit. "*its creation*").

Through the enjoining of prayer (*ṣalāt*) and of almsgiving (*zakāt*),[7] he meant worship because this injunction calls for the performance of works (*'amal*). This is because, from the viewpoint of practical worship (*'ibādah*) it is the most convincing, given that its existence needs no proof (*bayān*). By this injunction I mean the work which must be clarified and the form of which must be specified so that the one who is subjected to it performs it according to the prescribed conditions (*nash'a*). If this form of worship exists, this is proof that he (Jesus) does not cease being alive wherever he is, even if the temple (*haykal*) [that is, his body] is separated by

7. Reference to verse 19:31, *He has made me blessed, wherever I may be, and He has enjoined me to [maintain] the prayer and to [distribute] the zakat as long as I live.*

death. Thus, life is inseparable from him because life remains an attribute of essence (*ṣifāhnafsiyya*) for him, all the more so since He has infused into life the Spirit of God. (*rūḥAllāh*)

God has also said, *and* (*He has enjoined me*) *to be dutiful toward her who bore me* . . . (Qur'ān, 19:32), that is, to comport himself with excellence towards her. For his fundamental good comportment is to have exonerated his mother from what had been reported about her in a circumstance in which the sincerity of his testimony could not possibly have been doubted.

He ends his declaration in the following manner: . . . *He has not made me overbearing* (*jabbār*) *or miserable* (Qur'ān, 19:32). Now Invincibility (*jabarūt*) is majestic might (*'azhama*) as opposed to worshipping servitude (*'ubūda*) whereby Jesus is called 'servant of God' (*'abdAllāh*). "*Reformer*" should be understood to mean that he does not constrain (*ajbara*) the community to which he was sent with the Scripture, prayer, and almsgiving (*zakāh*). "I am only charged with conveying the Message from God and solely that." *You are not a warder over them* (Qur'ān, 88:22). "Therefore I am a reformer and I reform and communicate from God what He has prescribed: *O Messenger! Communicate that which has been sent down to you from your Lord* (Qur'ān, 5:57). . . . *And the Messenger's duty is only to communicate in clear terms* (Qur'ān, 24:54). *Therefore do remember, for you are but a reminder. You are not a warder over them* (Qur'ān, 88:21–22). Now, the one who reminds (*mudhakkir*) is concerned only with those who are in a state of forgetfulness. Had this not been the case, Jesus would have been a "teacher" (*mu'allim*) and not *"he who reminds."* Through this he shows that he reminds them only of their acceptance of His Lordship—exalted is He—over them at the moment when He seized posterity from the loins of Adam during the Primordial Pact (*mīthāqawwal*), cf. 7:172.

It is then that Jesus said: *Peace upon me the day I was born* . . . (Qur'ān, 19:33), for I have spoken to you of this saying that I am the servant of God. Thus I am safeguarded in my existence participating in sexual dissipation (*sifāh*) or marriage (*nikāh*).

. . . *and the day I die* . . . (Qur'ān, 19:33). He has therefore been protected from being killed (*qatl*), a claim made by the children of Israel: *Verily, we killed the Messiah, Jesus son of Mary* . . . (Qur'ān, 4:157). God showed their untruthfulness by saying: . . . *they did not kill him nor did they crucify him, but so it was made to appear to them* (*shubbiha-la-hum*) . . . (Qur'ān, 4:157). Thus, he tells them that peace shall be upon him the Day he dies, unharmed by killing, for had he been killed they would have martyred him, and a martyr is alive and not dead. And one does not speak of a martyr as being dead. (cf. 2:154, 3:169). Just as it is forbidden to say this about martyrs, in our view, the same situation is applied in the case of Jesus. God thus makes it known that Jesus died and was not killed. God has therefore mentioned that peace was upon him the Day he died. Then He mentions peace upon him the Day he is revived, that is, at the moment of the Resurrection. He is the abode of peace for those who are innocent of any evil, as is the case of the prophets and others like them among the people who are anxious about their faults (*'ināya*). He is thus the master of peace in all of these abodes. There is no third abode, but a life in this world and a final life: and between the two is death.

Had all of this not come about through a divine command, we would have been dealing with excessive outrageous statements from an individual (Jesus), which would only have demonstrated that person's station with God. Such statements are expressed in accordance with a pretentious approach and in this case in accordance with similitude (*amthāl*) and formal resemblances (*ashkāl*). May the folk of God be on guard against being distinguished through similitudes or boasting.

For this reason, an ecstatic utterance (*shaṭḥ*) is short-sightedness or a blunder (*ru'ūna*) and it never affects the realizer of the truth (*muḥaqqiq*), for such a person contemplates only his Lord. He is not discourteous towards his Lord and he claims nothing. Rather, he attaches himself to serving Him, ready to eagerly obey His orders. He takes into consideration all those who, in their existence, are also affected by this state. Then, the ecstatic utterance uncovers what has been created for this person, what he did not know about himself and his Lord. Had he been given all the virtue he claims through that utterance he would breathe his last and die, and he would place his trust, and would be dismissed and possess a function (*makān*) with God. But his status in this is like that of a soothing (*muhil*)or even astringent (*qābiḍ*) remedy (*dawā'*) which acts by virtue of the specification of his state and not in accordance with the power that he has with God; just as a magician acts in function of the specialty of the art in the eyes of those in attendance, by diverting their looks from the vision of truth to that which they receive from him.

The ecstatic utterance comes inadvertently. We have not seen or heard from a friend of God (*wali*) the manifestation of an ecstatic utterance due to short-sightedness of the soul (*ru'ūnanafs*), because a friend of God is necessarily poor and humble, and he returns to his fundamental principle (*aṣl*) and abandons pretension (*zuhuww*) which could assail him.

Such must be the condition of ecstatic language in the case of an authentic (*ḥaqq*) state although it is still blameworthy. But what if it comes from a liar? If one objects: what would the attitude of a liar appear during his ecstatic utterance considering the existence of its impact and the trace it leaves? We say that this question is relative regarding the disposition of a liar. In fact, the folk of God are only affected by an authentic state because they are the folk of God. In their case, the utterance is said to be ecstatic when it is not related to a divine command, as in the case of the prophets when it is indeed a divine command. It comes about from authentic extraordinary effects or reactions (*infi'ālāt*) for the initiate who knows the specifics (*khawwās*) of the (divine) Names. Such an initiate only utters what proceeds from the Names. This is manifested only among those around him who imagine that what is in question is the power of the spiritual state, the dignity with God, and authentic sanctity. However, such an individual is completely a liar, his utterance is not authentic and he is not said to be a possessor of ecstatic utterances (*shāṭiḥ*). Rather, it would be merely a vile sham (*mamqūt*).

The ecstatic utterance is a truthful word expressed in a moment of short-sightedness of the soul in which a remnant of the individual nature is manifested, whereby he is distanced from God.

This account will suffice in order to know what an ecstatic utterance is.

Chapter 198—vol. IV, p. 29—extracts

The Messenger of Allah existed before he knew that he was protected from the human beings. Allah has said: *O Messenger! Deliver what has been revealed to you from your Lord; and if you do it not, then you have not delivered His message, and Allah will protect you from the people; surely Allah will not guide the unbelieving people* (Qur'ān, 5:67). When the Revelation would descend upon him, he would say: "He who guards over us at night" although he knew that Allah is *Guardian over all things* (Qur'ān, 11:57). When affliction weighed hard on him and he faced certain oppositions (*addād*), he would say: "Lo, the fresh breath of the All-Merciful comes to me from Yemen." It referred to the Anṣār.

Know that the realities existentiated according to the Word of Allah (*kalimāt Allah*) which are inexhaustible. Regarding the existence of Jesus, it is said: *. . . and His Word* (kalimatu-Hu) *which He conveyed unto Mary . . .* (Qur'ān, 4:171). It is about Jesus. Regarding this, we will say that the existentiated realities are the words of Allah, according to the traditional facts (*al-dalālah al-sam'iyya*) for none of them adds to what we maintain regarding unveiling (*kashf*) or divine knowledge (*al-ta'rīf al-ilāhī*). The words which are accepted in the current use (*'urf*) are those which consist in the arrangement of the letters emanating from the breath emitted by he who pronounces them in the phonetic apparatus. The letters are manifested through this discontinuity (*taqāta'*) according to a particular relationship. Such are the words [. . .]

Chapter 198—section 2—vol. IV, pp. 43-45—extracts

Regarding the expression *Kalām Allāh,* the Word of God and *Kalimatu-Hu,* His one Word

The two terms *kalām:* word or verb, and *qawl*: to say, root word, expression are two qualifiers (*na'tān*) used for God:

1. *Al-qawl* is addressed to that which is not yet engendered (*al-ma'dūm*), as mentioned in the verse: *All that We say to a thing, when We will it, is to say to it 'Be!' and it is* (Qur'ān, 16:40).
2. *Al-kalām* is addressed to that which is engendered (*al-mawjûd*), according to the following verse: *and to Moses God spoke* (*kallama*) *directly* (*taklīman*) (Qur'ān, 4:164).

The term *kalām* is taken in the general meaning of expression (*tarjama*) [of a concept, thing, etc.] depending on the language in which one is expressing it (*mutarjima*). This term is then related to that which it expresses.

Al-qawl has an effect on that which does not yet exist and thus renders it existent.

Al-kalām has an effect on that which is existent in order to express knowledge. That which is formulated is capable of being modified (in interpretation), as stated in the following verses: *Are you then eager that they should believe you, though a part of them have heard the Word* (*kalām*) *of Allah or they alter it* (*yuharrifūna-Hu*) *willingly after having understood it?* (Qur'ān, 2:75). *They desire to modify* (*yabadillū*) *the word* (*kalām*) *of God* (Qur'ān, 48:15), namely in its interpretation (*tarjama*), which lends itself to modification (*tabdīl*) and to meanings which are implications of the Word. Furthermore, one can never establish anything of value by changing and modifying the meaning of the original (*aṣl*) text, because modification and alteration (*taḥrīf*) are added to this original text. If such is the case, the original text can accept neither alteration nor modification because it is a divine Word (*kalāmilāhī*) which can never be imitated or described, even by the quality of essence.

When Self-disclosure (*tajallī*) occurs in any form (*ṣūra*), this form may or may not be among the forms to which the word is related according to current usage (*'arf*). If this form is found among those forms to which the Word is related, then this Word is part of a modality of the Word that is related to this form due to the status it acquires as a consequence of the Self-disclosure, in conformity with the verse . . . *We have been taught the speech of the birds* . . . (Qur'ān, 27:16) or . . . *an ant said*: . . . (Qur'ān, 27:18).

Although Self-disclosure occurs to a thing which is not related to the Word in its common usage, the following possibilities are nevertheless not excluded:

1. That the form (taken by the Self-disclosure) is found in the mode of expression (*qawl*) to which it is related through faith, as in the verse: *This is Our book, which speaks truly against you* (Qur'ān, 45:29), or *They (both) said, 'We come heartily.'* (Qur'ān, 41:11), or again: *on the day when witness shall be given against them by their tongues, their hands, and their feet concerning what they used to do* (Qur'ān, 24:24), and finally *They will say, 'We were given speech by Allah* (Qur'ān, 41:21).

2. It may happen that this form is not found in one for whom the manner of expression (*qawl*) and pronunciation (*nutq*) are not related to the divine Word. This, then, is a mode of expression related to the formula of glorification (*tasbīḥ*) which escapes comprehension, except for that which God says which cannot be understood. In fact, the function of the Word (*kalām*) as well as speech (*qawl*) are linked to hearing and glorification. Had there been speech (*qawl*) or a word (*kalām*) which we were capable of understanding, our hearing would

> have refused it and our understanding, which is also knowledge (*'ilm*), would not have accepted it, for knowledge comes, or does not come, from the Word and from speech.

When Self-disclosure occurs in such forms, language (*nuṭq*) is established in accordance with the disclosed (God), depending on what befits the glorification emanating from this form, without being able to extend beyond it. Thus, one understands the glorification belonging to this form through the word of He Who is disclosed. This is remarkable knowledge understood by only a few of the folk of God, for the Word (*kalām*) is related to Him in forms that are what they are by their nature. Such is the case when Self-disclosure appears in the luminous and natural substances (*mawādd*). When it occurs in a substance which is neither luminous nor natural and when it takes place within pure principles (*ma'ānīmujarrada*), it is said that this is a Word (*kalām*)with respect to the imprint it leaves on that which is the object of this Self-disclosure, and not on one who speaks in this manner. All such influences come from the hierarchic categories of the Word (*kalām*) which was previously named "Words of God" (*kalimât Allāh*)—*kalimāt* being the plural of *kalima*, word. These words are the engendered beings themselves (*a'yān al-kā'ināt*).

God has said, *and His Word that He cast toward Mary* . . . (Qur'ān, 4:171). The 'Word' refers to Jesus himself (*'ayn 'Īsā*), introduced into Mary in a unique manner, (*ghayr dhālika*) and without her having prior knowledge (*ghayr dhalika*). Had the divine Word (*kalimailāhiyya*) been an utterance (*qawl*) coming from God or a Word (*kalām*) related to it, such as the Word (*kalām*) that God addressed to Moses, Mary would have been delighted and would not have said, *'I wish I had died before this and become a forgotten thing, beyond recall.'* (Qur'ān, 19:23). The divine Word that was cast toward her was none other than Jesus himself (*'ayn 'Īsā*), the Spirit of God and His Word, who is His servant and who speaks in order to exonerate his mother in unusual circumstances so that he can be *a Sign* (āya). What he expressed (*nutq*) was the Word of God (*kalāmAllāh*) conveyed through the Breath of the All-merciful (*nafasal-Raḥmān*). God thus comforted (*naffasa*) his mother against the words of her family, accusing her (of lewdness) regarding Jesus and from which he exonerated her. With respect to this (exceptional) situation, the Mu'tazilites have said that the speaker (*mutakallim*) is he who produces the word whereas it is not normal for the speaker to do so. The Word of God can also be manifested, but in an unusual way: minerals (*jamād*), plants (*nabāt*) or Jesus (in the cradle), are examples of accidental situations (*ashkālḥāditha*) coming about in existence.

We will clarify the meaning of the two expressions, *kalāmAllāh*, Word of God, and *kalīmatu-Hu*, His Words.

The Word (*kalām*) of God is His Knowledge and His Knowledge is His Essence. It is therefore not valid to maintain that His Word is not Him. However, it has been affirmed that His Word may be qualified as being additional to His Essence, yet this has no basis. Everything that is endowed with speech is described as capable of speaking and having in itself the power of doing so. Now God cannot be described as capable of speaking (His Word never being accidental) for then His Word would be created and also primordial (*qadīm*) according to Ash'arite doctrine, or it would be His Essence according to another position embraced by certain intellectuals (*'uqalā'*). The relationship between the Word and God is unknowable, just as His Essence (*dhāt*) cannot be known. One may argue thatthe Word belongs to God only through the revealed Law (*shar'*) and not because of the exercise of reason, because He cannot be attained bythought.

Understand, therefore, that the Breath (*nafas*) is linked with the All-merciful and that the Word (*kalām*) and speech (*qawl*) belong to God. The Breath thus results in words which are possible. The Breath exteriorizes speech following interiorization; and the Breath was extended outwards (*tafsīl*) after being synthesized inwardly (*ijmāl*).

If you object that the concern of the Word is to be heard even though in Existence it is only God Who speaks, who, then hears? We will respond that the condition of the hearer is to be (already) existent. Furthermore, God says to a thing which is not (yet) existent and in the very condition of its non-existence: *Be!* (*kun*), whereas that which was still inexistent becomes existent at the very moment of the dependence of its permanent capacity on hearing the Word of God and His engendering Command (*amr*).

Such is the case of he who reflects and is the source of his vision, the possibility (*jawāz*) of his vision being the very fact of existing, even though predisposition (*isti'dād*) and capacity (*tahayyu'*) concern both existence and non-existence.

The other reply (to the objection above) is that God speaks because He is qualified by the Word (*kalām*). He hears His Word in His quality as Hearer, although Speech and Hearing are two different attributes. If you further object that the benefit of hearing (*samā'*) of the Word is the obtaining of knowledge whereas God is Knowing through Himself, we would respond that not every word is (necessarily) conveyed to actualize that which is unknown. The speaker himself (*mutakallim*) offers praise because of the fact that he is a person of knowledge and has no need to acquire anything. On the contrary, he is satisfied with essential Perfection. The Real does not cease to speak and even if the word is incidental in the universe (*kawn*), this does not in itself prove its occurrence. God has said, *There does not come to them any new reminder from their Lord but they listen to it as they distract themselves* (Qur'ān, 21:2). That is, even though He has already spoken in this manner to others before this, for example, in the Torah or elsewhere, such as in the Qur'ān. It is thus so when we say that they want (to hear) the Word of God, which is one of His attributes.

It is clear that the hearer hears the word of the conveyer as coming from God, as He says: God expresses Himself through the tongue of His servant. "*God hears he who praises Him*" (*sami'a-Llāhu li-man ḥamida-Hu*) . . ..

CHAPTER 198—SECTION 11—VOL. IV, P. 83—EXTRACT

[. . .] Jesus, one of the prophets, Spirit of Allah and His Word appeared really as Word of Allah and manifested himself as Angel qua Spirit of Allah. So, the principle of this event is found among the knowers by Allah and the possessors of generosity among the folk of Allah who attach the Angel to this prophet and exempt God of this form.

As for the firmly rooted in knowledge (cf. 3:7), these are the folk of increase (in knowledge—cf. 20:114). The people of divine generosity are thus in accord with them when they say: "Divine Dignity (*janāb ilāhī*) is more capable of receiving forms than the universe." Then they attach themselves to the form of this prophet and cling to the form of the Angel, as it is, without explaining it away—particularly in the case of Jesus—for, at the moment when the Angel gave Jesus to his mother, he *assumed the likeness of a perfect human* (*bashar sawiyy*) (Qur'ān, 19:17) [. . .]

Chapter 298—vol. IV, pp. 475-476—extract

[. . .] Concerning the creation of Jesus [. . .] Allah has informed us that the Angel assumed for her (Mary) "*the likeness of a perfect man* (*bashar sawiyy*)" (Qur'ān, 19:17).

When Allah willed it, the voluptuousness (*lidhdha*) spread by the look (that Mary) took at the Angel after she had sought refuge from him (cf. Qur'ān, 19:18). He made known to her that he was the Messenger of God in order to bestow on her a pure boy (cf. Qur'ān, 19:19). She then became available to receive the child and the voluptuousness of the union (*lidhdhat al-nikāh*) seized him through a simple look. The water (*al-mā'*) from her was deposited in her womb and the body of Jesus was formed by this water, engendered by the necessary Insufflation in order for this voluptuousness to take hold of her. He came from the water of his mother.

However, the physiologists (*al-tabī'iyyūn*) deny this fact and claim that no thing can be generated from the water of a woman. Yet, this is not true. In our view, the human being is generated from the water of man and from the water of woman. It is certain that the Prophet, who does not speak out of his whim, has said: "When the water of man reaches first the water of woman, a boy is born to them, and when the water of a woman reaches first the water of man, a daughter is born to them." [. . .]

Chapter 302—vol. V, pp. 16-17—extract

[. . .] Furthermore, Allah made this world (*'ālam*) a synthetic summary (*mukhtaṣar majmū'*) gathering all the meanings in all aspects. He named him Adam, and Allah created him in His form (*'alā ṣūrati-Hi*). Also the human being is the synthesis (*majmū'*) of the world and constitutes a microcosm (*insān ṣaghīr*), and the world is a macrocosm (*insān kabīr*). Whether you name the human being a small world or microcosm you will have known this disposition as it is in itself and in its essential reality. See it in this way and admit it as you wish.

Thus the human being is not superior to the world in its totality, and the world is more excellent than man for it possesses an additional degree since man exists starting from the microcosmos. The world therefore has above him the degree of causality (*daraja al-saba'iyya*), given that man is generated from it.

Allah has said: *men have a degree above them* (*women*) (Qur'ān,

2:228), for Eve was issued from Adam and the degree he possesses over her does not cease to accompany him in the masculine quality (*dhukūra*) which overcomes the feminine quality (*unūtha*), even if the mother (*umm*) is the cause for the existence of the son (*ibn*). Her son therefore holds the masculine degree over her for he takes after his father in all aspects. The human being must therefore honor his two parents. His mother is [the symbol] of the world (*'ālam*) in all aspects, and his father is known and not unknown. The marriage (*nikāh*) being the face to face (*tawajjuh*), the child comes into the world according to the form of his parents. When the child is born, he is named after the name of his father and his name is not attached to the name of his mother, for the former possesses this degree and elevation (*'uluww*) which follows from him and attributed him the great nobility (*sharaf*).

Due to the fact that it is not possible to attach Jesus to him (the Angel) who was sent to Mary as a *human of perfect form* (*bashar sawiyy* , cf. Qur'ān 19:17) (but to God), she obtained the perfection (*kamāl*) that is the noblest (or most elevated, *ashraf*) station, and Jesus was attached to her. Therefore it is said, Jesus Son of Mary. By her perfection she obtained this nobility that is the degree through which man is situated above woman and, for this reason, the son is attached to his father. Thus, the Messenger of Allah bore witness to the perfection of Mary and Āsiya[8] the wife of the Pharaoh. For Āsiya the perfection was acquired due to the nobility of the station that the Pharaoh claimed.[9] Yet, at this station, it was suitable that the throne on which the Pharaoh sat concerned only perfection. It resulted for Āsiya as the perfection owing to the nobility of this station through which the Pharaoh was miserable and reduced to erratic behavior, whereas his wife gain happiness. Because of the nobility of this station thanks to which she realized her perfection, she said: *My Lord, build for me a house in Paradise . . .* (Qur'ān, 66:11). God did not make her speak in this way except by virtue of

8. Reference to certain traditions that mention the perfection attained by four women: Āsiya the wife of the Pharaoh, Mary the mother of Jesus, Khadīja, the first wife of the Prophet, and Fāṭima, the daughter of the Prophet and wife of 'Alī.

9. Reference to the following verses: *'Go to Pharaoh; he has waxed insolent. And say, "Hast thou the will to purify thyself; and that I should guide thee to thy Lord, then thou shalt fear?"'So he showed him the great sign, but he cried lies, and rebelled, then he turned away hastily, then he mustered and proclaimed, and he said, 'I am your Lord, the Most High!'* (Qur'ān, 79:17-24); *And Pharaoh said, 'Council, I know not that you have any god but me . . .'* (Qur'ān, 28:38)

the station of *in Thy presence* and she did not ask the protection of Moses, or any other creature. And this did not suit her for the state overcame her. Obviously, the perfect being cannot be inferior to a perfect being, inferiority being a descent in degree.

Because of the perfection of Mary linked to the case of Jesus, in the relationship he had with her, she did not say what Āsiya had said: *. . . and deliver me from Pharaoh and his work, and do Thou deliver me from the people of the evildoers* (Qur'ān, 66:11), in order for the sacredness of this relationship with Thou not to come to an end. Mary said: *Would I had died ere this, and become a thing forgotten!* (Qur'ān, 19:23). She was exculpated with Allah from [what they accused her], but she did not say this for Allah, whereas Āsiya had said *in Thy presence* (see supra). She gave Him precedence and asked His protection and exemption from the strength of His enemies whereas Mary uttered her words out of prudishness before the men for she knew [the requirements] of purity of her people and of her ancestors fearing that they would be dishonored because of her [. . .].

CHAPTER 345—VOL. V, P. 270—EXTRACT

[. . .] Allah has said: *and men a degree above them* (Qur'ān, 2:228). He did not make Jesus passive (*munfa'il*) with respect to Mary since man (*rajul*) is not passive with respect to woman (*mar'a*), as was the case of Eve with respect to Adam. Then Gabriel (Jibrīl) or the Angel (*malak*) *assumed for her the likeness of a perfect man* (Qur'ān, 19:17). He said to Mary: *He said: I am only a messenger of thy Lord, that I may bestow on thee a faultless son* (Qur'ān, 19:19). Therefore he bestowed Jesus on her who was passive vis-à-vis the Angel who assumed the likeness of a man (*rajul*). For this reason, he took the form of his father, a male of human likeness (*dhakar bashar*) and Spirit (*rūḥ*). Therefore, he unites the two forms that his father, the Angel, had assumed. He was Spirit from the point of view of his essence, and *bashar* from the point of view of the human form which he took [. . .]

CHAPTER 348—VOL. V, P. 298

[. . .] Jesus comes from a complexion (*mumtazij*) belonging to two worlds. He appeared between the angel and the human who are Gabriel and Mary respectively. Jesus is therefore spirit from a spirit and human from a human. This has not existed for anybody else in this species [. . .]

Chapter 358—vol. V, p. 395—extract

The statement of Jesus, . . . *Thou knowest what is within my soul, and I know not what is within Thy soul* . . . (Qur'ān, 5:116) are related to the soul of Jesus, which is really related to God. These words are more perfect to praise Allah, in order to free oneself from that which is attributed to Him and for the interrogation that took place regarding Him in the verse: *'Didst thou say unto men, "Take me and my mother as gods, apart from Allah"?'* (Qur'ān, 5:116). Jesus addresses Him with Thou in the remaining part of the verse: *Thou knowest what is within my soul, and I know not what is within Thy soul; Lo! Thou knowest the things unseen* (Qur'ān, 5:116). But how can He, to whom belong all of the creation (*khalq*) and the Command (*amr*), be interrogated? Jesus did not tell Him regarding what was being said about him: "I am a god that is worshipped" because of his knowledge, he who was vicegerent (*khalīfa*) and perfect man (*insān kāmil*), whereas the divine Names belong to Him. Jesus told Him: *I only said to them what Thou didst command me* (Qur'ān, 5:117) and I have not added anything therein. It can therefore be said that: "He was ordered to say that not everything that is presented must be said, and also he was not ordered to express that which falls out of the responsibility (*'uhda*) of that which is has been transmitted."

Muḥammad has said: ". . . or that Thou taught to certain of Thy creatures or that Thou hast chosen in the knowledge of Thy Mystery . . ." He mentioned that He chose something in the knowledge of His Mystery from that which He alone knows and which can only suit the Perfect Man. But Allah chose him in the knowledge of His Mystery that He alone knows. He only knew of the Human that which came to him and that Perfect Man did not know by himself: this is the Mystery of God for He is the Model (*mathal*). The statements of the prophet and of Jesus converge: Jesus said, *and I know not what is within Thy soul* (Qur'ān, 5:116), and Muḥammad said, ". . . or that Thou hast chosen in the knowledge of Thy Mystery."

The Perfect Man is the "locus" (*maḥall*) of all the Names the acquisition of which is within his capacity, but he cannot receive those which do not enter within his capacity. The latter are part of the Names which it is said that he is deprived of, like the names through which [ordinary] man is characterized. It is not possible to apply them to Allah or to say that Allah is deprived of such and such name that is attributed to Him. In the meaning it implies, each name receives the intimate reality of the named. Understand this!

He who knows the relationship between the Divine Names as they are and man, and the relationship between the names of the created realities (*asmā' kawniyya*) as they are and Allah, has known the station of man, his specificity with respect to the whole world and his nobility which makes him a synthesis like he who knows how to be diversified and who can savor all knowledge.

Chapter 380—vol. VI, p. 300—long extracts

[. . .] Know that the effort of interpretation (*ijtihād*) does not consist in innovating a ruling (*ḥukm*) for this is an error. The legally sound effort of interpretation (*ijtihād mashrū'*) must be exerted in looking for the proof starting from a book (*kitāb*), a tradition (*sunna*), a consensus (*ijmā'*), or [a clear] understanding of the Arabic in order to confirm (*ithbāt*) a ruling corresponding to the question posed by this proof that you strive to obtain. Knowledge in this matter that you claim to have obtained by your approach results from your effort of interpretation.

Obviously, Allah and His Messenger have not left anything without an explicit stipulation (*naṣṣ*), and they have never neglected anything. Indeed, Allah has said: . . . *Today I have perfected your religion for you* . . . (Qur'ān, 5:3). And after the affirmation of the perfection of religion, He does not accept any addition; for in matters of religion (*dīn*), addition is an imperfection (*naqs*). Therefore a law that Allah did not authorise becomes imperfection. Part of the intellectual heritage (*wirth ma'nawī*) is your comprehension of the Book and of all the activities of the universe. As for the divine inheritance, this you acquire in yourself (*dhāt-ka*) from the forms taken by theophany at the instant when God manifests Himself to you in them. Yet, you only see Him through Him, for God makes you see a theophanic form instead of and He does not repeat it in you, but He has diversified (*inṭalaqa*) it, and He provides you with an analogy (*naẓhīr*) thereof in your being and in what belongs to you. For this reason, in the hereafter in a general way, and also here below in a special way, when you want something you will say: *Kun*, and it will be.

God is for you, in the here below, the locus of your existentiation (*maḥall takwīni-ka*), and He is diversified due to your diversification; but in the hereafter, you shall be diversified due to His Diversification. In this life, He assumes your form, and in the hereafter you shall assume His Form. Therefore note the marvel of this disposition!

This is the case for you in the divine heritage (*mirath*) through the degrees of Number. God can be fourth of the three. When you come (to existence) and you are added to the three you become the fourth in the procession of numbers. But this shall not be possible for you as God is not transferred to the degree of five: He is then the fifth of the four after having been the fourth of the three. Thus, he leaves this degree to you so that you may inherit it. The same is true in all congregations which imply this status of heritage in the here below.

In the inheritance of election (*mīrāth al-khuṣūṣ*) and the inheritance obtained in the hereafter God is the fourth of the four while you are the fourth of these four, for in this world you arrive with an aspect of the truth (*ṣūra ḥaqq*), and in the same way you are an aspect of the truth in the hereafter. For this reason, he who said: *Lo, Allah is the third of the three . . .* (Qur'ān, 5:73) is an infidel who covers (*satara*) the truth. He covers his soul by His Lord for then he is indeed the third of the three and sees himself as God and not as creature (*khalq*), except from the aspect of the corporeal form and not that through which it is qualified. He is then God (*Ḥaqq*) in a creature. He covers (or conceals) his created nature because he contemplates God who sustains him, thus realizing in a general manner that which is mentioned in a tradition, namely that God constitutes all the attributes and faculties of His servant, for he is one of the elect.[10] Then he utters spontaneously, *Lo, Allah is the third of three . . .* (Qur'ān, 5:73). Furthermore, God says in the remaining part of the verse: . . . *No god is there but One God.* He is the third of three (*thuluth al-thalātha* or = one of the three) and two with respect to the whole (*ithnāni min al-'āmma*) and he who is their third (or = one of the three) in accordance with His creatures is the third (*al-thālith*) in relation to His creatures.

Furthermore, he knows well that God constitutes all of his faculties and that He takes him as witness that He is with God the same as He is with him, although it is just Him who hides this knowledge. Creatures speak of such beings instead of God. One such elect (*al-khāṣṣ*)

10. Reference to the famous *ḥadīth qudsi* which Ibn 'Arabī quotes so often: "My servant continues drawing near to Me through supererogatory works, until I love him, and when I love him, I am the hearing through which he hears, the sight through which he sees, the hand through which he grasps, and the foot through which he walks."

says: *Allah is the third of three* for he contemplates Him in both cases as he contemplates Him in Himself without them being conscious of this. Then he sees that God unites such beings in three forms and the saying of he who says that He is the third of three is true in two aspects: in creatures and in God. But the following divine saying is also true: *No god is there but One God* (Qur'ān, 5:73), for the essence of each of the three is none other than He who is One and three.

This is part of the prophetic divine inheritance. This contemplation is realized for us only through imitating the prophet and conformity to him. Therefore when we know, we inherit from him (the Prophet) and this inheritance is not effective for anyone, except after the transfer to the intermediary world (*'ilā al-barzakh*) of that which he inherits, but that which occur to you without this transfer is not an inheritance but only a gift, an expansion, and a freeing. In this you are a deputy (*nā'ib*), a successor (*khalīfa*), and not an heir (*wārith*). From the aspect of knowledge you are a heir and from the aspect of contemplation you are His Essence and not heir.

Have you not considered the prophetic saying: "Verily, your Lord is One like your father is one." Your father is none other than he from whom you have issued; then if you know him from whom you have issued, you know your father. The Prophet did not want to mention that our two parents (*abaway-nā*, lit. our two fathers) are two as it is obvious. We have issued forth from Adam and Eve in conformity to His word: *he lifted his father and mother* (*abaway-hi*) *upon the throne* (Qur'ān, 12:100). However, due to the fact that Eve is Adam himself—for she is the curve or the inclination (*dil'*) of Adam—there is one single father in two different forms as is the case with theophany. Eve's entity is therefore that of Adam but separated (*infisāl*) like right from left: he is therefore the source or the origin of growth (*'ayn zayd*). Such is the separation (*infisāl*) of Eve from Adam; she is therefore Adam himself and there is but one father (*ab wāḥid*). We have therefore stemmed from a single (being) just like the universe as a whole has issued from a single God. The essence (*'ayn*, or entity) is [at once] single-multiple (*wāḥida kathīra*) in relations, even though it does not seem so. Had it not been thus, we would have no existence, neither particular, nor principal existence (*ījādu ḥukmin*). Since He has existentiated us qua entity we give existence to the principle *for a suitable recompense* (Qur'ān, 78:26) for Him. If you are perspicacious [you will know that] He existentiates us qua entity and that we give for Him existence to a lord!

1. Had the Truth not been, existence would have not been,
   Had the generated being not been, the "worshiped god" (*ilāh*) would have not been.
2. To compensate this, the Truth has willed the question
   Of those who ask: "for whom" and "who is He?"
3. Thus, for the most part, it is not Him, no doubt.
   But for the elite, it is Him and not Him. [. . .]

CHAPTER 381—VOL. VI, P. 305—EXTRACT

Jesus descends at the end of time

1. O Mary, daughter of 'Imrān who was created
   A fertile field for an illustrious Spirit issued from a Spirit.
2. She kept her chastity and the Spirit came to her. It accorded her
   More than it did to the seven heavens issuing from the Tablet.
3. A sublime and noble gift to her
   More brilliant and illuminating among us than a beacon that shines.
4. She lives and there is no sword for her to kill.
   She was invited when she was invited to gentleness by the Spirit.

By gift we mean Jesus, the Spirit of Allah, in accordance with the words of Gabriel to Mary: . . . *to give thee a boy most pure* . . . (Qur'ān, 19:19). [. . .]

[. . .] Have you not considered the case of Zachariah when he entered in the sanctuary with Mary, a dedicated virgin, and Zachariah was well aware of this. He saw beside her of the sustenance that Allah gave her. Thus he immediately asked Allah to grant him a child (*walad*) when he was strongly seized by love before the spiritual state of Mary (*bi-ḥāli-hā*): *Lord, bestow me from Thee* . . . (Qur'ān, 3:38), that is, from near Thee, according to a relation of nearness (*'indiyyatan*), a mercy, a gentleness (*līn*), and a solicitude (*'aṭf*) . . . *a goodly offspring. Yea, Thou hearest the prayer.* And in his imagination, it Mary who was at issue (Zachariah's niece by marriage), due to the degree she possessed, which Allah had granted to her by way of divine solicitude: *And the angels called to him as he stood praying in the sanctuary* . . . (Qur'ān, 3:39). Indeed, he entered this place in which she was at the moment when she found sustenance beside her: *Allah giveth thee glad tidings of John* (*who cometh*) *to confirm a word from Allah lordly* . . . (Qur'ān, 3:39). It is a question of perfection (*kamāl*), for Mary was perfect like John (Yaḥyā) was in prophethood, . . . *of the righteous* . . . Allah had removed John from all carnal activity with women, just as He removed Mary from all carnal activity with men. According to us, John felt a disaffection for women (*'annīn*, or impotence). Thus, Mary is the Virgin (*wa hiya al-Batūl*).

Yaḥyā visited women just like Hanna (Mary's mother), who sought the company of men while guarding her virtue (*maryam*[an]), for *al-maryam*[u] expresses the type of woman who is detached from men. Her name is Hanna (she who sighs from compassion, according to the etymology of her name) and Maryam is a nickname by which she was described as we have already mentioned.

Consider attentively the influence of Zachariah's power of imagination on his son Yaḥyā at the moment when this faculty of Zachariah became available before the excellence of Mary's [spiritual] state due to the station that Allah had granted him: *a prophet of the righteous* (Qur'ān, 3:39). Yaḥyā never disobeyed Allah. All the prophets asked Allah to include His righteous servants in His mercy. No disobedience whatsoever took place with them, ever.

I have not mentioned a state more extraordinary than that of Zachariah, nor pointed out someone who manifested in himself, like Zachariah, the power of the human quality. It was he (Zachariah) who said: *Grant unto me from Thee a progeny most pure* (Qur'ān, 3:38). While he had not imagined the event yet, he did not utter this request only by his statement: *My Lord! How can I have a son when age hath overtaken me already and my wife is barren* . . . (Qur'ān, 3:40)? And what a relationship between this disposition and that which followed while there was no closeness of circumstances (*qarīna ḥāl*), and therefore he uttered such a statement to the extent that he said, in the remaining part of the verse: . . . *Even so. Allah doeth what He will* (Qur'ān, 3:40). His intention was for Allah to inform others of this matter in order for them to know that Allah does what He wills with the ordinary events which He derogates as He wishes to [. . .]

CHAPTER 382—VOL. VI, P. 316—EXTRACT

[. . .] According to the saying he has made known to us, Muḥammad is the pre-existing essence of prophethood which is proper to humankind: "I was a Prophet when Adam [was] between water and clay." In keeping with this divine word, he is by nature the Seal of the prophets: . . . *but he is the Messenger of Allah and the Seal of the prophets* (Qur'ān, 33:40). When he proclaimed himself the father of Zayd,[11] Allah interdicted to him to consider himself the father of any of the men among us in order to remove all comparison (with us) and any confusion of degrees.

Have you not considered: the Prophet fathered no male children (*walad dhakar*) who survived to honor him because from the origin, in the knowledge of Allah, he was destined to be the Seal of the prophets. He has said, "Verily, the Message (*risāla*) . . . ," in reference to the Prophethood (*nubuwwa*) and the Mission (*ba'tha*) of establishing a sacred legislation (*tashrī'*) among human beings. He continues, ". . . has been stopped . . . ," meaning that there can no longer be an authority (*ḥukm*) for one who would legislate in the Name of Allah after the law that we have received. The verse then says, ". . . After me, there is neither messenger . . ." who will come for the other human beings with a Law different from mine, ". . . nor prophet," according to a new legislation (*yanfaridu*) from his Lord upon which he will be based.

It is therefore clear that he is the Seal of the legislating prophethood (*khāṭim nubuwwa al-tashrī'*). Had he wished other than what we just mentioned, it would have been in contradiction with his other saying, "Jesus will descend amongst us with a statute of justice." To this we add faith, because according to our Law we do not doubt that he is indeed Messenger and Prophet.

We know that the prophet Muḥammad meant that there would be no other (sacred) Law after him which would abrogate his Law. In his sayings, he included in his community all the persons in the world from the time of his Mission (*ba'tha*) until the Day of Resurrection. He also mentioned al-Khiḍr, Ilyās, and Jesus, in relation to the visible Community of Muḥammad. As for his hidden Community, he included Adam up through the period of the Mission of the Messenger of Allah. He is therefore Prophet by precedence (*bi al-sābiqa*) and Prophet by Seal (*bi al-khāṭima*). For the Messenger of Allah, this precedence is the very Seal (*khāṭima*) of Prophethood.

---

11. A reference to the verse *When thou saidst to him whom God had blessed and thou hadst favoured, 'Keep thy wife to thyself, and fear God,' and thou wast concealing within thyself what God should reveal, fearing other men; and God has better right for thee to fear Him. So when Zayd had accomplished what he would of her, then We gave her in marriage to thee, so that there should not be any fault in the believers, touching the wives of their adopted sons, when they have accomplished what they would of them; and God's commandment must be performed* (Qur'ān, 33:37).

As for the ultimate function of Jesus, he seals the cycle of the Kingdom. He is the last messenger to appear and to be manifested according to the form of Adam. In this evolution (*nash'*), in which he does not come from a human father and wherein he was not like a son, I mean the posterity of Adam in its evolution. Not only did he have a unique period of time in gestation (*fi al-baṭn*), he also did not experience the usual timing of natural phases of growth. His transmission, or operative virtue (*intiqāl*), represents an analogy with Resurrection (*ba'th*). By Resurrection, I refer to the giving of life to the dead on the Day of Resurrection after a brief period of time, in contrast to those who reach there after a long time. This is included in the general meaning of the word: *As He originated you so you will return* (Qur'ān, 7:29) through the successive generation (*tanāsul*) and the transfer (*tanaqqul*) in the cyclical phases (*aṭwār*).

Furthermore, when Jesus will redescend to earth at the end of time, the Seal of the major Sanctity (*walāya kubrā*) from Adam to the last Prophet shall be given to him. This is attested to by the consideration given to Muḥammad; Allah has not sealed the universal Sanctity in each community, except through an Envoy who follows him (Muḥammad). Thus, he shall seal the cycle of the Kingdom (*dawra al-mulk*) and will end Sanctity, I mean the universal Sanctity (*walāya 'āmma*). He will be among the Seals (*khawāṭim*) of this world.

As for the Seal of Muḥammadan Sanctity, this [term] refers to the special Seal (*khaṭm khāṣṣ*) belonging to the sanctity of the visible Community of Muḥammad. Jesus and other prophets, such as Ilyās and al-Khiḍr, and all saints of Allah with respect to the visible Community, are therefore under the statute of his function of Seal (*khaṭmiyya*). Thus Jesus, qua Seal, is himself sealed (*makhtūm*) from the seal of this Muḥammadan seal. [. . .]

CHAPTER 397, VOL. VI, P. 379 (CHAPTER 394)

[. . .] . . . *And He taught Adam all the Names* (Qur'ān, 2:31). There is none here but the name and the named. Muḥammad had realized the knowledge of the Names, as he has said: "I have known the knowledge of the First ones and of the Last ones." He made known to us that he obtained the science of the Names, the primordial science, for Adam possessed primordiality (*awwaliyya*) due to the fact that he was among the first in sensory existence. The Prophet says of himself, with regard to that which distinguished him from the others, that he had received the *all-encompassing word* (*jawāmiʿ al-kalim*), the term "*kalim*" being the plural of "*kalima*." The words are the essences of the named realities. Allah has said: *and His Word, which He conveyed unto Mary* (Qur'ān, 4:171). His Word is none other than Jesus and the essences of all existentiated realities are the divine words that are never exhausted.[12]

The Prophet has therefore obtained the names and the named realities; thus he unites the best and he has been truly worthy of the preeminence (*siyāda*) over all the human beings, in conformity with his saying: "I am the prince (*sayyid*) of the human beings on the Day of Resurrection." His pre-eminence will therefore be manifested in the future life, the abode of the full Epiphany of God [. . .]

Chapter 463, vol. VII, p. 124—extract

[. . .] As for those who engage in interpretation (*aṣḥāb al-ta'wīl*) through rational speculation (*naẓhar*) on what precedes [the functional handling of the world], they do not possess knowledge when they arrive at it by coincidence.

In this knowledge, you will know that women are the halves (*shaqā'iq*: or the sisters in blood) of men. Have you not seen that Eve has been created from Adam? Thus she possesses two characteristics: masculinity (*dhukūra*) through origin (*aṣl*), and femininity (*unūtha*) through happenstance (*ʿaraḍ*) which is of the order of resemblance (*mutashābih*). For human nature implies the conjunction (*majmaʿ*) of the male and the female.

What is the reality of the agent (*fā'il*)—with respect to that which is receptive—(*munfaʿil*) when it acts only through conformation (*mushākala*)? It is so because what receptivity (*infiʿāl*) determines at first later manifests in him the form of what is received [from the other]. And through this disposition (*quwwa*), what it receives is in accordance to its own receptivity. Therefore it appears as initiator, innovator, and determinator.

We have already established that the realization of knowledge is carried out through the knower, that it is subordinated to the knowable reality, that it is the attribute of the knower, and that what constitutes it is in the knowledge of its object. In addition, the knower determines the latter just like the inventor gives existence to the thing he has envisaged and concretizes it.

12. Reference to verses 18:109 and 31:27 of the Qur'ān.

It results manifestly from the fact that Allah made women lovable to Muḥammad [as related in a *ḥadīth*] and that he who loves women like the Prophet loved them, loves Allah.

Therefore one calls 'knower' the person who possesses this receptivity when it permits one to apply knowledge to its object. One must possess this receptivity in principle in order to comprehend the knowable object.

It seems that the receptivity of Jesus with respect to Mary corresponds to the receptivity of Eve with respect to Adam: *Lo! therein verily is a reminder for him who hath a heart* (Qur'ān, 50:37). Therefore he understands this word of Allah: *O mankind! Lo! We have created you from a male* (like Eve)*and from a female* (Qur'ān, 49:13), like Jesus.

CHAPTER 474, VOL. VII, P. 160—EXTRACT

Commentary on verse 3:49, regarding the fashioning of the birds by Jesus

[. . .] Jesus insufflated a spirit into the bird which he had fashioned and which became a bird through the formal aspect (*ṣūra*) and the principal meaning (*ma'nā*). It is said that there was only a *form* of a bird and not a bird, and for this reason Allah says: *as the likeness of a bird* (Qur'ān, 3:49), and He did not say "a bird" since the Spirit did not penetrate it. According to us, it is certain that Dhu al-Nūn al-Miṣrī revived, with Allah's leave, Ibn al-'Ajūz whom a crocodile had swallowed, or again that Abū Yazīd (al-Basṭāmī) revived, with Allah's leave, an ant [which he had crushed]. [. . .]

CHAPTER 480—VOL. VII, PP. 171 TO 373

We gave him judgment, yet a little child (Qur'ān, 19:12)

1. All the faculties of man are part of his constitution,
   as spirit and body. Therefore do not deviate from the right path.
2. Through this, his exercise will diminish immediately
   It might be that the evolution of the body lends itself to it!
3. If that which disappeared from his habits becomes evident for you,
   This is the decision of God, the Unique, the Impenetrable.
4. Like Jesus and those like him
   among the humans, none
5. Is seen coming to you by violating his habits,
   Except He who has created man destitute.

Allah has said [of Yaḥyā]: *'Peace be upon him, the day he was born, and the day he dies, and the day he is raised up alive!'*(Qur'ān, 19:15). This peace comes to him from Allah.

Jesus says, regarding himself, in giving information on the state (*ḥāl*) which he has with Allah, in relation to the announcement that Allah makes (in verse 19:15) regarding His assistance for Yaḥyā: *'Peace be upon me, the day I was born, and the day I die, and the day I am raised up alive!'* (Qur'ān, 19:33) The Prophet Muḥammad [lit. the Muḥammadan], the Heir, added: "I was a Prophet when Adam was between water and clay."

1. The grace of the freshness of youth is intense
   for, as the Books says, it enjoys divine proximity.
2. The sciences of the initiates are taste (*dhawq*) and competence *khibra*) which stem from the sciences that cannot be grasped by analysis.

Having partly taken off his clothes while he was walking in the rain, the Messenger of Allah came out saying that this was a new knowledge coming from his Lord. It was an explicit statement which highlights in a legitimate manner that expected rain comes from the Lord. Indeed, all things which begin (*awwal*) in the world constitute new knowledge from the Lord, and everything that takes place in the world is a beginning (*awwal*). This thing in existing is a new knowledge coming from the Lord from the instant in which He says: "*Be!*" (*kun*). The world, in its totality, is the World of the Command (*'ālam al-amr*), regardless of the World of Creation (*'ālam al-khalq*).

We have already dealt with the World of the Command and of Creation in order to describe it according to the particular aspect (*wajh khāṣṣ*) that characterizes it in the World of Creation: this point ensnares certain theoreticians (*ahl al-naẓhar*) when it comes to the issue of divine knowledge. This is not the case with the folk of Allah, whose knowledge is intimately lived (*dhawq*).

A young child has two beginnings due to this proximity of constitution (*takwīn*) and audition (*samā'*). There is no separation between him and his consciousness of the proximity he has with Allah, a separation that would result from his distancing from the World of the Principles (*'ālam al-arkān*) due to [the process of] creation.

Jesus did not come from a father who has issued from the elemental world (*ab 'unsurī*), but rather he was *the Spirit of Allah* and *His Word* (Qur'ān, 4:171) which the Angel conveyed unto Mary. Nothing distanced him from He who had bestowed him his origin. He was well-informed about what he witnessed regarding this subject. In his cradle, he spoke in accordance with those surrounding him who forged calumnies about him against his mother, Mary, whom Allah exculpated both through the statements of Jesus and the creak of the palm tree for him. Indeed, the revealed Law (*shar'*) gives more authority to two righteous witnesses. Yet, there were no witnesses more righteous than these two.

Jesus said: *Lo, I am the servant of Allah . . .* (Qur'ān, 19:30). He himself established his servitude (*'ubūdiyya*) towards Allah, but he did not say "the son of Such and Such" for he was not. He was the reality of a theophany (*ḥaqq tajallī*) in the form of the spirit of Gabriel, and he had to speak on the issue of the nature of his own unusual composition (*takwīn khāṣṣ*).

. . . He hath given me the Scripture . . . (Qur'ān, 19:30). Before sending him with this mission, He granted him "his Gospel" (*injīla-hu*), he received an evident proof from his Lord and declared that he possessed "his divine Scripture" (*kitābi-hi al-ilāhī*).

. . . And hath appointed me a prophet . . . He establishes that the Prophet had been appointed, for Allah says: *Into whatever form He pleased He constituted you* (Qur'ān, 82:8). The matter of concern is the form that is appointed so that it is not imagined that this is in itself, but in accordance with a divine prerogative.

And hath made me blessed . . . (Qur'ān, 19:31), that is, he has given me an increase [in grace] which He has not accorded to anyone else. And this increase is the Seal of Sanctity, his descent at the end of time, and his status according to the Law of Muḥammad so that he may be found among those who see their Lord according to the Muḥammadan vision in the Muḥammadan form on the Day of Resurrection.

. . . wheresoever I may be . . ., in this life or in the next according to two gatherings: one in the rank of the Messengers, and the other as a follower of Muḥammad.

. . . and hath enjoined upon me prayer . . ., that is, I perform the obligatory prayer in the Community of Muḥammad, for the term *ṣalāt* is used with the article *al.*

. . . and almsgiving . . ., also according to the prescriptions imposed on this Community.

. . . so long as I remain alive, the duration of this legal obligation

(*taklīf*) during the life of here below.

And [hath made me]dutiful toward her who bore me (*wālidatī*) . . . (Qur'ān, 19:32). Here Jesus informs us that he was dutiful towards his mother as, for her, it was certainly a birth given that she was the locus of his constitution (*takwīn*). I have already dealt with the elementary kinship of Jesus (*nisbata-hu-'unsuriyya*) at the time of his creation; he was closer to his Lord, and had a newer knowledge in the worship of his Lord.

. . . *He hath not made me arrogant, unprosperous*, for this is possible only for the ignorant, as this ignorance arises from the power of the dark force of the fundamental constituting elements (*'anāsir*). We have already dealt with the degree of the natural world emanating from the domain of the fundamental elements in this work and in many instances.

Peace be upon me . . . (Qur'ān, 19:33), due to his knowledge of his station with his Lord and the destiny He had allocated to him.

. . . *the day in which I was born* . . . , that is, the peace (*salāma*) at the moment of his birth against the [malefic] assaults, in contrast to the influence exercised at birth on each servant, with which children are charged when they are born and which makes them cry from the reach [of Satan].[13] For Jesus did not cry, rather he prostrated to God.

. . . *and the day I die* . . . , thus disproving those who forged calumnies regarding him, namely that he had been killed, because he did not say: "the day I am killed."

. . . *and the day I am raised up alive*, that is at the moment of the great Resurrection. Thus, he confirmed his death. Allah granted him wise judgment (*ḥukm*) in the statement he had made when still an infant in the cradle. Yet, regarding access to his Lord, Jesus was more perfect than Yaḥyā', son of his maternal aunt, since he declared his own peace through the peace that his Lord granted him. For this reason, they claimed that he was a god who could be worshipped (*ilāh*). In the case of Yaḥyā, it is the Lord who proclaimed his peace and did not stipulate anything regarding the knowledge or lack thereof that Yaḥyā could attain from this peace.

Do you know that one is perplexed before the wisdom of an infant, unlike the grown person who possesses only apparent wis-

13. According to the tradition related by Abū Hurayra: "All children of Adam are touched by Satan at birth, except the son of Mary and his mother; at this contact, the child lets his first cry."

dom obtained by meditation (*tafakkur*) and reflection (*rawiyya*)? Babies usually lack this aptitude. It is said that Jesus expressed himself [in the cradle] under the influence of this wisdom. Allah's help can be manifested in this visible manner.

He granted Yaḥyā and Jesus an increase of knowledge in their way of expressing themselves which arises from tasted knowledge; for such an ability at that age and rate is valid only if experienced, and only if Allah grants to the infant Jesus the wise judgement belonging to the order of Prophethood which stems only from tasted knowledge. He who has this disposition possesses the inheritance proper to Jesus, even if he is Muḥammadan because of these two prophets or one of them according to the ability of his affiliation to both of them or to one of them. Jesus has clearly spoken in the cradle before a group of persons; I mean during the period of suckling.

We have already noted some facts that are far more important than this: we pointed out that he spoke in the belly of his mother and discharged an obligation when his pregnant mother sneezed. She praised God and the foetus said: "Allah may have mercy on you!" in a voice which could be heard by those present.

Regarding words: When my daughter Zainab was about one year old, I asked her in jest, in the presence of her mother: "Little daughter! What do you say about a man who unites with his wife without withdrawing?" She answered: "He must make the major ablution." Those who were present marvelled at this response.

I left during that same year and gave permission to her mother to perform the Pilgrimage in that year. I went through Iraq and reached Mecca. After having stopped at 'Arafah, I walked around with a group of people and was informed about my family by passing pilgrims. My daughter saw me while she was suckling. She cried: "O mother! Look, my father is coming!" Her mother looked and saw me coming from far away. My daughter said: "That is my father, that is my father." Her maternal uncle called me and I approached quickly. When she saw me, she started laughing and threw herself at me, saying: "O my father! O my father!"

Similar examples can also be found.

Chapter 500, vol. VII, p. 201—extract

Commentary on the verse: *If any of them says, 'I am a god apart from Him,' such a one We recompense with Gehenna; even so We recompense the evildoers* (Qur'ān, 21:29).

1. He who says, I am a worshiped god (*ilāh*)
   has said a word which is untrue
2. And he who says: I am a creature
   realizes truly the (divine) character traits.
3. The two (attitudes) amount to the same thing;
   thus He confers this realization.
4. And he who does not have in himself
   these two (dispositions) is in a condition of dependence.
5. (Whoever realizes them both) achieves this synthesis
   which for him is similar to what constitutes distinction.

Allah has said: *Lo! Gehenna lurketh in ambush, a home for the rebellious* (*tāghīn*) (Qur'ān, 78:21-22). *Lo! thy Lord is ever watchful* (Qur'ān, 89:14). Verify and observe, and you shall be led aright. It is Allah who guarantees success.

These people therefore obtain the opposite of their claim. Indeed, he who exceeds his limits (*tāghī*) rises himself (*murtafi'*). It is said that the water overflows when its level increases. Allah has said: *Lo, when the waters rose, We bore you in the running ship* (Qur'ān, 69:11).

However, whoever says: ". . . I am a worshiped god . . ." places himself at the limit of proximity. Allah informs us that the recompense for whoever pronounces this is at the limit of distancing: he is thus deprived of the felicity, since (according to the verse quoted in the beginning of this section) *his recompense is the Gehenna*. The sinking into the most profound abyss (*qa'r*) of the Gehenna is for he who desires to rise to the level of Divinity (*ulūha*) of He who maintains Himself (*istiwā'*) on the Throne by the divine name *al-Raḥmān*.

To my knowledge, no one has made such a statement in the grip of hunger, sickness, or another pressing need, except for the Pharaoh. Scorning his people, he said: *O chiefs! I know not that ye have a god other than me* (*ghayrī*) . . . (Qur'ān, 28:38). He was seized by suspicion after doubt or certitude (by adding at the end of this statement) *and set up for me a lofty tower in order that I may survey the god of Moses; and lo! I deem him of the liars*.

As for those who maintain that: *Allah, He is the Anoint son of Mary* . . . (Qur'ān, 5:72 and 5:17), they must not utter such statements, for the following two reasons:

First: A distinction is (generally) made between the human aspect (*nāsūt*) and the divine aspect (*lāhūt*), whereas those who utter such statements negate it.

Second: This statement indicates only that he who formulates it does so by himself and not by that which is said about him (Jesus). He who advances this argument does so in accordance with two modalities:

i) that which represents unity (*aḥadiyya*) for he who expresses himself in this way regarding Divinity (*al-Ulūha*); for him, the world, in its totality, is God Himself. For him, this world possesses the Unity of the Multiplicity, just as for another it will be the Unity of the multiplicity of the divine Names. This multiplicity exists in relationships (*nisab*) and properties (*aḥkām*), not in itself. According to the latter, the world in its totality is a set of accidents that occur to this entity (*'ayn*) among the fixed entities of the possible beings which have no real existence.

ii) the *min dūni-Hi—apart from Him*, which implies a lowering of the degree that belongs to Allah (*nuzūl 'an al-martaba al-latī li-Llāh*). This expression comprises a meaning analogous to that which is contained in the following verse: *And those who choose protectors apart from Him [say]: We worship them only that they may bring us near unto Allah . . .* (Qur'ān, 29:3). Even though these protectors are of a lower degree than Him, some consider them as a god (*ilāh*). By uttering this word, they state that God's manifestation in forms is of a lower rank than He (*qua* absolute Essence), even though God reveals Himself as independent of the worlds. Therefore, even if a theophany (*tajallī*) reaches this degree, it will be more perfect than His theophany in forms. The "rank" of His Independence from the beings of the world remains intelligible in itself. This can exist for he who sees Him as present in this world (literally as the essence of the world, or the world itself). For such a being, this indicator is His Ipseity (*huwiyya*), the proof for him resting in this prophetic statement: *I seek refuge from Thee in Thee . . .* [14] Seeking refuge takes place through Him and against Him, since there is no opposite for this except His Essence. All at once, God is He who gives the irresistible power and He who abases (*Huwa al-mu'izz al-mudhill*) [. . .]

14. This is part of a celebrated tradition which is found in the main Ḥadīth collections: Aḥmad I, 96, 118, 150; VI, 58, 201; Muslim Ṣalāt 222, Abū Dāwūd Ṣalāt 148, Tirmidhī Da'awāt 112; Ibn Mājah Du'ā' 3, etc. The complete tradition is: I seek refuge in Thy good pleasure from Thy displeasure and in Thy pardon from Thy punishment. I seek refuge in Thee from Thee. I cannot count Thy praises. Thou art as Thou hast praised Thyself."

Chapter 559—vol. VIII, p. 223—extract

Commentary on the Qur'ānic expression *min dūni-Hi: apart from Him*

He who says: "*I am a god apart from Him*" is not in ignorance except for the expression "*apart from Him,*" and not just by the formulation "*I am a single god.*" He is ignorant when he pronounces this formula in its entirety for it affirms the other (*al-ghayr*) by saying "*apart from Him.*" When the servant speaks through God, it is He who is his word: it is He who says "I am a god" and not the servant. The servant has no need to add "apart from Him" in what he pronounces through God, for the servant is not lord, especially when the issue is an experience of this order, without him, in a certain way, being his perfume.

In the following verse, *They indeed have disbelieved who say: Lo! Allah is the Messiah, son of Mary . . .* (Qur'ān, 5:17), it is specified that "son of Mary" is attributed to him. In other verses, prophethood is attributed to him as well. Had they said "the son of Allah" (*ibnu Allah*, as in verse 9:30), this would have been completely in error on their part and they would have been disbelievers (*kāfirīn*). Had they said "*Call upon Allah or the Anoint, whichsoever you call upon . . . ,*" as Allah says regarding al-Raḥmān (cf. Qur'ān, 17:110), they would have not excluded him from the divine degree (*al-martaba*) and they would not have associated someone with Allah, for Allah is worshipped as a singular God (*ilāh wāḥid*) [. . .]

Index of Qur'ānic Verses

Index of Qur'ānic Verse Translations